RISKS FACTORS FOR YOUTH SUICIDE

Bard—*Medical Ethics in Practice*
Benoliel—*Death Education for the Health Professional*
Brammer—*Coping with Life Transitions: The Challenge of Personal Change*
Corless, Pittman-Lindeman—*AIDS: Principles, Practices, and Politics, Abridged Edition*
Corless, Pittman-Lindeman—*AIDS: Principles, Practices, and Politics, Reference Edition*
Curran—*Adolescent Suicidal Behavior*
Davidson—*The Hospice: Development and Administration, Second Edition*
Davidson, Linnola—*Risk Factors in Youth Suicide*
Degner, Beaton—*Life–Death Decisions in Health Care*
Doty—*Communication and Assertion Skills for Older Persons*
Epting, Neimeyer—*Personal Meanings of Death: Applications of Personal Construct Theory to Clinical Practice*
Haber—*Health Care for an Aging Society: Cost-Conscious Community Care and Self-Care Approaches*
Leenaars, Wenckstern—*Suicide Prevention in Schools*
Leng—*Psychological Care in Old Age*
Lund—*Older Bereaved Spouses: Research with Practical Applications*
Prunkl, Berry—*Death Week: Exploring the Dying Process*
Riker, Myers—*Retirement Counseling: A Practical Guide for Action*
Sherron, Lumsden—*Introduction to Educational Gerontology, Third Edition*
Stillion—*Death and the Sexes: An Examination of Differential Longevity, Attitudes, Behaviors, and Coping Skills*
Stillion, McDowell, May—*Suicide across the Life Span—Premature Exits*
Turnbull—*Terminal Care*
Vachon—*Occupational Stress in the Care of the Critically Ill, the Dying, and the Bereaved*
Wass, Berardo, Neimeyer—*Dying: Facing the Facts, Second Edition*
Wass, Corr—*Childhood and Death*
Wass, Corr—*Helping Children Cope with Death: Guidelines and Resources, Second Edition*
Wass, Corr, Pacholski, Forfar—*Death Education II: An Annotated Resource Guide*
Wass, Corr, Pacholski, Sanders—*Death Education: An Annotated Resource Guide*
Weenolsen—*Transcendence of Loss over the Life Span*

IN PREPARATION
Bertman—*Facing Death: Images and Interventions*
Leviton—*Horrendous Death, Health, and Well-Being*
Leviton—*Horrendous Death and Health: Toward Action*
Lindeman, Corby, Downing, Sanborn—*Alzheimer's Day Care: A Basic Guide*
Lonetto—*Explaining Death and Dying*
Papadatos, Papadatou—*Children and Death*
Salloway, Matthiesen—*The Chosen Daughter: Women and Their Institutionalized Mothers*
Samarel—*Caring for Life and Death*
Wass, Corr—*Death in the Lives of Children: A Guide for Helping*

RISKS FACTORS FOR YOUTH SUICIDE

Edited by

Lucy Davidson, M.D.

Center for Environmental Health and Injury Control
Centers for Disease Control

Markku Linnoila, M.D.

National Institute on Alcohol Abuse and Alcoholism

●HEMISPHERE PUBLISHING CORPORATION
A member of the Taylor & Francis Group

New York   Washington   Philadelphia   London

Publishers's Note: This permanent edition contains the complete text of the Alcohol, Drug Abuse, and Mental Health Administration's, *Report of the Secretary's Task Force on Youth Suicide. Volume 2: Risk Factors for Youth Suicide,* prepared by a distinguished Project Staff and Advisory Panel.

RISK FACTORS FOR YOUTH SUICIDE

1 2 3 4 5 6 7 8 9 0   B R B R   9 8 7 6 5 4 3 2 1 0

Cover design by Debra Eubanks Riffe.
A CIP catalog record for this book is available from the British Library.

Library of Congress Cataloging-in-Publication Data

Risk factors for youth suicide / edited by Lucy Davidson, Markku
  Linnoila.
      p.   cm. — (Series in death education, aging, and health care)
   Originally published as v. 2 of: Report of the Secretary's Task
Force on Youth Suicide. Rockville, Md. : U.S. Dept. of Health &
Human Services, Public Health Service, Alcohol, Drug Abuse, and
Mental Health Administration, 1989.
   Includes bibliographical references and index.

   1. Youth—United States—Suicidal behavior. I. Davidson, Lucy.
II. Linnoila, Markku. III. United States. Dept. of Health and
Human Services. Secretary's Task Force on Youth Suicide. Report of
the Secretary's Task Force on Youth Suicide. IV. Series.
HV6546.R57   1990
616.85'8445'0835—dc20   90-37082
                                                              CIP

ISBN 1-56032-138-5
ISSN 0275-3510

CONTENTS

MEMBERS OF THE SECRETARY'S TASK FORCE ON YOUTH SUICIDE

Shervert Frazier, M.D.
Chairman
Formerly, Director
National Institute of Mental Health

Carolyn Doppelt Gray
Acting Deputy Assistant Secretary
Office of Human Development Services

M. Gene Handelsman
(served until June 1986)
Formerly, Deputy Assistant Secretary
Office of Human Development Services

Robert B. Helms, Ph.D.
Acting Assistant Secretary for Planning
and Evaluation
Office of the Secretary

Jerome H. Jaffe, M.D.
(served until June 1986)
Director, Addiction Research Center
National Institute on Drug Abuse

Stephanie Lee-Miller
Assistant Secretary for Public Affairs
Office of the Secretary

Markku Linnoila, M.D.
Clinical Director, Division of Intramural
Clinical and Biological Research
National Institute on Alcohol Abuse
and Alcoholism

Dodie T. Livingston
Commissioner, Administration for Children,
Youth, and Families
Office of Human Development Services

Robert G. Niven, M.D.
(served until January 1986)
Formerly, Director, National Institute on Alcohol
Abuse and Alcoholism

Everett R. Rhoades, M.D.
Director, Indian Health Service
Health Resources and Services
Administration

Mark L. Rosenberg, M.D., M.P.P.
Assistant Director for Science
Division of Injury Epidemiology and Control
Center for Environmental Health and
Injury Control
Centers for Disease Control

Charles R. Schuster, Ph.D.
Director
National Institute on Drug Abuse

Robert L. Trachtenberg
Deputy Administrator
Alcohol, Drug Abuse, and Mental Health
Administration

STAFF

Eugenia P. Broumas, Coordinator, Task Force Activities
Special Assistant to the Deputy Director
National Institute of Mental Health

Heather A. Pack, Policy Coordinator
Executive Secretariat
Office of the Secretary

ALTERNATES

Dorynne Czechowicz, M.D.
Assistant Director for Medical and Professional Affairs
Office of Science
National Institute on Drug Abuse

Jack Durell, M.D. (served until July 1986)
Formerly, Associate Director for Science
National Institute on Drug Abuse

Paget Wilson Hinch
Associate Commissioner, Family and Youth Services Bureau
Administration for Children, Youth, and Families
Office of Human Development Services

Chuck Kline
Deputy Assistant Secretary for Public Affairs - News
Office of the Secretary

Arnold R. Tompkins
Deputy Assistant Secretary for Social Services Policy
Office of the Assistant Secretary for Planning
   and Evaluation
Office of the Secretary

WORK GROUP ON RISK FACTORS FOR YOUTH SUICIDE

Lucy Davidson, M.D., Cochairperson
Medical Epidemiologist, Division of Injury Epidemiology and Control
Center for Environmental Health and Injury Control
Centers for Disease Control

Markku Linnoila, M.D., Cochairperson
Clinical Director, Division of Intramural Clinical and Biological Research
National Institute on Alcohol Abuse and Alcoholism

Susan J. Blumenthal, M.D.
Chief, Behavioral Medicine Program
Health and Behavior Research Branch
Division of Basic Sciences
National Institute of Mental Health

Dan Lettieri, Ph.D.
Psychologist, Division of Extramural Research
National Institute on Alcohol Abuse and Alcoholism

Alec Roy, M.B.
Visiting Associate
National Institute on Alcohol Abuse and Alcoholism

Review Panel–National Conference on Risk Factors for Youth Suicide

David J. Kupfer, M.D., Chairman
Professor and Chairman
Department of Psychiatry
School of Medicine
University of Pittsburgh
Western Psychiatric Institute and Clinic
Pittsburgh, Pennsylvania

Gerald L. Klerman, M.D.
Professor of Psychiatry
Cornell University Medical Center
New York Hospital
Payne Whitney Psychiatric Clinic
New York, New York

George Murphy, M.D.
Director, Psychiatric Outpatient Services
Department of Psychiatry
Washington University School of Medicine
St. Louis, Missouri

Herbert Pardes, M.D.
Chairman, Department of Psychiatry
College of Physicians and Surgeons of Columbia University
New York, New York

David B Pillemer, Ed.D.
Associate Professor of Psychology
Department of Psychology
Wellesly College
Wellesly , Massachusetts

Judith L. Rapoport, M.D.
Chief, Child Psychiatry Branch
Division of Intramural Research
National Institute of Mental Health
Bethesda, Maryland

Lee Robins, Ph.D.
Professor of Sociology in Psychiatry
Department of Psychiatry
Washington University School of Medicine
St. Louis, Missouri

Edwin Shneidman, Ph.D.
Professor of Thanatology
University of California, Los Angeles
Neuropsychiatric Institute and Hospital
Los Angeles, California

OVERVIEW OF THE WORK GROUP ON RISK FACTORS FOR YOUTH SUICIDE

INTRODUCTION

The first goal of the Task Force on Youth Suicide as stated by the Secretary was "to take the lead in coordinating activities about suicide among various Federal agencies, Congress, State and local governments, private agencies, and professional organization." The three work groups of the task force--risk factors, interventions and prevention, and strategies for the future--have worked toward establishing a model for the kind of coordination and sequential progress envisioned by the Secretary. The research conclusions and recommendations reached by the Risk Factors Work Group build on this foundation.

Another major charge to the task force was to "assess and consolidate current information." The work group generated a comprehensive list of potential risk factors, grouped them into specific risk factor domains, and identified experts in each area to review the scientific literature and write summary papers. In their papers, the commissioned authors were asked to catalog, analyze, and synthesize the literature on factors linked to youth suicide. These papers clarified the environmental, behavioral, socio-cultural, biological, and psychological factors which have been associated with an increased likelihood of suicide among young people. The papers were presented at the National Conference on Risk Factors for Youth Suicide in Bethesda, Maryland, May 8 and 9, 1986. They were critiqued by a review panel and opened for discussion and comment by those attending the conference. The following comments were distilled from

three sources: the commissioned papers, the review panel's work, and the reflections of the conference attendees.

Although research reviewed by the authors varied in quality as well as methodology, sufficient data were available to establish many characteristics as risk factors for youth suicide. Those biochemical, psychological, and social factors most clearly linked to youth suicide were the following:

- Substance abuse, both chronic and acute, in the context of the suicidal act. Substance abuse was also tied to the exacerbation of concurrent psychiatric disorders, themselves indicators of increased risk.

- Specific psychiatric diagnostic groups-- affective disorders, schizophrenia, and borderline personality disorders.

- Parental loss and family disruption.

- Familial characteristics including genetic traits such as predisposition to affective illness and the effects of role modeling.

- Low concentrations of the serotonin metabolite, 5-hydroxyindoleacetic acid (5-HIAA), and the dopamine metabolite homovanillic acid (HVA) in the cerebrospinal fluid.

- Other risk factors include homosexuality, being a friend of family member of a suicide victim, rapid socio-cultural change, a history of previous suicidal behavior, impulsiveness and aggressiveness, media emphasis on suicide, and ready access to lethal methods, such as guns.

The diversity of risk factors points to the need for targeting intervention and prevention strategies. Our ability to address specific populations at high risk for youth suicide will help focus research and evaluation components of planned interventions as well.

While clear trends were evident, the available research made quantifiable estimates of relative risk a goal as yet unreached. Many studies, while meticulously descriptive, lacked comparison groups. Other lines of research had not been conducted for youth and results were extrapolated from adult populations.

Recommendations for future research approaches were derived from the authors' assessments of the studies that had been done in each risk factor domain. The types of research envisioned by the work group would parallel other efforts at suicide prevention and promote a more precise identification of those young people likely to benefit from a particular intervention and of the circumstances under which directed interventions are most imperative.

CONCLUDING NOTE

The Work Group on Risk Factors for Youth Suicide has examined attributes and exposures that are associated with an increased likelihood of youth suicide. The careful identification and exploration of these risk factors forms the foundation for effective intervention and prevention planning. Given the nature of the work group's task and the limitations of the data available for review, most of our recommendations focus on the research process itself. However, where data were compelling, we have made the following recommendations in specific risk factor domains:

1. **Extend and verify knowledge of youth suicide by conducting well designed research.** Elements of sound design which address current deficiencies include: (a)

specifying the theoretical models upon which a study is based, (b) stating operational definitions for all variables, (c) designing a research protocol that will allow individual exposures to be assessed, (d) fostering interdisciplinary collaboration, (e) using comparison groups, and (f) using nonclinical populations.

Much of our knowledge of risk factors for youth suicide has been extrapolated from studies of adults or studies of suicide attempters. Methodologic deficiencies of many studies further limit our ability to quantify that risk. Stronger studies of youth suicide would provide the risk factor data upon which suicide intervention and prevention efforts could be more reliably based.

2. **Encourage collaborative behavioral and biochemical research into risk factors associated with youth suicide.**

Recently, behavioral and biological investigators have advanced our knowledge of risk factors associated with youth suicide. We expect that their combined efforts would be synergistic. Their collaboration could facilitate the translation of laboratory data into clinically useful information.

3. **Conduct long term, prospective studies of completed suicides among youth.** Such studies should be multi-center efforts with compatible data collection instruments.

Statistically, youth suicides are rare events. Collecting data at multiple sites could provide a larger sample size with power to detect more subtle risk factors. Clarifying the developmental course of various risk factors through prospective studies would facilitate the timing of treatment options.

4. **Establish surveillance systems for suicide attempts and suicide clusters.**

The incidence, prevalence and characteristics of suicide attempts among youth are unknown. Surveillance would provide population-based data to understand suicide attempts as a public health problem and to illuminate the relationship between suicide attempts and suicides.

Suicide clusters may represent an especially preventable type of youth suicide. Ongoing surveillance of clusters would allow for earlier detection and would address the following issues: the proportion of suicides occurring in clusters, their relative frequency among certain age groups, geographic differences, and changes in the pattern of suicide clusters over time.

5. **Assist death certifiers in implementing uniform operational criteria for the determination of suicide and assist States in expediting their mortality data recording and reporting.**

Nationally, death certificates comprise the primary data source for the epidemiologic analysis of suicide. However, suicide is a mode of death particularly subject to misclassification. Without explicit criteria for the determination of suicide, coroners and medical examiners do not reliably code suicide; medical examiners have estimated that half of all suicides may be inaccurately classified. Delays and errors in the vital registry system further compromise this data base.

6. **Develop valid and reliable mental health assessment instruments for youth.**

The personality variables and diagnostic groups associated with adult suicide also appear to be associated with youth suicide. However, the lack of appropriate assessment instruments for youth is an obstacle to early identification and early treatment.

7. **Conduct biochemical research to identify neuroendocrine markers for suicidal behavior which can be measured repeatedly over time, inexpensively, and at low risk and burden to the subject.**

Biochemical markers may be able to identify persons at high lifetime risk for suicide during periods of low immediate risk. Non-crisis-oriented interventions could be implemented for these potential suicides.

8. **Collaborate with the broadcast media in content analyses to identify the harmful and beneficial features of fictional suicide programs and news coverage of suicide.**

Some, but not all, fictional and nonfictional suicide programs have been associated with an increase in suicide attempts and suicides. Identifying which components of the programming were associated with an increase would allow for more responsible broadcasting.

9. **Increase gatekeepers' recognition of and ability to refer potentially suicidal youth by providing (a) information on acute and chronic risk factors for suicide, (b) information on behavioral manifestations of depression, schizophrenia, and conduct disorders, (c) information on indications and sources for referring youth at risk, and (d) training in communication skills for approaching and engaging youth at risk.**

Interested others, such as teachers, youth activity leaders, clergy, and peers have more opportunity for contact with potentially suicidal youth than clinicians. They constitute a prime source for detection and referral of troubled youth.

10. **Use risk factor information to target intervention and prevention services.**

Limits on the distribution of resources for suicide prevention compel us to direct our efforts to those persons in greatest need and those most likely to benefit. Risk factor information fosters prudent allocation of resources among those programs intended to prevent youth suicide.

11. **Avoid sensationalized or romanticized reporting in media coverage of suicides as well as attention to violence and according celebrity status to the decedents.**

Nonfictional media coverage of suicide has been associated with an increase in the number of suicides. Susceptible individuals may be affected by positively regarded qualities of the suicide reported and by perceived rewards for the behavior.

12. Incorporate suicide prevention strategies into treatment and outreach programs directed toward modifiable risk factors for youth suicide, such as alcohol and drug abuse.

These youth problems are intrinsically worth treating. Adding suicide awareness to extant programs for troubled youth can increase our capacity to reach potentially suicidal youth without initiating costly new programs.

13. Provide increased psychiatric and other youth services commensurate with predictable increases in the youth population.

Population increases among youth, which have been associated with increasing youth services, rather than catching up after a deficit, may offset adverse effects of the population increase.

14. Improve health professionals' treatment of depression and other psychiatric disorders associated with youth suicide.

Depression, conduct disorders, schizophrenia, and substance abuse are strongly associated with youth suicide. The risk of suicide is increased when these disorders occur singly or concurrently. Many health professionals are not trained in the effective treatment and management of these common disorders.

SUMMARY OF THE NATIONAL CONFERENCE ON RISK FACTORS FOR YOUTH SUICIDE

David J. Kupfer, M.D.

INTRODUCTION

In the past fifteen years, suicidal behavior among young people has become an increasingly important public health problem requiring the development and implementation of detection and information strategies at the national level. In 1985, suicide was the second leading cause of death in young people and the rate of suicide among our nation's youth had tripled over the past thirty years. For example, between 1970 and 1980, 49,496 of the nation's youth fifteen to twenty-four years of age committed suicide. Within this one decade, the suicide rate for this age group increased 40 percent (from 8.8 deaths per 100,000 population in 1970 to 12.3 per 100,000 in 1980); while the rate for the remainder of the population remained stable. Young adults twenty to twenty-four years of age had approximately twice the number and rate of suicides as teenagers fifteen to nineteen years old. This increase in youth suicide is due primarily to an increasing rate of suicide among young men. Rates for males increased by 50 percent (from 13.5 to 20.2 per 100,000) compared to a 2 percent increase in females (from 4.2 to 4.3 per 100,000) between 1970 and 1980, so that by 1980 the ratio of suicides committed by males to those committed by females in this age group was almost five to one.

Based on these startling statistics and the growing awareness of youth suicide by public health specialists and other concerned in-dividuals, the Secretary's Task Force on Youth Suicide of the Department of Health and Human Services convened three national conferences to develop a strategy to deal with this pressing public health problem. The first of these conferences on Risk Factors for Youth Suicide was held in May 1986, in Bethesda, Maryland. At this conference, a number of distinguished national and international speakers reviewed a variety of risk factors for youth suicide. After the day and a half of presentations, a group of panelists responded to individual papers and to a number of general themes. These panelists were David J. Kupfer, M.D. (chairman); Gerald L. Klerman, M.D.; George E. Murphy, M.D.; Herbert Pardes, M.D.; David B. Pillemer, Ed.D.; Judith L. Rapoport, M.D.; Lee Robins, Ph.D.; and Edwin Shneidman, Ph.D. They paid specific attention to the major themes of the conference as well as suggestions for further strategies which might begin to connect some of the risk factor areas with detection and intervention approaches.

CONFERENCE SUMMARY

The full text of the manuscripts by all the speakers is included in this volume and I will only highlight particular points that the authors made which were either not discussed completely or could benefit from further emphasis.

In their paper on sociodemographic,

epidemiologic, and individual attributes, Holinger and Offer discussed the need for increased accuracy in epidemiologic data. Both mortality data, local and national, and also the population denominators from which mortality rates are derived should be more reliable. They also argued that further long term, cross-cultural comparisons of suicide, homicide, and accident rates are necessary with a focus on period, cohort, and age effects.

In an extensive chapter on preparatory and prior suicidal behavior, Farberow concluded that prior suicidal behavior of any kind is unquestionably as strong a risk indicator for adolescents as it is for adults. On the other hand, indirect self-destructive behavior appears to play too complex a role in the personality of the individual to serve as a reliable risk indicator. Suicide attempters and completers among adolescents need to be appropriately viewed as separate but overlapping populations. While prior suicide attempts, threats, and suicidal ideation may be excellent clues for further suicidal behavior, it is also true that they are late clues in the progression towards suicide. Certain behaviors have been identified that appear consistently in the histories of adolescents who either attempted or committed suicide: school performance variables, including academic difficulties, disciplinary problems, and truancy; and antisocial behavior, especially assaultiveness. Finally, social isolation and impulsive behavior are also often noted. Such factors might be of greater value when they appear with specific evidence of active suicide potential. Other factors that may play a role in suicide are running away, suggestibility and imitation. Suicide notes may tell something about the person's style and pattern of thinking. Dichotomous thinking (cognitive thought processes) may serve as a useful clue in reflecting increasing rigidity and loss of ability to seek alternatives.

The manuscript by Huffine on social and cultural risk factors for youth suicide pointed to ways in which societies might influence the suicide rate among their members. She discussed social structures which might be supportive and protective of individuals or might produce stress. Secondly, the culture as well as social structure, influences the psychological development of its members. Finally, through such mechanisms as folklore and attitudes about suicide and death, the culture may play a role in influencing suicide risk factors and the incidence of suicide itself. The manuscript focused on social integration or the lack of it among various cultural groups including Hispanic Americans, American Indians, Blacks and Asians. Dr. Huffine also emphasized that cultural attitudes and socialization may contribute to increased suicide rates in populations by romanticizing suicide, presenting death as a positive state, or influencing the psychological development of individuals in such a way that they are susceptible to suicide.

In her chapter on family characteristics and support systems, Pfeffer concluded that family factors associated with a high risk of youth suicide are related to experiences characterized by the presence of intense levels of stress. Such stress appears to be chronic and seems to occur at an early phase of the individual's life. One implication of this position is that family risk factor research on youth suicidal behavior needs to adhere to a developmental perspective. Such an orientation could facilitate the examination of continuities and discontinuities in family variables that may be precursors to youth suicide. In identifying a number of stressors, Pfeffer pointed to the loss of social supports, variability and parental functioning which also includes a violation of personal boundaries. She concluded that perspective longitudinal research designs of high-risk populations were indicated. Such studies may evaluate the long term outcome of children who previously had suicidal tendencies. These studies may also evaluate children who are the offspring of parents prone to abuse or affective disorders, or parents who have separated, divorced, or died. Finally, factors such as family disorganization, parental psychopathology and family violence were vectors that could enhance suicidal behavior. Efficient screening techniques for identifying high-risk families as well as screening devices for identifying high-risk children and adolescents in such situations are implied needs for youth suicide prevention. Another approach is to plan interventions that focus on ameliorating family disorganization and parental psychopathology so that stress may decrease and stability may be enhanced.

In their chapter on contagion as a risk factor, Davidson and Gould argued convincingly for further investigation of suicide clusters. After reviewing various epidemic suicide reports in the literature and investing medial influence on suicide, they concluded that time-space clusters of suicide do occur and are not a new phenomena of the 1980's. Nonfictional media coverage of suicides is associated with an increase in the observed number of suicides over those expected, and susceptible individuals may be affected by direct or indirect exposures to suicide. Obviously, a number of questions were raised, such as, what proportion of suicides may occur in clusters and in what ways youth may be differentially exposed and susceptible to suicide contagion. Since youth suicide clusters are of particular concern and may be potentially more preventable, the sorts of prevention and intervention efforts for averting cluster suicides are extremely important. Therefore, recommendations concerning media coverage, further research investigations, and the establishment of a surveillance system for potential suicide clusters seemed valuable.

In his review of stress and life events, Paykel concluded that there still is a dearth of studies of recent life events in the role of youth suicidal behavior. Relatively few studies of early parental loss or studies examining completed suicide have been published. Studies of older suicides and suicide attempters examining early loss due to breakup of parental marriage consistently show suicide and attempt rates higher than in normal control groups or psychiatrically disordered controls.

Since the interpretations of these associations are not fully clear-cut, the implications for prevention are also not easy to summarize. Most of the recent events may serve as signals for high-risk periods when crisis interventions might be attempted.

In reviewing sexual identity issues, Harry argued that suicide attempts among homosexuals of both sexes are two to six times more likely than in heterosexuals. This conclusion, however, is somewhat unclear due to a lack of control groups, especially nonclinical control groups. Harry argues that it would be desirable to obtain both experimental and control groups for nonclinical populations through population-based surveys.

In assessing major psychiatric disorders, Kovacs and Puig-Antich concluded that the "condition" of psychiatric patienthood in adolescents and young adults is associated with an alarmingly high mortality risk from suicide. These psychiatric disorders include psychosis and manic-depressive illness. They also suggested a need to focus on prepubertal children; since their suicidal intent may be profound, while their physical and cognitive limitations may render them less lethal. Although suicidal ideation occurs frequently among prepubertal children their rate of suicide remains quite low. This is probably due to prepubertal child's lack of cognitive maturity and skills necessary to complete suicide. Therefore, this age group provides an opportunity to study suicidality untruncated by suicide completion. Suicidality of very early onset may enable attempters to be selected for future studies who are at most risk and most closely approximate completed suicides. These children, therefore, are a very interesting model for intervention. Finally, Kovacs and Puig-Antich concluded that more efficacious treatment and care of psychiatrically ill youths may be the most feasible way to alter their risk of suicide.

In their assessment of the role of personality disorders and characteristics, Frances and Blumenthal strongly suggested that even though conduct disorders and borderline personality disorders are highly associated with adolescent suicide, assessment of personality factors has been impeded by lack of standardized measures for these characteristics in young people. In addition, assessment of underlying personality at the time of a suicide attempt is confounded by the distress experienced by the individual around the time of the event. However, from personality studies that have been done, a continuum of the traits and disorders associated with suicidal behavior in adolescence appears to be associated with such behavior in adulthood. Therefore, stability in personality characteristics, such as impulsiveness and aggressiveness, appears to be present over the life cycle. It is proposed that certain diagnostic categories from the DSM-III Infancy, Childhood, and Adolescence section correspond to, and may in some individuals eventually develop into particular personality disorders in adulthood. For example, schizoid disorder of childhood and adolescence may become schizoid personality disorder; avoidant disorder of childhood and adolescence may become avoidant personality disorder; conduct disorder may become antisocial personality disorder; oppositional disorder may become passive aggressive personality disorder; and identity disorder may become borderline personality disorder. The presumption is that the childhood or adolescent condition is diagnosed if the individual is under age eighteen, and the adult personality diagnosis is used after age eighteen whenever the personality psychopathology has persisted at an intensity sufficient to meet disorder criteria. In addition, these personality variables may also have biological correlates, i.e., serotonin deficiency related to increased impulsiveness and aggressiveness, and may interact with environmental factors.

The authors noted that the coexistence of depression and conduct disorder or borderline personality disorder may represent an extremely risky combination of factors. The implications of these findings suggest careful clinical assessment and further development of "kiddy" personality measures and better

definitions. They also lead to the notion that various prevention studies for conduct disorders should be attempted more vigorously. In essence, it appears that the same disorders are predicting suicidal behavior in adults and in children.

In reviewing methods, Worden argued that although the numbers may be few, suicide statistics should be diligently collected for children under the age of 10. Methods of suicide should also be studied in context. Therefore, those who are collecting data on suicide methods should use one of the existing scales that account for the context of the event. If that were to take place, we would have a better grasp of the relative lethality of various age, sex, and ethnic groups as well as important distinctions between methods chosen by youth versus adults.

In his examination of substance use and abuse, Schuckit suggested that controlled substances and/or alcohol are frequently used as the means of attempting self-harm, especially among younger women. Alcohol is often taken as a prelude to the suicidal act. Adolescents, alcoholics, and drug abusers have an elevated risk for suicide attempts and completions. Children of alcoholics and of patients with depressive or schizophrenic disorders may themselves be a elevated risk for suicide attempts and completions. Almost all substances of abuse are likely to exacerbate the preexisting emotional or psychiatric disturbances. Efforts aimed at minimizing the risk for suicide should include educating young people and their families about the need to refrain from all recreational psychotropic substances during times of mood swings or anger. Finally, the children of alcoholics may themselves have inherited problems of impulsiveness or hyperactivity or a propensity to misuse substances with subsequent mood swings, anger, and frustration in their own lives.

In reviewing various biological factors, Asberg argued that a low output serotonin system or perhaps even more likely a "low stability system" might render an individual more vulnerable to self-destructive or impulsive action in time of crisis. Asberg also pointed out that although relatively little is known about the biochemical linkages between the serotonergic system and suicidal behavior, the evidence that personality features (impulsiveness and aggressiveness) may represent intervening variables is highly suggestive. At the present time, it might be recommended that cerebrospinal fluid (CSF) measures could be used as an aid to suicide risk prediction in highly specialized clinical settings, but not on a larger scale.

The next presentation reviewed receptor studies and the ways in which postmortem research might contribute to our understanding of the biological aspects of suicidal behavior. Stanley argued that postmortem research would necessitate interviewing next of kin to obtain the needed personality descriptives and diagnostic information. He also suggested that in an effort to maintain a link between postmortem findings and the clinical application of such findings, investigators should obtain samples of postmortem CSF wherever possible.

In a third presentation on biological factors with an emphasis on neuroendocrine aspects, Meltzer suggested that the thyroid stimulating hormone (TSH) response may be blunted in persons who commit violent suicide. Methodologically, he examined differences between violent versus nonviolent attempts and also persons who attempted suicide versus those individuals with suicidal ideation. He found a significant relationship between serum cortisol and hopelessness. His review, therefore, suggested that there may be relationships between cortisol and suicidal behavior.

Finally, in reviewing genetic factors, Roy suggested that the Copenhagen adoption studies strongly suggest a genetic factor for suicide independent of or added to genetic transmission of psychiatric disorders. Interestingly, support for this possibility comes from the recent Amish studies which show that suicide was much more likely to occur when an individual had genetic vulnerabilities to both suicide and to affective illness. Roy also pointed out that Kety's recent data pointed to a genetic factor which represents the inability to control impulsive behavior triggered by depression, stress, or other stimuli. Therefore, he concluded that important goals were first the identification of genetic factor, next the examination of genetic transmission of psychiatric disorders per se, and then the examination of an additive genetic factor relating to impulsive behavior.

In summarizing the biological factors, Goodwin discussed a cluster of biological findings emphasizing again the difference between persons with suicidal ideation versus those who are suicide attempters and completers. He argued that the presence of a psychiatric illness was the single most predictive factor for a serious suicide attempt. In pointing to specific psychiatric illnesses, he felt that the key psychiatric diseases were affective disorders with an emphasis on hopelessness, alcoholism with an emphasis on loss of impulse control, and schizophrenia with an emphasis on psychosis.

At the end of these presentations, the discussants each presented brief overview of their thoughts as well as specific points on various chapters.

Klerman stated that the conference contained a number of omissions such as discussion of some high-risk populations including the American Indians. He also pointed out that relatively little of the existing epidemiological methodology for assessing risk has been applied to youth suicide. Techniques such as attributable relative risk and logistic regression, which are the standbys of epidemiology, have not been applied by and large to most of these studies. Murphy reinforced the notion of expanding Shafii's recent study (Louisville, Kentucky) to other places. He also stressed Frances' argument about comorbidity, such as, the combination of personality disorder and substance abuse. Pardes discussed the need to find ways of fostering interactions among various disciplines working on this topic. Pillemer argued that one way to try to firm up conclusions from correlational studies involves improving the database through more careful matching of controls with suicide groups. Another strategy would involve applying survey methods to nonclinical populations. He also stated that intoxication with alcohol or drugs often precedes suicidal behavior and that the suicide rate among substance abusers is much higher than in the general population. It, therefore, might be possible to partially disentangle this risk factor from associated factors by conducting planned intervention studies.

Rapoport reemphasized the role of psychiatric disorders, especially impulsive conduct disorders, in relation to suicidal behavior. Robins suggested that we should try to study the whole spectrum of suicidal ideation through attempts to successful suicide rather than keeping them as separate enterprises. Many factors are highly correlated with suicide attempts and suicide completions but we do not yet know to what extent these are separate populations and to what extent they are overlapping populations. The only way we can find out is by studying multiple variables simultaneously. The intersection of two areas traditionally separated in psychiatric diagnosis--the internalizing disorders of depression and the externalizing disorders of conduct and drug abuse--predicts an explosive situation. This is an opportunity, therefore, to integrate genetic and stress research. Another notion is to examine children who have had antisocial fathers and depressive mothers who would then be very likely to have a double genetic dose which might be the critical thing in the research reported. Shneidman stressed other points in the conference preceedings which have already been described. In particular, Schneidman argued for "individual case autopsies."

Kupfer suggested that several workshops be held to examine the gaps in methodology. For example, there may be several areas where we already have multiple assessment instruments and we need to decide which is the most appropriate. The notion of launching several prospective studies with an intervention component might be the most economical way to go in the long run. Which risk factors do we know enough about to design such trials and which risk factors are modifiable? These are crucial questions since part of the strategy of public health intervention is to identify risk factors which are modifiable.

In conclusion, considerable attention should be paid to the differences between vulnerability factors and protective factors, the need for longitudinal prospective studies, comorbidity, and interdisciplinary research. In understanding the application of risk factors we must plan for the education of primary care practitioners and pay attention to teachers in dealing with early detection and recognition of children in trouble. Other goals are planned interventions where the disentanglement of risk factors is very appropriate and the development of a child brain bank. Along these lines would be setting up criteria as well as the actual completion of a national registry for suicide completers. With respect to some of the methodology gaps, the notion of developing child personality measures would be important.

Davidson pointed out that we need to understand much more about the circumstances of directed interventions, we need to study nonclinical populations, and we need to replicate studies in children similar to what we have carried out with adults. An important point to be emphasized in this report is the issue of weighting the various risk assessment factors and developing a bridge between risk factor identification and intervention planning. (In a later presentation, Davidson pointed to five criteria for developing this bridge: the prevalence of the risk factor in the population, the strength of the risk factor (relative risk), how the population at risk might be reached (identification), the acceptability of the proposed intervention, and the effectiveness of the intervention (the percent of those treated who will benefit). Shaffer has previously pointed out that the implications for prevention rest very much on which model for suicidal behavior is accepted, whether there is an overlap model or a continuous model.

In assessing the various risk factor domains that were covered in this conference, it becomes clear that the 14 or 15 risk factor domains can be reduced in number. For example, those relating to CSF determinations, neurochemical receptors, and neuroendocrine studies can be grouped together as biological risk factors. Also substance use and abuse can be included under the major psychiatric disease segment. Some of the first several risk factor domains can also go under a larger category concerning psychosocial factors and social supports. In short, although these risk factor domains can be teased out separately, one might argue that a smaller set of risk factor domains might be more useful for ascribing weights and attempting to deal with prediction and the establishment of various detection and intervention strategies.

Although one can provide different models, it has been previously suggested that five domains organized as a matrix or multi-axial set of domains may provide a simple model for looking at most of these risk factors. Whether a model of risk should be a series of interlocking Venn diagrams or some other additive model, it does appear that a major clinical research strategy will be the need to develop weights for each of its major components. For example, in applying this model, the breakup of a relationship might be a final humiliating experience that triggers a depressive episode in a young person with a family history of affective disorder. Such an individual may also have poor social supports, which interact with the other identified risk factors to increase the individual's vulnerability to suicide.

The question is, at what level and in what degree do each of these factors contribute to suicide potential? Or is the degree of overlap of all factors the most significant criterion? Or we may wish to pose such questions as: What makes 15 percent of the people who suffer from an affective disorder end their lives by suicide while the other 85 percent do not? Using this overlapping model, we may learn that the subgroup of affective disorder patients who commit suicide have a greater overlap of other risk domains such as increased hopelessness, impulsiveness, decreased social supports, a recent humiliating life experience, and/or an increased family history of affective disorder or suicidal behavior.

From this example, it is clear that psychiatric diagnoses are key risk factors. Current research shows that affective disorders, conduct disorder, and substance abuse are the psychiatric diagnoses most highly associated with suicide in young people. In the adult literature over 90 percent of persons who end their lives by suicide have an associated psychiatric illness. The few studies on adolescent suicide suggest high percentages as well.

Secondly, personality traits relating to suicide, such as aggression, impulsiveness, and hopelessness are intrinsically important in characterizing suicide since they may represent personality styles that cut across diagnostic groupings. In addition, this domain includes certain personality disorders, such as borderline personality disorder and antisocial personality disorder, which are more highly correlated with suicidal behavior and represent risk factors. The comorbidity (or co-occurrence) of antisocial and depressive symptoms appears to be a particularly lethal combination in adults and young people. The third risk factor domain is concerned with psychosocial factors, social supports, life events, and chronic medical illness. For example, early loss, increased negative life events, the presence of a chronic medical illness, and decreased social supports increase the risk for suicide.

In addition to these three risk factor domains, two others stand out. One is the identification of both genetic and family factors that predispose an individual to suicide. Previous investigators have suggested that the genetics of suicide may be independent of the genetics in a family history relating to specific psychiatric disorders, such as affective disorder or alcoholism. The final factor may be the neurochemical and biochemical variables currently under active investigation in an attempt to identify either a biologic abnormality or a vulnerable state for suicide. I would advocate that intervention strategies incorporate these factors into the research design (if only to track them) as an essential feature. This material may represent a somewhat personal view of the proceedings of the risk meeting and may need to be more "objectively" reviewed to achieve a consensus of the scope of the problem, the risk factor characteristics, what kinds of detection and interventions can be carried out now, and what we can do to improve our detection and intervention strategies.

On a broader note, it would appear that politically the time is ripe to advocate partnerships between various agencies and funding sources, e.g., Federal-State-local; foundation-Federal; university-community. Aside from the obvious problems of partnership, there is a tendency in the suicide area to promise too much too quickly. Perhaps if one does not only advocate research or education or intervention, one might have a better balanced shot at achieving the sustained longitudinal push one will need to redevelop this area of public health concern.

Our own recent experience in the Commonwealth of Pennsylvania last winter was proposing a model center to capture all three components. We will establish at Western Psychiatric Institute and Clinic (WPIC), in conjunction with our ongoing program for adolescents and young adults, a Center for Teenagers at Risk to serve the western Pennsylvania region. This center will have three major components: (1) outreach, education and prevention; (2) demonstration intervention and treatment programs; and (3) research on adolescent suicide. The goal of the mobile outreach component will be to teach targeted school and agency personnel to identify the signs and symptoms of depression and potential suicide. The intervention component will involve the development of therapeutic strategies based on the known risk factors for suicide in this age group. The research component will work toward the goal of more accurate identification of teenagers at risk of suicide.

COMMISSIONED
PAPERS

SOCIODEMOGRAPHIC, EPIDEMIOLOGIC, AND INDIVIDUAL ATTRIBUTES

Paul C. Holinger, M.D., M.P.H., Associate Professor of Psychiatry, Rush-Presbyterian-St. Luke's Medical Center, Chicago, Illinois

Daniel Offer, M.D., Professor and Chairman, Department of Psychiatry, Michael Reese Hospital and Medical Center, Chicago, Illinois

INTRODUCTION

From an individual, clinical point of view, it is difficult to overestimate the distressing, disastrous impact of the suicide of a young person. The impact on parents, siblings, friends, and the community seems almost inexpressible. However, the extent to which one views self-destructiveness among the young as an issue in the public health and epidemiologic realms seems dependent on the context and perspective. On the one hand, suicide is the second leading cause of death among 15 to 24 year olds in the United States (following only accidents) (National Center for Health Statistics, 1985) and, primarily because of the number of suicides, homicides, and accidents among young people, violent deaths* are the **leading** cause of number of years of life lost in this country (Holinger, 1980). On the other hand, young people have the **lowest** suicide rates of any age group and are at **least** risk of dying by suicide (Holinger, Holinger, and Sandlow, 1985).

The purpose of this paper is twofold. First, we will present and evaluate the epidemiologic data related to suicide among adolescents. Second, we will discuss the potential for the prediction of youth suicide

*Violent deaths refer to suicide, homicide, and accidental deaths (Weiss, 1976).

on an epidemiologic level. The focus will be on completed suicides, and we will utilize a developmental model emphasizing early (10-14 years old), middle (15-19 years old), and late (20-24 years old) adolescence, with an emphasis on the 15 to 19 and 20 to 24 year olds. The paper is divided into six sections; sections on literature, methodology, data, discussion, and future research will follow this brief introduction.

LITERATURE

This section on literature will focus on the epidemiology and potential prediction of adolescent suicide.

Of the many tasks of science, perhaps one of the most important is that of prediction, especially if such prediction can lead to effective intervention. Two types of studies over the past five years have begun to suggest that prediction of certain violent deaths may be possible for some age groups. One type of study involved the use of a population model (Holinger and Offer, 1983; Holinger and Offer, 1984; Holinger and Offer, 1986; Holinger, Offer, Ostrov, et al., unpublished data), and the second type of study utilizes cohort analysis (Solomon and Hellon, 1980; Hellon and Solomon, 1980; Murphy and

Wetzel, 1980; Klerman, Lavori, Rice, et al., unpublished data).

In our 1981 examination of the increase in suicide rates among 15 to 19 year olds during the past two decades (Holinger and Offer, 1981), we reported that simultaneous with an increase in suicide rates was a steady increase in the population of 15 to 19 year olds from just over 11 million in 1956 to nearly 21 million in 1975. A subsequent study then related the changes in the adolescent population and changes in the proportion of adolescents in the total U.S. population to the adolescent suicide rates during the twentieth century in the United States (Holinger and Offer, 1982). Significant positive correlations were found between adolescent suicide rates, changes in the adolescent population, and changes in the proportion of adolescents in the population of the United States, i.e., as the numbers and proportion of adolescents increased or decreased, the adolescent suicide rates increased and decreased, respectively. It should be recalled that while one might assume that the number of deaths from a particular cause will increase with increases in the population, the mortality rates do not necessarily increase with an increase in population because the denominator is constant (i.e., deaths/100,000 population).

Cohort analyses have also provided data to demonstrate the increase in suicide rates among the young (Solomon and Hellon, 1980; Hellon and Solomon, 1980; Murphy and Wetzel, 1980; Klerman, et al., unpublished data). Solomon and Hellon (1980), studying Alberta, Canada, during the years 1951 to 1977, identified five-year age cohorts, and followed the suicide rates as the cohorts aged. Suicide rates increased directly with age, regardless of gender. Once a cohort entered the 15 to 19 year old age range with a high rate of suicide, the rate for that cohort remained consistently high as it aged. Murphy and Wetzel (1980) found the same phenomenon, in reduced magnitude, in larger birth cohorts in the United States. Not only does each successive birth cohort start with a higher suicide rate, but at each succes-

sive five-year interval it has a higher rate than the preceding cohort had at that age. Klerman, et al. (unpublished data), noted a similar cohort effect in their study of depressed patients.

There are both similarities and differences between the population-model and the cohort-effect studies. The similarities lie in the emphasis on recent increases in suicide rates among the younger age groups. The differences are in the predictive aspects. The cohort studies suggest that the suicide rates for the age groups under study would continue to increase as they are followed over time. Implicitly, the cohort studies also seem to suggest that the suicide rates for younger age groups will continue to increase as each new five-year adolescent age group comes into being. The predictions by the population model are different. The population model suggests that suicide rates for younger age groups will begin leveling off and decreasing, inasmuch as the population of younger people has started to decrease. In addition, the population model suggests that as the current group of youngsters gets older, suicide rates will increase less than the cohort studies would predict. It is well known that male suicide rates increase with age in the United States while female rates increase with age until about 65 and then decrease slightly (Kramer, et al., 1972; Holinger and Klemen, 1982). Therefore, one would expect an increase in suicide rates age consistent with this long-established pattern. However, the current group of adolescents and young adults make up an unusually large proportion of the U.S. population. The population model suggests that the larger the proportion of adults in the population, the lower will be their suicide rates. Thus, the population model would suggest that the suicide rates for the adult populations would decrease over the next several decades compared with adult rates in the past, consistent with the movement of the "baby boom" population increase through those adult age groups. This is not to say that the rates for the older groups of the future might be expected to have smaller suicide rates than the older groups of the past.

Other literature is also relevant to the issue of violent deaths, population shifts, and potential prediction. Positive relationships between population increases and upsurges in the rates of various forms of violent death are described by Wechsler (1961), Gordon and Gordon (1960), and Klebba (1975). These findings were not supported by the work of Levy and Herzog (1974, 1978), Herzog, et al. (1977), and Seiden (1984) in their reports of negative or insignificant correlations between both population density and crowding and suicide rates.

The work of Easterlin (1980) and Brenner (1971, 1979), with extensive research of population and economic variables, respectively, and other related studies (Seiden and Freitas, 1980; Peck and Litman, 1973; Klebba, 1975; Hendin, 1982) began to suggest the potential for prediction of suicide and other violent deaths. Turner, et al. (1981), showed that the birth rate increased with good economic conditions, and decreased with poor conditions. Previous studies specifically examined the potential of a population model to predict the patterns of violent deaths (Holinger and Offer, 1984). This model was also related to economic changes, with a suggested interaction of economic and population variables (e.g., good economic conditions leading to an increased birth rate with subsequent population changes) that helped explain violent death rates from an epidemiologic perspective.

Other Factors. Summaries of other risk factors for suicide among children and adolescents have been presented elsewhere (Holinger and Offer, 1981; Seiden, 1969), but brief mention should be made here of three other variables: geographics, divorce rate, and teenage pregnancy. With respect to geographics, the western States have the highest suicide rates among adolescents, and the eastern States tend to have lower rates (Seiden, 1984; Vital Statistics of the United States, 1979). The birth rates for teenagers and the divorce rate for all ages have increased recently, paralleling the recent increases in suicide rates among the young, but these parallels were not consistent early in the century (Vital Statistics of the United States, 1979; Shapiro and Wynne, 1982).

METHODOLOGIC ISSUES

Methodologic Problems. Although we present elsewhere detailed discussions of the methodologic problems in using epidemiologic data to analyze violent deaths (Holinger and Offer, 1984; Holinger, in press, 1987), we will note the more important issues here.

Two major types of methodologic problems occur when using national mortality data to study violent death patterns: (1) under- and overreporting; and (2) data misclassification. Underreporting may result in reported suicide data being at least two or three times less than the real figures (Hendin, 1982; Seiden, 1969; Toolan, 1962, 1975; Kramer, et al., 1972). The underreporting may be intentional or unintentional. In intentional underreporting, the doctors, family, and friends may contribute to covering up a suicide for various reasons: guilt, social stigma, potential loss of insurance or pension benefits, fears of malpractice, and so on. Unintentional underreporting refers to deaths labeled "accidents," e.g., single car crashes or some poisonings, which were actually suicides but were unverifiable as such because of the absence of a note or other evidence. Studies of violent deaths among youth involve additional methodologic problems. There may be greater social stigma and guilt surrounding suicide in childhood and adolescence because of the intense involvement of the parents at that age and the parents feeling that they have failed and will be labeled "bad parents." In addition, it may be much easier to cover up suicide in the younger age groups. Poisonings and other methods of suicide are more easily perceived as accidents in those age groups than in older age groups.

Two types of data classification problems exist. One involves classification at the national level and the changes in this classification over time. The changes in Federal classification over time have been outlined in various government reports (Dunn and Shackley, 1944; Faust and Dolman, 1963a, 1963b, 1965; Klebba and Dolman, 1975; National Center for Health Statistics, 1980; Vital Statistics - Special Reports, 1941, 1956). There has been little change over the century in Federal classification for suicide. The second type of data classification problem concerns classification at the local level, e.g., the legal issue involving the requirement of some localities for a suicide note as evidence of suicide; this practice both decreases numbers and biases results because only the literate can be listed as having committed suicide.

Sources of Data. Sources of population and mortality data are noted in the respective tables and figures of this report. The data used from 1933 to the present are for the complete population, not samples: they include all U.S. suicides among the age groups indicated. With the exception of Figure 1, data prior to 1932 are not utilized in the present report as they are sample data and include only death registration States and areas utilized by the Federal government during any specific year. It was only after 1933 that all States were incorporated into the national mortality statistics (with Alaska added in 1959 and Hawaii in 1960).

Other Forms of Violent Death. Suicide, homicide (homicide mortality rates refer to those killed, not the killers), and accidents have been studied in aggregate (Weiss, 1976; Holinger and Klemen, 1982), and have been related in that all may represent some expression of self-inflicted mortality (Wolfgang, 1959; Menninger, 1938; Freud, 1901; Farberow, 1979). Homicide and accidents may be self-inflicted in that some victims may provoke his or her own death by "being in the wrong place at the wrong time" (Tsuang,

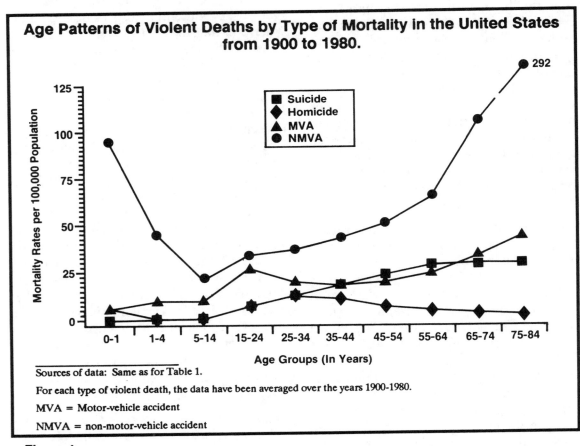

Figure 1.

Boor, and Fleming, 1985; Wolfgang, 1959, 1968; Doege, 1978). Although suicide is the most overt form of self-inflicted violence, homicide and accidents can be more subtle manifestations of self-destructive tendencies and risk-taking (Holinger and Klemen, 1982). However, this paper focuses primarily on that most overt form of self-destructiveness: suicide.

Methodologic Issues in Studying Adolescent Suicide and Population Shifts. The general methodologic considerations were discussed above. The sources of population, suicide, and homicide data are noted in the respective tables and figures of this section. With respect to population data, both the figures and the correlations utilize the proportion of the population of a given age in the entire U.S. population (e.g., the proportion of 15 to 24 year olds in the entire U.S. population). Homicide data as well as suicide data will be noted, and the focus will be on 15 to 24 year olds. The correlations were derived as described previously (Holinger and Offer, 1984).

In addition to the possibility discussed below that there is a meaningful relationship between violent death rates and population shifts, one must also consider the possibility that either artifact or other variables are responsible for correlation. The possibility that the correlations are artifact because of change in Federal classifying of suicide and homicide is unlikely: as described above, the comparability ratios for suicide and homicide have been rather consistent over the decades. However, the possibility that another variable is involved, specifically period effects due to economic trends, needs to be addressed. In the early 1930's (the starting point of these data, when the entire U.S. population was included in the mortality figures), the mortality rates were at their peaks, probably because of the economic depression. The violent death rates decreased for several years following, reaching low points during the early 1940's (World War II).

During the time of this decrease in rates,

however, the population of the adults (35 to 64 years) in the United States increased steadily. These economic shifts could then be seen to contribute to the inverse correlations, with the population variable having a coincidental, rather than etiologic, relationship with the violent death rates. The time trends of violent deaths in the United States (e.g., the tendency of violent death rates to increase in times of economic depression such as the early 1930's and decrease during war as in the early 1940's with World War II) have been presented in detail elsewhere (Holinger and Klemen, 1982).

DATA

Epidemiologic Data. Figure 1 presents age patterns of violent deaths by type of mortality in the United States, averaged over the years 1900- 1980. Non-motor-vehicle accidents tend to have the highest rates, followed by motor-vehicle accidents, suicide, and homicide, respectively. Of particular importance to this paper are the age effects* seen in suicide. When male and female rates are combined, suicide rates can be seen to increase steadily as age increases. Separating male and female rates indicates that male rates increase steadily as age increases, whereas female rates tend to increase to peaks during the 35 to 64 age range, with a subsequent decrease. Perhaps the most salient finding in Figure 1 is that children and adolescents, despite the recent attention on the increases in their rates, have the **lowest** suicide rates of any age group in the United States (National Center for Health Statistics, 1984). That is, children and adolescents are at lower risk of dying by suicide than any other age group in this country. This finding allows one to address the question of adolescent suicide from a different and perhaps more fruitful perspective: What factors protect adolescents from suicide? And what intrapsychic and external factors break down to create a suicidal outcome in an adolescent?

---
*Age effects involve changes in specific rates of mortality or illness over the life span of the individual (Holford, 1983).

7

Although the national mortality age groupings somewhat awkwardly separate various psychological developmental stages, the age groups roughly correspond to late childhood and early adolescence (10 to 14 years), middle adolescence (15 to 19 years), and late adolescence and young adulthood (20 to 24 years). Suicides are not recorded in national mortality figures for the 0-4 year age group, and recorded suicides for 5 to 9 year olds are very rare, usually less than 10 per year. Among the age groups under study here, 20 to 24 year olds have the highest rates, followed by 15 to 19 year olds and 10 to 14 year olds, respectively.

For 10 to 14 year olds, of interest are the low rates (less than 2 per 100,000 population), the recent increases in rates, and the fact that boys tend to have higher rates than girls. White boys have the highest rates.

Figure 2 shows the suicide rates for 15 to 19 year olds, and here the trends are clearer. The rates are higher (currently about 8 per 100,000 population), young men tend to have higher rates than young women, and whites higher than nonwhites. White men are at highest risk. In addition, the time trends, or period effects*, are more apparent, with increased rates during the 1930's, decreases during the 1940's and 1950's, increases from the mid-1950's through the 1970's, and the very recent tendency toward a leveling off of this increase.

Figure 3 presents suicide data for 20 to 24 year olds. Rates for 20 to 24 year olds are higher than the younger age groups (currently about 15 per 100,000 population), men have rates higher than women, whites have higher rates than nonwhites, and white men tend to have the highest rates. Trends over time show the familiar period effects: increased rates during the 1930's, decreased rates during the 1940's to about the mid-1950's, increases through the late 1970's-- when suicide rates for adolescents were higher than ever recorded in this country-- and a recent leveling off and decrease in rates.

Data on Youth Suicide and Population Shifts. The data indicate that significant positive correlations exist between adolescent and young adult suicide rates and the proportion of that age group in the United States (Figures 4, 6, and Table 1). That is, increases (and decreases) in the proportion of 15 to 24 year olds are accompanied by in-

*Period effects involve changes in rates of mortality or illness during a particular historical period (Holford, 1983).

Correlation Coefficients Between Suicide and Homicide Rates and Population Ratios for 15 to 24 and 34 to 44 Year Olds, United States, 1933-1983.

	Suicide Rate	Homicide Rate
Proportion of 15 to 24 Year Olds in Total U.S. Population	+ .34**	+ .41*
Proportion of 35 to 44 Year Olds in Total U.S. Population	-.52*	-.68*

* p < .001

** p < .01

Sources of suicide and homicide data:

Vital Statistics - Special Reports Vol. 43 (for 1933-1953); Grove RD, Hetzel AM: Vital Statistics Rates in the United States: 1940-1960, U.S. Government Printing Office, 1968 (for 1954-1960); Vital Statistics in the United States, Mortality 1961-1979 (for 1961-1979); and National Center for Health Statistics, unpublished data (for 1980-1983).

Sources of population data:

Grove Rd, Hetzel AM: Vital Statistics Rates in the United States: 1940-1960, U.S. Government Printing Office, 1968 (for 1933-1960); Vital Statistics in the United States, Mortality 1961-1979 (for 1961-1979); and National Center for Health Statistics, unpublished data (for 1980-1983).

Table 1.

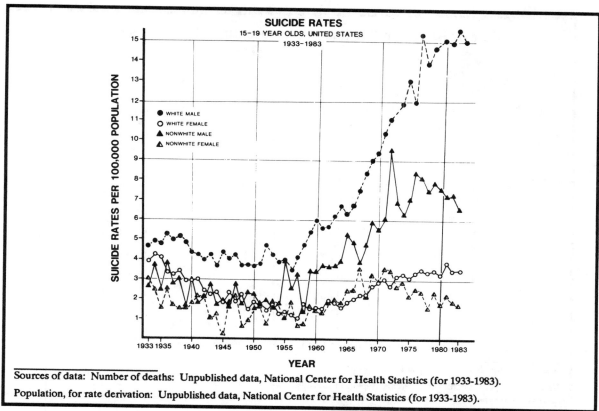

Figure 2.

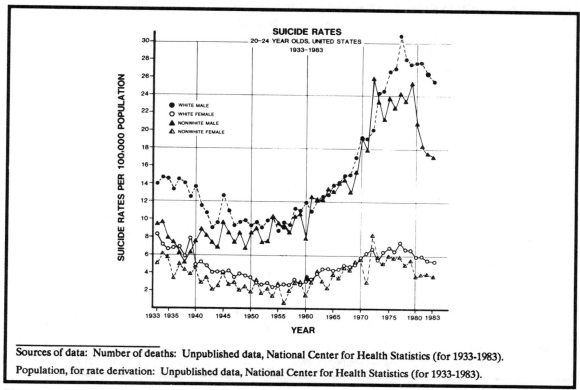

Figure 3.

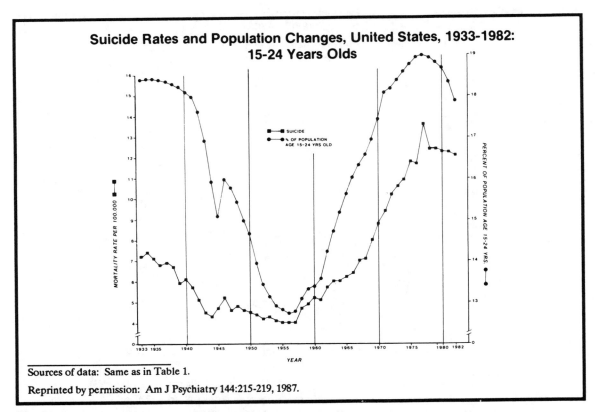

Sources of data: Same as in Table 1.

Reprinted by permission: Am J Psychiatry 144:215-219, 1987.

Figure 4.

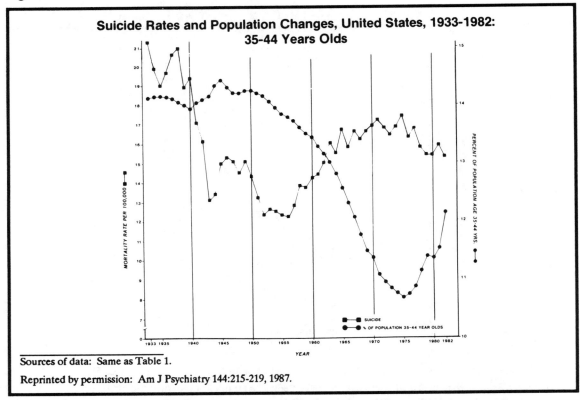

Sources of data: Same as Table 1.

Reprinted by permission: Am J Psychiatry 144:215-219, 1987.

Figure 5.

10

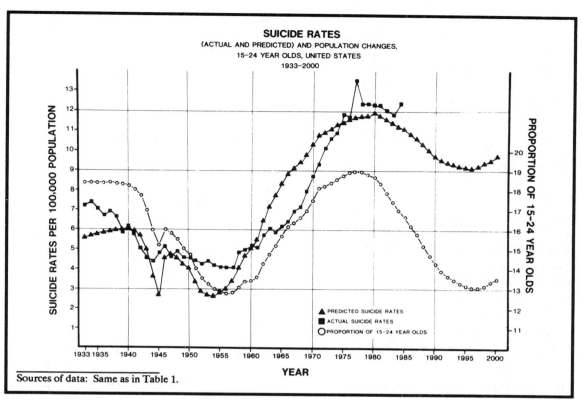

SUICIDE RATES
(ACTUAL AND PREDICTED) AND POPULATION CHANGES,
15–24 YEAR OLDS, UNITED STATES
1933–2000

▲ PREDICTED SUICIDE RATES
■ ACTUAL SUICIDE RATES
○ PROPORTION OF 15–24 YEAR OLDS

Sources of data: Same as in Table 1.

Figure 6.

creases and decreases, respectively) in their suicide rates. Opposite trends are seen for adult and older age groups, i.e., as the proportion of adults increase, their suicide rates decrease. Homicide data follow the patterns of suicide data for both younger and older age groups. These findings and resulting hypotheses regarding prediction should be viewed with caution, because of the methodologic problems inherent in utilizing national mortality data, as well as the number of years required to adequately test such epidemiologic propositions over time.

Figures 4 and 5 focus on suicide and homicide rates, and these figures present examples from 2 age groups to depict the differences between the younger and adult age groups. Figure 4 shows the changes over time in mortality rates for suicide and homicide rates for 15 to 24 year olds, and the proportion of 15 to 24 year olds from 1933 to 1982 in the United States. The mortality rates and proportion of 15 to 24 year olds in the population can be seen to be rather parallel: increases (and decreases) in the proportion

of 15 to 24 year olds are accompanied by increases (and decreases) in their suicide and homicide rates. Figure 5 shows the relationship between suicide and homicide rates and population changes among 35 to 44 year olds, an age group whose trends are similar to the adult groups in general (35 to 64 year olds) (Holinger and Offer, unpublished data). For the 35 to 44 age group, rates can be seen to have time trends somewhat opposite to the population changes: decreases in the proportion of 35 to 44 year olds are accompanied by increases in their suicide and homicide rates. For 35 to 44 year olds, suicide and homicide rates were high during the early 1930's to the mid-1970's, and leveled off recently. In contrast, the proportion of 35 to 44 year olds in the population reached high levels during the 1940's, decreased throughout the 1950's and 1960's into the mid-1970's, and recently increased.

Prediction of Adolescent Suicide Rates to the Year 2000. Inasmuch as the population shifts among adolescents over the next 15 years can be approximated, based on the cur-

11

rent number of children and adolescents in the United States (Current Population Reports, 1984), we can use the population model to try to predict the suicide rates for 15 to 24 year olds from the present time to the year 2000. Figure 6 presents the actual suicide rates for 15 to 24 year olds (1933 to 1982), their predicted rates (1933 to 2000), and the proportion of 15 to 24 year olds can be seen to be rather parallel, as noted previously: somewhat high levels in the 1930's, decreases during the 1940's and 1950's, and increases throughout the 1960's and into the late 1970's. The actual suicide rates show a peak in the later 1970's with a recent leveling off and slight decrease. The recent rates correspond to the recent peak (nearly 19%) in the proportion of 15 to 24 year olds in the United States. As noted earlier, this relationship between suicide rates for 15 to 24 year olds and their population shifts is statistically significant.

The proportion of adolescents is expected to decrease throughout the 1980's to the mid-1990's with a subsequent increase. These data for the proportion of adolescents in the United States (Current Population Reports, 1984). The predicted suicide rates for 15 to 24 year olds show a decrease throughout the 1980's and into the 1990's, corresponding to the decrease in the proportion of adolescents.

While at least decades will be needed to evaluate the population model, recent data lend some support to the hypothesis. The actual suicide rates for 15 to 24 year olds, 1977 to 1983, were reported as follows:

1977:	13.6
1978:	12.4
1979:	12.4
1980:	12.3
1981:	12.3
1982:	12.1
1983:	11.9
1984:	12.5
1985:	12.2 (10% sample)*

The 1977 rate of 13.6 is the highest suicide rate recorded in this country for 15 to 24 year

olds, and it corresponds to the peak in the proportion of 15 to 24 year olds in the population.

Understanding the recent leveling off and decrease in suicide rates among adolescents is aided by Figures 2 and 3, which provide a race and sex breakdown of rates for 15 to 19 and 20 to 24 year olds. For all race and sex groups among 20 to 24 year olds, the recent leveling off and decrease in rates can be seen in Figure 3. Similarly, in Figure 2, 15 to 19 year old nonwhite men and nonwhite women also show recent decreases in rates. However, for 15 to 19 year old white men and white women, the rates do not appear to have leveled off recently. To examine the recent trends among white 15 to 19 year olds, we examined in detail the rate of rise in suicide for these two groups. We found that the rates of increase show a statistically significant decrease over the past several years for white men and white women in the 15 to 19 year age group (Holinger, Offer, and Zola, unpublished data).

DISCUSSION

Self-destructiveness among the young presents us with something of a paradox. On the one hand, young people are at lowest risk of suicide, and their suicide rates are lower than for any other age group. Each year, only about one adolescent per 10,000 commits suicide, whereas the rates for older ages may be ten times that figure. In addition, even among those adolescents identified as needing treatment (Offer, Ostrov, and Howard, 1985), i.e., a high risk group, there is only about one suicide per 1,000 disturbed adolescents. This forces us to ask a number of questions: Why are adolescents at such low risk of suicide? What intrapsychic and sociologic factors protect adolescents from suicide?

*Sources of data: Vital Statistics of the United States, 1977-1979 (for 1977 to 1979 data); National Center for Health Statistics: Advance report, final mortality statistics, 1981. Monthly Vital Statistics Report, Vol. 33, No. 3 Supp. (for 1980 and 1981 data); National Center for Health Statistics: Advance report, final mortality statistics, 1982. Monthly Vital Statistics Report, Vol. 33, No. 9 Supp. (for 1982 data); and National Center for Health Statistics, unpublished data, for 1983 to 1985.

Why does suicide among youth seem to attract so much more research and media attention than does suicide among age groups with much higher rates? Given the relatively low rates of adolescent suicide, can the issue of youth suicide be conceived of as a major public health problem?

On the other hand, suicide is the second leading cause of death among adolescents. Suicide, homicide, and accidents, all of which may reflect self-destructive tendencies, are, in the aggregate, the leading cause of death for persons aged 1 to 39 years in the United States. Such deaths account for more years of life lost in this country than any other cause. In addition, suicide in particular appears to create a ripple effect; it seems to have a life-long traumatic impact on the survivors.

Throughout the 1970's, during studies of the descriptive epidemiology of adolescent suicide, we began focusing on the population shifts among various age groups over time. Specifically, we began examining the relationship between population changes among the young and their violent death rates. We found that increases and decreases, respectively, in the proportion of adolescents in the U.S. population were accompanied by increases and decreases, respectively, in their suicide and homicide rates, and we began publishing these findings (Holinger and Offer, 1982, 1984). The opposite trend was found for older people, i.e., as their proportion in the general population increased, their suicide and homicide rates decreased. The works of Brenner (1971, 1979) on the economy and Easterlin (1980) on population variables were particularly useful in rounding out the sociologic-epidemiologic perspective by which to understand these findings. As the data emerged on population changes and violent deaths, the predictive aspects of the population model assumed particular importance. Inasmuch as we knew the numbers of children and preadolescents in the population, it was possible to approximate the numbers of teenagers over the next two decades.

We projected the proportion of teenagers over the next 20 years and then made predictions of the trends in suicide rates based on those population changes. We began constructing the prediction model up to the year 2000 as described earlier. With the proportion of adolescents peaking in the late 1970's and then beginning to decrease, we suggested that the suicide rates among youth would peak then as well and then begin to level off and decrease. This prediction contrasted with predictions based on cohort studies which implied continued increases. The importance of the attempt at prediction of suicide rates using the population model lies in the possibility of intervention and prevention on a large-scale, epidemiologic level.

It is our task to examine risk factors in youth suicide from primarily one perspective, the epidemiologic. There are other, obviously important risk factors, such as familial, biologic, and affective disorders. The epidemiologic perspective may, however, provide a somewhat different view of the concept of risk factors in general. While white male adolescents are still at greatest risk of suicide among the young, the youthful population as a whole may be at less risk of suicide over the next decade if the hypothesis regarding the population model continues to be supported. However, with the next increase in the proportion of adolescents in the total United States population (probably beginning in the mid-1990's), the youthful population as a whole once again may be at greater risk, as was the case during the 1970's. Various preventive interventions are implied by the population model when the suicide risk increases for the youthful population. For example, as detailed below, high schools, colleges, mental health services, governmental agencies, and businesses will all have a role in addressing this increased risk.

Adolescent Suicide and Population Shifts. One seems obliged to attempt preliminary explanations of the findings at this point. At least three levels of interpretation seem necessary and need to be subjected to further hypothesis-testing: an epidemiologic-sociological level, a psychodynamic-clinical level, and a nosological level.

On the epidemiologic-sociological level, suicide and homicide rates may increase with increases in the proportion of 15 to 24 year olds for a variety of reasons; for example, increased competition for jobs, college positions, academic and athletic honors results in an increased number of adolescents who fail to get such places (Holinger and Offer, 1982, 1984; Holinger and Offer, 1986). Such reasoning is consistent with Barker's (1964, 1968) extensive data on large and small schools. In addition, the younger members of the 15 to 24 year olds may be the least powerful and attractive force in society with respect to political pressure, jobs, and so on. On the other hand, the adults in the 35 to 64 year old groups are much more powerful politically and, with the exception of the older adults, attractive with respect to employment (experience, schooling completed, etc.). Thus, the population increases in the adult age group may lead not so much to increased competition and failure but rather to more economic benefits (greater and more successful pressure on government and union leaders to enlarge the job market, obtain more health services, etc.). Therefore, suicide and homicide rates would decrease with the increased population ratio in the adult age groups.

Briefly, explanations for the two other levels follow somewhat similar reasoning. For example, on the psychodynamic-clinical level, depressed adolescents with marginal ego capabilities and an inadequately internationalized sense of self-esteem may be at increased risk of suicide during times when the increased number of adolescents lead to heightened competition for much-needed external sources of self-esteem (e.g., academic honors, places on athletic teams, etc.). On the nosological level, when the proportion of young people is high, adolescents with thought disorders or major affective disorders may be at greater risk of suicide not only for the above reasons, but also because of a relative decrease in psychiatric services, and counseling that is available for diagnosis and treatment.

Potential Prediction: Psychiatric and Public Health Implications. One of the main features of published reports utilizing a population model has been the potential for prediction of suicide, specifically among the young (Hendin, 1982; Holinger and Offer, 1982, 1985): it was suggested that as the absolute numbers and proportion of adolescents and young adults began to decrease in the late 1970's and 1980's, the suicide rates for those ages (which had been increasing over the previous 20 years with the increase in the youthful population) would begin to level off and decrease as well. This hypothesis has some support from the recent data noted earlier, showing a peak in adolescent suicide rates in 1977 with a subsequent decrease in the proportion of adolescents in the population. Therefore, several researchers (Maris, 1985; Holinger and Offer, 1982, 1984; Hendin, 1982) have explicitly or implicitly predicted that with the leveling off and decreasing of the population of 15 to 24 year olds would come a corresponding leveling off and decrease in the suicide rates of that age group during the late 1970's and 1980's.

There are important psychiatric and public health implications in this model. Based on current population projections, the decrease in the numbers and proportion of 15 to 24 year olds will be ending in the mid-1990's, with another increase in 15 to 24 year olds beginning at that time (Current Population Reports, 1984). Thus, the population model would suggest that the government, schools, employers, health services, etc., should be ready to respond to that increase in terms of increased psychiatric services, counselors, jobs, high school and college expansion, and so on. A preventive response would thus be created, rather than "after-the-fact" reactive model.

The psychiatric implications of the population model are particularly important when one considers epidemiologic data on the number of adolescents who need help but do not get it. Offer, Ostrov, and Howard (1985) found that 20 percent of adolescents in their sample needed psychiatric help but that only 4 percent received help. Thus, 16 percent of adolescents in their sample were in need of treatment but did not get it. With an increased number of adolescents in the population will come even higher numbers of adolescents who do not receive treatment, for whatever reason, and it would be especially critical that this issue of treatment availability and utilization be addressed before periods of increase in the adolescent population.

IMPLICATIONS FOR FUTURE RESEARCH

Four areas of future research appear particularly important with respect to violent deaths, their potential for prediction, and population changes. First, it is critical that the epidemiologic data be increasingly accurate, both in terms of mortality data (local and national) as well as the population bases from which mortality rates are derived. Epidemiology that utilizes national mortality data is a relatively young field in the United States; only since 1933 have complete population data, not just samples, been available for all States in the United States. Therefore, many more decades of data and study will be needed to test various hypotheses involved in these epidemiologic trends.

Second, prospective studies are needed to test specifically the hypotheses on the potential for predicting violent deaths, using a model of population shifts. To this end, mathematical models should be developed to predict violent death rates based on projections of the future population. These predictions of rates then could be measured against the actual findings over the next several years. Such models are currently being developed.

Third, at least two types of cross-cultural studies of violent mortality would help enhance understanding of this leading cause of

death: (1) Further long-term, cross-cultural comparisons of suicide, homicide, and accident rates with a focus on period, cohort, and age effects, and (2) cross-cultural studies that examined violent deaths and population changes to evaluate the predictive and preventive aspects of the population model.

Fourth, and finally, we have attempted in this paper and others (Holinger and Offer, 1982, 1984) to examine violent death mortality rates primarily from the perspective of the single variable of population changes. We have focused on this variable because of its potential for prediction, with changes in population for the various age groups being known years in advance. Yet, it is apparent that understanding something as complex as violent deaths (whether from an intrapsychic or epidemiologic perspective) requires a concept of a general systems approach. From an epidemiologic perspective, the work of Easterlin (1980) on population changes and Brenner (1971, 1979) and others (Wasserman, 1984; MacMahon, Johnson, and Pugh, 1963; Colledge, 1982; Courmier and Klerman, unpublished manuscript) on economic variables have been particularly important. The relationship between economy and mortality rates is well documented, with poor economic conditions (as indicated by high unemployment rates) being related to higher mortality rates (Brenner, 1971, 1979; Wasserman, 1984; MacMahon, Johnson, and Pugh, 1963; Colledge, 1982; Courmier and Klerman, unpublished manuscript). In addition, the birth rate in the United States (which, with immigration and increased life expectancy, will be responsible for most of the relevant population changes) tends to be inversely related to economic changes in the United States: bad economic conditions correspond to low birth rates and vice-versa (Turner, et al., 1981). Thus, an interacting system emerges, within which violent death mortality may be understood from an epidemiologic perspective; this system includes such variables as economic conditions, birth rates, and population shifts. However, despite the well documented relationship between the economy and mortality rates, one cannot predict future violent death rates from this relationship because of the difficulty in predicting future economic conditions. Thus, another important area of future research emerges: further work is needed to determine if the population model discussed in this paper will make possible predictions not only for violent death rates but also for economic conditions for specific age groups (as per Easterlin's work (1980)), inasmuch as the population shifts for certain age groups are known years ahead.

REFERENCES ················

1. Barker RG: Ecological Psychology. Stanford, California, Stanford University Press, 1968.

2. Barker RG, Gump PV: Big School, Small School: High School Size and Student Behavior. Stanford, California, Stanford University Press, 1964.

3. Brenner MH: Time Series Analysis of Relationships between Selected Economic and Social Indicators. Springfield, Virginia: National Technical Information Service, 1971.

4. Brenner MH: Mortality and the national economy. Lancet 1979:568-573.

5. Colledge M: Economic cycle and health. Soc. Sci. Med. 16:1919-1927, 1982.

6. Cormier HJ, Klerman GL: Unemployment and male-female labor force participation as determinants of changing suicide rates of males and females in Quebec. Unpublished manuscript.

7. Doege T: An injury is no accident. NEJM 298:509-510, 1978.

8. Dunn HL, Shackley W: Comparison of cause of death assignments by the 1929 and 1938 revisions of the International List: Deaths in the United States, 1940. Vital Statistics-Special Reports, Vol. 19, No. 14, 1944.

9. Easterlin RA: Birth and Fortune. New York, Casic Books, 1980.

10. Farberow N: The Many Faces of Suicide. New York, McGraw-Hill, 1979.

11. Faust MM, Dolman AB: Comparability of mortality statistics for the fifth and sixth revisions: United States, 1950. Vital Statistics-Special Reports, Vol. 51, No. 2, 1963a.

12. Faust MM, Dolman AB: Comparability ratios based on mortality statistics for the fifth and sixth revisions: United States, 1950. Vital Statistics-Special Reports, Vol. 51, No. 3, 1963b.

13. Faust MM, Dolman AB: Comparability of mortality statistics for the sixth and seventh revisions: United States, 1958. Vital Statistics---Special Reports, Vol. 51, No. 4, 1965.

14. Freud S: The Psychopathology of Everyday Life. London, The Hogarth Press, 1960 (1901).

15. Gordon RE, Gordon KK: Social psychiatry of a mobile suburb. Int J Social Psychiatry 6:89-106, 1960.

16. Hellon CP, Solomon MI: Suicide and age in Alberta, Canada, 1951-1977. Arch Gen Psychiatry 37:505-510, 1980.

17. Hendin H: Suicide in America. New York, WW Norton & Co., 1982.

18. Herzog A, Levy L, Verdonk A: Some ecological factors associated with health and social adaptation in the city of Rotterdam. Urban Ecology 2:205-234, 1977.

19. Holford TR: The estimation of age, period and cohort effects for vital rates. Biometrics 39:1311-1324, 1983.

20. Holinger PC: Violent Deaths in the United States, 1900-1980: An Epidemiologic Study of Suicide, Homicide and Accidents. New York: Guilford Press, 1987 (in press).

21. Holinger PC, Holinger D, Sandlow J: Violent deaths among children in the United States, 1900-1980: An epidemiologic study of suicide, homicide, and accidental deaths among 5-14 year olds. Pediatrician 12:11-19, 1983-1985.

22. Holinger PC, Klemen EH: Violent Deaths in the United States, 1900-1975. Soc Sci Med 16:1929-1938, 1982.

23. Holinger PC, Offer D: Perspectives of suicide in adolescence. In Research in Community and Mental Health, Volume 2 (Simmons R, ed), Greenwich, CT, JAI Press, 1981, pp. 139-157.

24. Holinger PC, Offer D: Prediction of adolescent suicide: A population model. Am J Psychiatry 139:302-307, 1982.

25. Holinger PC, Offer D: Toward the prediction of violent deaths among the young. In Suicide Among the Young (Sudak, et al, eds) New York, Wright PSG, 1984.

26. Holinger PC, Offer D: The epidemiology of suicide, homicide, and accidents among adolescents, 1900-1980. In Advances in Adolescent Mental Health, Vol. 1, Part B (Feldman R, ed.), Greenwich, CT, JAI Press, 1986, pp. 119-145.

27. Klebba AJ: Homicide trends in the United States, 1900-1974. Public Health Reports 90:195-204, 1975.

28. Klebba AJ, Dolman AB: Comparability of mortality statistics for the seventh and eighth revisions of the International Classification of Diseases, United States. Vital and Health Statistics, Series 2, No. 66, Washington DC, US Government Printing Office, 1975.

29. Klerman GL; Lavori PW; Rice J; et al.: Birth-Cohort trends in rates of major depressive disorder among relatives of patients with affective disorder. Arch Gen Psychiatry 42:689-693, 1985.

30. Kramer M, Pollack ES, Redick RW, Locke BZ: Mental Disorders/Suicide. Cambridge, MA, Harvard University Press, 1972.

31. Levy L, Herzog A: Effects of population density and crowding on health and social adaptation in the Netherlands. J Health Soc Behavior 15:228-240, 1974.

32. Levy L, Herzog A: Effects of crowding on health and social adaptation in the city of Chicago. Urban Ecology 3:327-354, 1978.

33. MacMahon B, Johnson S, Pugh TF: Relation of suicide rates to social conditions. Public Health Reports 78:285-293, 1963.

34. Maris R: The adolescent suicide problem. Suicide Life-Threatening Beh 15:91-109, 1985.

35. Menninger KA: Man Against Himself. New York, Harcourt Brace and Co. 1938.

36. Murphy GE, Wetzel RD: Suicide risk by birth cohort in the United States, 1949-1974. Arch Gen Psychiatry 37:519-523, 1980.

37. National Center for Health Statistics: Annual Summary for the United States, 1979. Monthly Vital Statistics Report 28:28, 1980.

38. National Center for Health Statistics: Advance Report, final mortality statistics, 1982. Monthly Vital Statistics Report, Vol. 33, No. 9, Supp. DDHS Pub. No. (PHS) 85-1120. Public Health Science, Hyattsville, MD, Dec. 20, 1984.

39. Offer D, Ostrof E, and Howard KI: Epidemiology of Mental health and mental illness among adolescents. In

Significant Advances in Child Psychiatry (Call J, ed). New York: Basic Books Inc., 1986, in press.

40. Peck M, Litman RE: Current trends in youthful suicide. Tribuna Medica 14:13-17, 1973.

41. Seiden RH: Suicide among youth: A review of the literature, 1900-

1967. Bull Suicidology (Suppl), 1969.

42. Seiden RH: Death in the West - A regional analysis of the youthful suicide rate. West J Med 140:969-973, 1984.

43. Seiden RH, Freitas RP: Shifting patterns of deadly violence. Suicide Life - Threatening Beh 10:195-209, 1980.

44. Shapiro J, Wynne EA: Adolescent alienation: Evaluating the hypotheses. Social Indicators Research 10:423-435. 1982.

45. Solomon MI, Hellon CP: Suicide and age in Alberta, Canada, 1951-1977. Arch Gen Psychiatry 37:511-513, 1980.

46. Toolan JM: Suicide and suicidal attempts in children and adolescents. Am J Psychiatry 118:719-724, 1962.

47. Toolan JM: Suicide in children and adolescents. Am J Psychiatry 29:339-344, 1975.

48. Tsuang MT, Boor M, Fleming JA: Psychiatric aspects of traffic accidents. Am J Psychiatry 142:538-546, 1985.

49. Turner CW, Fenn MR, Cole AM: A social psychological analysis of violent behavior. In Violent Behavior: Social learning approaches to Prediction, Management and Treatment (Stuart RB, ed) New York, Brunner/Mazel, 1981.

50. U.S. Bureau of the Census, Current Population Reports, Series P-25, No. 952, Projections of the Population of the United States by Age, Sex, and Race: 1983 to 2080. U.S. Government Printing Office, Washington, DC, 1984.

51. Vital Statistics of the United States, 1979: Mortality. Washington DC, US Government Printing Office, 1984.

52. Vital Statistics-Special Reports. Vol. 14, No. 2. Washington DC, US Government Printing Office, 1941.

53. Vital Statistics-Special Reports: Death rates by age, race and sex, United States, 1900-1953. Vol. 43, Washington DC, US Government Printing Office, 1956.

54. Wasserman IM: The influence of economic business cycles on the United States suicide rates. Suicide Life-Threatening Beh 14:143-156, 1984.

55. Wechsler H: Community growth, depressive disorders, and suicide. Am J Sociology 67:9-16, 1961.

56. Weiss NS: Recent trends in violent deaths among young adults in the United States. Am J Epidemiology 103:416-422, 1976.

57. Wolfgang ME: Suicide by means of victim-precipitated homicide. J Clin Exp Psychopathol 20:335-349, 1959.

58. Wolfgang ME: Patterns in Criminal Homicide. Philadelphia, PA, University of Pennsylvania Press, 1968.

PREPARATORY AND PRIOR SUICIDAL BEHAVIOR FACTORS

Norman L. Farberow, Ph.D., Cofounder, The Institute for Studies of Destructive Behaviors, and Suicide Prevention Center, Los Angeles, California

INTRODUCTION

Suicide does not just occur. Experience has shown that it is more often the end result of a process that has developed over a period of time and within which have been many fluctuations in the course of reaching the decision to act against oneself. Fortunately, experience has also shown that during that period, the individual engages in a number of behaviors that have become available as signs and portents. There are, of course, many kinds of signs such as epidemiological, demographic, family characteristics, personality disorders, cultural factors, and others. Although inevitably there will be some overlap with other areas, this paper will focus on behavioral factors only; that is, acts and actions engaged in by the person that indicate the potential for a self-destructive act to occur in the future.

Because of the large amount of pertinent research in the area of behavioral factors, this review, necessarily, is arbitrary and selective. For example, no effort has been made to examine all the so-called suicide potential scales containing predictive items. First, there are no scales specifically constructed to evaluate suicide potential in adolescents; second, the behavioral items on the scales are almost all considered individually in this paper anyhow; and third, many of the scales depend on clinically reported items rather than on research-substantiated factors. Finally, it must be remembered that, while considering each factor separately, the factors almost always will appear in a context that will contain other clues, some of which may affect considerably the significance of the factor discussed.

PRIOR SELF-DESTRUCTIVE BEHAVIOR

Prior self-destructive behavior, whether in the form of suicide attempts, threats, ideation, or gestures, has been identified by many investigators as a powerful indicator of completed suicide risk (1,2,3,4,5). However, the research was conducted primarily on adults in psychiatric settings, general hospitals, and in the community. This paper will focus on children, adolescents, and youth. For the most part, studies reviewed are limited to those whose subjects are aged 20 or below, but occasional research that includes older ages are included. The format will look at studies of completed suicides, then attempted suicides within each risk variable. The research on children or young adolescents are presented first. In addition, the studies are further divided on the basis of the presence or absence of control or comparison groups.

PRIOR SUICIDAL BEHAVIOR

Completed Suicides - Control Groups

The risk factors of previous self-injuries, suicide attempts, threats, ideation, and gestures have been grouped under the general heading of prior suicidal behavior. Most of the time, the prior suicidal behavior refers to suicide attempts. However, many researchers have not differentiated between suicide attempts and gestures, or between suicidal ideation and threats, and often, not between suicide attempts and threats. When such distinctions appear it is uncertain how much overlap has occurred, for suicide attempts are almost always preceded by threats and ideation. The best approach was deemed the conservative one of assuming that all the forms of suicidal activity, verbal and behavioral, are equivalent for the purposes of risk evaluation and prediction. As seen later in this paper, this view is substantiated by other investigators. Dorpat and Ripley's (5) review of studies of committed suicides from the United States and England led them to the conclusion that between 20 percent and 65 percent of individuals who commit suicide have made prior suicide attempts. In an additional 15 studies (5) that determined the incidence of completed suicides in groups of attempted suicides by followup, the authors found that the percentages ranged from 0.03 percent in one short followup study to 22.05 percent in the longest followup study. The researchers estimate the incidence of committed suicide among the suicide attempts to be between 10 percent and 20 percent, but add their belief that the actual number of attempted suicides who go on to commit suicide is greater than the percentage given.

Relatively few investigators over the past 10 to 15 years have used control groups in their studies of completed adolescent suicides, a fact that does not surprise too much in terms of the problems involved in obtaining appropriate groups for comparison. One approach has been through the use of matched

peers. Shafii, Carrigan, Whittinghill and Derrick (6) at the University of Louisville conducted psychological autopsies on 20 adolescents, ages 12-19, who committed suicide in Jefferson County, Kentucky. Their highly relevant control group was made up of 17 matched-pair living peer friends, the same age and sex as the adolescent suicide, from whom the same extensive set of data were gathered. The researchers found that the suicides were significantly more often likely to have a history of suicide threats (p <.02) and suicidal ideation with expressions of the wish to die (p <.02) than did the controls.

Rich, Young, and Fowler (7) also conducted psychological autopsies. The subjects were all 283 completed suicides in San Diego County over a period of 20 months. The investigators compared the 133 suicides under the age 30 with the 150 suicides age 30 and over and found that prior suicide threats and attempts were high in all ages of completed suicides. Prior "suicide talk," 71 percent, and suicide attempts, 42 percent, were noted in the under 30 age group, but were not significantly different from the frequencies of 63 percent suicide talk and 35 percent attempts found in the over 30 age group. The comprehensive psychological autopsy study of Maris (8) compared completed suicides (from Cook County, Illinois) with attempted suicides and natural deaths (from Baltimore, Maryland). The study covered all ages, including 36 young adults, adolescents and children ages 10 to 29, among his study population of 414 subjects. In analyzing his data on all subjects with highly sophisticated statistical methods, Maris found that the single factor with the greatest discriminatory power (beta .64) was the number of prior suicide attempts; however, that factor separated the two suicidal groups from the natural deaths, but not from each other. The interesting factor that distinguished the completed suicides was that they had one relatively serious prior attempt, while the attempters had several low-lethality prior suicide attempts. When Maris (9) later compared his group of 36 young completed suicides with the remainder of his completed suicide group, using the same statistical procedures, he found that the factor most significant in differentiating the young suicides from the older suicides continued to be the greater number of prior suicide attempts in their histories.

Seidin's (10) study compared a group of 25 students at the University of California at Berkeley who committed suicide over a 10-year period, with the entire UCB student body population during the same period. Information from newspaper clippings, police files, university records and reports of friends and acquaintances indicated there were "numerous warnings" in almost every case of suicide, and 22 percent had made prior suicide attempts. They had also given subtle warnings, such as making wry jokes about killing themselves, or crossing out the word emergency in the question "Whom shall we notify in case of emergency?" on the medical history form, and substituting the word, death.

PRIOR SUICIDAL BEHAVIOR

Completed Suicide - No Control Group

Control groups for completed suicide are often neither available nor feasible. Non-controlled studies are nevertheless valuable in providing information and generating direction and hypotheses for further study. Some of the following suicide studies of children and adolescents are marked by extensive exploration into background, personality, behavioral, physical, and communication factors. As in the case of controlled studies, prior suicidal behavior is referred to often as a significant risk-indicator in the histories of the completed suicides the investigators studied.

Shaffer's (11) study is well-known and often referred to because of its study population completeness--all the children and younger adolescent suicides under age 14 occurring in England and Wales over a 7-year period, 1962 to 1968--and its exhaustive search for

information from a wide variety of sources-- government, school, medical, social service, and family. The histories of his 30 cases disclosed that 46 percent, almost half, had previously attempted or threatened suicide, or revealed their suicidal thoughts before their death, with 27 percent having done so in the 24-hour period before their death.

Three studies, in widely separated parts of the world, using coroner's office reports and hospital records, where available, of completed suicides, found that prior suicide attempts were significant. Cosand, Bourque, and Kraus (12), gathered data on 315 suicides between ages 10 and 24 that occurred in Sacramento County, California, between the years 1925 and 1979. They compared the older youth with the adolescents aged 15 to 19 and found that the older age group had made significantly more suicide attempts than the younger age suicides and that the females in both age groups had significantly more prior suicide attempts than the males. In another long term study, Marek, Widacki, and Zwarysiewicz (13) compared 76 cases of committed suicides among "juveniles" occurring between the years 1881 to 1960, with 76 similar cases occurring over 15 years, 1960 to 1974, in Cracow, Poland. Data were obtained from hospital records and coroners' offices. In the more recent 76 cases, they found prior suicidal attempts in 17 percent of the cases and suicide threats and ideation in an additional 13 percent. In a large-scale study of Ontario, Canada, Garfinkel, Chamberlin, and Golombek (14) examined all the data available in the coroner's office records for the 1,554 suicides aged 10 to 24 that occurred between January 1971 and August 1978. They found that a history of threats, note-leaving, general manifestations of depression, and other suicidal behavior "accounted for the majority of prior symptoms" in the cases for which information on prior conditions was available.

In summary, studies of the histories of completed suicides, whether control or comparison groups are used or not, indicate that prior suicidal behavior in the form of attempts, threats, or ideation, or combination of these, is one of the strongest indicators of high risk in adolescents as well as in adults. Percentages of frequency of this factor, supported by good methodology and statistical evaluation, vary from 22 percent to 71 percent in study populations from university, government, and city hospital settings; in psychiatric and general populations; and from coroner's office records.

PRIOR SUICIDAL BEHAVIOR

Suicide Attempts, Threats, Ideation — Control Groups

The presence or absence of prior suicidal behavior has been explored in controlled studies even more frequently among suicide attempters than among completed suicides. Some studies have been retrospective, others prospective.

Two studies serve as landmarks in this area. Jacobs' (15) and Teicher's (16) carefully designed research compared 50 adolescent suicide attempters treated at Los Angeles County General Hospital with a matched control group of 31 adolescents at a suburban high school. They reported 44 percent of the attempters had one or more previous suicide attempts, while there were no attempts among the controls. The other landmark early study was a total population study in Sweden carried out by Otto (17) on all the children and adolescents under age 21 who made a suicide attempt and came to the attention of health authorities. A control group consisted of adolescents from the general population matched for age, sex, and geographical region. Otto found that 16 percent of his study population of the 1,727 young suicide attempters had made previous suicide attempts. Prior attempts were more common among boys (21%) than girls (14%).

In three studies of overdosers, prior suicide attempts were frequent in the experimental groups and absent in the controls. McIntire and Angle (18) found that 26 percent of 50 poison center patients ages 6 to 18, had made similar suicide gestures in the past, whereas

no such gesture was reported by any of the controls. McKenry, Tishler, and Kelley (19) noted that prior suicide attempts were marked in their study population of 46 adolescent attempters admitted to a university hospital primarily for overdoses. The nonsuicidal comparison group from the same hospital had no prior suicide attempts in their history. In a study from England, Hawton, Osborn, O'Grady, and Cole (20) followed up 50 adolescents who were treated for suicide overdoses at the Oxford General Hospital Psychiatric Service in England. The investigators found that 40 percent of the attempters--versus none of the controls from a sample of the general population--had either taken an overdose or injured themselves prior to the attempt that brought them into the study.

Clarkin, Friedman, Hurt, Corn, and Aronoff (21) studied two different age groups of adolescents with suicidal behavior in a New York Hospital; the first group had a mean age of 16 and the second a mean age of 25.5. The researchers noted that 58 percent of the adolescents and 75 percent of the young adults had made at least one prior attempt. Apparently, prior suicide attempts appear in significant numbers in the younger, as well as the older, adolescents and youth.

PRIOR SUICIDAL BEHAVIOR

Attempts, Threats, Ideation — No Control Groups

Selected studies of young suicide attempters seen in psychiatric hospitals and in private practice note the presence of prior suicide attempts in the history. Shafii and Shafii (22) reviewed 340 cases of children and younger adolescents mostly aged 13 to 15, for suicidal or severe self-destructive behaviors seen on an emergency basis at the Child Psychiatric Services at the University of Louisville Hospital; Diekstra (23) reviewed 158 admissions of adolescent suicide attempters to a hospital in Holland. Both studies noted that the risk of suicide is significantly increased when a previous suicide attempt has been made. Diekstra found that previous suicide attempts and suicide threats or ideation ranked first and second in significance among the indicators.

Schneer, Perlstein, and Brozovsky's (24) interesting study reported that the admissions during one year for a hospital in Brooklyn at two different times, 11 years apart, indicated that the number of suicidal adolescents had almost doubled, from 13.6 percent to 26.7 percent, although the census of admissions had remained practically the same. Concomitantly, the percentage of admissions with repeated episodes of suicidal behavior had increased five-fold, from 4 percent to 20 percent. Gabrielson et al. (25) studied a special risk group, 14 pregnant females, aged 13 to 17, who had made suicide attempts and were admitted to the Yale-New Haven Hospital, and found that 21 percent had histories of prior suicide attempts. Crumley (26) reviewed the histories from his own private practice of 40 adolescents, aged 12 to 19, in treatment following a suicidal attempt. He found a history of numerous prior attempts was common in 17, or 40 percent.

In summary, retrospective studies of histories of adolescent suicide attempters, all except one from hospital populations where they were treated, indicated substantial levels of prior suicidal behavior, ranging from 16 percent to 38 percent. At least half the studies were controlled.

SUBSEQUENT SUICIDAL BEHAVIOR

Followup Studies — Control Groups

The preceding studies were retrospective; they started with groups of completed suicides or attempted suicide and then sought information in the young people's histories that indicated identifying or predictive behavior, especially prior suicidal behavior. The following group of studies use a prospective approach, taking groups from their index suicidal behavior and following them for various periods of time, noting the kinds and

frequencies of suicidal behaviors that subsequently appeared.

As in the previous studies of attempted suicides, the presence of a prior suicidal behavior is a good predictor of the index suicidal behavior, which in turn, becomes a valuable clue to predict suicidal behavior in the followup period. Barter, Swaback, and Todd (27) and Stanley and Barter (28) provide two reports on a followup study of a group of adolescents, under the age of 21, hospitalized for suicide attempts in the Colorado Psychiatric Hospital over a 3-year period. A followup interview on 45 patients indicated continued suicidal behavior by 42 percent of the youngsters. Stanley and Barter (28) extended the study to include psychiatrically ill adolescents hospitalized at the same time but with with no history of suicidal behavior. The followup data indicated that suicide attempts occurred in 50 percent of the experimental subjects and in only 16 percent of the controls, a highly significant difference.

Otto's (17) study, referred to earlier, was actually a 10-year followup of 1,727 child and adolescent suicide attempters in Sweden. They were compared with nonsuicidal children equivalent demographically. A huge undertaking, it was possible only in a country where data are routinely kept on its citizens from the time they are born until they die. Otto found that mortality was significantly higher in the suicidal group than in the controls, with 5.4 percent deceased in the experimental group and 1.8 percent deceased among the controls. Of the attempters who died, 80 percent committed suicide. Repeated attempts were more common among boys than girls, 21 percent versus 14 percent.

Four additional controlled studies reported on the occurrence of suicidal events following treatment for suicide attempts. Cohen-Sandler and Berman's (29) well-designed investigation conducted with young suicidal children, ages 6 to 16, followed for 3 years 20 suicidal children, 21 depressed but not suicidal children, and 35 psychiatric controls, nonsuicidal and nondepressed. Five percent of the children had engaged in multiple suicide attempts before the index hospitalization. Twenty percent of the suicidal children were suicidal again after discharge. No further suicidal behavior was reported in the other two groups.

Rauenhorst (31) followed a group of 50 Caucasian female attempters, ages 16 to 30, and compared them with matched controls, who had been treated for minor or accidental trauma. Followup continued for 14 to 21 months after discharge. Among the 38 experimentals and 44 controls located and interviewed, 5 of the experimentals, 38 percent, and none of the controls had made a subsequent suicide attempt. One person made several subsequent attempts.

As part of his larger study, Motto (32) followed for 10 years male adolescents who had been admitted and treated in psychiatric inpatient hospitals in San Francisco because of a suicidal state or depressive mood. He focused on the 122 boys in this population who were ages 10 to 19 and found that 11 suicides, 9 percent, occurred within a mean of 38 months after discharge. Motto further reports that 43 percent of the 119 subjects had a history of one or more attempts before the index hospitalization, and that 9 percent of those who reported no prior suicide attempts went on to commit suicide, whereas 10 percent of those with a history of prior attempts did so.

In a study in Oxford, England, Hawton, et al. (20) did two followups of 50 adolescent overdosers aged 18 and under, at 1 month and 12 months after discharge. He compared his group, divided into two sub-groups, one 15 and below and the second 16 to 18, with a general population sample previously collected. In the year following the overdose, 14 percent of the patients made further suicide attempts, all but one of them in the 16 to 18 year age group.

SUBSEQUENT SUICIDAL BEHAVIOR

Followup Studies — Not Control Groups

Two researchers report followup studies but do not use control groups. White (33) surveyed 50 consecutive patients aged 14 to 19 admitted to a general hospital in Birmingham, England, following suicidal overdoses. Information on 40 of the cases in 1 year of followup indicated that 10 percent of the patients had further self-poisoning episodes. Crumley's (26) group of 40 adolescents in his private practice who had entered treatment following a suicide attempt yielded one patient, 3 percent, who committed suicide within 2 years following his treatment.

In summary, the followup studies of suicidal behavior support further the usefulness of prior suicidal behavior as an indicator of suicide risk. Further suicide attempts ranged from 10 percent to 50 percent, and completed suicides occurred in from 3 percent to 10 percent subsequently. As one would expect, most of the study populations were hospital patients. The followup times varied considerably, ranging from several months to 10 years.

In general, from the studies of completed suicides, attempts, threats, and ideation suicidal behavior--with and without control groups and retrospectively in case histories or prospectively through followups--prior suicidal behavior is a significant and valuable clue for further self-destructive behavior. The risk factor seems valid both for children and adolescents and for boys and girls and also seems to increase in significance with increasing age among adolescents.

RELATIONSHIP BETWEEN COMPLETED SUICIDE, SUICIDE ATTEMPTS AND SUICIDE THREATS

Most efforts to explore the relationship between the various kinds of suicide have approached the problem from two directions--similarities and differences between demographic characteristics, suicide methods and motivations, and/or the extent to which all the suicide behaviors occur in the same persons. Stengel and Cook (38) were the first to demonstrate the demographic and personality differences between completed and attempted suicides in their London study. Those differences, that is, that attempters are younger, use less lethal methods, have more women than men, more often occur where others can rescue, have been substantiated regularly. The role of intention to die has been found to be critical, with the attempters more often motivated to influence others than to die. The concept of attempted suicide has been incorporated in Kreitman's term, parasuicide, in which he emphasized the nonfatal aspect of the act when an "individual deliberately causes self-injury or ingests a substance in excess of any prescribed or generally recognized therapeutic dosage" (63, page 3). Kreitman and his colleagues (39) find their studies have confirmed the traditional view that parasuicides and suicides are epidemiologically distinct. Sex and age patterns are different, rates are very different and motivations may be different. At the same time they note the close relationship between the two, with one percent of parasuicides going on to commit suicide within one year and 41 percent of the completed suicides having a history of parasuicide. Although Kreitman's populations refer to the general population, their studies included ages down through 15.

Marks' and Haller's (40) large scale study on the relationship between attempts and threats compared adolescents who had made suicide attempts with adolescents referred for both suicide attempts and for suicidal thoughts and threats, and with adolescents referred for suicidal thoughts and/or threats but with no suicide attempts. The comparison group was the rest of their large sample of disturbed adolescents not referred for suicidal behavior. The groups were compared on family, school, friends, leisure time interests, emotions, etc. using psychological tests, interviews and therapists ratings. Marks and Haller concluded that there was little evidence to support the assertion that those teenagers that threatened suicide were markedly different from those who attempted it. The results also indicated the same distinctions in personality and demographic characteristics between commits and threats as had been found between commits and attempts. For suicide attempts, the 3:1 ratio of females to males was confirmed; for suicidal thoughts, the ratio was more 2:1 female to male. There were apparently enough sex differences to emphasize the need to study the sexes separately.

Goldberg's (41) study aimed at identifying characteristics that may be the same for people with suicide ideation, those who attempted suicide and those who completed suicide. A variety of schedules were administered to 489 persons and the presence or absence of thoughts of suicide during the previous month were related to the various factors as the outcome variables. Goldberg concluded from the similarities reported by the subjects, that suicide ideation, attempts, and completions, if not on a continuum, are at least overlapping phenomena. Persons with these different kinds of suicidal manifestations, she felt might be essentially equivalent.

In summary, the overlap to which all the suicide behaviors, commits, attempts, threats, and education occur in the same population has been noted at length in the studies surveyed in the preceding sections of this paper. While it is possible, as Kreitman (39) has done, to focus on the differences between the populations, it is the similarities and overlap that seem more impressive. It is also unlikely that an "overlap" group exists as a separate group, as has been suggested. In general, it seems justifiable to conclude that the presence of any of the overt forms of suicidal behavior, such as attempts, threats and/or ideation in the prior history of any individual can be considered valuable indicators of high risk for further self-destructive acts. The usefulness of the presence of high levels of indirect self-destructive behaviors as predictive clues is much more uncertain.

PREPARATORY BEHAVIORS

While the risk factors reviewed above, prior and subsequent attempts, threats and ideation, rate as excellent indicators of suicide risk, they have the disadvantage of occurring late in the process of identification, and mark the fact that a suicidal state has already existed. The obvious aim is to identify factors that occur earlier, before any overt suicidal behavior has appeared, so that intervention to prevent possible injury or death can take place. The following section reviews studies that note activities aptly termed "preparatory behaviors" that may be considered as risk factors for potential suicide.

INDIRECT SELF-DESTRUCTIVE BEHAVIOR

Indirect self-destructive behavior (ISDB) has long been recognized as an important aspect of self-destructive behavior (34) but it has not been systematically investigated until relatively recently. Menninger (35) developed the concept psychodynamically as "focal or partial suicide" while Farberow (36) has conducted research on a number of the behaviors felt to be indirectly self-destructive, or suicidal equivalents. Whereas a number of behaviors have been identified as indirect self-destructive behavior (36), only the research by Farberow will be discussed in this paper.

No studies, except those of Farberow and his colleagues, have specifically explored the parameters of these behaviors from the point of view of determining the personality characteristics, attitudes, prevalence and demographic features of persons who consistently engage in this kind of behavior. Farberow (36) selected various groups of persons engaging in indirect self-destructive behavior (ISDB) and conducted controlled studies of their characteristics. One specifically involved young people, juvenile delinquents. Studies were conducted of groups of patients who were diabetic, had thromboangiitis obliterans or Buerger's Disease, were elderly and chronically ill, hyperobese, or on renal hemodialysis. Control groups were made up of cooperative patients in each disease group. In addition, a file survey determined the presence and kind of ISDB in five treatment groups: two drug rehabilitation programs, a youth delinquency program and two hospital populations, one of completed and one of attempted suicide. Briefly summarized, the major results obtained from these studies characterized the patients with levels of ISDB as: high impulsivity, low frustration tolerance, present orientation, minimal tolerance for frustration or delay, and little future orientation or concern. These characteristics were frequently accompanied by strong drives toward risk taking, pleasure seeking, and a need for excitement. In the case file study, the methadone maintenance group had the highest ISDB scores, especially on noncompliance with medical regimen, not making recommended changes in life activities, and disregarding treatment requirements. Alcohol abuse was one of the most frequent forms of ISDB, appearing in from one-half to one-third of the drug abusers. In the youth diversion group, where the ages were 18 and under, 5 percent were noted to be problem drinkers and 20 percent to be drug abusers. Overt suicidal behavior in any of the groups was absent or minimal, except among the elderly chronically ill. There was a high inverse correlation between suicide potential and life satisfaction, leading to the conclusion that ISDB among the elderly, chronically ill was generated by feelings of isolation and loss, variables also known to arouse direct suicidal behavior. It may be that the elderly, chronically ill person uses ISDB as a way of avoiding the stigma and taboos characterizing overt suicide. The extent to which the ISDB frustrates the hospital staff may also bring some feeling of power into an environment in which the patients have, for the most part, lost control of their lives.

In general, indirect self-destructive behavior as an indicator of suicide risk is behavior about which there is still far too little understood to function as a reliable clue. The difficulty seems to lie in its complexity in that different degrees of certain kinds of ISDB may serve different purposes in the same individual, protecting the individual in some instances (as substitute behavior) or putting him at greater risk (by becoming part of the problem and making it even larger). Substance abuse seems to be at least a low level indicator of risk but will be useful only if accompanied by other, more reliable indicators.

SCHOOL PROBLEMS

School plays an important role in the life of the young person, eventually occupying at least a third of the individual's day. As the second major social system in which children and adolescents are involved, it adds its own pressures and stresses to the traditional ones of family and home. A number of investigators of suicide have found school behaviors such as failures, discipline, and truancy significant as risk factors for potential suicidal behavior.

Academic Performance

A number of investigators noted school failures and falling behind the appropriate grade among both completed and attempted adolescent suicides. Seiden (10) found that although undergraduate suicides did much better than their fellow classmates in terms of grade point average, 3.18 versus 2.50,

there was a continuous deterioration of their performance as they progressed through school. The students were filled with doubts of adequacy and were despondent over their general academic aptitude. Iga (42) describes the pervasive concern about gaining entrance into school and performing in school well enough to stay in it as primary contributing factor in suicides of Japanese youth. Education is virtually the only means for achieving security in a society that is highly status conscious. Preparation for the examination begins in early childhood for many Japanese. At least 80 percent of the children attend a neighborhood cram school for further preparation after school hours.

Shafii, et al. (6) report conflicting data about school performance from their studies of committed suicides versus attempted suicides. They found that poor academic performance or being a school drop-out did not differentiate their suicide subjects from their control subjects. However, acting-out behavior resulting in disciplinary problems and suspension from school did significantly differentiate the suicides from the controls. In contrast, Shafii and Shafii (22) found that failure in academic performance was a marked characteristic of young suicide attempters, 15 and younger, when compared with nonsuicidal psychiatric patients.

Pfeffer, et al. (43,44) found differences in suicidal behavior between inpatients and outpatients of latency age. As a result of a higher incidence of multiple deficits in ego functioning in both the suicidal and nonsuicidal inpatients groups, at least three-fourths of each group tested below grade level. However, the suicidal children were much more worried about doing poorly in school than the nonsuicidal controls, 48 percent versus 19 percent. In contrast, among the outpatients, both suicidals and controls worried about doing poorly in school, but showed no significant difference in the percentage functioning at the appropriate school grade level.

The percentage performing poorly in school was noted as high (78%) in the study by

Barter, Swaback, and Todd (27); 58 percent by Hawton, et al. (20); and 35 to 38 percent by Garfinkel and Golombek (37). Garfinkel and Golombek (37) found that more than half were experiencing failure in school or were drop-outs, but closer inspection indicated that the severity of the attempt made a difference. Those attempts rated most severe were correlated most highly with success at school while minor or moderate ratings of severity of suicide attempts was more significantly associated with failure at school. They felt this corroborated results in a previous study of completed suicides in which the suicides had been associated with industrious and productive performances.

Stanley and Barter (28) found that disturbance in school adjustment was an early and frequent indicator of emotional disturbance in adolescence. However, they were not able to demonstrate a significant difference in adequate school adjustment between their experimental and control groups. In their followup, they did find a difference with patients who repeated suicide attempts after discharge having significantly poorer school records than the control groups.

Otto (17) noted school problems also in his extensive followup of suicide attempters. However, the levels of school problems he found for his experimental group, 7 percent, was considerably lower than those reported in the preceding studies. The nature of the school problems were primarily unsatisfactory school results, desire to quit school, problems relating to teachers and school friends, and severe fear of examinations. Otto said that it is unusual for the school to be the direct cause of a suicide attempt. When an attempt does occur it is more likely to be in the higher grades where the demands may be too much for some children. Marek, et al. (13) found school failures to be the primary motive for suicide deaths in their study of juvenile suicides in Poland.

Among uncontrolled studies, Rohn, et al. (45) found that 75 percent of the teenagers hospitalized for a suicide attempt at the University of Maryland Hospital had exceptionally poor school records. Tishler, McKenry and Christman-Morgan (46) felt that deteriorating school marks and worry about failing school were typical of their adolescent suicide attempters seen at a children's hospital in Columbus, Ohio.

Strong contradictory evidence is reported by Cohen-Sandler, Berman, and King (30) in their well controlled study that divided subjects into four developmental stages from birth to 15 years. Their control groups were depressed and nonsuicidal psychiatric children. They found, in contrast to the high frequency of school adjustment problems reported by other investigators, that school refusal, poor concentration and poor school work failed to discriminate among the children. Indeed, school problems were reported generally for only 20 percent or fewer children in the entire sample.

Disciplinary Problems

Shaffer (11) found that it was primarily in this school behavioral area that children and adolescents who committed suicide were expressing their emotional problems. The most frequent precipitant was a disciplinary crisis, occurring in 31 percent of his cases. Five of his subjects had learned that a letter describing their anti-social behavior in school and their truancy was about to be sent to their parents. For had been in a fight with another child and two had been dropped from a school sporting team. Three had presented school problems because of a dispute with one or the other parent.

Rohn, et al. (45) found 35 percent of his suicide attempters were having behavior or discipline problems. White (33) found adverse school reports more likely to occur in the younger adolescents than in the older. He reported 67 percent were labeled as idle trouble-makers or a bad influence. When the subjects were in secondary schools there were only 14 percent with similar adverse reports. Barter, Swaback, and Todd (27) noted disciplinary actions in 78 percent of their suicide attempters.

Truancy or Drop-outs

Shaffer (11) noted truancy in 7 boys and 2 girls, and that 12 of the 21 boys had not been in school the day before their death. Three of these had been chronic school refusers while 5 had been absent for less than a week. Two had been away from home and school during the 24 hours preceding their deaths. Truancy was also noted as a problem by Barter, Swaback, and Todd (27), Otto (17), and Garfinkel and Golombek (37).

Isolation and Withdrawal

Otto (17) noted a desire to quit school in 12 percent of his subjects. Nilson (47) found a number of school problems in her study of runaways. However, she felt that school problems and the process of running away are interactive so it was useless to decide which was primary or to determine the relationship of school problems to suicidal behavior in her runaway group.

Wenz (48) conducted an interesting sociological study related to this problem by looking for sociological correlates of alienation among 200 adolescents, aged 12 through 18, who were telephone callers to a crisis intervention center or suicide attempters treated in emergency medical facilities. He found significant negative correlations of school performance with alienation in 20 percent of the above-average students, 25 percent of the average students, and 56 percent of the below-average students. Like Nilson, he assumes that school difficulties themselves are not a primary factor in the suicide attempt but rather problems that have been present for a long time and are the result of alienation.

In summary, almost all the researchers confirm the use of school problems and poor school performance as significant risk factors. However, the evidence produced in the well-controlled studies of Pfeffer, et al. (43,44) and Cohen-Sandler, Berman, and King (30) indicates that caution needs to be used in evaluating the presence or absence of this factor, for school problems may be more generally predictive of emotional disturbance (which would include suicide) than primarily of suicide alone. However, school problems may be highly age-related, and so less differentiating in the younger ages than in the older ages. While still an important clue, school problems rank more as moderately predictive, but clues that provide considerable additional supporting weight when other factors are present.

ANTI-SOCIAL BEHAVIOR

Anti-social behaviors appear in many forms. We have included in this category such behaviors as aggression, rage, hostility, violence, delinquency, homicidal impulses, fire-setting, stealing, and disobedience. References are primarily to behavior indices although at least one investigator, McAnarney (49) relates the tendency to national attitudes. She sees Denmark, Sweden, and Japan as suppressing aggression and notes the higher rates of suicides occurring in their countries, and contrasts them with the Norwegians who enjoy more freedom in expressing anger and have a markedly lower rate of suicide.

Some of the most intensive work in evaluating the role of aggression in suicidal behavior has come from two sources, Pfeffer and her colleagues (43,44,50,51) in New York, and Cohen-Sandler, Berman, and King (30) in Washington, D.C. Earlier studies from Pfeffer, et al. (43,44) on inpatient and outpatient children of latency age compared four groups: children who were suicidal recently, suicidal in the past, nonsuicidal recently, and nonsuicidal in the past. They found aggression high in all groups, 90 percent for the suicidal groups and 80 percent for the nonsuicidal groups, a nonsignificant difference. All the children displayed severe aggression that included fights, temper tantrums, a tendency to hurt and tease others, a destructiveness toward objects, defiance, and restlessness. Fire-setting and stealing were prevalent among both suicidal and nonsuicidal children. When their desires were not fulfilled, they displayed intense rage.

Often both suicidal and homicidal impulses were present, and to defend against the rage, the children denied, projected and displaced hostile feelings onto others. A similar research design applied to a group of outpatient children who were latency-aged yielded exactly the same results (44). The sole specific indicator of potential suicidal behavior was an increase in hypermotor behavior both within the inpatients and the outpatients.

Pfeffer and her colleagues (50,51) then conducted two studies of children aged 6 to 12, with one group predominantly from a low social status and the second from a middle social status. The subjects were divided into four groups: those with suicidal tendencies alone, those who showed assaultive tendency alone, those with both suicidal and assaultive tendencies, and those with neither suicidal nor assaultive tendencies. The results showed that the degree of expression of aggressive tendencies was a significant predictor of group membership for each of the four groups of children. Aggression was greatest in the group classified as both assaultive and suicidal; lying, stealing, and truancy were present among both children who were suicidal only and assaultive only. One important contribution to this study was the delineation of two types of children: the first, an assaultive and suicidal group who had distinct ego deficits and exhibited rage episodes and serious assaultive tendencies; the second, a group with relatively stable ego functioning who decompensated and were more likely to become overtly depressed under extreme environmental stress. The authors pointed out that from a theoretical point of view, the results did not deal directly with the question whether suicidal behavior is an expression of inhibited aggression or aggression turned inward. Rather, different groups of variables were producing different patterns of behavior expressed as assaultiveness and suicidal behavior. These different sets can occur in isolation, producing groups of children who are assaultive alone or suicidal alone. However, they can also occur together, in which case they produce highly intense aggression.

In Washington, Cohen-Sandler, Berman, and King (30) noted especially the appearance of aggression in their four progressive developmental life stages from infancy to 15 years of age. They concluded that, as a result of experiencing a disproportionate number of losses of all kinds, suicidal children, in contrast to the experiences of depressed and psychiatric controls, developed a greater loss of self-esteem and an increase in aggrieved rage. A review of their life events showed that suicidal children remained more intensely involved with family members and peers during childhood than the children in the control groups who were more often separated from their families. The frustrated investment of the suicidal children in these relationships was expressed as rage. Nearly two-thirds of the suicidal children made homicidal threats, gestures and, even attempts.

The presence of aggressive, violent feelings in the young suicidal child was reported by Paulson, et al. (52) who found violence, internalized hate and anger, marked preoccupation with fire-setting, and homicidal behavior toward family members and peers in 20 percent of suicidal children hospitalized for suicidal behavior.

Aggressive, violent and anti-social behaviors have been noted in varying proportions by a number of investigators of older adolescents. Among those with control subjects, Jacobs (15) and Teicher (16) hypothesized that rebelliousness of suicidal adolescents is one phase they go through until they reach the final suicidal stage. McIntire and Angle (18) found a mean score for hostility significantly higher for their experimental group of self-poisoners than for control subjects. Tishler and McKenry (46) found suicide attempters between ages 12 and 18 had a significantly higher score on the hostility scale of the Brief Symptom Index when compared with a group of nonattempters, and Otto (17) reported that one group of youngsters in his extensive followup of suicide attempters in Sweden could be characterized as showing increased irritability, aggressiveness, instability, and peevishness. Otto hypothesized that it was depression that was hidden behind the anti-social activities such as vagrancy, theft, and truancy. Smith (53), comparing highly suicidal teens with highly suicidal adults, found that the high-risk teens were much more overtly angry, explosive, and less well behaved than the adults.

Two of the three psychological autopsy studies using controls, Shafii, et al. (6) and Rich, Young, and Fowler (7) found that anger, irritability, and outbursts characterized the subjects who committed suicide. Rich, Young, and Fowler classified 9 percent of their under-30 cases as anti-social personality compared with only 1 percent of the group aged 30 and over. The under-30 aged group also experienced legal trouble more significantly, p<.001. Shafii, et al.(6) reported anti-social behavior including involvement with legal authorities, shoplifting, fire-setting, fighting, school disciplinary problems, drug selling, and prostitution significantly more often in the suicidal group than in the control group, p<.003. Maris (9) reported that younger subjects who completed suicide were significantly more often motivated by revenge and likely to commit suicide based in anger and irritability than were older suicides.

In studies of committed suicide with no control groups, Shaffer (11) reported anti-social symptoms in 73 percent of 30 children he studied. Crumley (26) found anti-social and violent behavior a prominent feature in two studies of suicide attempters from his private practice, with intense rage appearing when the teenager was disappointed when the person on whom he was leaning was unavailable. Hendin (54) related the increase in the suicide rate of young blacks in the United States to their struggle to deal with conscious rage and murderous impulses.

Among studies of attempted suicides with no controls, Goldberg's (41) extensive epidemiological investigation of suicidal ideation found that persons who denied

overt aggression had the highest percentage of suicidal thoughts, 16.5 percent. Rosenberg and Latimer (55) found evidence, in the records of 77 suicidal adolescents at a State hospital, of patterns of sexual delinquency, running away, truancy, and destructive behaviors for the girls, and considerable acting-out, running away, destructiveness, stealing, and defying authority for the boys. Alessi, et at. (56) found that 63 percent of juvenile delinquents considered seriously suicidal were committed for one or more violent felonies and 31 percent had a history of assaultive in-program behavior.

Summarizing, anti-social behavior, especially assaultiveness, when expressed along with suicidal behavior, seems to be an excellent risk factor for suicidal potential. All of the researchers quoted noted its significance in contrast to control groups. It seems likely that anti-social behavior is more important as a clue in the younger ages, so long as it is accompanied by suicidal expressions. It does not appear to be as significant in adult suicides, as indicated by Rich, Young, and Fowler (7) and Maris (9).

POOR IMPULSE CONTROL AND ACTING-OUT

Impulsive and acting-out behavior are closely related to the anti-social behaviors just discussed and are frequently included among the list of various behaviors when anti-social behaviors are identified by researchers. For example, Maris (9) found that younger children who completed suicide had more intense deep feelings, more aggressive feelings, and higher levels of impulsivity and dissatisfaction with their life accomplishments than older completed suicides. Shafii and Shafii (22) found the risk of suicide was significantly increased when there was impulsivity and lack of regard for danger in the histories of suicidal children and adolescents.

Impulse and acting-out behavior were both noted by Crumley (26) in his review of his private practice patients and by McIntire and Angle (18) in their study of self-poisoners in children and adolescents. The researchers in both studies considered the impulsivity and the activity as part of the anti-social, hostile, and aggressive behavior that characterized their populations.

Among suicidal children of latency age, Pfeffer, et al. (43,44) found an inability to tolerate frustration, delay actions, tolerate deprivation, or plan for the future. However, this poor impulse control was present for both suicidal and nonsuicidal children. The researchers found an increase in hypermotor behavior, possibly providing an increased potential for dangerous acting-out behaviors. Finally, Pfeffer (57) noted in an earlier study that an unrealistic, repetitive acting-out of life-endangering and omnipotent fantasies, such as being a superhero, was another important clue of high risk. The confusion and loss of reality from acting out such fantasies were thought to arise from feelings of intense vulnerability and helplessness.

In summary, poor impulse control and acting-out behavior are often seen as part of the pattern of behaviors included as anti-social. Impulsivity appears to characterize suicidal persons in the studies reviewed, although Pfeffer, et al. (43,44) found it did not differentiate suicidal children from the nonsuicidal children. In general, impulsivity and acting-out serve as good clues especially when found in the context of anti-social behavior. It may be that, because of the lack of preparation and planning, impulsivity will produce more suicidal events, but that they are less likely to be lethal.

SUGGESTIBILITY

Involvement in Fantasy Games and Imitation

In recent years increasing attention has been focused on the growing degree of violence appearing in television programs, many of them screening at times when they can be watched by adolescents and children. Sometimes the violence has involved suicidal behavior, as in the Russian roulette scene of the

Academy Award-winning film, *The Deer Hunter.* Concomitantly, there has been widespread popularity of various fantasy games involving an array of violent activities, including instructions to the youngsters that they should try to become in real life the characters that they are fulfilling in the game. Now in its seventh year, the National Coalition on Television Violence (NCTV) has been conducting lobbying and educational campaigns both among the public and the government in an effort to control the violence shown on television and the continuing development of violent fantasy games. They point out that prime time violence has increased over the recent years. For the fall-winter season shows on the major television networks, ABC, NBC, and CBS in 1980 to 1981 the average number of acts of violence per hour was 5.6. By the winter of 1985, the average had increased to 13.9 acts of violence per viewing hour.

To illustrate the process of imitation and the way in which violence on TV can stimulate similar acts of violence in young viewers, NCTV gathered information on verified imitations of the Russian roulette suicide that was featured in *The Deer Hunter*. The Coalition was able to find 41 shootings with 37 deaths. Most of the time the information about the event was attributed to newspaper reports; in other instances it was attributed to notification by a friend or the family. In each instance, the act was reported to have occurred within a short time of having seen the movie, or with specific identification of the action as an imitation of the movie scene by friends or family. Of the 41 shootings, approximately half, or 20 of the victims were below the age of 19.

NCTV has also been concerned with toys requiring violence in fantasy, such as war games and fantasy games. A survey of 50 different fantasy role-playing games found that all had a basic violent theme, such as medieval sorcery and combat, wild west battles, outer space combat, post-nuclear holocaust violence, urban thievery, espionage, assassinations, samurai brutality, war violence, and others. Frequently the violence is intense and gruesome.

One of the most popular and widely played games is the adolescent fantasy role-playing game Dungeons and Dragons (D&D). The game has been claimed to be a major factor in causing at least 50 suicides and murders, according to the evidence accumulated by the NCTV and by a group calling itself Bothered About D&D (BADD), founded by the mother of one of its victims. The game requires attacks, assassinations, spying, theft, and poisonings. The players arm their characters with any of 62 different types of weapons. An extreme number of monsters from horror and demonology are involved including 22 types of satanic demons and devils. Players can be cursed with 20 different types of insanity. D&D is played in groups under the direction of a Dungeon Master, primarily by males, age 12 to 20, and there are an estimated 3 to 4 million players in the United States. The game can last for months and even years with the goal being not to get killed and to accumulate as much power as possible. Power is earned by the murder of opponents. Players can be good or evil and are encouraged to identify with their own character in the game. In the group of related deaths, 22 or 44 percent of the suicides or murders involved youngsters aged 19 and under.

All the evidence about the game is primarily anecdotal. The publishers of NCTV quote, without sources, various authorities on whose work they rely for their evidence of the harm from violent, fantasy role-playing games, violent toys and play, and the desensitization effect of continued exposure to role-playing violence.

Although specific research is lacking on the relationship between magical thinking/fantasy and suicide, a hypothesis might be drawn from the results of the study by Gould (58). Magical thinking implies a loss of ability to recognize the boundary between fantasy and reality. Thus, for young people or children who have either lost or not developed the ability to maintain the boundary, fantasy games, such as war games and Dungeons and Dragons, become more and more engrossing and all-encompassing.

The games themselves become the reality. Pfeffer (60) calls attention to this in her comments on ego functioning often seen in suicidal children "As the pace, pitch, and content of the child's play intensify, suicidal children may lose the ability to discriminate between themselves and play objects. . . Another aspect of ego boundary diffusion of suicidal children is manifest when play ceases and becomes a form of personal acting out (p. 201)."

SOCIAL ISOLATION

Social isolation appears in many forms including withdrawal, alienation, asocial behavior, poor or inadequate peer relationships, and similar behaviors. It is usually considered fairly often to be the hallmark of a depressive syndrome. However, social isolation may appear in suicidal persons even when depression is not evident.

In their comprehensive description of the development of the suicidal state, Jacobs (15) and Teicher (16) identify one stage as a process of progressive social isolation from meaningful social relationships. The first stage of exacerbated problems is followed by a period of dissolution and disappearance of meaningful social relations. The feelings of isolation that follow then become both the problem and the barrier that prevents resolution of it. Withdrawal into self appears as gloominess, silence, and social alienation and the physical withdrawal frequently takes the form of running away from home. Sometimes the adolescent will try to reestablish a relationship with a significant other in a romance. About 36 percent of the suicide attempters were found to be engaged in a serious romance that was failing or terminating.

Both Seiden (10) and Hendin (61) found in their studies of suicidal college students that they were often asocial, withdrawn, shy, friendless, and alienated from all but the most minimal social interactions. Often, they almost totally absorbed themselves in their school work, which may then have served as a protective device. Hendin hypothesized the psychodynamics as one in which the students saw their relationship with their parents as dependent on their emotional, if not physical, death. The depression and isolation that developed was actually a form of protection that sometimes shielded the individual and even made suicide unnecessary.

The adolescent suicide attempters treated by Shafii and Shafii (22) and Rohn, et al. (45) at their university hospitals and the self-poisoners seen by McIntire and Angle (18) at their poison control center were characterized as loners, preoccupied with self, involved in failed romantic relationships, withdrawn, and isolated. Rohn, et al. (45) found the social aspects were characteristic of the boys in his study. However, Marks and Haller (40), found that their suicidal girls were more likely to have few or no friends during their childhood, to be socially isolated, and to be unable to talk about their personal problems with anyone.

In two followup controlled studies, Stanley and Barter (28) in Colorado found that young people who went on to make further attempts after their hospital discharge were much less likely to have adequate peer relationships, less likely to be living with their parents, and to have more social agency contact than those who did not make further suicide attempts. Otto (17) found social isolation much more prominent in his suicide attempters than in his nonsuicidal controls. He hypothesized that behind much of the anti-social behavior may be found loneliness and isolation, listlessness, contact difficulties, feelings of guilt, emptiness, and apathy.

Wenz's (48) interesting sociological approach hypothesized alienation as a highly significant factor among adolescent suicide attempters. Applying Dean's Measure of Alienation to adolescents who called a suicide prevention center and adolescent attempters treated at emergency rooms, he found the variable with the strongest negative association was social contact with peers, indicating the less the relational involvement with peers, the greater the feelings of social isolation. Wenz concludes that alienation sets in motion a train of events that leads to attempted suicide. As a result of alienation there is an atrophy of interpersonal relations. The greater the communication blockage, the greater the adolescent's sense of isolation and the more the person withdraws from further contact with others. The process is circular and leads to ever-greater degrees of isolation and withdrawal. His reasoning is strikingly similar to that of Jacobs (15).

Summarizing, controlled studies indicate that social isolation consistently identifies the suicidal person when comparisons with nonsuicidal persons are available. It thus appears to be a good clue, but not in and of itself; social isolation appears in depressed persons who are not suicidal and in nondepressed nonsuicidal persons. However, when social isolation appears with suicidal expression, it emerges as a significant high risk predictor.

RUNNING AWAY

Runaways are inherently a suicide risk group inasmuch as the behavior is associated with emotional disturbance, family conflicts and strife, school and learning problems, social alienation, and other negative conditions, all of which are associated with suicidal risk. Nilson's (47) study of 18 runaways compared them with other court referrals who were not runaways. Half the runaway group, 14, made suicide attempts or gestures and 12 showed suicidal ideation only. In the nonrunaway control group, only 2 of the 18 made an attempt or gesture, while 11 showed signs or ideations. The difference between the two groups is significant, $p < .02$.

The presence of a history of having been a runaway is noted by Rosenberg and Latimer (55) and White (33) in their research on attempted suicides among adolescents, and Shaffer (11) also notes the presence of runaways in the histories of younger adolescents who completed suicides.

Four well controlled studies sharply diverged on the usefulness of a history of running away. Jacobs (15) considers it the third stage in his theory of the development of the suicidal state, following the second stage of withdrawal. Marks and Haller (40) find the presence of running away a significant differentiator between suicidal boys and emotionally disturbed nonsuicidal boys, but not a differentiating factor between the girls. The strongest evidence against running away as a distinguishing feature comes from the studies by Pfeffer, et al. (43,44) and Cohen-Sandler, Berman, and King (30). Their carefully designed studies find that running away is more a symptom of emotional disturbance than necessarily of suicidal risk.

In summary, the usefulness of running away as a significant risk factor, while seemingly positive, has been thrown into doubt by the results of Pfeffer's and Cohen-Sandler, et al.'s studies. It is true, however, that the population of their studies are young, ranging in age from 5 to 14 at the most. It may be that the usefulness of this factor changes with older adolescents. At this point, the value of a history of running away as a suicide risk indicator is useful, but not necessarily predictive unless accompanied by other self-destructive clues.

THINKING PATTERNS AND STYLES

Shneidman (62) has pioneered in the study of suicidal thinking. His approach has been an analysis of the logical substructures of syntax in the writings of suicidal people, primarily through the comparison of genuine suicide notes with simulated suicide notes. Shneidman stimulated a number of other researchers. Using the matched pairs of real and simulated suicide notes, Tripodes (63) applied 24 aspects of reasoning patterns, including the cognitive maneuvers, and the idio-, contra-, and psycho-logic categories of analysis to the thinking of suicidal people.

The picture of the suicide note-writer obtained was impressively similar to that described in clinical face-to-face contact, but with the added special features of the suicide logic and style of thinking.

Tripodes used a comprehensive approach, covering all aspects of style of thinking. Neuringer and his colleagues (64) focused on dichotomous thinking or the tendency to polarize thought in an extreme manner. Using the semantic differential with groups of suicide attempters, psychosomatic patients and normal patients, Neuringer (65) found in two separate studies that suicide attempters were overwhelmingly more dichotomous in their thinking on the activity and potency factor scales than were the other two groups of subjects. While polarization of values was apparently a common characteristic of individuals in psychological stress, the dichotomization of the activity and potency factors seemed to be an exclusive hallmark of suicidal thinking. The results were even more extreme when only highly serious suicide attempters were compared with the psychosomatic and normal patients. Neuringer and Lettieri (66) extended the earlier studies by taking daily measures of dichotomous thinking from high-risk, medium-risk, and zero-risk individuals over a three-week period following a suicidal crisis. The results were the same but the investigators were even more alarmed that the extreme dichotomous thinking did not seem to diminish over time. They raised the concern that the process of dichotomous thinking associated with suicidal action might always be present, ready continuously to distort the world in such a way that suicide is an ever-present possibility.

Levenson and Neuringer (67,68) conducted a number of studies on rigidity and constriction of thinking in the suicidal individual and found that person to be more socially rigid and inflexible, to show an inability to shift in problemsolving strategies (as did Lineham, et al. 69), to be consistently high in field dependency, and to have difficulty solving arithmetic problems.

Summarizing, Neuringer (64) stated that suicidal individuals seemed to have difficulty in utilizing and relying on internal, imaginative resources; to polarize their value systems; and to tend to be rigid and constricted in their thinking. The process was the result of emotional stress affecting the cognitive structures, and decreasing cognitive capacity.

Kaplan and Pokorny (70) tested the hypothesis that the level of self-derogation in the thinking of individuals might predict subsequent suicidal behavior. In a longitudinal study of junior high school students in Houston, they administered a questionnaire three times at annual intervals, and obtained measures of self-derogation over periods of time. By correlating them with the number of self-destructive behaviors appearing between the measures, the investigators confirmed their hypothesis that high level of self-derogation were positively associated with suicidal thoughts, threats, and suicide attempts.

In summary, style of thinking, while apparently useful and intriguing, is limited in its predictive value for suicide because few professionals have the specialized knowledge of logic and language to apply the suggested analysis. Dichotomous and self-derogatory thinking seem like positive risk factors, especially after suicidal behavior appears. Such modes of thinking serve as evidence of increasing constriction and rigidity, boding ill for an individual's ability to see alternative possible courses of action.

SUICIDE NOTES

Shneidman (71) is also the person who discovered and initiated the use of suicide notes and personal documents as a source of valuable insights, not only into the thinking and reasoning styles of suicidal persons, but also as a means of determining his personality and emotional state immediately preceding the suicide.

Researchers in this area have indicated that suicide notes do not appear until about age 15. Shneidman and Farberow (72) collected notes in Los Angeles County from people ranging in ages from 13 through 90, with the median age in the 50s. Suicide notes come primarily from completed suicides; they are rarely obtained from attempted suicides. In a statistical comparison of attempted and committed suicides, Shneidman and Farberow (73) found suicide notes in 36 percent of the committed suicides and only 1 percent of the attempted suicides.

Shneidman (71) has held three different positions on the relationship of suicide notes to suicidal phenomena since he began their study. At first, the notes would offer special opportunities for observing the thinking and feeling that went into the act; second, that it is understandable that the views into the thinking and feeling were so limited considering the stress under which the notes were written; and third, that the notes' value was increased measurably when seen in the context of the history of the suicidal person. In such instances the note then "illuminates many aspects of the life history."

Shneidman (74) reviewed all the studies that have been conducted on suicide notes up to 1976 and reported that research has been carried out on the logic of suicide, changes in suicidal dynamics over age, the socioeconomic and psychological variables of suicide, suicidal life space, the emotional content, the effects of motivational level on language, comparisons with ordinary letters to friends and relatives, language characteristics, relations to persons and computer count of key tag words.

Shneidman summarized by saying that, as a whole, the studies have indicated that it was possible to distinguish between genuine and simulated suicide notes, and that the genuine suicide notes were primarily characterized by dichotomous logic, and greater degree of hostility and self-blame, more use of specific instructions to the survivors, less evidence of thinking about how one is thinking, and much evidence of the variety of meanings attributed to the word love. The content of the notes frequently reflect unrequited love, intellectual self-assertion, shame and guilt related to disgrace, the wish to escape from the pain of insanity, the wish to spare loved ones from further anguish, and a sense of inner pride and autonomy connected to one's own fate in the manner of one's own death. Often the writing is directed to his survivors-to-be as though he were going to be alive to supervise his wishes.

Peck (75) conducted a content analysis of suicide notes of suicide victims below the age of 35 (15.3% below age 25) in a large Midwest city. He found that elements of fatalism were most prevalent in victims under the age of 20, that they decreased for each of the subsequent older age groups, and that they were more frequent among single persons. The author concludes that the young fit a fatalistic model of suicide, which is described as a condition of excessive constraint or regulation that may trigger a reaction when the individual moves from excessive regulation to a state of alienation and a break in social ties. This almost seems a definition of adolescence.

Edland and Duncan (76) categorized the notes written by about 23 percent of the committed suicides in Monroe County, New York, into a system that focused on the psychodynamics and attitudes toward death. The authors felt that indications of such thoughts and concerns in individuals, while they were alive, should serve as significant predictive clues for high-risk potential suicide.

In summary, suicide notes have yielded much information about suicidal persons, information that has been useful in identifying risk factors, such as dichotomous thinking, constriction, ambivalence, and age-related dynamics. Further exploration will undoubtedly yield more. As predictive clues, however, the usefulness of suicide notes seems limited, for they are rarely discovered until after the fact of a suicide and so serve more to indicate what did happen rather then what might.

CONCLUSIONS AND SUMMARY

A number of summary conclusions can be made about behavioral clues as risk factors.

1. Prior suicidal behavior of any kind is unquestionably as strong a risk factor indicator for adolescents as it is for adults. It is consistently substantiated in both retrospective and prospective studies, in both well-controlled and no-control studies, and identifies from 22 percent to 71 percent of completed suicides and from 16 percent to 38 percent of attempted suicides retrospectively, and from 3 percent to 10 percent of completed suicides and 10 percent to 50 percent of attempted suicides prospectively.

2. Indirect self-destructive behaviors seem to play too complex a role in the personality of the individual to serve as reliable risk indicators. For some individuals, such behavior may play a protective role against suicidal behavior, whereas for other persons, the same behavior can become a significant self-destructive behavior on its own. Much more needs to be learned of the role of indirect self-destructive behaviors in the personality of the individual before they can achieve a consistent value as a risk factor.

3. Suicide attempters and committers among adolescents still seem most appropriately viewed as separate but overlapping populations.

4. While prior suicide attempts, threats, and ideations may be excellent clues for further suicidal behavior, it is also true that they are late clues in the progression toward suicide, indicating that a suicidal state has already occurred. Primary prevention objectives encourage the identification of preparatory suicidal risk behaviors at earlier states that may prevent the development of an overt suicidal state.

5. School problems have been identified consistently in histories of children and adolescents who have either committed or

attempted suicide. These problems include deteriorating academic accomplishments, disciplinary problems, and truancy. However, they also identify general emotional disturbance and need other suicidal clues to be most useful as risk factors.

6. Anti-social behavior, especially assaultiveness and threatening people, and including rage and hostility, are highly useful clues of suicide potential, especially among children and younger adolescents.

7. Social isolation and impulsivity are also often noted. However, these behaviors are found to characterize the general psychiatric population just as frequently as they do the suicidal group. These factors appear to be of greater value when they occur with other evidence of suicide potential and help to substantiate the evaluation.

8. Suggestibility and imitation probably play a role in suicide. However, this has been shown primarily in large-scale group and social reactions. The role suggestibility and imitation play, especially in violent role-fantasy games and television violence, in stimulating suicidal behavior in the individual is unclear.

9. Suicide notes can be highly useful in delineating the suicidal person's style and pattern of thinking. Dichotomous thinking, especially, may serve as a useful clue in reflecting increasing rigidity and loss of ability to seek alternatives as the person becomes more and more suicidal.

10. Running away might also be considered another kind of indirect self-destructive behavior, possibly substitutive or protective, possibly overtly self-harmful, probably both. Because running away and suicidal behavior are both highly associated with family conflict, it is highly likely they will be found together.

REFERENCES ·······························

1. Farberow NL, Shneidman ES: Attempted, threatened and completed suicide. J Abnorm Soc Psychol 1955;50:230.

2. Shneidman ES, Farberow NL: Clues to suicide. New York: McGraw Hill, 1957.

3. Shneidman ES, Farberow NL: Statistical comparison between attempted and completed suicides. In: Farberow NL, Shneidman ES, eds. The Cry for Help. New York: McGraw Hill, 1961.

4. Farberow NL, Shneidman ES, Neuringer C: Case history and hospitalization factors in suicide of neuropsychiatric hospital patients. J Nerv Ment Dis 1966;142:32-49.

5. Dorpat TL, Ripley HS: The relationship between attempted suicide and committed suicide. Comp Psychiat 1967;8:74-79.

6. Shafii M, Carrigan S, Whittinghill JR, Derrick A: Psychological autopsy of completed suicide in children and adolescents. Am J Psychiatry 1985;142:1061-1064.

7. Rich CL, Young D, Fowler RC: San Diego suicide study: I. Young vs. old cases. Department of Psychiatry, University of California San Diego School of Medicine, 1984. (Unpublished observation).

8. Maris R: Pathways to suicide. Baltimore: Johns Hopkins Press, 1981.

9. Maris R: The adolescent suicide problem. Suicide & Life Threatening Behavior 1981;15:91-109.

10. Seiden RH. Campus tragedy: A study of student suicide. J Abnorm Psychol 1966;71:389-399.

11. Shaffer D: Suicide in childhood and early adolescence. J Child Psychol & Psychiat 1974;15:275-291.

12. Cosand BJ, Bourque LB, Kraus JF: Suicide among adolescents in Sacramento County, 1950-1979. Adolescence 1982;17:917-930.

13. Marek Z, Widacki J, Zwarysiewicz W: Suicides committed by minors. Forensic Sciences 1976;7:103-108.

14. Garfinkel BD, Chamberlin C, Golombek H: Completed suicide in Ontario youth. In: Proceedings of the 10th International Congress for Suicide Prevention and Crisis Intervention. Ottawa, Canada: IASP, 1979:126-131.

15. Jacobs J: Adolescent suicide. New York: New York-Wiley-Interscience, 1971.

16. Teicher JD: Children and adolescents who attempt suicide. Pediatr Clin North Am 1970;17:687-696.

17. Otto U: Suicidal acts by children and adolescents. Acta Psychiat Scandinav 1972;233:7-123.

18. McIntire MS, Angle CR: Psychological "biopsy" in self-poisoning of children and adolescents. Am J Dis Child 1973;126:42-46.

19. McKenry PC, Tishler CL, Kelley C: The role of drugs in adolescent suicide attempts. Suicide & Life Threatening Behavior 1983;13:166-175.

20. Hawton K, O'Grady J, Osborn M, Cole D: Adolescents who take overdoses: Their characteristics, problems and contacts with helping agencies. Br J Psychiat 1982;140:118-123.

21. Clarkin JF, Fieman RC, Hurt SW, Corn R, Aronoff M: Affective and character pathology of suicidal adolescent and young adult inpatients. J Clin Psychiat 1984;45:19-22.

22. Shafii M, Shafii SL: Pathways of human development. New York: Thieme and Stratton, 1982:164-180.

23. Diekstra RFW: Adolescent suicidal behavior: Building blocks for a social learning theory. In: Pfeffer Cr, Richman J, eds. Proceeding of the 15th annual meeting of the American Association of Suicidology. New York City: AAS, 1982:30-31.

24. Schneer HI, Perlstein A, Brozovsky M: Hospitalized suicidal adolescents: Two generations. J Am Acad Child psyhiat 1975;14:268-280.

25. Gabrielson IW, Klerman LV, Currie JB, Tyler NC, Jekel JF: Suicide attempts in a population pregnant as teenagers. J Am Pub Health 1970;60:2289-2301.

26. Crumley FE: Adolescent suicide attempt. JAMA 1979;214:2404-2407.

27. Barter JT, Swaback DW, Todd D: Adolescent suicide attempts: A followup study of hospitalized patients. Arch Gen Psychiatry 1968;19:523-527.

28. Stanley EJ, Barter JT: Adolescent suicidal behavior. Am J Orthopsychiat 1970;40:87-96.

29. Cohen-Sandler R, Berman AL: A followup study of hospitalized suicidal children. Proceedings of the 14th annual meeting of the American Association of Suicidology, 1981:42-44.

30. Cohen-Sandler R, Berman AL, King RA: Life stress and symptomatology: Determinants of suicidal behavior in children. J Am Acad Child Psychiat 1982;21:178-186.

31. Rauenhorst JM: Followup of young women who attempt suicide. Dis Nerv Sys 1972;33:792-797.

32. Motto JA: Suicide in male adolescents. In: Sudak HS, Ford AB, Rushforth NB, eds. Suicide in the young. Boston: John Wright/PSG, 1984:227-244.

33. White HC: Self-poisoning in adolescence. Br J Psychiat 1974;124:24-35.

34. Durkheim E: Suicide. Glencoe, Illinois: Free Press, 1951.

35. Menninger K: Man against himself. New York: Harcourt, Brace, 1938.

36. Farberow NL: The many faces of suicide. New York: McGraw Hill, 1980.

37. Garfinkel BD, Golombek H: Suicide behavior in adolescence. In: Golombek H, Garfinkel BD, eds. The adolescent and mood disturbance. New York: International Universities Press, 1983:189-217.

38. Stengel E, Cook N: Attempted suicide. London: Oxford University Press, 1958.

39. Kreitman N: Parasuicide. London: John Wiley & Son, 1977.

40. Marks PA, Haller DL: Now I lay me down for keeps: A study of adolescent suicide attempts. J Clin Psychol 1977;33:390-400.

41. Goldberg E: Depression and suicide ideation in the young adult. Am J Psychiat 1981;138:35-40.

42. Iga M: Suicide of Japanese youth. Suicide & Life Threatening Behavior 1981;11:17-30.

43. Pfeffer CR, Conte HR, Plutchik R, Jerrett I: Suicidal behavior in latency aged children: An empirical study. J Am Child Psychiat 1979;18:679-692.

44. Pfeffer CR, Conte HR, Plutchik R, Jerrett I: Suicidal behavior in latency aged children: An outpatient population. J Am Child Psychiat 1980;19:703-710.

45. Rohn RD, Sarles RM, Kenney TJ, Reynolds BJ, Heald FP: Adolescents who attempt suicide. J Pediatr 1977;90:636-638.

46. Tishler C, McKenry P, Christman-Morgan K: Adoescent suicide attempts: Some significant factors. Suicide & Life Threatening Behavior 1981;11:86-92.

47. Nilson P: Psychological profiles of runaway children and adolescents. In: Wells CFj, Stuart IR. eds. Self-destructive behavior in children and adolescents. New York: Van Nostrand, Reinhold, 1981:2-39.

48. Wenz FW: Sociological correlates of alienation among adolescent suicide attempts. Adolescence 1979;14:19-30.

49. McAnarney ER: Adolescent and young adult suicide in the United States—A reflection of societal unrest? Adolescence 1979;14:765-774.

50. Pfeffer CR, Solomon G, Plutchik R, Mizruchi MS, Weiner A: Suicidal behavior in latency-age psychiatric inpatients: A replication and cross validation. J Am Acad Child Psychiat 1982;21:564-569.

51. Pfeffer CR, Plutchik R, Mizruchi MS. Suicidal and assaultive behavior in children: classifaciation, measurement and interrelations. Am J Psychiat 1983;140:154-157.

52. Paulson MJ, Stone D, Sposto R: Suicide potential and behavior in children ages 4-12. Suicide & Life Threatening Behavior 1978;8:225-242.

53. Smith K: Family and individual characteristics of suicidal adolescents and adults. In: Vorkoper C, Smith K, eds. Proceedings of the 16th annual meeting of the American Association of Suicidology. Dallas, Texas: AAS, 1983:58.

54. Hendin H: Youth suicide: A psychosocial perspective. Paper presented at Symposium on Adolescent Suicide: Understanding and Responding. Los Angeles, 1985. (Unpublished observations).

55. Rosenberg PH, Latimer R: Suicide attempts by children. Mental Hyg 1966;50:354-59.

56. Alessi N, McManus M, Brickman A, Grapentine A: Suicidal behavior among serious juvenile offenders. Am J Psychiat 1984;141:286-287.

57. Pfeffer CR: Clinical observations of play of hospitalized suicidal children. Suicide & Life Threatening Behavior 1979;9:235-244.

58. Gould RE: Suicide problems in children and adolescents. Am J Psychother 1965;19:228-246.

59. Sebastiano SdeF, Rieder C, Berk SE: The organization of fantasied movement in suicidal children and adolescents. In: Pfeffer CR, Richman J, eds. Proceedings of the 15th annual meeting of the American Association of Suicidology. New York: AAS, 1982:25-26.

60. Pfeffer, CR: The suicidal child. New York: Guilford Press, 1986.

61. Hendin H: Growing up dead: Student suicide. Am J Psychother 1975;29:327-338.

62. Shneidman ES: Psychologic: A personality approach to patterns of thinking. In: Kagan J, Lesser G, eds. Contemporary issues in thematic apperception methods. Springfield, Illinois: Charles C. Thomas, 1961.

63. Tripodes P: Reasoning patterns in suicide notes. In: Shneidman ES, ed. Suicidology: Contemporary Developments. New York: Grune & Stratton, 1976.

64. Neuringer C: Current developments in the study of suicidal thinking. In: Shneidman ES, ed. Suicidology: Contemporary Developments. New York: Grune & Stratton, 1976.

65. Neuringer C: Dichotomous evaluations in suicidal individuals. J Consult Psychol 1961;25:445-449.

66. Neuringer C, Lettieri DJ: Cognition, attitude and affect in suicidal individuals. Life Threatening Behavior 1971;1:106-124.

67. Levenson M, Neuringer C: Problem solving behavior in suicidal adolescents. J Consult Clin Psychol 1971;37:433-436.

68. Levenson M, Neuringer C: Suicide and field dependency. Omega 1974;5:181-186.

69. Linehan MM, Ivanov A, Graham BJ, Chiles JA, Sadin P, Nielson SL: Interpersonal response styles of parasuicides. In: Proceedings of the 14th annual meeting of the American Association of Suicidology. Albuquerque, NM: AAS, 1981:28-30.

70. Kaplan HB, Pokorny AD: The self-derogation and suicide - 1: Self-derogation as an antecedent of suicidal responses. Social Science & Medicine 1976;10:113-118.

71. Shneidman ES. Voices of death. New York: Harper and Row, 1980.

72. Shneidman ES, Farberow NL: Sociopsychological investigation of suicide. In: David HP, Brengelmann JC, eds. Perspectives in personality research. New York: Springer, 1960:270-293.

73. Shneidman ES, Farberow NL: Statistical comparisons between attempted and committed suicides. In: Farberow NL, Shneidman ES, eds. The cry for help. New York: McGraw Hill, 1961:19-47.

74. Shneidman ES: Suicide notes reconsidered. In: Shneidman ES, ed. Suicidology: Contemporary Developments. New York: Grune & Stratton, 1976..

75. Peck DL: Towards a theory of suicide: A case for modern fatalism. Omega 1980-81;11:1-14.

76. Edland JF, Duncan CE: Suicide notes in Monroe County: A twenty-three year look (1950-1972). J of Forensic Sciences 1973;18:364-369.

SOCIAL AND CULTURAL RISK FACTORS FOR YOUTH SUICIDE

Carol L. Huffine, Ph.D., Director of Research, California School of Professional Psychology, Berkeley, California

INTRODUCTION

Our attention to suicide among young people has been drawn by the extraordinary number of adolescents and young adults who killed themselves during the decade of the 1970s. Although there is evidence that the rate of suicide among youth is declining, it is still very high, and, more importantly, we are left feeling powerless to explain the unanticipated increase or to prevent such a social tragedy from recurring. In the following pages, I will briefly review the pattern of youth suicide in the United States over the past 25 years and, where possible, compare United States rates and patterns with those of other countries. Following that, I will summarize Emile Durkheim's explanation of suicide, which I will then use to organize the literature on social and cultural risk factors and to assess the usefulness of explanatory models.

From 1960, the rate of suicide among 15 to 19 year olds and 20 to 24 year olds increased steadily until the late 1970s, when some decrease could be seen in the older group. This pattern is most apparent among men, but is also evident among women [1,2]. The United States tends to be about mid-way among the countries from whom data are available with regard to suicide rates [3], and it appears that only Canada [4] and Australia [5] have experienced a pattern of increase similar to that of the United States.

Although the suicide rate among young Japanese dropped between the 1960s and 1970s, it has been rising again [2,6]. In other Near Eastern and Asian countries, suicide rates generally have been low but increasing slowly and steadily over time [7]. Exceptions are Hong Kong, where there is considerable variation year by year [8], and Taiwan, where the suicide rate has dropped, from its mid-1960s high, to the low point in about 30 years [9]. With the exception of countries such as Japan, Thailand, and Sri Lanka, which have U-shaped curves, suicide rates in Asian countries tend to be high among adolescents and young adults, and to decrease with age.

Age-related patterns of suicide tend to be the same for both sexes in those Asian countries from which data are available. Differences in rates **between** the sexes tend to be much smaller than in the United States. There is, in fact, almost parity in a number of countries, and in Taiwan, Singapore, and Thailand, rates of suicide among female adolescents exceed those of male adolescents.

We have come to recognize the United States and Canada suicide rate increases as, at least in part, cohort phenomena. That is, the suicide rates for successive birth cohorts are higher, at each age, than the rates for preceding cohorts [4,5,10,11]. This means that the jump in rates among adolescents and young adults in the 1970s should be "echoed" in future suicide rate increases among the middle aged and then among the elderly. Recognizing the phenomenon as a cohort effect is important because of the predictability it provides, but also because it refocuses our search for explanation. Rather than look only at what was, or is, going on at the time of the observation (i.e., in the era of the 1970s), we seek a more pervasive factor that can affect the risk for suicide of successive waves of babies. And if, as seems to be the case here, there is an extraordinary jump, what might we say about the life experiences of this particular birth cohort that can help us explain their amplification of the general trend?

The suicide rates that have captured our attention are those of the "baby boomers," persons born during the 1950s. This group of individuals stands out, not only because of its absolute number, but also because it was preceded and followed by exceptionally small birth cohorts, the depression and the "baby bust" cohorts. In Europe, fertility increased for a few years following World War II, but only Canada, Australia, and New Zealand experienced fertility trends similar to that of the United States (12).

My search for risk factors was guided initially by the findings described above: that in the United States, successive birth cohorts have had higher suicide rates than antecedent ones, that the increase in rate of suicide at ages 15 to 19 and 20 to 24 among persons born in the 1950s was especially sharp, and that the only countries with similar patterns of youth suicide over time are also among the few countries demonstrating a post World-War II fertility pattern similar to that of the United States. Subsequently, the search widened in response to (1) the discovery of other phenomena calling for discussion, and (2) the wish to use a theoretical frame for the analysis that would give it coherence.

Sociocultural theorists do not presume to explain individual instances of suicide. Rather, they focus on rates and patterns of rates as phenomena in and of themselves. We tend to see the social group as the context within which an individual acts, and to see contexts as varying in the degree to which they increase or decrease the probability of group members killing themselves. I will touch upon three general ways in which societies might influence the suicide rate among their members; these might be considered sets of risk factors.

1. Social structures might support and protect individuals, or they might produce stress.

2. The culture, as well as social structure, of a social group influences the psychological development of its members.

3. The culture produces, through such mechanisms as folklore, attitudes about suicide and death.

Most of the work in suicide has focused on the first set of influences, and the review that follows reflects this emphasis.

BACKGROUND

In looking at the literature produced in the past fifteen years or so, I have been impressed with the continuing importance of the work Emile Durkheim (13) did so many years ago, and I have been reimpressed with the genius of that work. Much of what is said by contemporary writers about today's youth and their suicide rates is a restatement, generally in more specific terms, of some part or another of the model developed by Durkheim. Durkheim described four basic "types" of suicide (anomic, egoistic, fatalistic, and altruistic), which represent extremes of two processes he considered essential to a healthy social order-- integration and regulation of its members.

Social integration refers to the degree to which members identify with the group. It is a structural condition that binds persons together as members of a collective body with which they identify and that provides part of their identity. Too little or too much integration, according to Durkheim, constitutes a suicide risk. Too little integration results in individuals feeling isolated, set apart from, or different from, their fellows. This state is referred to as "egoistic" and is characterized by excessive individuation. In some form or another, this part of Durkheim's model has been the most widely used by contemporary analysts of suicide rates. Its relative popularity may be attributable to the relative ease with which the concept can be operationalized and linked to psychological concepts.

A social group may be too integrated, as well as not sufficiently so, in which case its members are at risk of altruistic suicide. Here the problem is one of insufficient individuation; the person may be said to have no identity other than the social group or that which is conferred by his/her social status. In such instances, individuals may be called upon to sacrifice themselves in the name of the group or to preserve it. Although some writers have dismissed altruistic suicide as irrelevant for modern analyses (14,15,16), it is important, I suggest, for reasons I shall develop later.

The other dimension of importance to Durkheim's theory is that of regulation, the social condition that "restrains the passions" of the individual. Current theorists have tended to interpret social regulation in terms of norms. The idea is that individual aspirations, and the methods by which those aspirations may be achieved, are defined by social norms. A state of anomie is said to exist when individuals do not have a set of clearly defined goals, or when there is a disparity between goals and the possibility of their being achieved because the social structure fails to provide access to the means for goal achievement. Anomic conditions are generally seen as resulting from rapid social change, but it is theoretically possible for them to be chronic for some segments of a society. At the other end of the regulation continuum is fatalism, a condition created by excessive regulation. Here individuals' futures are foreclosed, and lives are oppressively dictated. As with altruistic suicide, fatalistic suicide as a theoretical "type" has not been much used, and has been viewed as not particularly useful. I turn now to a review of social and cul-

tural risk factors for youth suicide using Durkheim's model as a general frame for the discussion.

REVIEW

Egoism/Social Integration

Without even looking at data, one might expect relatively high rates of suicide among adolescents and young adults in contemporary societies because they are in stages of life characterized by identity change and consolidation. Konopka (17) argues that adolescence is a period of high risk because the individual undertakes a series of "firsts," including questioning childhood precepts that were provided by parents and which guided his/her life for so many years, reassessing old values, and evaluating potential new ones. The adolescent needs to move beyond a very small interpersonal circle to find warm supportive relationships, and to cope with the yearning for the warmth and support of family ties. Maris makes the point that adolescence is a "time marked by marginality, confusion, and ambiguity" (18, page 100). In suggesting that the greatest problem young people have today is their uselessness, he reminds us of Sabbath's (19) definition of suicidal adolescents as expendable children. In short, adolescence and young adulthood are, in Western civilization, characterized by loose and uncertain social integration and identity.

Social integration and rates of youth suicide. Some authors have attributed the steady increase in suicide rates over time to concomitant changes in social integration. Sudak, Ford, and Rushford (20), for instance, suggest that increasing divorce rates and diminishing importance of religious and moral values have contributed to increased personal alienation (egoism, in our terms,) and, thereby, to increased suicide. Hawton (2) also discusses the loosening of family ties over time as a causal agent in suicide among the young, while Holinger and Offer (21) note the increase in broken families, and the implications of this increase for social integration of the young. They suggest further that the large impersonal high schools of today make it difficult for adolescents to find a sense of self-worth and to establish friendships.

A final bit of evidence that social integration is a useful explanatory concept for adolescent suicide rates is the regularity with which minority group suicide rates are especially high in adolescence. It is only in adolescence and young adulthood that suicide rates of blacks approximate those of whites, and at times they have exceeded them (20,22,23,24). Similar patterns are found among American Indians (25,26,27) and Hispanic-American residents of the southwestern United States (28). This relative parity with white Anglo men in suicide rates of young men of ethnic minority status suggests that the effects of uncertain social integration on all adolescents and young adults are compounded for minority groups. Investigators of Indian suicide have been the most likely to discuss this possibility, describing the young American Indian as caught between two cultures. The profoundness of the identity problems the Indian might experience is poignantly reflected in Tonkin's observation that, in British Columbia, native Americans may "lose their Indian status when they live off the reserve" (27, page 175). Resnick and Dizmang similarly describe the young American Indian as caught between two cultures: "he is unprepared for the one and feels the other, toward which he is ambivalent, has failed him" (29, page 886).

Social Integration and Rates of Suicide Among Youth. Social isolation is sometimes used, explicitly or implicitly, in discussing differences among subsets of young people in terms of their potential for suicide. For instance, social integration has been used to explain racial differences in suicide rates (20). Bush (30) posits the existence of a "black perspective" that can protect individuals from the pain caused by racism. He suggests that, to the extent that individuals differ from, or move away from, the intragroup perspective, they are vulnerable to the ef-

fects of racism, among them, suicide. Seiden takes a somewhat different approach but with the same concepts. He suggests that changing racial attitudes in this country have led to increased individual freedom and, ironically, to decreased social integration for black people. Specifically, he argues that "as racial discrimination decreases, the stability of shared social relationships, the sense of community based upon discrimination by a common enemy, is likewise decreased" (24 page 5).

Data are available from two studies undertaken to test hypotheses about social integration and suicide among blacks. To test their hypothesis that black adolescents living in a black subculture would have lower suicide rates than black adolescents living in "nontraditional" areas, Shaffer and Fisher (31) compared rates in two Southern and two Northern regions. The specific regions were selected because blacks accounted for more than 95 percent of their nonwhite population, and the investigators could then safely assume that "suicide among nonwhites" meant "suicide among blacks." The results of the comparison confirmed the hypothesis. That is, blacks were underrepresented in the suicides in the Southern areas, but they accounted for almost the same proportion of suicide as of the population in the Northern areas. This finding helps put into perspective the extraordinarily high rates of suicide among young blacks that Morris et al. (23) found in Philadelphia.

In the other test of the hypothesized relation between social integration and black suicide, Davis (22) compared suicide rates and racial composition of the 18 States with the largest black populations. He does not interpret his finding of a negative correlation between the percentage of blacks in the population and the nonwhite suicide rate, but one might well make an argument that blacks living in states where there are a large number of blacks are more socially integrated than blacks living where there are few other blacks. However, it should also be noted that among the ten States where the proportion of blacks in the population decreased between 1970 and 1975, the nonwhite suicide rate was as likely to go down as to go up over the same period of time. Among the eight States in which the proportion of blacks increased or remained stable, the suicide rate went up in seven and down in only one.

It may be, as Shaffer and Fisher acknowledge, that their and Davis' findings reflect the disintegrative effects of migration, or the vulnerability to suicide of persons who migrate, rather than the protective effects of social integration. Direct evidence of migration as a suicide risk is sparse and not very compelling. In Israel, suicidal behavior is high among young immigrants, especially those from Asia or Africa (32). It should be noted, however, that Amir's data include attempted, as well as completed, suicide and that the rate of suicide for Israelis under the age of 19 years is extremely low. We should also remember that Sainsbury and Barraclough (33) found suicide rates of first-generation immigrants to be more similar to the rates of their countries of origin than to those of the host countries.

One final point about racial differences in suicide rates and social integration: In Durban, South Africa, the rate of suicide among colored persons, those of mixed black and white heritage, is considerably higher than among the other major racial groups, Africans, whites, and Indians. The differences are, however, greater among the middle aged than among the youth or the elderly (34).

Holinger and Offer (21) point out that, among teens, those who are or have been married have much higher rates of suicide than those who have not been married. Although marriage is a primary form of social integration and, therefore, protection against suicide for adults, Holinger and Offer's data suggest it is a suicide risk factor for teenagers. This apparently anomalous finding would have been predicted by Gibbs and Martin's extension of Durkheim's theory (35). They operationalize social integration as "status integration," which means, essentially, the extent to which one's status configuration is a configuration common within the population. Few teenage persons in this society are married, so those who are have low status integration and, therefore, low social integration, and are at high risk for suicide. We should note that Durkheim also would have expected high suicide rates among married teens, especially men, because early marriage forecloses options. In this respect, it would lead to fatalistic suicide.

There is evidence that, among students, those who commit suicide are less well integrated into their social groups than are the others. Petzel and Riddle (36) observed that school nonattendance and multiple school changes may be associated with suicidal behavior. There is no consistent evidence that college students are more likely than their nonstudent age peers to commit suicide, but there is some evidence suggesting that students of elite universities are at relatively high risk (2,37,38). While one might suggest that these institutions are characterized by their emphasis on individualism and lack of integrative mechanisms, Peck and Schrut (37) point out that the populations at elite universities are likely to be more disproportionately male than are populations of other postsecondary institutions, and they are likely to be older.

In the descriptive material provided by Peck and Schrut from their study of suicide among college students in Los Angeles county, one can discern a pattern of behavior that suggests failure to conform to the norms or expectations of the college student of the 1960s. For instance, compared with other students, those who committed suicide were more likely to spend a lot of time in solitary activities, and to attend religious services and express belief in an afterlife. They were less likely to use drugs and they were less experienced sexually. Although we typically think of religiosity as inversely related to suicide (see below) and drug abuse as associated with it, we should consider that failure to use drugs at all and attendance at religious services were not normative behaviors for college students in the 1960s, at least not in California. These behaviors might, then, be seen as evidence of failure to fit into the social group.

Peck and Schrut, as well as Sanborn, Sanborn, and Cimbolic (39) who studied adolescent suicide in New Hampshire, found that, compared with other students, those who committed suicide were doing poorly academically. Shaffer (40) did not report on the academic standing of the adolescent suicides occurring in England and Wales in the 1960s, but he did describe them as tending to be above average in intelligence as well as height. Nonstatistical analysis of the data he had amassed on 31 cases of suicide led Shaffer to suggest that they clustered into two personality types, the solitary isolate and the impetuous individual prone to aggressive outbursts.

As noted earlier, religion was seen by Durkheim as a key mechanism for social integration, and his findings of strong associations between suicide and religion have been replicated many times. These are findings of higher rates of suicide among Protestants than among Jews who, in turn, have higher rates than Catholics. The interpretive principle of interest here is orthodoxy. In more recent work the connection between religion and suicide is less consistently located, and is less clear than in early studies. For instance, when level of religious commitment or involvement is controlled, investigators tend no longer to find differences in rate of suicide across religious denominations. Stack, for instance, found no correlation between the percentage of Catholics in the population and the suicide rate when he controlled for the divorce rate. The divorce rate was seen as a proxy for Catholic orthodoxy and Stack interpreted his findings as follows: "We hold that the convergence of Catholic and Protestant normative structures is responsible for the lack of a relationship between Catholicism and suicide" (41, page 69). Minear and Brush (42) attributed the lack of difference in attitude toward suicide between Jews and agnostics in their sample of college students to the absence of religious Jews in the sample. Smith and Hackathorn (43) failed to find a relationship between religious integration and suicide across 69 primitive societies, although they found strong correlations between suicide and family integration and economic integration. It may be, however, that their measure of religious integration was not as valid as were the measures of family and economic integration.

There is no good evidence of a direct association between level of religiosity and risk of suicide among individuals, because valid data on the religious views of the deceased are scarce. However, there is evidence from a number of studies that religious involvement is associated with low rates of **acceptance** of suicide (42,44,45). The studies cited all compared religiosity and attitudes toward suicide in samples of young persons, a category much more "liberal" toward suicide than older persons (46).

We need to be very careful in interpreting findings about "attitudes" toward suicide. Respondents, especially the young, clearly differentiate between "right" as a moral concept and right as a perquisite. Eighty-eight percent of Boldt's adolescent respondents said suicide is wrong (46). Yet, 35 percent of them said it is a basic human right, and 47 percent said people should not be restrained from killing themselves, or should be restrained only under certain circumstances. Minear and Brush warn that the liberal attitudes of their sample of students toward the right to kill oneself "does not imply that a majority of college students could personally accept the idea of their own suicide. Most, in fact, could not imagine committing suicide" (42, page 321).

Anomic Suicide

As noted earlier, anomic conditions are generally associated, in the mind of the social theorist, with rapid social change. The change needs to be of the type that leaves the social group, or some subset of it, without a set of "rules" by which members can regulate their lives. Without a set of expectations about what they should aspire to and how to achieve the valued goals, the affected individuals are at increased risk for suicide. The clearest example of this process I encountered is that presented in the very nicely written article by Rubinstein (47) about an epidemic of suicide among Micronesian adolescents. Rubinstein describes the transformation of Micronesian communities from subsistence fishing and agriculture groupings to reliance on a cash economy and government employment. Among the changes in life this transformation has wrought is the extinction of the traditional men's clubhouses and community-level men's organizations. These clubhouses and organizations had socialized young males into their adult roles, providing them a sense of social identity and self-esteem, and compensating for the structural tensions and distance they encountered in family relations. It was among young men, of course, that the rate of suicide increased dramatically and, as Rubinstein was able to demonstrate, among the young male residents of the district centers, which were the foci of social change.

Goldney and Katsikitis (5) suggest that the surge in adolescent suicide among mid-century Australian birth cohorts is related to the social and economic changes in Australia over the past 50 years. Rin and Chen (9) suggest that the first of two surges in the Taiwanese rate of suicide is related to the migration to Taiwan of 2 million mainland Chinese within a ten-year period. They see the second surge as related to a period of modernization, industrialization, and changing value orientations. Socioeconomic changes resulting from political independence are designated as likely causal factors in the marked jump after 1969 in the suicide rate in Sri Lanka (48). None of these investigators provides an analysis of **how** socioeconomic or political changes affected the lives of the population stratum in which the suicide rates have increased.

The widely-recognized high rate of suicide among American Indians is often characterized as a manifestation of anomie. For instance, Resnick and Dizmang (29) point out that the dominant culture in this country has vacillated widely in its judgment of what Indians should be, and Indians themselves have been unable to make their own adjustments to the cultural changes they have experienced. Reznick and Dizmang point especially to the problems of once-valued behaviors being no longer possible because of the restrictions and limitations of reservation life, and to the loss of role models to young men. The arguments they make in this work are, in large measure, illustrated in Dizmang's earlier description of changes in the lives of the Shoshone-Bannock Indians (49) and the apparent suicidogenic effects of these changes on young men. In 1974, Dizmang, Watson, May, and Bopp (25) presented the results of a case-controlled analysis of suicide on the Fort Hall reservation. Their goal was identification of personal factors associated with suicide. The childhood experiences of the suicide group were much more chaotic than were those of the controls, and they were much more likely to have attended boarding school and to have done so at young ages. One could argue that the experience of attending the off-reservation boarding school, unless it is a step in the process of assimilation into the dominant culture, is likely to accentuate the cultural confusion experienced by the young American Indian.

Resnick and Dizmang (29) point out that suicide rates vary tremendously across Indian groups, a point taken up in greater detail by Shore (50), who presents data revealing variation across tribes from 8 to 120 per 100,000. The figures he presents suggest that suicide rates generally are low among southwestern United States tribes (Navaho and Papago) relative to northwestern tribes. Extrapolating from homicide rates, Shore suggests that suicide rates are high among traditionally nomadic tribes and lower among agricultural village tribes. Although he does not offer interpretation or analysis, it is evident that the controls of the Federal government, including movement of Indians to reservations, was more disruptive of the cultural patterns of nomadic, than of the village-based, groups.

Some writers have suggested that social change during the 1960s resulted in anomie among black Americans and may account for increased suicide rates among blacks. Hendin, for instance, suggests that changes in what are considered acceptable forms of response to racial oppression can create anomic situations for older blacks. "They become suicidal only when an adaptation that has been distinctly Negro in our culture fails them" (51 page 419). Seiden (24), although focusing on theories of social integration, points out that, during times of marked social change such as we experienced in the 1960s, there is confusion about customs and moral codes. One may infer that this resultant anomie put young blacks at higher-than-usual risk for suicide.

Another recent social change that might be expected to have disproportionately influenced the birth cohort known as the "baby boomers" is the women's movement. With the emphasis during the 1960s and 1970s on acquiring and using access to educational and professional opportunities, changing sexual mores, and altering the nature of intimate as well as formal relations between the sexes, expectations about the American woman's role, goals, and behavior were seriously challenged. The female members of the 1950s birth cohort grew up without the certainty about their roles that had characterized their mothers' lives. One might expect, then, that they would demonstrate increased rates of suicide as adolescents and young women. Although rates of suicide among young white women have increased, the change has not been nearly as great as for young men. The rate among 20 to 24 year old nonwhite women has increased tremendously, so that it is now almost equal to that of their white age and sex peers. This is an interesting and potentially important phenomenon, but it probably cannot be taken as an effect of sex-role changes in the past 20 years. We should not forget, however, that changes in women's roles and expectations have profound chan-

ges on the world in which **men** live. Thus, it is feasible that the effects of the women's movement, insofar as they produce change in the suicide rate, are more evident among men than women.

There is, as noted at the beginning of the paper, a condition other than rapid social change that has become identified as anomic. That is the social condition in which structural mechanisms fail to provide opportunities for individuals to achieve culturally valued goals. A number of authors assert that this condition has been produced by the high rate of fertility in the 1950s. Borrowing from Easterlin (52), they suggest that this large cohort of young people has been confronted with increased competition for rewards and reduced opportunity to acquire them (20,52).

The concept of anomie has, then, been used less often, and with less attention to the theory of which it is a part, than has egoism (isolation) in analyses of changes in suicide rate among American subpopulations. In fact, one sees the concept of anomie employed primarily in anthropological studies of traditional societies. It may be that contemporary societies are not as vulnerable to rapid social change as are those like postwar Micronesia, and/or that the effects of change are buffered by countervailing forces. Except for the case of the nomadic American Indian, the only United States group to which we can point as having demonstrated anomic suicide in recent history is businessmen who responded to the crash of the stock market in the late 1920s by killing themselves.

Altruistic Suicide

As noted earlier, there has been a tendency among modern theorists to dismiss the concept of altruistic suicide from serious consideration because of its lack of relevance to modern society. I consider this tendency unwise for a variety of reasons. First, of course, we saw altruistic suicide re-emerge in Jonestown with tragic results of astounding magnitude. Second, it appears to be very much a part of what drives suicide rates up in some societies. Third, where some form of altruistic suicide is part of the cultural tradition, it is likely to influence a society's suicide rate as an "enabling factor," a factor that makes suicide acceptable, if not prescribed or expected.

It may be that part of the impetus to dismiss altruism as an important factor in suicide, is the word itself. We tend to emphasize the connotation of benevolence in thinking of this term. Yet, "altruism" also refers, perhaps even more strongly, to selflessness. The word was formed by Comte from an Italian term meaning "of, or to, others." It was translated into English as "devotion to the welfare of others" and as an antonym to "egoism." In 1876, Marlborough described the law and duty of life in altruism as living for others (54). My point is that the aspect of altruism that constitutes a suicidal risk is the abnegation of the self, the giving up of one's own identity, or the dominance of the identity by a single social role or social tie. If we focus on this aspect of altruism, we can understand the acquiescence of hundreds of persons to the call from their leader that they murder their children and commit suicide.

In societies such as the modern United States, in which there is such strong emphasis on autonomy and the development of individual identities, we seldom see cases of suicide we might identify as altruistic. However, in other societies, group loyalties and family ties are such that the individual might be said not to exist and, in those societies, some suicides appear very much to be sacrifices of the self for the group. For instance, Amir (32) says that suicide rates were very high among the Israeli pioneers, and he attributes this phenomenon to a very intense social solidarity and the attribution of failure to individual shortcomings.

One can see traces of altruism in the very high rates of suicide among the youth of Japan. It is widely accepted that the tortuous process of gaining access to higher education in Japan precipitates a good many suicides among those who fail. Whereas it appears that this is an instance of a highly valued goal

to which there is very limited access and, thus, potentially an anomic situation, it also seems that the young Japanese man's suicide is motivated less by disappointment in his failure to achieve **his** goals than by his failure to fulfill his responsibility to his family. Fuse (55) describes the tendency of many Japanese to become overinvolved with their social role as "role narcissism." He means by this that the social role becomes cathected by the individual as the ultimate meaning for life. Threat of loss of that social role creates such shame and chagrin that the individual may well choose to end his life rather than continue it in an altered or degraded social role. Iga (56) describes Japanese culture similarly, as one in which the basic social structure is a small group and in which the supremacy of the group goal is stressed. Emphasis on education and the entrance examination, which is the student's single opportunity to enter a university, have become Japanese tradition. Iga vividly describes the pressures brought to bear by his parents, especially his mother, on the Japanese adolescent to achieve a university education. The family may pay enormous costs, financial and emotional, to prepare him for the examination. The student who fails does not just fail to realize a personal goal; he fails his family and he fails, on behalf of his family, to achieve a group goal. My interpretation is supported by Hirsch (57), who describes the Japanese culture as consistently emphasizing an intense, life-long, parent-child relationship. He identifies cultural values stressing self-discipline and subservience of the self to a whole system of hierarchies leading to shame and guilt when role expectations are not met. Hirsch cites DeVos in describing the need for children to achieve and bring honor to the household in order to fulfill their duty to their parents, and to repay them for their sacrifices. Although there is no evidence that suicide is expected of a young Japanese man who fails to gain access to a university, the guilt he feels for failing his family, combined with the failure to achieve the goal that has, for many years, been his single focus, and cultural enabling factors I will refer to later, constitutes a serious risk factor for suicide.

Hoskin, Friedman, and Carote (58) investigated an area of New Britain which had a high incidence of suicide. In describing the social structure of the communal groups, they speak of the extreme importance to the individual of personal ties and affiliations, and they discuss some historical rationale for the critical importance of the individual's affiliative tie to a small group of others. In their investigation of suicide among the population, they learned of the primacy of the loss of personal ties among the deceased. While the authors seems to lean toward anomie as an explanation for the high incidence of suicide, the social fragmentation they speak of has, in fact, a very long history and could be seen as the reason why the individual Kandrian is so dependent upon relations with a very small group of others for his/her continued well-being. In effect, I am suggesting that the role relation is one in which the individual is as role-cathected as are the Japanese described by Fuse and Hirsch. The individual's identity is extraordinarily dependent on the role relationship.

In sum, I would argue that we not dismiss the concept of the altruistic suicide but, in fact, be wary of its potential for young people. Blos (59), among others, describes adolescence as an individuation process and, thereby, an opportunity for the young person to confront and resolve conflicts associated with dependency. There are a variety of ways, such as use of drugs, that the adolescent might avoid managing those development tasks. An alternative available in the past 20 years or so is the cult. The cult provides alternatives to the threatening and difficult experiences of young adulthood, and it involves relinquishing one's own sense of self which, for the troubled or fearful young person, can be experienced as a relief (60). In so doing, however, the young individual is trading off the risk of egoistic suicide, which is likely to exist for a short period and for which there are social buffers, for the risk of altruistic suicide which is present as long as cult membership is maintained and against which there is likely to be precious little protection.

Fatalistic Suicide

Fatalistic suicide is relatively infrequent and there is little evidence of high rates where one would expect them, e.g. among prisoners serving life sentences, victims of incurable debilitating disease. The one report of what I might call fatalistic suicide describes situations in which other risk factors are also present. Gehlot and Nathawat (61) describe suicide in India where the overall rate is quite low but where, relative to other segments of the Indian population, the rate among young people is quite high. The authors label a large proportion of young Indian suicides as "performance" suicides, but it is not clear just what that term means and what its theoretical background and implications are. However, in their case studies, I find evidence of fatalistic suicide. They describe the deaths of two young women, well-educated professionals, who had been forced, by the absence of their husbands, to live with, and under the control of, strict and traditional in-laws. These women were unable to pursue their professional activities, they were unable to escape the situations they were in, and they were unable, by virtue of their education and/or personal characteristics, to fulfill traditional roles as subservient and dutiful daughters-in-law. In this sense, their suicides take on a fatalistic quality. Headley (7) similarly suggests that self-inflicted death among Asian women and young people tends to be fatalistic suicide. She focuses on the very limited opportunities these categories of persons have. "The options for women to refuse marriages they do not want, for support should they be divorced, and for status in society other than as wife and mother are limited" (7, page 355). Thus, although fatalistic suicide has long been discounted as a virtually empty cell in Durkheim's paradigm, excessive regulation may, in fact, be an important cultural risk factor in some parts of the world.

Cultural Attitudes and Socialization

Cultures do not contribute to suicide rates of populations only through the kinds of structural variables described in the preceding pages. They may also facilitate suicide in such ways as romanticizing suicide, presenting death as a positive state, or influencing the psychological development of individuals in such a way that they are susceptible to suicide.

In the traditions of India and Japan, suicide has been an acceptable, even prescribed, practice. Suttee, the form of suicide among Indian widows with which we are familiar, was practiced by women who simply had no other choices, or by those for whom the sacrificial pyre was a way to achieve social admiration. Another form of self-immolation, Johar, was practiced by Indian women whose husbands had been killed in battle. Here, the suicide was to avoid being raped by the conquerors (61). Thus, in India, suicide has traditionally been a way for women to resolve dilemmas created by their social role and the dependence on their husbands that role imposed on them. **Acceptable** forms of suicide in India were those associated with religious motives and committed by ascetics, and those committed by the very old, the very feeble, or the incurably ill (62).

Japanese culture also prescribed suicide under some circumstances, but it was men who were to kill themselves, and their doing so was valued as demonstrating the highest of virtues. Suicide is, of course, proscribed in Japan today, but the influence of the past is clear in the conflicting and confusing reactions to the suicide in 1970 of Mishima Yukio. Proclaiming the values of the samurai, he invaded the headquarters of the Japanese Self-Defense Force and, in front of the commanding general of that force, Mishima committed seppuku, the time-honored ritualistic suicide by disembowelment. The initial reaction to this event was to declare Mishima insane and fanatical. However, the day after Mishima's suicide, the Japanese people were asked to respect his motives, and various spokespersons described themselves as empathic with Mishima, who came to be described as a martyr, an exemplar of what it means to be Japanese, and as dying splendidly (63).

The goal of Fuse's paper was to explore the "deep relationship between suicide and culture in Japan," and he demonstrates quite eloquently how "ritualized suicide such as seppuku was a culturally approved and reinforced means of safe-guarding self-esteem and honor" (55, page 63). Given that, he pleads for restraint in what he sees as an increasing tendency to define suicide in terms of psychopathology. Hirsch sums up his discussion of the cultural determinants of suicide by stating that Japan historically sanctioned ritualistic suicide and "condoned other forms of suicide as acceptable means of dealing with life's problems" (57, page 339). Prominent among the cultural factors cited by Tatai as underlying Japanese suicides are "an historical tradition of suicide as an honorable solution to harsh and difficult personal solutions" and "a romanticizing of suicide as an escape from the stresses of life under a mantle of acceptability" (6, page 19).

In two studies of suicide in nonindustrialized societies, there is evidence that suicide is, in some form, ritualized or accepted. The primary method of killing oneself among the Kandrian is hanging, and there appears to be a ritualistic procedure known to members of the society. Kandrian children represent it in their drawings (58). Rubinstein describes the development of what he terms a "suicide subculture" among Micronesian youth. It is "a set of coherent meanings which organize, provide significance for, and contribute to the frequency of adolescent suicides in Micronesia" (47, page 664).

Cultural views of death that might facilitate or enable suicide are illustrated by writers about Japan more than others. Iga for instance, talks about how there is little separation between this world and the afterworld in Japanese culture, and how the Japanese romanticize impermanence (e.g., treasuring most highly the most fragile of flowers, the cherry blossom) (56). Tatai (6) describes

Shintoists as viewing death as an opportunity to become a kami, or spirit, and Buddhism as presenting the idea of reincarnation and survival after death.

The only study I found that tested a hypothesized relationship between personality and suicide across cultures is Smith and Hackathorn's (43) comparison of 69 "primitive and peasant" societies in terms of suicide rates and a number of potential correlates, including expression of affect, and the importance of pride and shame. The potential predictor variables were selected on the basis of review of existing literature and availability of measures in the data files they used. The personality characteristics are two of the three variables accounting for 69 percent of the variance in a 7-point suicide rating scale. The data revealed that suicide rates are high where societies expect very restrained, or very open, expression of emotion, and where they place a great deal of importance on individual pride and shame. Certainly we see the emphasis on these characteristics (emotional restraint and shame) in the description of socialization of Japanese children. It would be very informative to assess child-rearing practices in other industrialized societies, and to test the hypothesis that cultures encouraging these characteristics in their populations have high suicide rates when compared with societies where moderation in expression of affect is endorsed and individual pride and shame are not emphasized.

SUMMARY

During the decade of the 1970s, the United States witnessed a startling increase in suicide rates among adolescents and young adults. The increase has been described as part of a cohort effect, an increase in suicide rates in each successive birth cohort. It has also been attributed to the coming of age-at-risk of the baby boom generation, and the only countries showing similar patterns of change in youth suicide are those with similar post World War II fertility patterns.

The risk factors found to be most closely and consistently associated with youth suicide in this country are those that, in some way, operationalize Durkheim's concept of egoism. These risk factors reflect weak social integration and the concomitant isolation that individuals experience. Weak social integration may be endemic to adolescence and young adulthood in countries such as the United States. The ubiquitous isolation felt by adolescents and young adults might be amplified in minority groups, whose adolescent members experience the combination of age-related problems of egoism, and problems created by the prejudice of the majority group, preventing integration of minorities into the social mainstream.

Whether or not adolescence is a period in which social ties are vulnerable and tenuous, many social critics feel that ours is an increasingly egoistic society, and they cite as evidence such social changes as increasing divorce rates and decreasing importance in people's lives of religion. Risk factors reflective of weak social integration have been used to "explain" differential suicide rates among subgroups of youth, as well as the increase over time of youth suicide in general. The integrative function of identification with the minority group and its "perspective" has been identified as protecting young blacks from suicide. Students who kill themselves tend to have histories of behavior that is not normative; that is, they tend to look like social isolates.

Religion was seen by Durkheim as a major form of social integration, and social theorists have tended to continue to see social integration as a critical function of religion. It appears that the degree to which individuals are committed to orthodox religious beliefs continues to predict levels of suicide fairly consistently. However, religious affiliation is no longer a dependable index of orthodoxy and is, therefore, not useful as a predictor of suicide.

Risk factors that can be clustered because they reflect Durkheim's second major "type" of suicide, anomic, are less useful in analyzing suicide in the United States than are those discussed under the label "egoistic." However, anomie continues to be a productive concept when suicide rate changes in traditional societies are under consideration. The societies in which anomie is readily available as an explanatory principle are those in which major and rapid social change can and does occur. The relative unavailability of the concept for analysis of suicide in the United States may be a function of the resistance of western social structures to rapid major change. That is, these societies may be relatively invulnerable to anomie.

The problem in using the concept of anomie in reference to suicide in our society may stem from the concept's resistance to operationalization rather than, or as well as, society's resistance to rapid change. For instance, although writers may speculate on the suicidogenic effects of changes (such as those in the status of blacks and women), we have seen no specification of measures that would reflect anomie, which then may be used in comparative analyses of group suicide rates or rates across time.

Altruism as a suicide risk factor has tended to be dismissed by social scientists. I have argued that this tendency is unwise, and that we need to think once more about the risks posed when persons abdicate their egos for a group identity and subordinate individual goals and desires to group needs and dictates.

A second reason for not dismissing the altruistic suicide as relevant in the world of today is that it may be a powerful enabling factor. There is evidence that where altruistic suicide is part of a society's cultural tradition, suicide continues, even in the face of official proscriptions, to be seen as an acceptable, even honorable, way to deal with shame. The attractiveness of altruistic suicide is likely to be especially strong for persons at an age when they are confronted with the painful hard work of individuation.

Evidence for the presence of risk factors that might predict fatalistic suicide is sparse and tenuous. However, interpretation of suicide among some Asiatic subgroups has been facilitated by Durkheim's predictions about the effects of excessive social regulation. We might be well advised to re-explore this part of the theory.

In sum, cultures contribute to high suicide rates by failure to provide supportive structures such as those that integrate individuals into the social group, by creating stress for members of the social group (e.g., rapid social change leaving individuals without a set of norms to follow), by influencing the personalities of individuals through socialization practices (e.g., promoting repression of affect), and by promoting positive or accepting attitudes toward suicide (e.g., ennobling certain forms of suicide or making the suicides of certain persons heroic).

CONCLUSIONS

The major conclusion I drew from this analysis is that we need more theory-driven research. It is important that more and better work be done in the following:

- Specification of theories, models, and concepts related to suicide
- Operationalization of relevant concepts into measures
- Derivation of hypotheses from theories and models of suicidal behavior
- Testing hypotheses using valid and reliable data and appropriate analytic techniques

We need, for instance, to think about Easterlin's assertions that the fertility rates of one period determine the opportunity structure 20 years later, and that the opportunity structure influences the probability of suicide among young adults. What hypotheses can be derived from his model and how might they be tested empirically? What opportunities does his model provide us for being more effectively proactive in preventing, or at least tempering, increases in rates of suicide among specified groups in the population?

The second conclusion from this work is that there is continued need for clarification and assessment of theoretical issues and questions. What, for instance, is the relation between integration and anomie? I speculated earlier that contemporary societies might be relatively invulnerable to anomie because of their resistance to rapid social change. We have seen that contemporary societies tend to be characterized as relatively egoistic. This suggests that the more integrated a society is, the more vulnerable it is to anomie. Might this conclusion be derived from Durkheim's work or from that of the social theorists who have followed in his footsteps? I am not the first to suggest that social integration and social regulation are related processes. I do not believe, however, that they are the same, and I feel we can profit from trying to describe, not only how they influence one another, but also how they are independent.

We know that social systems are not static but are dynamic. Might use of some of the basic principles of systems theory help us understand variations in suicide rate across societies and time? For instance, might the recent emergence and proliferation of cults and fundamentalist groups in the United States be understood as reaction to a social system that has become excessively egoistic? What I am proposing here is that societies might be thought of as oscillating between the extremes of the integration and the regulation continua. This way of looking at societies and social change might constitute a more productive framework for assessing and interpreting change in rates of suicide over time than any of the models currently in use.

REFERENCES

1. Centers for Disease Control. Violent deaths among persons 15-24 years of age - United States, 1970-78. Morbidity and Mortality Weekly Report 32:453-457, 1983.

2. Hawton K: Suicide and Attempted Suicide Among Children and Adolescents. Beverly Hills, California, Sage Publications, 1986.

3. Holinger PC: Adolescent suicide: An epidemiological study of recent trends. American Journal of Psychiatry 135:754-756, 1978.

4. Solomon MI, Hellon CP: Suicide and age in Alberta, Canada, 1951 to 1977. Archives of General Psychiatry 37:511-513, 1980.

5. Goldney RD, Katsikitis M: Cohort analysis of suicide rates in Australia. Archives of General Psychiatry 40:71-74, 1983.

6. Tatai K: Japan. In LA Headley (ed) Suicide in Asia and the Near East Berkeley, California, University of California Press. pp 12-58, 1983.

7. Headley LA: (Ed) Suicide in Asia and the Near East Berkeley, California, University of California Press, 1983.

8. Headley LA: Hong Kong. In LA Headley (ed) Suicide in Asia and the Near East Berkeley, California, University of California Press, pp 87-100, 1983.

9. Rin H, Chen T: Taiwan. In LA Headley (ed) Suicide in Asia and the Near East Berkeley, California, University of California Press, pp 59-86, 1983.

10. Murphy GE, Witzel RD: Suicide risk by birth cohort in the United States, 1949-1974. Archives of General Psychiatry 37:519-523, 1980.

11. Cosand BJ, Bourque LB, Kraus JF: Suicide among adolescents in Sacramento County, California 1950-1979. Adolescence 17:917-930, 1982.

12. Bouvier LF: America's baby boom generation: The fateful bulge. Population Bulletin 35:1-35, 1980.

13. Durkheim E: Suicide: A Study in Sociology JA Spaulding and G Simpson (Trans) New York, Free Press 1951.

14. Giddons A: A typology of suicide. European Journal of Sociology 7:276-295, 1966.

15. Johnson BD: Durkheim's one cause of suicide. American Sociological Review 30:875-886, 1965.

16. Martin WT: Theories of Variation in the Suicide Rate, in Gibbs JP (ed): Suicide. New York, Harper and Row, pp 74-96, 1968.

17. Konopka G: Adolescent suicide. Exceptional Children 49:390-394, 1983.

18. Maris, R: The adolescent suicide problem. Suicide and Life-Threatening Behavior 15:909, 1985.

19. Sabbath JC: The suicidal adolescent—the expendable child. Journal of the American Academy of Child Psychiatry 8:272-285, 1969.

20. Sudak HS, Ford AB, Rushforth NB: Adolescent suicide: An overview. American Journal of Psychotherapy 38:350-363, 1984.

21. Holinger PC, Offer D: Perspectives on suicide in adolescence. Research in Community and Mental Health 2:139-157, 1981.

22. Davis R: Black suicide in the seventies: Current trends. Suicide and Life-Threatening Behavior 9:131-140, 1979.

23. Morris JB, Kovacs M, Beck AT, Wolffe A: Notes toward an epidemiology of urban suicide. Comprehensive Psychiatry 15:537-547, 1974.

24. Seiden RH: Why are suicides among blacks increasing? HSMHA Health Reports 87:3-8, 1972.

25. Dizmang LH, Watson J, May PA, Bopp J: Adolescent suicide at an Indian Reservation. American Journal of Orthopsychiatry 44:43-49, 1974.

26. Ogden M, Spector MI, Hill CA Jr: Suicides and homicides among Indians. Public Health Reports 85:75-80, 1970.

27. Tonkin RS: Suicide methods in British Columbian adolescents. Journal of Adolescent Health Care 5:172-28, 1984.

28. Smith JC, Mercy JA, Warren CW: Comparison of suicides among Anglos and Hispanics in five Southwestern states. Suicide and Life Threatening Behavior 15:14-26, 1985.

29. Resnick HLP, Dizmang LH: Observations on suicidal behavior among American Indians. American Journal of Psychiatry 127:882-887, 1971.

30. Bush JA: Suicide and blacks: A conceptual framework. Suicide and Life-Threatening Behavior 6:216-222, 1976.

31. Shaffer D, Fisher P: The epidemiology of suicide in children and young adolescents. Journal of the American Academy of Child Psychiatry 20:545-565, 1981.

32. Amir M: Suicide among minors in Israel. The Israel Annals of Psychiatry and Related Disciplines 11:219-269, 1973.

33. Sainsbury P, Barraclough B: Differences between suicide rates. Nature 220-1252, 1968.

34. Meer F: Race and suicide in South Africa London, Routledge & Kegan Paul, 1976.

35. Gibbs JP, Martin WT: Status Integration and Suicide. Eugene, Oregon, University of Oregon Press, 1964.

36. Petzel SV, Riddle M: Adolescent suicide and cognitive aspects. Adolescent Psychiatry 9:343-398, 1981.

37. Peck ML, Schrut A: Suicidal behavior among college students. HSMHA Health Reports 86:149-156, 1971.

38. Ishii K: Backgrounds of higher suicide rates among "name university" students: A retrospective study of the past twenty five years. Suicide and Life-Threatening Behavior 15:56-68, 1985.

39. Sanborn DE III, Sanborn CJ, Cimbolic P: Two years of suicide: A study of adolescent suicide in New Hampshire. Child Psychiatry and Human Development 3:234-242, 1973.

40. Shaffer D: Suicide in children and early adolescence. Journal of Child Psychology and Psychiatry 15:275-291, 1974.

41. Stack S: Religion and suicide: A reanalysis. Social Psychiatry 15:65-70, 1980.

42. Minear JD, Brush LR: The correlations of attitudes toward suicide with death anxiety, religiosity, and personal closeness to suicide. Omega 11:317-324, 1980-81.

43. Smith DH, Hackathorn L: Some social and psychological factors related to suicide in primitive societies: A cross-cultural comparative study. Suicide and Life-Threatening Behavior 12:195-211, 1982.

44. Best JB, Kirk WG: Religiosity and self-destruction. Psychological Record 32:35-39, 1982.

45. Hoelter JW: Religiosity, fear of death and suicide acceptability. Suicide and Life-Threatening Behavior 9:163-172, 1979.

46. Boldt M: Normative evaluations of suicide and death: A cross-generational study. Omega 13:145-157, 1982-83.

47. Rubinstein DH: Epidemic suicide among Micronesian adolescents. Social Science and Medicine 17:657-665, 1983.

48. Dissanayake SAW, De Silva P: Sri Lanka. in LA Headley (ed) Suicide in Asia and the Near East Berkeley, California, University of California Press, pp 167-209, 1983.

49. Dizmang LH: Observations on suicidal behavior among the Shoshone-Bannock Indians. Presented at 1st National Conference on Suicidology, Chicago, 1968.

50. Shore JH: American Indian suicide - fact and fancy. Psychiatry 38:86-91, 1975.

51. Henden H: Black suicide. Archives of General Psychiatry 21:407-422, 1969.

52. Easterlin RA: Birth and Fortune. New York, Basic Books, 1980.

53. Hendin H: Suicide among the young: Psychodynamics and demography, in Peck ML, Farberow NL, Litman RE (eds): Youth Suicide. New York, Springer, pp 19-38, 1985.

54. Old English Dictionary. Compact Edition Oxford, Oxford University Press, 1971.

55. Fuse T: Suicide and culture in Japan: A study of seppuku as an institutionalized form of suicide. Social Psychiatry 15:57-63, 1980.

56. Iga M: Suicide of Japanese Youth. Suicide and Life-Threatening Behavior 11:17-30, 1981.

57. Hirsch J: Cultural determinants of suicide: The perspective of the Japanese. Mental Hygiene. 3:337-339.

58. Hoskin JO, Friedman MI, Carote JE: A high incidence of suicide in a preliterate primitive society. Psychiatry 32:200-209, 1969.

59. Blos P: The Adolescent Passage. New York, International Universities Press, 1979.

60. Wellisch DK, Ungerleider JT: Destructive Aspects of the Cult Experience, in Peck ML, Farberow NL, Litman RE (eds): Youth Suicide. New York, Springer, pp 80-87, 1985.

61. Gehlot PS, Nathawat SS: Suicide and family constellation in India. American Journal of Psychotherapy 37:273-278, 1983.

62. Rao V: India. In LA Headley (ed) Suicide in Asia and the Near East Berkeley, California, University of California Press, pp 210-237, 1983.

63. Kristeller JL: Mishima's suicide: A psycho-cultural analysis. Psychologia 16:50-59, 1973.

FAMILY CHARACTERISTICS AND SUPPORT SYSTEMS AS RISK FACTORS FOR YOUTH SUICIDAL BEHAVIOR

Cynthia R. Pfeffer, M.D., Associate Professor of Clinical Psychiatry, Cornell University Medical College, and Chief, Child Psychiatry Inpatient Unit, New York Hospital-Westchester Division, White Plains, New York

The search for etiological, correlational, and early warning signs of child and adolescent suicidal behavior has intensified, especially because of the heightened awareness that the incidence of suicide and nonfatal suicidal behaviors have been increasing in the last three decades. Current evidence suggests that suicidal behavior is a complex, multi-determined symptom. An implication of this concept of youth suicidal behavior is that investigations aimed toward elucidating the most important determinants of suicidal behavior—including diagnosis, personality traits, family and environmental factors, and biological variables—require an integrated approach that gives credence to the role of interactive effects of a number of variables.

Research Design Limitations

A variety of approaches have been used to evaluate family factors associated with suicidal behavior. Nevertheless, knowledge gained about family risk factors for youth suicidal behavior has been limited by the designs of previous investigations. There is minimal information about family characteristics of youngsters who commit suicide and a paucity of prospective studies of child and adolescent suicide victims. Almost all the existing studies describing family features are of individuals who exhibit nonfatal suicidal behavior. Furthermore, of these studies, a large number have not focused primarily on family factors but describe them as aspects of the more extensive investigation of multiple factors associated with youth suicidal behavior. Since these studies evaluated factors after suicidal tendencies were expressed, they do not provide information about family factors that are precursors for youth suicidal behavior. This issue can be studied in prospective longitudinal investigations which, currently, are absent in this field of investigation.

Other important limitations exist in previous studies of family risk factors for youth suicidal behavior. Whereas most studies provide a definition of suicidal tendency, the methods to evaluate the suicidal tendencies are often not described and certainly not systematic or uniform. The studies vary in the type of suicidal tendency being investigated. Some studies assess subjects with only suicidal ideation, others evaluate suicide attempters, and still others investigate subjects with a range of suicidal tendencies that include suicidal ideation, threats, and attempts.

Biases in selection of subjects may exist. Most studies use patients who were admitted to medical or psychiatric emergency, inpatient or outpatient facilities. There are limited data on subjects in other settings such as schools and correctional facilities or for those who drop out of treatment. There are almost no studies of nonpatient populations.

The methods of collecting data predominantly have used chart reviews or clinical interviews. These chart reviews are limited by informant, interviewer, and recording variability. The clinical interview techniques varied. Most studies did not use systematic interview approaches. In some studies, the procedures for interviewing were not stated. Only a few studies used standardized interview instruments or self-report ratings.

Finally, the statistics are reported in inconsistent ways. For example, the greatest limitation is that most research papers do not include complete statistical data needed to compare the findings from different investigations. As a result, it is difficult to meaningfully compare the effect sizes of results.

Nevertheless, although the studies of family factors were limited by a number of methodological features, the information acquired in these studies have a number of consistent trends that lend support to the importance of family risk factors for youth suicidal behavior. These findings will be described in the next sections.

Studies of Adult Suicidal Individuals

Before there was an extensive interest in studying youth suicidal behavior, the role of early childhood experiences on suicidal behavior was investigated in retrospective studies of adults. These studies indicate that family instability due to early parental loss and deprivation is related to adult suicide and nonfatal behavior (1-9). In fact, studies of adult suicidal individuals suggest that the critical time period for sensitization to the effects of parental loss is during the preadolescent and early adolescent years (10-12).

These retrospective studies are important not only in suggesting ways in which early life events may be associated with long term outcome of suicidal symptom expression but also in pointing out the need for cross-sectional

prospective studies of high risk child populations. For example, children who suffered parental loss, family breakup, and environmental instability are appropriate subjects for investigations of high risk populations to examine the precursor factors of suicidal behavior. Another issue to be evaluated is whether there is a proximal association between stressful live events and suicidal behavior among children and adolescents. The next sections will discuss research on this issue.

Studies of Multiple Factors Associated with Youth Suicidal Behavior

Table 1 outlines family factors in the cross-sectional studies of children and adolescents that evaluated multiple psychosocial variables associated with suicidal behavior. (Tables appear at the end of this chapter.) Definitions for suicidal behavior were clearly presented in most of these studies, but varied. All youngsters were studied after they expressed suicidal tendencies. In most studies, data were collected during interviews of the youngsters and their parents. Most of these studies were of youngsters admitted to psychiatric or medical emergency facilities. In this way, generalization of the findings to the general population, medically ill, or untreated youngsters was limited. The sample sizes ranged widely from 37 to 1010 youngsters. The comparison groups consisted predominantly of youngsters evaluated in the same setting as the index sample, so there was control over demographic and other variables that were not the specific focus of study.

There was only one study of suicide victims (27). This pilot study utilized the psychological autopsy method of interviewing relatives and friends of 20 children and adolescents who committed suicide. There were 17 nonsuicidal controls who were matched by age, sex, race and social status to the suicide victims. Significantly higher prevalences of family breakup, violence, emotional problems, and suicidal tendencies were found in families of the suicide victims than the controls. Although the number of suicide victims was small in this study, the types of family turmoil reported have also been found in many investigations of nonfatal suicidal behavior of children and adolescents (see Table 1).

Among the studies of nonfatal suicidal behavior, three types of family factors have been consistently associated with suicidal behavior. First, there were family stresses involving changes in the composition of the families because of losses, deaths, and parental separation/divorce (13,17,21,23,24,26).

Second, family violence especially involving physical and sexual abuse was highly represented in these studies (21,22,24,26,28). Third, symptoms of family depression and/or suicidal behavior were found to be associated with suicidal behavior of the children and adolescents (13-15,17,22,23,26). The findings of these studies, therefore, suggest that more indepth assessment of these three types of family factor correlates of youth suicidal behavior is warranted.

Life Stress and Social Supports

Most of the previously described studies indicate an association between a variety of family problems and suicidal behavior in children and adolescents but they do not indicate whether the occurrence of these problems during specific periods of the youngster's life is an important element associated with suicidal behavior. Of note is the study by Rosenthal and Rosenthal (24), which indicated that severe stresses of abuse and parental rejection were common in the histories of preschool children who expressed suicidal ideas and/or attempts.

Only a few studies evaluate the relation between developmental periods, social support stresses, and child and adolescent suicidal behavior. Table 2 indicates some of the recent studies that address this issue.

Stanley and Barter (29), in a chart review, compared 38 adolescent psychiatric in-

patients who attempted suicide with 38 psychiatric inpatient controls matched by age and sex. The authors determined that, although there were no differences in incidence of parental loss in the two groups of adolescents, the suicide attempters had a greater incidence of parental loss before they were 12 years old than the nonsuicidal inpatients. Furthermore, parental discord expressed as threats of parental separation and/or divorce were significantly more common for the suicidal adolescents.

A further indication of the relation between lack of social supports and suicide attempts was found when Stanley and Barter followed up on the outcome of these hospitalized adolescents. The previously suicidal adolescents were significantly more likely to express future suicidal behavior ($X^2 = 7.87$, df = 1, p<.01). For example, approximately 50 percent of the previously suicidal adolescents continued to exhibit suicidal behavior after hospital discharge in contrast to four adolescents in the comparison group who showed postdischarge suicidal behavior.

Stanley and Barter compared adolescents who made a suicide attempt after discharge (N=15) with adolescents who were previously suicidal but made no suicide attempts after discharge (N=21) and with initially nonsuicidal adolescents who did not make a suicide attempt after discharge (N=24). The adolescents who made a postdischarge suicide attempt had less adequate peer relations than the other previously suicidal adolescents ($X^2 = 6.61$, df = 1, p<.05) and the nonsuicidal controls ($X^2 = 5.02$, df = 1, p<.05). In addition. the repeat suicide attempters were less likely to be living with their parents after discharge than the other previously suicidal adolescents ($X^2 = 4.007$, df = 1, p<.05) and the nonsuicidal adolescents ($X^2 = 4.7$, df = 1, p<.05). These findings support the notion that early and continued lack of social supports are important factors related to suicidal behavior in adolescents.

Cohen-Sandler, Berman and King (31) provided a longitudinal perspective on the types and degree of stress in social supports associated with youth suicidal behavior. In this retrospective chart review study, 20 suicidal psychiatric inpatients, 5 to 14 years old, were compared with 21 depressed non-suicidal child inpatients and 35 psychiatric inpatient controls. The two comparison groups, who were hospitalized in the same inpatient unit, provide good controls for the effects of depression and other factors associated with psychiatric inpatients. Only 38 percent of the depressed inpatients engaged in suicidal behavior but 65 percent of the suicidal children were depressed. Thus, depressed children were not necessarily suicidal, and not all of the suicidal children were diagnosed as depressed.

The results revealed that the suicidal children had higher lifetime stress scores than the other children and that by the age of 4-1/2 years, the suicidal children began to experience more family stresses. Furthermore, in the year prior to hospitalization, the suicidal children had significantly higher degrees of stress than the other inpatients. This study suggests that measures of life stress can distinguish suicidal from non-suicidal children and that particular types of stresses were important. Loss of adult support was an important factor and was a consequence of hospitalization of a parent, death of a grandparent, and birth of a sibling. Furthermore, problematic parenting could be inferred from the finding that the suicidal children were more likely to have parents who abused drugs and/or alcohol.

Adam and associates (30) used a high risk population to determine the relation between early losses and suicidal ideation. They interviewed 41 students, referred to a university mental health service, who reported the death of at least one parent before age 16 years, and compared these students to age-, sex-, and religion-matched students at the same clinic; the control group included 35 students with a history of parental separation and/or divorce before 16 years of age and 61 students from intact homes.

The main findings revealed that 50 percent of the subjects with a history of early parental loss were preoccupied with suicide and 18 percent made one or more suicide attempts. There was more suicidal ideation among those subjects who experienced both an early loss and greater family instability after the losses. When there was greater family instability before, during, or after the parental loss, suicidal ideation was more frequent than in those subjects who experienced a restoration of family stability after the loss.

Among the rare studies of adolescent suicide, an innovative approach was taken by Salk and colleagues (32) in their study of prenatal, birth, and neonatal distress factors and their relation to adolescent suicide. The birth records of 52 adolescents who committed suicide before age 20 were compared with the records of 52 adolescents whose births preceded and 52 adolescents whose births followed those of the index subjects. The results indicated that the suicide victims had more prenatal and postnatal problems than the two control groups. The three most common problems found among the suicide victims were respiratory distress for more than one hour after birth, no antenatal care before 20 weeks, and chronic disease of the mother during the pregnancy. The types of chronic diseases for the mothers of the suicide group included chronic persistent anemia, rheumatic fever at age 12, residual heart murmur and arthritis, chronic anxiety with treatment, kidney infection, polio, chronic hypertension, asthma, high blood pressure, repeated gonococcal infection, muscular dystrophy with incapacitation, multiple surgery, extreme obesity, infectious hepatitis, and fibroid uterus. While it was noted that socioeconomic factors or family conflicts did not distinguish the groups, no specific information was provided about specific psychosocial variables before or at the time of birth or during the lifetime of the adolescents. This limitation makes it difficult to evaluate the results with respect to whether the reported features of infant pre- and postnatal distress were indicators of more fundamental features of psychosocial stresses associated with adolescent suicide. Nevertheless, this study reinforces others that indicate the important relation between early childhood stress and risk for adolescent suicide.

Child and Adolescent Abuse

Although violent deaths attributed to accidents and homicide are the leading causes of death in adolescents (33), the relation between family violence and youth suicidal behavior has been relatively neglected as a topic for investigation. Two studies, described in Table 3, provide information about this issue.

Deykin, Albert, and McNamarra (35) surveyed the Massachusetts Department of Social Services records for evidence of contact with this agency for abuse and/or neglect for 159 adolescents admitted to an emergency service after a suicide attempt. For each of these adolescents, two age- and sex-matched comparison subjects treated for other medical conditions in the same emergency service were studied. The suicide attempters were approximately 5 times more likely to have contact with the Massachusetts Department of Social Service. The strength of this study is that the data from the social service department were unbiased because the contacts were recorded before the subject's emergency room visit and by personnel who had no awareness of the future psychological status of the subjects. The study provides strong evidence for an association between child abuse and/or neglect and adolescent suicide attempts. However, it could not discern whether there were differential effects of abuse or neglect with regard to adolescent suicidal behavior.

An earlier study (34) used a high risk population to evaluate self-destructive behavior in 60 physically abused children, 30 neglected children, and 30 normal children. In this study, Green noted that there was a higher incidence of self-destructive behavior in abused children than in the two comparison groups. Five of the abused children at-

tempted suicide, two made suicide gestures, and eleven exhibited suicidal ideation.

These two studies support the need for further research into the association between family violence and youth suicidal behavior.

Parental Psychiatric Symptoms and Disorders

A number of studies evaluating multifactoral elements associated with childhood and adolescent suicidal behavior have suggested that the parents of suicidal youngsters exhibit a variety of symptoms that include depression, violence, alcohol and drug abuse, and suicidal tendencies (14-17,22-24,26-28). These findings are in keeping with a number of studies of adult suicidal individuals that indicate a consistent relation between family suicidal behavior, family affective disorders, and an individual's suicidal behavior (36-38). Surprisingly, even in view of the important implications of these findings, there has been a relatively minimal number of investigations of the family pedigees for psychiatric problems among suicidal children and adolescents.

Table 4 highlights two recent investigations of types of parental psychopathologies found among suicidal youngsters. These two studies (39,40) suggest that parental symptoms of depression, alcohol abuse, suicidal impulses, and chronic psychiatric illness are important features associated with the histories of adolescents who attempt suicide. These studies suggest that further investigation of the psychiatric problems of parents of suicidal youngsters is warranted.

Another approach of study is to use a high risk population involving the offspring of parents with psychiatric problems. Most of the current research employing this methodology involves children of parents with affective disorders. These studies vary with respect to the types of comparison groups, methods for assessment of the youngsters, ages of the youngsters who were evaluated, time of parental assessment in relation to the parents' degree of illness, criteria for diagnosing the youngster, and degree of blindness of raters. Nevertheless, consistent trends in the results of these studies have emerged.

Children with an affectively disordered parent are likely to exhibit behavior problems and psychopathology (41-49) and have a distinct risk of developing an affective disorder (47,50-52). Child-rearing patterns of affectively disordered parents include disturbances in mother-child attachment (53), lack of parental encouragement of the child's ability to regulate affects (48,53,54) and unstable caretaking characterized by parental hostility, abuse, rejection, and separations (41,48,49,54,55).

In spite of these findings, the relation between youth suicidal behavior and parental affective disorders and/or suicidal behavior has been a relatively unexplored issue. Table 5 highlights the results of the existing studies. Only two studies of affectively disordered parents (44,47) mention that there is a higher association of suicidal tendencies in children of depressed parents than nondepressed control parents. For example, rates of suicidal ideation of 6.5 percent to 9 percent and lower rates of 0.9 percent to 3 percent for suicide attempts were noted for children of depressed parents. These studies did not evaluate whether there were certain parental characteristics, such as the presence of suicidal tendencies, that distinguished the depressed parents with suicidal youngsters from those depressed parents without suicidal children.

The relation between parental suicidal behavior and quality of child care has been minimally studied. However, some preliminary data exists on the relation between parental suicide attempt and child abuse (see Table 5). Hawton, Roberts, and Goodwin (56) looked in the child abuse bureau records for reports on mothers who attempted suicide, mothers at risk for depression, and control mothers who were not depressed or suicidal. There was significantly more child abuse reported for the suicide attempter mothers than either of the comparison mothers. In the majority

of cases, child care problems were identified before the suicide attempt. However, there were no differences among the mothers for other clinical chracteristics such as history of psychiatric treatment, previous suicide attempts, alcoholism, and drug addiction. The main findings suggest that mothers who attempt suicide may be more at risk for serious child care problems involving child abuse than mothers in the general population or for mothers who are at risk for depression. An implication of this study is that there may be a relation between parental violence and parental suicidal behavior. Furthermore, since the children were all 5 years of age or younger, no information was provided about the children's potential for suicidal behavior, a behavior that other studies have associated with child abuse.

There is only one study of the effects of parental suicide on children (57), and it has a number of limitations. The main methodological shortcoming is that data about the children were obtained from the surviving parents rather than by direct assessment of the children. The results indicate a higher frequency of psychiatric referrals for the children of the suicide victims than for comparison children whose parents were recruited from general medical practice and matched to the suicidal parents for age, sex, and marital status. No children of the suicide victims, however, exhibited suicide attempts. Family life was more unstable before the parental suicide than among the comparison families. This feature suggested that the effects on the children may be related not to the parental suicide as a sudden isolated disaster but rather to a chronically stressful environment in which the suicide was a major event. Since this study had serious methodological problems, the results must be considered to be quite tentative.

DISCUSSION

This review of research on family variables and social supports as risk factors for suicidal behavior in children and adolescents indicates that there is much variation in the research methods, populations studied, types of suicidal behavior investigated and manner in which statistical results are reported. In fact, most studies are of nonfatal suicidal behavior and, therefore, most of the findings must be considered to be about putative risk factors. However, a number of consistent trends have emerged when the issues are appraised from the multiple perspectives of investigations of suicidal youngsters, offspring of parents with psychopathology, and retrospective accounts of adults.

The studies reviewed in this report support the notion that the nature of family characteristics and social supports are important factors associated with youth suicidal behavior. Family factors associated with high risk are related to experiences characterized by the presence of intense levels of stress. Such stress, suggested by the investigations of children, adolescents, and adults, appears to be chronic and/or occurs at an early phase in the life of the individual. An important implication of these findings is that future research on family risk factors for youth suicidal behavior should adhere to a developmental perspective. Such an orientation can facilitate the examination of continuities and discontinuities in family variables that may be precursors to youth suicidal behavior.

Studies suggest that a variety of stresses exist. One type is related to loss of social supports through death, parental separation and/or divorce, mobility involving school changes, and problems with peer relationships. A second type of stress is associated with variability in parental functioning that is liked to parental psychopathology. This affects the quality of the parent-child interactions and/or may necessitate the temporary absence of the parent who requires intervention that removes him or her from the home. It also involves violation of personal boundaries best characterized when a youngster is witness to, or the victim of, sexual or violent abuse.

Important shortcomings of the studies described in this report are that they do not address hypotheses about the mechanisms underlying the relation of these family characteristics and social supports to youth suicidal behavior. For example, early loss of social supports may be an important stress that affects the development of personality characteristics and/or biological systems and thereby enhances chronic vulnerability to suicidal behavior. On the other hand, an acute loss of social supports may alter existing psychological and/or biological functioning. This may create a temporary and an acute crisis in ego functioning that affects the quality of a youngster's affect regulation, impulse control, judgment, cognition, and fantasies.

Another mechanism may involve genetic vulnerability. In this case, stress involving features of parent-child discord may be of secondary importance. For example, the mechanism involving the relation between parental violent abuse and youth suicidal behavior may be determined by some factor, such as a biological correlate, and the stressful parent-child experiences may be of secondary value. In connection with genetic vulnerability, there must be an interaction with levels of experiential stress to promote risk for suicidal behavior.

Evaluation of these mechanisms requires different research strategies than those used in the investigations reviewed in this report. Prospective longitudinal research designs of high risk populations are indicated. Such studies may evaluate the long-term outcome of children who previously had suicidal tendencies, as well as evaluate children who are the offspring of parents prone to abuse, affective disorders, separation/divorce, or death. The time required and cost involved in these investigations can be manageable, and the yield of potentially valuable information may be great.

From a more theoretical perspective, youth suicidal behavior is a multidetermined symptom with many associated factors. The studies described in this review focus mainly on risk factors and do not address issues involving protective variables against suicidal behavior. Factors associated with invulnerability of an individual, such as ways in which adaptive skills can be enhanced, must be documented. Such an approach may be consistent with a theoretical framework for youth suicidal behavior that suggests opposing vectorial components related to the expression of the suicidal symptom. For example, qualities of a supportive individual such as an ability to provide empathy, consistent availability, capacity to set limits and offer structure, and ability to gratify individual needs to enhance self-esteem may be important social support vectors that prevent suicidal behavior. The factors described in this review such as family disorganization, parental psychopathology, and family violence are vectors that enhance suicidal behavior. This model of opposing vectors, illustrated below, may elucidate approaches to assessment and interventions for suicidal risk.

Finally, important implications for prevention of suicidal behavior among children and adolescents can be derived from these studies. There is a need for efficient screening techniques to identify high risk families. Also of value would be screening devices for identifying high risk children and adolescents in such situations. Another approach is to plan interventions that focus on ameliorating family disorganization and parental psychopathologies so that stress may decrease and stability may be enhanced.

REFERENCES

1. Greer S: The relationship between parental loss and attempted suicide: A control study. British Journal of Psychiatry 1964; 110:698-705.

2. Dorpat TL, Jackson JK, and Ripley HS: Broken bones and attempted and completed suicide. Archives of General Psychiatry 1965; 12:213-216.

3. Greer, S: Parental loss and attempted suicide: A further report. British Journal of Psychiatry 1966; 112:465-470.

4. Levi LD, Fales CH, Stein M, and Sharp VH: Separation and attempted suicide. Archives of General Psychiatry 1966; 15:158-164.

5. Crook T, and Raskin A: Association of childhood and parental loss with attempted suicide and depression. Journal of Consulting and Clinical Psychology 1975; 43:277.

6. Luscomb RL, Clum GA, and Patsiokas T: Mediating factors in the relationship between life stress and suicide attempting. The Journal of Nervous and Mental Disease 1980; 168:644--650.

7. Goldney RD: Parental loss and reported childhood stress in young women who attempt suicide. Acta Psychiatrica Scandanavia 1981; 64:34-59.

8. Roy A: Early parental death and adult depression. Psychological Medicine 1983; 13:1-5.

9. Yesavage JA, and Widrow L: Early parental discipline and adult self-destructive acts. The Journal of Nervous and Mental Disease 1985; 173:74-77.

10. Hill, OW: The association of childhood bereavement with suicidal attempt in depressive illness. British Journal of Psychiatry 1969; 115:30I-304.

11. Birtchnell J: The relationship between attempted suicide, depression and parental death. British Journal of Psychiatry 1970; 116:307-313.

12. Adam KS, Bouckoms A, and Streiner D: Parental loss and family stability in attempted suicide. Archives of General Psychiatry 1982; 39:1081-1085.

13. Teicher JD, and Jacobs J: Adolescents who attempt suicide: Preliminary findings. American Journal of Psychiatry 1966; 122:1248-1257.

14. Pfeffer CR, Conte HR, Plutchik R, and Jerrett I: Suicidal behavior in latency-age children: An empirical study. Journal of the American Academy of Child Psychiatry 1979; 18:679-692.

15. Pfeffer CR, Conte HR, Plutchik R, and Jerrett I: Suicidal behavior in latency-age children: An outpatient population. Journal of the American Academy of Child Psychiatry 1980; 19:703-710.

16. Carlson GA, and Cantwell DP: Suicidal behavior and depression in children and adolescents. Journal of the American Academy of Child Psychiatry, 1982; 21:361-368.

17. Garfinkel BD, Froese A, and Hood J: Suicide attempts in children and adolescents. American Journal of Psychiatry, 1982; 139:1257-126I.

18. Miller ML, Chiles JA, and Barnes VE: Suicide attempters within a delinquent population. Journal of Consulting and Clinical Psychology, 1982; 4:491-498.

Risk Factors for Increased and Protective Factors for Decreased Youth Suicidal Risk

Increased Suicidal Risk ← Risk Factors For: ← Youth Suicidal Risk → Protective Factors For: → Decreased Suicidal Risk

1. Loss of Social Support
   a. Death
   b. Parental Separation/Divorce
   c. School Changes
   d. Peer Problems

2. Variability in Parental Functioning:
   a. Affective Disorders
   b. Suicidal Tendencies
   c. Alcohol Abuse

3. Violence
   a. Sexual Abuse
   b. Physical Abuse

1. Presence of Social Support
   a. Empathy
   b. Constant Availability
   c. Limit Setting
   d. Environmental Structure

2. Individual Adaptive Skills
   a. Appraisal of Stress
   b. Seek Alternative Solutions
   c. High Frustration Tolerance
   d. Self-esteem
   e. Good Impulse Control

20. Pfeffer CR, Solomon G, Plutchik R, Mizruchi MS, and Weiner A: Suicidal behavior in latency-age psychiatric inpatients: A replication and cross validation. Journal of the American Academy of Child Psychiatry, 1982; 21:564-569.

21. Kosky R: Childhood suicidal behavior. Journal of Child Psychology and Psychiatry, 1983; 24:457-468.

22. Pfeffer CR, Plutchik R, and Mizruchi MS: Suicidal and assaultive behavior in children: Classification, measurement, and interrelations. American Journal of Psychiatry, 1983; 140:154-157.

23. Pfeffer CR, Zuckerman S, Plutchik R, and Mizruchi MS: Suicidal behavior in normal school children: A comparison with child psychiatric inpatients. Journal of the American Academy of Child Psychiatry, 1984; 23:416-423.

24. Rosenthal PA, and Rosenthal S: Suicidal behavior in preschool children. American Journal of Psychiatry, 1984; 141:520-525.

25. Taylor EA, and Stansfeld SA: Children who poison themselves. I. A clinical comparison with psychiatric controls. British Journal of Psychiatry, 1984; 145:127-135.

26. Myers KM, Burke P, and McCauley E: Suicidal behavior by hospitalized preadolescent children on a psychiatric unit. Journal of the American Academy of Child Psychiatry, 1985; 24:474-480.

27. Shafii M, Carrigan S, Whittinghall JR, and Derrick A: Psychological autopsy of completed suicide in children and adolescents. American Journal of Psychiatry, 1985; 142:1061-1064.

28. Pfeffer CR, Newcorn J, Kaplan G, Mizruchi MS, and Plutchik R: Suicidal behavior in adolescent psychiatric inpatients. 1986; presented at the Annual Meeting of the American Psychiatric Association, Washington, D.C.

29. Stanley EJ, and Barter JT: Adolescent suicidal behavior. American Journal of Orthopsychiatry, 1970; 40:87-96.

30. Adam KS, Lohrenz JG, Harper D, and Streiner D: Early parental loss and suicidal ideation in university students. Canadian Journal of Psychiatry, 1982; 27:275-281.

31. Cohen-Sandler R, Berman AL, and King RA: Life stress and symptomatology: Determinants of suicidal behavior in children. Journal of the American Academy of Child Psychiatry, 1982; 2:178-186.

32. Salk L, Lipsett L, Sturner WQ, Reilly BM, and Levat RH: Relationship of maternal and prenatal conditions to eventual adolescent suicide. The Lancet, 1985; March 16.

33. Monthly Vital Statistics Report-National Center for Human Services, 1984; 33.

34. Green AH, Self-destructive behavior in battered children. American Journal of Psychiatry, 1978; 135:579-582.

35. Deykin EY, Albert JJ, and McNamarra JJ: A pilot study of the effect of exposure to child abuse or neglect on adolescent suicidal behavior. American Journal of Psychiatry, 1985; 142:1299-1303.

36. Murphy GE, and Wetzel RD: Family history of suicidal behavior among suicide attempters. The Journal of Nervous and Mental Disease, 1982; 170:86-90.

37. Roy A: Family history of suicide. Archives of General Psychiatry, 1983; 40:971-974.

38. Roy A: Family history of suicide in manic-depressive patients. Journal of Affective Disorders, 1985; 8:187-189.

39. Tishler CL, and McKenry PC: Parental negative self and adolescent suicide attempts. Journal of the American Academy of Child Psychiatry, 1982; 21:404-408.

40. Friedman RC, Corn R, Hurt SW, Fibel B, Schalick J, and Swirsky S: Family history of illness in the seriously suicidal adolescent: A life-cycle approach. American Journal of Orthopsychiatry, 1984; 53:390-397.

41. Weissman MM, Paykel ES, and Klerman GL: The depressed woman as a mother. Social Psychiatry, 1972; 7:98-108.

42. Garmezy N: Children at risk: the search for antecedents of schizophrenia II. Ongoing research programs, issues, and intervention. Schizophrenia Bulletin, 1974; 9:55-125.

43. Garmezy N, and Streitman S: Children at risk: The search for the antecedents of schizophrenia I. Conceptual models and research methods. Schizophrenia Bulletin, 1974; 8:14-90.

44. Welner Z, Welner A, McCrary D, and Leonard MA: Psychotherapy in children of inpatients with depression: A controlled study. The Journal of Nervous and Mental Disease, 1977; 164:408-413.

45. Decina P, Kestenbaum CJ, Farber S, Kron L, Gargan M, Sackeim HA, and Fieve RR: Clinical and psychological assessment of children of bipolar probands. American Journal of Psychiatry, 1983; 140:548-553.

46. Weissman MM, Leckman JF, Merikangas KR, Gammon GD, and Prusoff BA: Depression and anxiety disorders in parents and children: Results from the Yale Family Study. Archives of General Psychiatry, 1984; 41:845-852.

47. Weissman MM, Prusoff BA, Gammon GD, Merikangas KR, Leckman JF, and Kidd KK: Psychopathology in the children (ages 6-18) of depressed and normal parents. Journal of the American Academy of Child Psychiatry, 1984; 23:78-84.

48. Zahn-Waxler C, McKnew DH, Cummings EM, Davenport YB, and Radke-Yarrow M: Problem behaviors and peer interactions of young children with a manic-depressive parent. American Journal of Psychiatry, 1984; 141:236-240.

49. Williams H, and Carmichael A: Depression in mothers in a multi-ethnic urban industrial municipality in Melbourne. Aetiological factors and effects on infants and preschool children. Journal of Child Psychology and Psychiatry, 1985; 26:277-288.

50. Cytryn L, McKnew DH, Bartko JJ, Lamour M, and Hamovitt J: Offspring of patients with affective disorders II. Journal of the American Academy of Child Psychiatry, 1982; 21:389-391.

51. Leckman JF, Weissman MM, Prusoff BA, Caruso KA, Merikangas KR, Pauls DL, and Kidd KK: Subtypes of depression: Family study perspective. Archives of General Psychiatry, 1984; 41:833-838.

52. Beardslee WR, Klerman GL, Keller MB, Lavori PW, and Padorefsky DL: But are they cases? Validity of DSM III major depression in children identified in a family study. American Journal of Psychiatry, 1985; 142:687-691.

53. Gaensbauer TJ, Harmon RJ, Cytryn L, and McKnew DH: Social and affective development in infants with a manic-depressive parent. American Journal of Psychiatry, 1984; 141:223-229.

54. Davenport YB, Zahn-Waxler C, Adland ML, and Mayfield A: Early child-rearing practices in families with a manic-depressive parent. American Journal of Psychiatry, 1984; 141:230-234.

55. Ghodsian M, Zajicek E, and Wolkind S: A longitudinal study of maternal depression and child behavior problems. Journal of Child Psychology and Psychiatry. 1984; 25:91-109.

56. Hawton K, Roberts J, and Goodwin G: The risk of child abuse among mothers who attempt suicide. British Journal of Psychiatry, 1985; 146:486-489.

57. Shepherd DM, and Barraclough BM: The aftermath of parental suicide for children. British Journal of Psychiatry, 1976; 129:267-276.

Studies of Multiple Factors Associated with Youth Suicidal Behavior

Citation	Definition of Suicidal Behavior	Population Studied	Sample Size	Comparison Group	Time of Study	Data Source	Test Results	Statistics
(13) Teicher, J. D. and Jacobs, J. Adolescents who attempt suicide: preliminary findings. Am. J. Psychia. 1966; 122:1248-1257.	None given	20 adolescent inpatients with suicide attempts.	70	50 non-suicidal adolescent inpatients matched for age, race, sex, SES	1964	Interviews of adolescents and parents.	44% of suicide attempts had a relative or friend who attempted or committed suicide and in 25% there was a suicide attempt by a parent. Progressive social isolation over time.	No comparison between samples described.
(14) Pfeffer, C.R., Conte, H.R., Plutchik, R., and Jerrett, I. Suicidal behavior in latency-age children: an empirical study. J. Amer. Acad. Child Psychia. 1979;18:679-692.	Thoughts or acts which may lead to death or serious injury. A spectrum of suicidal behavior was defined that included non-suicidal, suicidal ideas, threats, mild and serious attempts.	42 suicidal children.	58 children 6-12 years old; psychiatric inpatients.	18 nonsuicidal children.	1976-1978	Interviews of children and parents.	No difference in parental separations of suicidal (94%) and nonsuicidal (75%) children. Mothers of suicidal children more depressed. An association between severity of child suicidal behavior and parental depression and suicidal tendencies. 48% suicidal children and 19% non-suicidal children worried about poor school performance.	$t=2.11$, $p<.05$ $t=2.61$, $p<.01$ $t=2.01$, $p<.01$
(15) Pfeffer, C.R., Conte, H.R., Plutchik, R., Jerrett, I. Suicidal behavior in latency-age children: an outpatient population. J. Amer. Acad. Child Psychia. 1980; 19:703-710.	Suicidal behavior included thoughts and/or acts which may lead to death or self-injury. A spectrum of suicidal behavior was defined.	13 suicidal outpatients.	39 child psychiatric outpatients, age 6-12 years in municipal hospital center.	26 non-suicidal outpatients.	1977-1979	Interview of parents and children.	No difference in parental depression, psychiatric hospitalization, alcohol/drug abuse, marital separations, parental violence, and child abuse in suicidal children. Suicidal children had more parental suicidal ideation than nonsuicidal children.	$p<.05$
(16) Carlson, G.A. and Cantwell, D.P. Suicidal behavior and depression in children and adolescents. J. Amer. Acad. Child Psychia. 1982; 21:361-368.	Suicide attempt was an act leading to self-injury.	22 youngsters attempted suicide.	102 children and adolescents in psychiatric inpatient and outpatient care.	80 nonsuicidal attempters.	1977-1978	Interview of children and parents.	59% suicide attempts had families with depression and alcoholism compared to 50% in non-attempter group - no difference between groups.	Not given.
(17) Garfinkel, B.D., Froese, A. and Hood, J. Suicide attempts in children and adolescents. Amer. J. Psychia. 1982; 139:1257-1261.	Deliberate self-inflicted injury with conscious decision to die.	505 children and adolescents in emergency service for suicide attempts (mean age 15.3 years - range = 6-21 years).	1010 children and adolescents.	505 non-suicidal youngsters matched for age, sex, and time of evaluation.	1970-1977	Hospital chart review.	Suicide attempters had more family history of mental illness (51.6%, N = 442) than non-attempters (16.4%, N = 452). Suicide attempters had more family history of medical illness (51.5%, N = 445) than non-attempters (44.5%, N = 468). Suicide attempters had more family history of suicidal behavior (8.3%, N = 443) than non-attempters (1.1%, N = 442). Suicide attempters had more paternal unemployment (14.1%, N = 242) than non-attempters (6.7%, N = 193). Suicide attempters had more parental absence (n = 442) than non-attempters (N = 437).	$X^2=122.3$, df=1, $p<.01$ $X^2=3.96$, df=1, $p<.05$ $X^2=23.95$, df=2, $p<.01$ $X^2=6.89$, df=1, $p<.01$ $X^2=129.3$, df=3, $p<.001$

Table 1.

Studies of Multiple Factors Associated with Youth Suicidal Behavior

Citation	Definition of Suicidal Behavior	Population Studied	Sample Size	Comparison Group	Time of Study	Data Source	Test Results	Statistics
(18) Miller, M.L., Chiles, J.A., and Barnes, V.E. Suicide attempts within a delinquent population. J. Consulting and Clinical Psychol. 1982: 4:491-498.	A nonfatal act in which the individual deliberately causes self-injury.	50 adolescents admitted to correctional facility for delinquent behavior and who made suicide attempts (ages 13-15 years).	170	120 nonsuicidal delinquents in same facility matched for age, sex, race, SES.	1980	Interviews of adolescents.	Suicide attempters (mean = 4.8) had greater parental conflict than non-attempters (mean 2.5). No difference in parental absence for attempters (63.3%) or non-attempters (72.2%).	p < .01
(20) Pfeffer, C.R., Solomon, G., Plutchik, R., Mizruchi, M., and Weiner, A. Suicidal behavior in latency-age psychiatric inpatients: a replication and cross validation. J. Amer. Acad. Child. Psychia. 1982;21:564-569.	Thoughts or acts which may lead to death or self-injury. A spectrum of suicidal behavior defined.	51 suicidal children.	85 child psychiatric in-patients, 6-12 years old.	14 nonsuicidal children.	1978-1981	Interviews with children and parents.	No association between spectrum of suicidal behavior and number of children in family, parental violence, medical illness, psychiatric hospitalization, alcoholism, suicidal behavior, history of prenatal and neonatal problems.	
(21) Kosky, R. Childhood suicidal behavior. J. Child Psychol. and Psychia. 1983; 24:457-468.	Self-injurious behavior with intent to die.	20 suicidal attempter psychiatric in-patients (age range 5.2-14 years, mean age 11 years).	70 children	50 psychia-in-patients who were not suicidal.	1975-1978	Clinical psychiatric evaluations.	Family losses were greater for suicidal (70%) than non-suicidal (20%) children. 60% suicidal children living with one parent but 82% non-suicidal living with both parents. Suicidal children from lower income families. No difference in number or ordinal position of children in families. 15% suicidal children's parents and 6% nonsuicidal children's parents attempted suicide. Psychiatric or physical illness high in both groups. Intrafamilial aggression higher for suicidal (60%) than non-suicidal children (4%). High rate of pre and perinatal problems in both groups.	$X^2 = 29.2$, df=2, p < .01 $X^2 = 12.8$, df=2, p < .01 $X^2 = 10.4$, df=3, p < .05 No significant difference p < .01

Table 1 continued.

Studies of Multiple Factors Associated with Youth Suicidal Behavior

Citation	Definition of Suicidal Behavior	Population Studied	Sample Size	Comparison Group	Time of Study	Data Source	Test Results	Statistics
(22) Pfeffer, C.R., Plutchik, R., and Mizruchi, M.S. Suicidal and assaultive behavior in children: Classification, measurement and interrelations. Am. J. Psychia. 1983; 140:154-157.	Thoughts or acts which may lead to death or self-injury.	11 suicidal only children and 48 assaultive suicidal children.	102 children, 6-12 years old, in psychiatric inpatient and outpatient treatment, mean age 9 years.	26 assaultive only children and 17 non-assaultive nonsuicidal children.	1976-1979	Clinical interview of children and parents.	Assaultive-only (3.0) and assaultive-suicidal (3.8) children experienced more parental assaultive behavior than nonassaultive-non-suicidal (1.8) and suicidal only (2.0) children. Assaultive-suicidal (0.9) and suicidal only (0.5) children experienced more parental suicidal behavior than nonassaultive-nonsuicidal (0) and assaultive only (0.1) children.	$F=5.7$, $df=3, 101$, $p<.001$; $F=4.3$, $df=3, 101$ $p<.01$
(23) Pfeffer, C.R., Zuckerman, S., Plutchik, R., and Mizruchi, M.S. Suicidal behavior in normal school children: a comparison with child psychiatric inpatients. J. Amer. Acad. Child Psychia. 1984; 23:416-423.	Thoughts or acts which may lead to death or self-injury.	12 suicidal school children and 51 suicidal inpatients.	101 school children and 65 psychiatric inpatients matched for age, sex, race. Mean age of school children 9.7 years and inpatients 10.1 years.	89 nonsuicidal school children and 14 non-suicidal inpatients.	1979-1982	Interview of children and parents.	Spectrum of suicidal behavior scores for mothers were lower for nonsuicidal school children than suicidal school children. 26% of school children's mothers reported suicidal ideas. 0% school children's mothers attempted suicide. 15.6% inpatients' mothers had suicidal acts. When hospitalization status was matched, children with suicidal ideas compared to nonsuicidal children had more: parental separation parental depression parental psychiatric hospitalization maternal suicidal ideas	$t=2.42$ $p<.02$ F ratio = 4.56 $p<.05$ F ratio = 8.38 $p<.01$ F ratio = 6.86 $p<.01$ F ratio = 13.37 $p<.001$
(24) Rosenthal, P.A., and Rosenthal, S. Suicidal behavior in preschool children. Am. J. Psychia. 1984; 141:520-525.	Serious injury or attempt to injure self.	16 suicidal children in psychiatric outpatient clinic.	32 children age range 2.5-5 years, mean 3.5 years.	16 nonsuicidal children in psychiatric outpatient clinic. Matched for age, sex, race, SES.	1981-1982	Interview of parents and child.	More child abuse or neglect in suicidal (81%) than non-suicidal (38%) children. Suicidal children were more rejected (81%) than nonsuicidal (25%) children.	$X^2=4.66$ $df=1$, $p<.05$ $X^2=8.03$, $df=1$, $p<.005$
(25) Taylor, E.A., Stansfeld, S.A. Children who poison themselves. I. A clinical comparison with psychiatric controls. Brit. J. Psychia. 1984; 145:127-135.	Deliberate self-poisoning.	50 children admitted as medical emergency for self-poisoning (age 8-17 years).	100	50 nonsuicidal admitted to psychiatric clinic. Matched for age and sex.	Not given.	Records.	Greater disturbed mother-child relations for suicidal (57.4%) than nonsuicidal children (34.0%). Greater disturbed father-child relation for suicidal (60.4%) than nonsuicidal (24.5%) of children. More lack of family warmth in suicidal (60%) than nonsuicidal (8%) children. No family differences between suicidal and nonsuicidal for family mental disturbance, inadequate living conditions, inadequate communication or control, stresses.	$p<.05$ <.002 $p<.004$

Table 1 continued.

Studies of Multiple Factors Associated with Youth Suicidal Behavior

Citation	Definition of Suicidal Behavior	Population Studied	Sample Size	Comparison Group	Time of Study	Data Source	Test Results	Statistics
(26) Myers, K.M., Burke, P., and Mc-Cauley, E. Suicidal behavior by hospitalized preadolescent children or a psychiatric unit. J. Amer. Acad. Child Psychia. 1985; 24:474-480.	Same as in studies by Pfeffer, et al.	61 suicidal children admitted to psychiatric inpatient unit.	348 child inpatients.	287 nonsuicidal inpatients.	1979-1982	Chart review.	Suicidal children had more family history of suicidal behavior (25%) than nonsuicidal children (6%). Suicidal children had more father abuse (36%) than nonsuicidal children (18%). Suicidal children experienced more recent stressful life events than nonsuicidal children.	$x^2=4.50$, $df=1$, $p<.04$ $x^2=5.02$, $df=1$, $p<.03$ $x^2=6.32$, $df=1$, $p<.02$
(27) Shaffi, M., Carrigan, S., Whittinghall, J.R., Derrick, A. Psychological autopsy of completed suicide in children and adolescents. Am. J. Psychia. 1985; 142:1061-1064.	Suicide was self-inflicted death.	20 children and adolescents, age 12-19 years committed suicide.	37	Non-patients. 17 control matched for age, sex, race, SES.	1980-1983	Interview families of suicide victims and controls.	Suicide victims had more exposure to family or peer suicidal behavior (85%) than controls (18%). Suicide victims had more family emotional problems (60%) than controls (24%). Suicide victims had more parental absence and abuse (55%) than controls (29%).	$x^2=6.12$, $df=1$, $p<.008$ $x^2=5.14$, $df=1$, $p<.02$ $x^2=3.20$, $df=1$, $p<.04$
(28) Pfeffer, C.R., Newcorn, J., Kaplan, G., Mizruchi, M.S., and Plutchik, R. Suicidal behavior in adolescent psychiatric inpatients. Presented at 1986 Annual Meeting of the American Psychiatric Association, Washington, D.C.	Thoughts and/or acts which may lead to death or injury of self. A spectrum of suicidal behavior was defined.	117 suicidal adolescent inpatients.	200 adolescent inpatients, age range = 13-19 years.	83 nonsuicidal adolescent inpatients.		Chart review.	History of suicidal behavior in families and peers noted for entire group. Severity of suicidal behavior associated with: conflicts with boy/girlfriend friend sexual abuse recent school change family assaultive behavior recent parental arguments recent physical abuse	r=.249, p<.001 r=.213, p<.005 r=.188, p<.01 r=.180, p<.005 r=.176, p<.02 r=.162, p<.05

Table 1 concluded.

Studies of Life Stress and Social Supports and Youth Suicidal Behavior

Citation	Definition of Suicidal Behavior	Population Studied	Sample Size	Comparison Group	Time of Study	Data Source	Test Results	Statistics
(29) Stanley, E.J., and Barter, J.T. Adolescent suicidal behavior. Amer. J. Orthopsychia. 1970; 40:87-96.	Not given.	38 Adolescent psychiatric in-patients with suicide attempts.	76	38 Adolescent psychiatric in-patients without suicide attempts, age and sex matched.	1962-1965	Chart review.	No difference in incidence of parent loss. Greater percentage of parent loss before age 12 years for suicide attempters (16 out of 17) than controls (9 out of 16). More threats of parental separation or divorce in suicide attempters. No difference in peer relations, school performance, delinquency, sexual adjustment.	$p < .026$ $X^2 = 4.546$, df = 1, $p < .05$
(30) Adam, K.S., Lohrenz, J.G., and Harper, D., and Streiner, D. Early parental loss and suicidal ideation in university students. Can. J. of Psychia. 1982; 27:275-281.	Suicidal ideation included moderate to high levels of frequency, intensity and/or duration of wishes to kill oneself.	41 Students referred to university mental health service reporting the death of one or both parents before age 16 years. AGes of students were 17-27 years (mean age 20.9 years).	137	35 Students in same mental health service with history of parental divorce or permanent separation prior to age 16 years and 61 students in mental health service from intact homes. These controls matched for age, sex, religion.	1967-1971	Semi-structured clinical interview.	Significantly more suicidal ideation in 76 subjects with early loss than controls. Suicidal ideation not related to any particular age of loss. Death of father and death of both parents greater in subject with suicidal ideation than those without suicidal ideation. Greater family instability after death for those with suicidal ideation than those without. Greater family instability after separation/divorce for those with suicidal ideation than without.	$X^2 = 18.81$, df = 2, $p < .001$ $X^2 = 8.15$, df = 2, $p < .025$ $X^2 = 16.84$, df = 2, $p < .001$ $X^2 = 9.52$, df = 2, $p < .01$
(31) Cohen-Sandler, R., Berman, A.L., and King, R.A. Life stress and symptomatology: determinants of suicidal behavior in children. J. Amer. Acad. Child Psychia. 1982; 2:178-186.	Engaged in overt, potentially self-destructive behavior and verbalized either intent to inflict lethal self-harm or a wish to kill self.	20 suicidal psychiatric in-patients ages 5-14 years.	76	21 depressed, nonsuicidal in-patients and 35 psychiatric in-patient controls who were neither depressed or suicidal, all matched for age, sex, race.	1977-1979	Chart review.	No difference in family size in the groups. Suicidal more likely to be first born. Suicidal children more likely to have parents who abused alcohol and/or drugs. Suicidal children had higher life stress score (mean = 486.6) than depressed children (mean = 329.0) or controls (mean = 360.2). Suicidal children experienced more stress (mean 182.7) than depressed (mean 74.2) and controls (mean 84.4) in the year prior to admission. By age 4-1/2 years, suicidal children experienced more sibling births and parental divorce. In lifetime suicidal children experienced greater number of marital separations, divorce, remarriages (mean 2.35) than depressed (mean 0.86), or control (mean 1.57).	$X^2 = 4.52$, df = 1, $p < .02$ $X2 = 4.86$, df = 1, $p < .02$ $F = 6.80$, $p < .005$ $F = 9.00$, $p < .0005$ $X^2 = 8.00$, df = 1, $p < .005$, and $X^2 = 3.78$, df = 1, $p < .05$ $F = 4.01$, df = 2.73, $p < .025$

Table 2.

Studies of Life Stress and Social Supports and Youth Suicidal Behavior

Citation	Definition of Suicidal Behavior	Population Studied	Sample Size	Comparison Group	Time of Study	Data Source	Test Results	Statistics
(32) Salk, L., Lipsett, L., Sturner, W.Q., Reilly, B.M., Levat, R.H. Relationship of maternal and perinatal conditions to eventual adolescent suicide. The Lancet 1985; March 16.	Medical examiner classification of suicide as cause of death.	52 adolescents who committed suicide before age 20 years.	156	Control 1, 52 closest birth preceding subject matched for sex, race, hospital of birth, and Control 2 52 closest birth following subject matched for sex, race, and hospital of birth. No difference in SES.	1975-1983	Hospital and medical examiner records.	Greater number of risk factors of subjects (mean = 4.62, S.D. = 4.96), then Control 1 (mean 3.52, S.D. = 3.72) or Control 2 (mean = 3.67, S.D. = 3.71).	Cases vs. Control 1, p <.01 Cases vs. Control 2, p <.05 Cases vs. Control 1 and 2, p <.01

Table 2 concluded.

Studies of Abuse and Youth Suicidal Behavior

Citation	Definition of Suicidal Behavior	Population Studied	Sample Size	Comparison Group	Time of Study	Data Source	Test Results	Statistics
(34) Green, A.H. Self-destructive behavior in battered children. Am. J. Psychia. 1978; 135:579-582.	Self-destructive behavior included self-cutting, self-burning, hair pulling, head banging, suicide attempt.	60 physically abused children; 5-13 years, Black, Hispanic, low SES.	120 children	30 neglected children from family court, 30 "normal" Children from pediatric out-patient volunteers, age, sex, SES matched.	1978	Interview of mother or guardian.	Higher incidence of self-destructive behavior in abused children (40.6%) compared to in neglected children (17.2%) or normal children (6.7%). The difference in self-destructive behavior between abused and neglected children was significant.	$\chi^2 = 13.52$, df = 2, p <.01 p <.05
(35) Deykin, E.Y., Albert, J.J., and McNamarra, J.J. A pilot study of the effect of exposure to child abuse or neglect on adolescent suicidal behavior. Am. J. Psychia. 1985; 142:1299-1303.	Suicide attempt was any intentional, self-inflicted injury accompanied by a statement of suicidal intent.	159 adolescents admitted to an emergency service for a suicide attempt, ages 13-17 years.	477	2 age and sex matched comparison subjects in the same week's emergency room and treated for other medical conditions.	1979-1982	Emergency room records and records of the Massachusetts Department of Social Services.	Suicide attempters were 3-8 times more likely to have social service contact. The suicide attempters had a significantly higher relative risk of having a previous social service department contact. The estimated proportion of suicide attempts explained by events requiring social service department assistance.	Odds ratio = 4.2, 95% confidence level = 2.2-8.1, p <.001 12% for both sexes

Table 3.

Parents of Suicidal Youth

Citation	Definition of Suicidal Behavior	Population Studied	Sample Size	Comparison Group	Time of Study	Data Source	Test Results	Statistics
(39) Tishler, C.L., and McKenny, P.C. Parental negative self and adolescent suicide attempts. J. Amer. Acad. of Child Psychia. 1982; 21:404-408.	Suicide attempt included situations in which a person performs a life-threatening behavior with the intent of jeopardizing life.	42 adolescents, ages 12-18, who were seen in a hospital emergency service for attempted suicide. Mean age 15.8 years. Their parents also evaluated.	88	46 nonsuicidal adolescents admitted for minor injuries to the same emergency service. Their parents also evaluated.	1979-1980	Questionnaires administered to the adolescents and their parents.	Fathers of suicide attempters had: Lower self-esteem scores (1.28) than nonattempters (0.84); Were more depressed (0.47) than nonattempters (0.20). Abused alcohol more (3.08) than nonattempters (2.00). No difference for attempter and nonattempter fathers for suicidal ideation or anxiety. Mothers of attempters: Were more anxious (0.90) than nonattempters (0.62). Abused alcohol (2.28) more than nonattempters (1.74). Had more suicidal ideation (34%) than nonattempters (9%). No difference for attempter and nonattempter mothers for depression or self-esteem.	p < .05 p < .05 p < .05 p < .01 p < .05 p < .05
(40) Friedman, R.C., Corn, R., Hurt, S.W., Fibel, B., Schulick, J., and Swirsky, S. Family history of illness in the seriously suicidal adolescent: a life-cycle approach. Amer. J. Orthopsychia. 1984; 53:390-397.	No definition given.	18 adolescent inpatients with serious suicide attempt and depression.	34	18 Non-suicidal adolescent inpatients with depression.	1982-1983	Parental interview SADS and family history using Family History-RDC.	No difference in family histories for affective disorders or suicide attempts or suicide for attempters and nonattempters. Suicide attempters had family with a chronic psychiatric illness before patient was 14 years (53%) more than non-attempters (22%).	p < .02

Table 4.

Suicidal Behavior of Children with Depressed and/or Suicidal Parents

Citation	Definition of Suicidal Behavior	Population Studied	Sample Size	Comparison Group	Time of Study	Data Source	Test Results	Statistics
(44) Weiner, Z., Weiner, A., McCrary, D. and Leonard, M.A. Psychopathology in children of inpatients with depression: a controlled study. J. of Nervous and Mental Disease 1977; 164:408-413.	No definition given.	75 white children of 29 parents hospitalized for depression.	227	152 normal children of 41 parents who were not hospitalized or depressed.	1975	Interviews of parents.	7% of children of depressed parents met diagnostic criteria for depression. Suicidal ideas more common in probands (9%) than control children (1%). No difference in suicide attempts among probands (3% or control children (1%).	$p < .02$
(47) Weisman, M.M., Prusoff, B.A., Gammon, G.D., Merikangas, K.R., Leckman, J.F., and Kidd, K.K. Psychopathology in the children (ages 6-18) of depressed and normal parents. J. Am. Acad. Child Psychia. 1984; 23:78-84.	No definition given.	107 children 60 depressed parents (ages of children 6-18 years).	194 children	87 children of 40 normal parents (ages of children 6-18 years).	1975	Questionnaire administered to parent about child.	Children of depressed parents had more symptoms (33.8) than children of normal parents (16.1) and DSM III diagnoses (24.2 and 8.1 respectively). Common DSM III diagnoses of children of depressed parents were: major depression (13.1%), attention deficit disorder (10.3%), and separation anxiety (10.3%). Suicidal behavior was reported in children of depressives but not of normals. 6.5% of children of depressives reported suicidal ideas. 0.9% of children of depressives threatened suicide. 0.9% of children of depressives attempted suicide.	$p < .01$ $p < .01$
(56) Hawton, K., Roberts, J. and Goodwin, G. The risk of child abuse among mothers who attempt suicide. Brit. J. of Psychia. 1985; 146:486-489.	No definition given.	114 mothers with at least one child age 5 or under, in emergency service for suicide attempt.	223	45 control mothers who gave birth in same place and times as proband mothers, and 64 mothers, with a child age 5 or under who were at for depression.	1981-1982	Local child abuse index records and records of local children's hospital.	Abuse documented in 20% of attempter mothers and 0% of controls. Abuse greater before attempts in attempt mothers than the mothers at risk for depression.	$x^2 = 8.40$ df $= 1$, $p < .01$ $x^2 = 3.69$ df $= 1$, $p < .05$
(57) Shepherd, D.M. and Barraclough, B.M. The aftermath of parental suicide for children. Brit. J. Psychia. 1976; 129:267-276.	Documented suicide.	36 children whose parent committed suicide when child was 2-17 years old.	186	150 children whose parents were matched with the suicidal parent for age, sex, marital status and drawn from general practice registers.	1970	2 interviews with surviving parents, one interview a few weeks after death, second interview was 5-7 years after death.	No child of suicide victim attempted suicide, one child made threats. Higher frequency of psychiatric referrals for children of suicide victims than controls. Marital separation and disharmony greater before suicide (55%) than in controls.	$x^2 = 6.32$ df $= 1$, $p < .02$ $x^2 = 8.96$ df $= 1$, $p < .01$

Table 5.

CONTAGION AS A RISK FACTOR FOR YOUTH SUICIDE

Lucy Davidson, M.D., Ed.S., Medical Epidemiologist, Division of Injury Epidemiology and Control, Center for Environmental Health and Injury Control, Centers for Disease Control, and, Clinical Assistant Professor in Psychiatry, Emory University School of Medicine, Atlanta, Georgia

Madelyn S. Gould, Ph.D., M.P.H., Assistant Professor of Clinical Social Sciences, in Psychiatry and Public Health (Epidemiology), Columbia University, College of Physicians and Surgeons, and Research Scientist, New York State Psychiatric Institute, New York, New York

INTRODUCTION

"The sole approach to the youth suicide problem lies in recognizing beforehand the susceptible individuals and in their proper management." Harry Bakwin reached this conclusion in his seminal article entitled, "Suicide in Children and Adolescents" in 1957 (1). In 1987, we are still struggling with these tasks and, during the intervening three decades, our task has expanded enormously. Suicide has become the third leading cause of death for persons in this country aged 15 to 24 (2) and reducing youth suicide is a priority objective for the Department of Health and Human Services (3). We are still working to clarify risk factors for youth suicide in order to identify "susceptible in-dividuals" and develop effective suicide prevention programs. In this paper we focus on the processes by which one suicide be-comes a compelling model for successive suicides or facilitates other suicides. We review two bodies of literature: (1) reports of suicide epidemics or clusters for evidence of contagion and possible mechanisms and (2) research on the effects of suicide stories in the mass media. The term "suicide con-tagion" has been used to describe this pat-tern.

Until recently, contagion as a risk factor for youth suicide had not stimulated much public awareness or research interest. However, widely publicized clusters of youth suicides in places such as Plano, Texas; Westchester County, New York; and Omaha, Nebraska, have focused attention on the possible role of contagion in suicides that occur close together in time and space.

Suicide contagion is a hybrid term that ap-pends to suicide the medical meaning of con-tagion as the transmission of a disease through direct or indirect contact. Although suicide is not a disease, per se, applying the infectious disease model to suicide contagion can clarify for whom and through what sorts of contact the likelihood of suicide is in-creased. Components of the infectious dis-ease model that illustrate analogous factors in suicide contagion are host susceptibility, modes of transmission, degree of virulence, and dose dependency.

Host susceptibility measures an individual's intrinsic ability to ward off or resist an illness. For example, an immunized child would not be very susceptible to measles, even if ex-posed to an outbreak of measles at school.

For adolescents, host susceptibility to suicide is multidetermined. Genetics play a part--we know that depression is a common antecedent to suicide and that some forms of depression have a strong genetic component. Good baseline emotional health might be like an effective immune system in being highly capable of warding off challenges. Finally, the cognitive and affective ability to identify and speak about feelings may make an individual less susceptible to suicide.

Infectious agents have different modes of transmission. We can classify routes as direct (person-to-person) or indirect. Person-to-person spread may be implicated in subsequent teen deaths following the suicide of another member of the same social network. The suicide of someone famous, such as Marilyn Monroe, may be an indirect exposure to suicide for millions of people. Thus, various suicide contagion pathways may exist: direct contact or friendship with a victim, word-of-mouth knowledge, and indirect propagation through the media.

Infective agents differ in their degree of virulence. Beta-hemolytic streptococci are more virulent than other types of streptococci. Similarly, for youth suicide, the virulence of the agent may be greater when the first death in a potential cluster is that of a highly esteemed role model, such as the class president, rather than a loner who was always perceived as odd or disturbed.

The likelihood of an infection is dose dependent. Not all persons who consume salad contaminated with staphlococci will get food poisoning, but those who had two helpings are much more likely to become ill than the ones who only tasted the salad. The risk to an individual youth for suicide may increase as the number of suicides increases in his or her peer group or in the community. The seventh youth suicide in a widely publicized series of seven is likely to have been more exposed to suicide than his predecessors and, in effect, to have received a higher dose.

Infectious processes, though, can result in a wide variety of clinical effects ranging from inapparent infection to severe clinical illness or death (4). Persons susceptible to suicide contagion may have an "inapparent infection" and not be registered among suicides or suicide attempters. The consequences of suicide contagion may be inapparent, either because the illness was arrested before the appearance of effects (suicides or suicide attempts) or because the apparent effect was unobserved, ignored, misclassified or unreported (an actual suicide recorded on the death certificate as an accident). Inapparent infections are not available for study and their absence may result in an understatement of the significance of contagion as a risk factor for youth suicide.

Evidence of Suicide Epidemics or Clusters

If contagion does play a role in suicidal behavior, one might expect clusters of suicides to occur. That is, an excessive number of suicides would occur in close temporal and geographic proximity. Evidence for suicide contagion has been reported in accounts of epidemic suicides from ancient times through the 20th century. In England in 665, distraught persons crowded to the seaside cliffs and threw themselves over. They preferred a speedy death to the lingering torture from the plague which was rampant at that time. In 1190 in York, over 500 Jews committed suicide to avoid religious persecution. In 1928, an epidemic of 150 suicidal drownings in the Danube occurred during 2 months. The epidemic was finally controlled by establishing a "suicidal flotilla," a boat squadron to patrol the river (1). Youth have not been immune to epidemic suicide. Between May 1908 and October 1910, 70 children in one school district in Moscow killed themselves (5).

More detailed accounts of epidemic or cluster suicides can be examined for characteristics that suggest that suicide contagion may be part of the etiology. Table 1 summarizes the reports that we have compiled from the literature, newspaper accounts, and our personal knowledge. There is no systematic surveillance or reporting system for suicide clusters. These accounts have selection biases that affect their representativeness. They are merely descriptive studies. No comparison groups or statistical analyses are included. Furthermore, most of these studies describe suicides among adults. Youth may be differentially exposed and susceptible to the characteristics of suicide contagion presented in these reports.

A number of studies highlight the choice of identical methods among suicides in a cluster (6-12). Most striking is Walton's report of an unintentional death by antifreeze poisoning, which was headlined in the evening paper. Five suicides from antifreeze poisoning ensued. One decedent was found on the bed next to the newspaper featuring the article; another told her husband before here death that she drank the antifreeze because she read about it in the paper (6). Seiden described five cases of suicide by jumping that occurred within a month on a college campus. Each successive case was given extensive news coverage (7). In these two series, as in a report of suicides in Great Britain by burning (9), decedents were not acquaintances, and the route of contagion was presumed to be indirect via the mass media or word-of-mouth.

Subsequent suicides in clusters in which the victims use flamboyant methods automatically access a degree of celebrity. This notoriety may convey the illusion of immortality in a way that counteracts the potential suicide's more realistic appreciation of the finality of death. Nalin has described the "aura" that a particular method of suicide may assume. In Guyana, suicide by malathion insecticide poisoning became associated, through press reports, with unrequited love. Suicides, in this case, were making a publicly recognizable statement through their choice of method. The potential suicide attempter also may have imagined that attendant newspaper publicity would manipulate others (12).

In reviewing epidemic suicide, Forbes Winslow observed that "all human actions are under the influence and power of example more than precept." He attributed the outbreak of suicides to "the force of imitation being so great and acting prejudicially on weak-minded persons or on those predisposed to mental disorders" (13). Another 19th century writer who considered the role of the potential suicide's intrinsic vulnerability and the impact of outside events said that "...it is difficult to determine how much was due to the psychopathic tendencies of the actors ... and how much to the external circumstances which probably served only as the spark applied to the inflammable material" (11). Contemporary researchers have also considered the impact of poor baseline emotional functioning on susceptibility suicide in a cluster (6,9,14-16). Emotional well-being, then, could lessen and emotional disability increase host susceptibility. However, the proportion of non-cluster suicides with psychiatric problems (17) may not differ from proportions reported in case series of cluster suicides.

The mechanisms most often associated with epidemic suicides among those who are susceptible are imitation and identification (15, 18-22). Imitation represents the action derived from an identification with another person's needs, the identification being conscious or unconscious (23). Ward and Fox studied a suicide epidemic on an Indian reserve, during which 8 adolescents and young adults died from among the 37 families in that community. The researchers examined the way that one suicidal youth can serve as a role model to be imitated: "The stimulus of one suicide could suggest to others a similar mode of escaping an intolerable life situation" (14). The role model also may be an unintentional death, as in the series of antifreeze suicides reported by Walton (6). Sacks and Eth explored the idea of pathological identification in a cluster of suicides among hospitalized patients. They held that these pathological identifications were "fostered by the individual's past history that may contain many points of common experience" (19).

Although imitation and identification may be powerful mechanisms, emphasizing these components exclusively, as in the term "copycat suicides," trivializes the many other factors contributing to suicide. The simplistic notion that one person merely copied another's suicide does not explain why the suicide was copied by that particular individual and not be hundreds of others who were similarly exposed. Suicides remain multidetermined events even when they occur in clusters. Explaining cluster suicides by imitation alone does not take each decedent's susceptibility and stresses into account.

Some researchers have considered the social environment and the ways in which disruptions in that environment or negative social expectations within the milieu may foster cluster suicides. Rubenstein looks at rapid sociocultural change as an environmental setting that fostered clusters of youth suicides (20). Cluster suicides in hospital settings have been attributed to social disruption creating anomie or a sense of hopelessness (24-26). Hankoff felt that the prospect of secondary gain (i.e., reassignment or relocation) was the major environmental influence for a cluster of suicide attempts among Marines. The environmental response to the first attempt provided significant secondary gain; this became the harbinger of other attempts, which were finally averted by minimizing the secondary gains (8).

These accounts of epidemic suicides indicate that temporal and geographic clustering of suicide does occur. Cluster suicides appear to be multidetermined, as are noncluster suicides, but imitation and identification are factors hypothesized to increase the likelihood of cluster suicides. Among those susceptible, the route of exposure to the model may be direct or indirect. The nature of existing research, however, limits conclusions that might be drawn, and also suggests areas for further clarification.

The absence of a standard operational definition for the time and space parameters of a suicide cluster limits our ability to compare results. Without a clear and replicable definition for suicide clusters, we cannot undertake surveillance. Surveillance could determine what proportion of youth suicides appear to occur in clusters and how representative these case-series findings may be. Suicide clusters are more commonly reported now, but without comprehensive surveillance, we cannot be certain that these episodes occur any more frequently than would be expected by chance variation. Without reference to a comparison group, descriptions of the demographic and psychological characteristics of suicides that occur within the context of a cluster are speculative. What may appear to be a ubiquitous characteristic of cluster suicides may not differentiate them from noncluster suicides or nonsuicides and, therefore, may be of limited value in preventing this particular type of death.

Studies in Progress

Researchers are currently attempting to address the problems identified in the previous section. Field studies are using a psychological autopsy protocol with several cluster outbreaks and including comparison groups and detailed analyses of the relationships between the suicides in an attempt to identify possible mechanisms of contagion. The Centers for Disease Control (CDC) and the New York Psychiatric Institute are conducting two such studies using the psychological autopsy--a procedure that involves reconstruction of the life style and circumstances of the victim, together with details of behaviors and events that led to the death of that individual" (27). Data collection and analysis are still in progress for these studies. Additional suicide clusters have been reported to the CDC. Some recent known clusters are highlighted in Table 2.

These recent clusters indicate that it is not necessary for the decedents to have had direct contact with each other. In the Westchester County outbreak, indirect knowledge of the suicides appears to have been obtained through the news media.

Other clusters had a mixture of members from one social network and individuals who were unknown to each other directly. Among those who knew another decedent, the degree of acquaintance varied--from closest friends to those in the same school or church who knew of each other but had little direct personal contact.

Methods may be similar for most deaths within a cluster, indicating a possible underlying imitative mechanism. The clearest imitation of method is seen in a cluster of suicides by jumping from an expressway overpass in Seattle. Jumping from overpasses had previously been extremely rare in that community. Identical methods, however, may not always reflect direct imitation of another decedent in the cluster. Although all of the Wind River suicides were by hanging, cultural factors may have predominated in that choice of method. Hanging has been the method favored by most native American suicides in that community.

Time-space cluster analysis is another type of ongoing study in which epidemiological techniques are used to detect and statistically assess temporal and geographic clustering of suicides (Gould MS, Shaffer D: A study of time-space clustering of suicide. RFP #200-85-0834 (P), Centers for Disease Control, 10-85-4/87). Several epidemiologic techniques had been developed to examine the occurrence and significance of time-space clusters of diseases (28-30). These methods are being adapted to establish clustering. They can demonstrate an excess frequency of suicide in certain times and places or show a significant relationship between the time and space distances between pairs of suicides. These techniques are being applied to U.S. mortality data on suicides occurring during the two 5-year periods 1978 to 1982 and 1955 to 1959, and also to data from a consecutive series of adolescent suicides in the Greater New York Metropolitan area in 1984. The principal aims of the study are to determine whether outbreaks of suicide are real; that is, (1) whether clusters are occurring more frequently than by chance alone; (2) what proportion of suicides occur in clusters; (3) whether clustering of suicides is predominantly a phenomenon of youth; and (4) whether the proportion of cluster outbreaks is increasing. The analyses will also provide guidelines on the time and space parameters that should define a suicide cluster.

A limitation of statistical time-space cluster analyses is that they cannot indicate whether clusters are due to the influence of a model suicide, or whether the model merely happened to be the first individual who committed suicide in response to conditions that then led others to die. Field studies are better suited to identifying the mechanisms of the clusters. A goal of the time-space cluster analytic study is to identify a representative sample of clusters for future complementary field investigations.

Media Influence

Most of the research on imitative suicide has focused on the impact of suicide reporting in the mass media. This research strategy examines the possibility of contagion being transmitted indirectly through the media, in contrast to direct, person-to-person propagation. Phelps conducted a prototypic ecological study of media influences on suicide in 1911 and concluded:

> The practically universal increase in the mortality of suicides of late years, however, can be demonstrated by official figures of at least comparative accuracy; and as this increase historically parallels that in the number and percentage of sensational, crime-inciting books and newspapers, at least a semblance of positive evidence of the relations of the two is thereby afforded--though not for a moment, of course, can the open-minded student of the painfully complex problem of the increase in suicide forget the fact that the suggestion of printers' ink is but one of the many factors involved (32).

More current studies of the impact of nonfictional suicide reporting will be reviewed

(Table 3A) as well as the impact of fictional suicide stories (Table 3B).

Nonfictional Suicide Stories

Phillips and his colleagues have provided increasing evidence suggesting that imitative behavior follows media coverage of nonfictional suicides (33-37). They reported that prominent newspaper coverage of a suicide has the effect of increasing suicidal behavior within the readership area of the newspaper. The magnitude of the increase is related to the "attractiveness" of the individual whose death is being reported and the amount of publicity given to the story. This finding has been replicated with data from the United States (38) and from The Netherlands (39). In addition, Wasserman found that a significant rise in the national suicide rate occurred only after celebrity suicides were covered on the front page of the New York Times (40).

Sex- and age-specific imitative effects have been noted by Barraclough, Shepherd, and Jennings (41), who found an association between reports of suicide inquests in a local paper and the subsequent suicide of men under 45 years of age. Further support for a sex- and age-specific effect was reported by Motto (42), who found a reduction in suicides among women younger than 35 years of age during a newspaper strike in Detroit. This specific reduction was replicated in another city (43).

Although these investigations support the role of imitative behavior in suicides following nonfictional suicide stories, results of a number of studies have demonstrated no effect (44-47). Baron and Reiss reported that the findings of Bollen and Phillips indicating a significant imitative effect of nonfictional television news stories, were due to statistical artifact and the timing of media events (44). Upon reanalyzing Phillips' data, they reported that the media events had their effects only during periods when suicides were already high; the variables measuring the purported effects of the media events were actually capturing regularities in the distribu-

tion of suicides. Bollen and Phillips did report, however, an excess in suicides that could not be predicted by any day-of-the-week, month, year, or holiday effect and confirmed the excess with two analytic strategies (38).

Stack found no relationship between the monthly national suicide rate and the amount of television coverage per month on suicide stories (46). This lack of a relationship, however, may have been an artifact of the methodology used in the study. Monthly rates of suicide may not be sensitive enough to detect imitative influences, since a contagion effect of the media has been reported not to extend beyond 10 days (35,38). Methodological artifacts may also account for Littmann's not finding a relationship between suicide-related newspaper reports and the occurrence of subway suicides in Toronto. Littman reported that there was no significant excess of newspaper reports before subway suicides in both epidemic and non-epidemic years (47). There were overlaps, however, in the "before" time periods for one suicide with the "after" time periods for another suicide, making independent examination of the "before" period impossible. The examination was limited to subway suicides. An examination of all suicides might have yielded a different result.

The core independent variable in Stack's study was the number of seconds of television coverage of suicide stories included in the 6 o'clock news. There is evidence that it is not only the amount of coverage, but also the type of story that has an impact on subsequent suicides (37,40,45). Articles, reports, features, and editorials are likely to have differential effects. In another study, Stack commented on the tenor of news reporting that may offset imitative effects (45). He found no increase in U.S. suicide rates after widespread coverage of the Jonestown mass suicides. He attributed the lack of imitation to the labeling of decedents as cultists, the presentation of many deaths there as involuntary, and the horror conveyed by postmortem photos.

Differential susceptibility to the imitative effects of the media may also reflect selective coverage in even routine reports. Shepherd and Barraclough analyzed reports of suicides appearing in the Portsmouth News between 1970 and 1972. They found that longer reports were written on violent suicides than on less violent suicides and that violent suicides were more likely to stimulate multiple reports ($p < .001$). Suicides of the very young or very old were more often reported than suicides of other-aged persons. They regarded this distortion of the news as a publishing commitment to entertainment and to the belief that violence is intrinsically newsworthy (48).

Fictional Suicide Stories

Very little research has been carried out on the impact of fictional representations of suicide. In the context of an epidemiological study of childhood suicide, Shaffer implicated this mechanism as a precipitant in one of the 30 consecutive suicidal deaths he studied (49). A teenage victim was found dead with copy of Graham Greene's novel *Brighton Rock*, in which the young, central character commits suicide. There have been anecdotal reports of suicide rates increasing in response to the publication and popularity of other novels and poems. Publication of Goethe's *The Sorrows of Young Werther* in 1774 launched a fad among young men of wearing blue tailcoats and yellow waistcoats like Werther and, in many cases, imitating his suicide (50,51).

Results of recent studies that focus on the effects of media coverage of fictional suicide stories are controversial. Kessler and Stripp (52) failed to replicate Phillips' (37) finding that fictional television suicide stories on daytime television serials--or "soap operas"-- triggered imitative deaths. They attributed the discrepancy to Phillips' misspecification of the dates of 8 of the 13 television suicide stories, invalidating Phillips' one attempt to examine the impact of fictional suicide stories.

Holding (53,54) examined the impact of an 11-episode weekly series that was presented by the BBC in Edinburgh to dramatize the suicide prevention work of the Samaritans. The series resulted in a significant increase in new client referrals to the Samaritans in the 4 weeks following the programs. If the series had produced a preventive effect, the rise in referrals should have been associated with a fall in completed suicides. To the contrary, suicides did not decrease during the 10-week period following the series. Moreover, this period did not show the decline that was evidenced in corresponding weeks in comparison years. These results suggest a deleterious effect of fictional suicide stories in the media.

Gould and Shaffer (55) examined the variation in youth suicide and attempted suicide before and after four fictional television films that were broadcast in the fall and winter of 1984/1985. They reported that the observed number of attempted suicides after the broadcasts was significantly greater than expected and that there was significant excess of completed suicides after three broadcasts. Their findings are consistent with an imitation mechanism.

Critique of Methods

The major limitation of the studies in which investigators examined the impact of media coverage of suicides is that all have employed aggregate data (see Tables 3A and 3B). A major constraint of such a design is that it cannot demonstrate whether the suicide victims were actually exposed to the media events. There is always the danger of an ecological fallacy, therefore, which involves making spurious individual-level inferences from aggregate relationships.

As early as 1911, Hemenway outlined a study to determine the effects of newspapers on suicides. He proposed using coroners to collect data in such a way as to avoid making conclusions from aggregate relationships. Coroners would obtain the following information:

1) Dates of prominent publication of

details of suicides, with the method selected by the unfortunates. 2) Dates of subsequent suicides with special references to the grouping of cases according to methods. 3) Direct evidence, by asking at inquests for information as to the possible relationship of the suicide being investigated as to previous cases either read about or known of (56).

As Table 3 indicates, Hemenway's proposals have not been acted upon.

Despite the limitation imposed by the use of aggregate data, the investigators in the studies taken as a whole, have employed rigorous statistics, comparison periods, and control variables. Their findings meet a number of criteria that assist judgments about the causal significance of associations. Five criteria for judging causal relationships are time sequence of variables, consistency of associations on replication, strength of association, specificity of association, and coherent explanation (57).

Results of several studies (33,34,36,39,40) established the time sequence of the variables, for instance, that the increase in mortality occurred only after the media events. The suicide stories, it was shown, did not occur during a "suicide wave," but before it.

Consistent findings in support of an imitation hypothesis were reported by the most investigators, despite their differences in method, location, and types of variables. A number of investigators examined an excess of deaths following the appearance of suicide stories (33,34,36,38,40,41,55). Others examined the decrease in deaths during the cessation of newspaper stories (42,43). Different types of control periods were employed, varying from control periods immediately before the suicide story (36), to control periods in different years (34,42), and indirect control periods used in time-series analyses (40). Both quasi-experimental designs (33) and regression analytic strategies (36) were employed. Despite the consistency in the findings, however, the possibility of confounding variables cannot be entirely ruled out.

The strength of the association is indicated by the reports that suicide stories had larger effects on suicide rates than did day of the week, month, or holidays, which are variables known to affect the suicide rate (38). Furthermore, reports of suicides by celebrities resulted in a large increase in suicides (40).

The final criterion suggested for judging a causal association is whether it is coherent or consistent with existing knowledge. Media coverage of suicides is associated with an increase in subsequent suicides. This increase in suicides relates to the amount of publicity and is restricted to the area in which the stories are publicized. This is consistent with the consensus of laboratory findings that mass media violence can elicit aggression (58). The association is also consistent with a number of mechanisms of contagion, such as imitation and familiarity with the idea of suicide. These mechanisms will be discussed in a subsequent section.

In summary, growing evidence forcefully supports the contention that imitative suicides follow media coverage of nonfictional suicides. The effect extends to both newspaper and television coverage. Some of the inconsistencies that exist among studies could have arisen as a result of significant methodological differences among them. Although there is some evidence that fictional suicide stories have an impact, little information is available and the results of available studies are contradictory.

Mechanisms of Suicide Contagion

Mechanisms underlying the phenomenon of contagion have not been studied in the context of cluster suicides. In social-learning theory, however, behavioral scientists have constructed a foundation on which many aspects of suicide contagion may build. According to this theory, most human behavior is learned through observation and modeling (59). People learn from example. Imitative learning is influenced by a number of factors, including the characteristics of the model and the consequences or rewards associated with the observed behavior (59). Models who possess engaging qualities or who have high status are more likely to be imitated. Behaviors depicted as resulting in gains, including notoriety, are more effective in prompting imitation.

Consistent with these principles, Phillips and his colleagues have reported that the magnitude of the increase in suicide behavior after prominent newspaper coverage is related to two factors: (1) the "attractiveness" of the individual whose death is being reported, and (2) the amount of publicity given to the story. Likewise, Wasserman found that the national suicide rate rose significantly after suicides of celebrities were reported on the front page of the New York *Times* but not after less prominent suicides (40).

People cannot learn much by observation unless they attend to the modeled behavior (59). A number of factors, some involving the observers' characteristics, regulate the amount of attention to witnessed or reported behavior. Research thus far has only roughly sketched the host characteristics that may yield a greater susceptibility to imitating suicide. Sacks and Eth proposed as one such characteristic a history of similar past experiences that lead to "pathological identification" with the victim (19).

In addition to imitative effects, the occurrence of suicides in the community or in the media may produce a familiarity with, and acceptance of, the idea of suicide. Rubinstein postulated this mechanism in his study of a suicide epidemic among Micronesian adolescents. Familiarity with suicide may eliminate the "taboo" of suicide. It may also lower the threshold point at which the behavior is manifested and may introduce suicide as an acceptable alternative response or option to life stresses (20).

CONCLUSIONS

A review of (1) reports of suicide epidemics, of ongoing studies of suicide clusters, and of investigations of the news media and their relationship to suicide and (2) work in the behavioral sciences indicates four conclusions:

- Time-space clusters of suicide occur, have been reported among various age groups, and are not a new phenomenon.

- Nonfictional media coverage of suicides is associated with an increase in the observed number of suicides over the number expected. The increase may not be uniform for all age-sex groups.

- Susceptible individuals may be affected by direct or indirect exposures to suicide.

- Imitative learning is fostered if the model is held in high regard and if rewards are expected for the behavior.

Remaining questions are legion. Only substantial research will resolve them. Some of the questions for future research follow:

- What proportion of suicides occur in clusters? Are clusters more common in certain age groups, geographic locations, or times? Is the proportion of cluster outbreaks increasing?

- In comparison with other age groups, in what ways are young people exposed to and susceptible to suicide contagion?

- Which characteristics of model suicides are most likely to cause an increase in suicides?

- Which combination of host susceptibility and contagion factors are most lethal?

- What sorts of prevention and intervention efforts could most effectively avert cluster suicides?

- Does media coverage create new suicides or accelerate suicides that would have occurred anyway?

Youth suicide clusters are a particularly grievous loss of life and are potentially more preventable than single suicides. Interim recommendations are needed even though our knowledge base has sobering gaps. Five basic recommendations follow:

- News media representatives should be encouraged to avoid romanticizing suicide, emphasizing violent aspects, and making celebrities of persons who die by suicide.

- News media representatives should be invited to collaborate in studies to identify the destructive and constructive components of fictional accounts of suicide. Before a decision is made to broadcast such a story, these components should be identified and assessed, and a warning that the program might adversely affect some persons should precede any such broadcast.

- In research studies, variables should be operationally defined, comparison groups used, and individual rather than aggregate- only exposures assessed.

- Surveillance for potential suicide clusters should be established so that potential clusters could be averted and existing clusters kept from spreading. Surveillance would alert researchers to suicide clusters which might be more thoroughly investigated.

- Intervention efforts should be directed toward those who are most exposed (either directly or indirectly) to the "model" suicide and toward those who are most susceptible, for example, those whose emotional health is poor and those who strongly identify with the person who has taken his or her life.

REFERENCES

1. Bakwin H: Suicide in children and adolescents. J Pediatr 1957; 50:749-69.

2. Centers for Disease Control: Violent deaths among persons 15-24 years of age--United States, 1970-1978. MMWR 1983; 32:453-7.

3. Public Health Service: Promoting health/preventing disease: Objectives for the nation. Washington, D.C.: U.S. Government Printing Office, 1980.

4. Hackett TP, Cassem NH: (eds). Massachusetts General Hospital handbook of general hospital psychiatry, 2nd edition. Littleton, Mass.: PSG Publishing Co., Inc., 1987.

5. Popow NM: The present epidemic of school suicides in Russia. Nevrol Nestnik (Kazan), 1911; 18:312-55, 592-646.

6. Walton EW: An epidemic of antifreeze poisoning. Med Sci Law 1978; 18:231-7.

7. Seiden RH: Suicidal behavior contagion on a college campus. In: Farberow, NL (ed.), Proceedings of fourth international conference for suicide prevention, 1967; 360-5.

8. Hankoff LD: An epidemic of attempted suicide. Comprehensive Psychiatry 1961; 2:294-8.

9. Ashton VR, Donnan S: Suicide by burning as an epidemic phenomenon: An analysis of 82 deaths and inquests in England and Wales in 1978-9. Psychol Med 1981; 11:735-9.

10. Crawford JP, Willis JH: Double suicide in psychiatric hospital patients. Br J Psychiatry 1966; 112:1231-5.

11. Rovinsky A: Epidemic suicides. Boston Medical and Surgical Journal 1898; 138:238-9.

12. Nalin DR: Epidemic of suicide by malathion poisoning in Guyana. Tropical & Geographical Medicine 1973; 25:8-14.

13. Winslow F: Suicide considered as a mental epidemic. Bulletin of the Medico-Legal Congress. New York, 1895, 334-51.

14. Ward JA, Fox J: A suicide epidemic on an Indian reserve. Can Psychiatr Assoc J 1977; 22:423-6.

15. Niemi T: The time-space distances of suicides committed in the lock-up in Finland in 1963-1967. Israel Annals of Psychiatry and Related Disciplines 1978; 16:39-45.

16. Robbins D, Conroy RC: A cluster of adolescent suicide attempts: Is suicide contagious? J Adolesc Health Care 1983; 3:253-5.

17. Robins E: The final months. New York: Oxford University Press, 1981.

18. Rosenbaum M: Crime and punishment--the suicide pact. Arch Gen Psychiatry 1983; 40:979-82.

19. Sacks M, Eth S: Pathological identification as a cause of suicide on an inpatient unit. Hosp & Community Psychiatry 1981; 32:36-40.

20. Rubinstein DH: Epidemic suicide among Micronesian adolescents. Soc Sci Med 1983; 17:657-65.

21. Bunch J, Barraclough B: The influence of parental death anniversaries upon suicide dates. Br J Psychiatry 1971; 118:621-26.

22. Crawford JP, Willis JH: Double suicide in psychiatric hospital patients. Br J Psychiatry 1966; 112:1231-5.

23. Hinsie LE, Campbell RJ: Psychiatric dictionary 4th edition. New York: Oxford University Press, 1970.

24. Kahne MJ: Suicide among patients in mental hospitals. Psychiatry 1968; 31:32-43.

25. Anonymous: A suicide epidemic in a psychiatric hospital. Diseases of the Nervous System 1977; 38:327-31.

26. Kobler AL, Stotland E: The end of hope: A social-clinical study of suicide. London: The Free Press of Glencoe, 1964.

27. Farberow NL, Neuringer C: The social scientist as coroner's deputy. J of Forensic Sci 1971; 16:15-39.

28. Ederer F, Myers MH, Mantel N: A statistical problem in space and time: Do leukemia cases come in clusters? Biometrics 1964; Sept.:626-38.

29. Knox G: The detection of space-time interactions. Applied Statistics 1964; 13:25-29.

30. Mantel N: The detection of disease clustering and a generalized regression approach. Cancer Res 1967; 27:209-20.

31. Wallenstein S: A test for detection of clustering over time. Am J Epidemiology 1980; 111:367-73.

32. Phelps EB: Neurotic books and newspapers as

factors in the mortality of suicide and crime. Bulletin of the American Academy of Medicine 1911; 12:264-306.

33. Phillips D: The influence of suggestion on suicide: Substantive and theoretical implication of the Werther effect. Am Sociological Review 1974; 39:340-54.

34. Phillips DP: Suicide, motor vehicle fatalities, and the mass media: Evidence toward a theory of suggestion. Am J Sociology 1979; 84:1150-74.

35. Phillips DP: Airplane accidents, murder, and the mass media: Towards a theory of imitation and suggestion. Social Forces 1980; 58:1001-24.

36. Bollen KA, Phillips DP: Suicidal motor vehicle fatalities in Detroit: A replication. Am J Sociology 1981; 87:404-12.

37. Phillips DP: The impact of fictional television stories on U.S. adult fatalities: New evidence on the effect of the mass media on violence. Am J Sociology 1982; 87:1340-59.

38. Bollen KA, Phillips DP: Imitative suicides: A national study of the effects of television news stories. Am Sociological Review 1982; 47:802-9.

39. Ganzeboom HBG, de Haan D: Gepubliceerde zelfmoorden en verhoging van sterfte door zelfmoord en ongelukken in Nederland 1972-1980. Mens en Maatschappij 1982; 57:55-69.

40. Wasserman IM: Imitation and suicide: A reexamination of the Werther effect. Am Sociological Review 1984; 49:427-36.

41. Barraclough B, Shepherd D, Jennings C: Do newspaper reports of coroners' inquests incite people to commit suicide? Br J Psychiatry 1977; 131:529-32.

42. Motto JA: Newspaper influence on suicide. Arch Gen Psychiatry 1970; 23:143-8.

43. Blumenthal S, Bergner L: Suicide and newspapers: A replicated study. Am J Psychiatry 1973; 130:468-71.

44. Baron JN, Reiss PC: Reply to Phillips and Bollen. Am Sociological Review 1985; 50:372-6.

45. Stack S: The effect of Jonestown on the suicide rate. J Soc Psychol 1983; 119:145-6.

46. Stack S: The effect of suggestion on suicide: A reassessment. Paper read at the Annual Meetings of the American Sociological Association, San Antonio, Texas, 1984.

47. Littmann SK: Suicide epidemics and newspaper reporting. Suicide and Life-Threatening Behavior 1985; 15:43-50.

48. Shepherd D, Barraclough BM: Suicide reporting: Information or entertainment? Brit J Psychiat 1978; 132:283-87.

49. Shaffer D: Suicide in childhood and early adolescence. J Child Psychol Psychiatry 1974; 15:275-91.

50. Spender S: Foreward to JS Goethe: The sorrows of young Werther. New York: New American Library, 1962.

51. Goethe JS: Reflections on Werther. New York: New American Library, 1962.

52. Kessler RC, Stipp H: The impact of fictional television suicide stories on U.S. fatalities: A replication. Am J Sociology 1984; 90:151-67.

53. Holding TA: The B.B.C. "Befrienders" series and its effects. Brit J Psychiatry 1974; 124:470-2.

54. Holding TA: Suicide and "The Befrienders." British Medical Journal 1975; 3:751-753.

55. Gould MS, Shaffer D: The impact of suicide in television movies: Evidence of imitation. N Engl J Med 1986; 315:690-4.

56. Hemenway HB: To what extent are suicide and other crimes against the person due to suggestion from the press? Bulletin of the American Academy of Medicine 1911; 12:253-63.

57. Susser, M: Causal thinking in the health sciences: Concepts and strategies in epidemiology. New York: Oxford University Press, 1973.

58. Comstock B: Television and human behavior: The key studies. Santa Monica, CA: Rand, 1975.

59. Bandura A: Social learning theory. New Jersey: Prentice-Hall, 1977.

60. Motto JA: Suicide and suggestibility--the role of the press. Am J Psychiatry 1967; 124:252-6.

Descriptive Studies of Epidemic or Cluster Suicide

Reference	Data Source	Population Studied	Description/Findings	Proposed Mechanism
Anonymous, 1977 (25)	Case histories	Psychiatric inpatient suicides	—3 suicides on 1 ward occurred within 8 months and no others in 10 years in that psychiatric hospital.	—"fragmented leadership, faulty supervision, and staff demoralization and anomie may contribute to poor psychiatric care and to epidemics of suicide in psychiatric hospitals."
Ashton and Donnan, 1981 (9)	Coroner's reports and death certificates	82 suicides by self-immolation, 1978-79 in England and Wales	—Between 10/78 and 9/78, there were 82 suicides by burning compared with a yearly average of 23 between 1963 and 1978. —Most of the suicides were known to be psychiatrically ill and were predominately young men or older married women.	—Imitation, "mediated by news coverage."
Crawford and Willis, 1966 (10)	Psychiatric hospital records	24 inpatient suicides at Stone House Hospital, England, between 1876 and 1965 from which "similar" suicides occurring within 12 months were identified	—3 pairs of similar suicides were identified plus 1 suicide that imitated that of a patient from another psychiatric hospital whose body was found on the hospital grounds. —Each of the 4 pairs used the same method: cut throat, hanging (2 pairs), jumping. —1 pair were close friends. —2 pairs used identical locations.	—The second patients were "infected" by the success of the first. —Suicide as an effort to join a deceased friend. —Imitation.
Hankoff, 1961 (8)	Case histories	12,000 U.S. Marine Corps troops stationed in a remote, isolated place	—16 suicide attempts and 1 suicide occurred in 12 months. —7 of the attempts occurred in July and August and were knife wounds. The suicide occurred during this span.	—The suicide attempts represented infectious acting-out, the epidemic being "an emergent event of a shared group process..." —Choice of method seemed "more a matter of suggestion or conformity than of specific motivational significance." —July-August attempts were "inaugurated by an attempt which attained 'maximum' secondary gains (no hospitalization)."
Kahne, 1968 (24)	Questionnaires and interviews	Psychiatric inpatients	—An "epidemic" of 8 suicides occurred.	—"all eight suicide cases occurred ruling a period of marked social disorganization within the hospital, a period which is most appropriately described as anomic."
Kobler and Stotland, 1964 (26)	Hospital records, interviews	Psychiatric inpatients, average census = 26	—1 patient attempted suicide 12/23/59 and 3 others committed suicide between 1/1 and 1/19/60. Another suicide occurred 6/60.	—Social expectations among hospital staff of helplessness and hopelessness were communicated to patients as an implicit or explicit expectation of suicide.
Nelin, 1973 (12)	Hospital records, and case reports	Suicides and suicide attempts by malathion poisoning in Guyana	—Malathion was introduced to Guyana between 1960-62, and malathion poisoning cases increased from 16 in 1962 to 100 in 1964. —From hospital records the malathion suicide attempt rate was 31 per 100,000 and increasing.	—"Retroflexed rage, impulsively expressed and without obvious depression" —Uncontrolled availability of malathion. —"Widespread press publicity exploiting the dramatic aspects of cases in which rejected love is the motivation for poisoning has helped to give malathion an aura of lethality." —Attempters may expect newspaper publicity of their act to affect their families.
Niemi, 1978 (15)	Questionnaires sent to police districts	Suicides in jail in Finland, 1963-1987. N=28	—"the number of suicides committed in the lock-up within 24 and 48 hours counted from the previous suicide in the lock-up was significantly greater than expected"	—Identification and a "mental state of readiness"

Table 1.

Descriptive Studies of Epidemic or Cluster Suicide

Reference	Data Source	Population Studied	Description/Findings	Proposed Mechanism
Robbins and Conroy, 1983 (16)	Case reports of patients seen at a psychiatric hospital	Chappaqua high-school students, New York, who presented with suicide attempt or ideation	—After 2 suicides in a high school population, 5 students attempted and 1 was admitted with severe suicidal ideation within 7 weeks. The first attempter was visited ruling his hospitalization by the other 5. They comprised a peer group at school.	—"suicide attempts may cluster among groups of young people with risk factors for self-destructive behavior."
Rovinski, 1896 (11)	Interviews	"Epidemic" suicides near Odessa, Russia	—Members of a religious sect committed suicide by being buried alive. —Deaths occurred in groups on 4 occasions during a 3-month period. —N=9, 5, unknown, 5.	—The sect leader convinced followers that death from the Anti-Christians was imminent and unavoidable and that it was preferable to "die for Christ" volitionally by suicide. —Influence of the charismatic leader on "psychopathic tendencies" of the members—"the spark applied to the inflammable material."
Rubinstein, 1983 (20)	Hospital and medical records, all death certificates, police records, church records; and 250 semi-structured interviews with suicide attempters and friends and relatives of suicide victims	Micronesia (the U.S. Trust Territory of the Pacific Islands)	—Over 12 years, 25 suicides occurred in clusters of 3 or 4 in several months, then none for a year or so. —8-fold increase in suicide rates since 1960 among 15- to 24- year-old males.	—"as suicide grows more frequent in these communities, the idea itself acquires a certain familiarity if not fascination to young men, and the lethality of the act seems to be trivialized." —Prominence of role model a factor. —"suicides have acquired subcultural significance among male youth, giving use to fad-like and imitative acts." —"the significance of the act acquires an aspect of collective identification and familiarity, making it less aversive to troubled youth."
Sacks and Eth, 1981 (19)	Case histories	Psychiatric inpatients	—1 patient's suicide precipitated another's suicide attempt and suicidal preoccupation in another. —The suicide attempter used the same method as the suicide (jumping). Patient with suicidal preoccupation had made a previous attempt by this method and had visited the attempter in ICU after his fall.	—Risk is high in "those who have formed pathological identifications with the victim as the result of a history of similar past experience, especially that of a suicidal or abandoning parent." —The schizophrenic's impaired object relations and reality testing may increase "vulnerability to the partial and bizarre identifications that might have contributed to their suicidal preoccupation and behavior."
Seiden, 1967 (7)	Hospital records, police reports, coroner's reports, newspapers, interviews	Suicides on a college campus	—5 male suicides by jumping occurred on the University of California, Berkeley campus during 1 month in 1967. —Subjects had histories of chronic and severe mental disorders.	—Hypothesis of symbolic location rather than behavioral contagion. —"particular locations maybe highly valued and perhaps even necessary for the commission of suicide."
Welton, 1978 (8)	Case reports	Accidental poisonings, suicides and suicide attempts by antifreeze in England	—After a widely publicized unintentional death from antifreeze, 5 suicides and 8 attempts occurred by that method. —All of the suicides had preexisting psychiatric illness.	—"There is little doubt that the publicity attached to the first unfortunate accident resulted in five imitative suicidal deaths."
Ward and Fox, 1977 (14)	Interviews with family, neighbors, police & coroner's reports, hospital records	Native Americans in Ontario	—Eight suicides occurred within 12 months in a small rural community of 3,000.	—"The stimulus of one suicide could suggest to others a similar mode of escaping an intolerable life situation." —Contagion among vulnerable persons.

Table 1 concluded.

CHARACTERISTICS OF RECENT SUICIDE CLUSTERS

Location	Number of Suicides	Sex	Age Range	First Date of Death	Last Date of Death	Methods	Social Relation to Another in Cluster
Plano, Texas	8	7M 1F	14-18	2/23/83	5/8/84	4 Gunshot 4 Carbon monoxide	Some
Westchester and Putnam Counties, New York	5*	5M	13-19	2/4/84	3/13/84	3 Hanging 1 Gunshot 1 Carbon monoxide	None
Clear Lake, Texas	6	5M 1F	14-19	8/9/84	10/11/84	3 Gunshot 2 Hanging 1 Carbon monoxide	Some
Seattle, Washington	3	3M	20's-42	7/9/85	7/14/85	3 Jumping from expressway overpass	Unknown
Wind River, Wyoming	9†	9M	14-25	8/10/85	10/1/85	9 Hanging	Some
Omaha, Nebraska	3	2M 1F	15-18	2/3/86	2/7/86	1 Gunshot 2 Overdose	Some

* An unintentional hanging also occurred
† 4 other suicides of tribal members ages 17-34 occurred between 1/2/85 and 10/18/85. All were by hanging.

Table 2.

STUDIES EXAMINING MEDIA INFLUENCES ON SUBSEQUENT IMITATIVE SUICIDES*

A. Nonfictional Suicide Stories

Citation	Period and Population Studied	Methodology	Comparison Group/Period	Findings	Statistics	Support of Imitation
Baron, and Reiss, 1984 (44)	Daily U.S. suicides for 1972-1976 (also examined homicides for 1973-1976—only the portion pertaining to the suicides is presented here).	Employed a list of publicized suicide stories carried on network news programs, a list originally used by Bollen & Phillips (1982). A different set of publicized stories was used also (details of added stories not given). The study was designed to extend the earlier study by Bollen & Phillips. Regression analytic design. Ecological design.	Indirect control periods through the use of regression analysis.	Suicide stories only had their effects during periods when suicides were already high. Explained the discrepancy between this finding and Bollen & Phillips' earlier finding by the fact that the earlier regression model did not include a term to represent an interaction between the day of the week and suicide story. However, Bollen & Phillips did control for main effects of day, week and holidays in their regression model.	Time series regression analysis. Most coefficients of story by day variable were not significant.	No
Barraclough, Shepherd, and Jennings, 1977 (41)	Suicides and undetermined deaths in Portsmouth, England, between 3-year period—1/1/70 to 12/31/72. There were 76 deaths (54 suicides and 22 undetermined).	Newspaper reports about suicide inquests were identified in the local daily newspaper in the area (128 reports were identified). They determined the number of days that had been preceded within 2, 4, and 7 days by one or more reports to derive an "expected" distribution. They compared this to the "observed" distribution of the number of days on which a suicide occurred that had been preceded by a report. Four age/sex groups (aged 44 and younger; 45 and older) were independently tested. Ecological study—cannot determine whether suicides need the newspaper.	Observed-to-expected distribution of days preceded by a newspaper report.	Association between newspaper reports of suicide inquests and men under 45, but not for other age and sex groups. Characteristics of the suicides did not correspond to the reports.	Chi-square goodness of fit test (or binomial test, if the expected frequency was binomial) $p < .03$. 4 days before: $X^2 = 7.30$ $p < .01$. 7 days before: $X^2 = 5.03$ $p < .05$.	Yes. Sex- and age-specific
Blumenthal and Bergner, 1973 (43)	Period of major newspaper strike in NYC: 4/26/66 to 9/1/66 (140 days) 3/6 newspapers on strike.	The age, sex and method of each suicide during the strike period was determined and suicide rates per 100,000 were calculated. The same data were obtained for each of the preceding 3 years. Designed as replication of Motto (1970) study. Ecological study.	Period of strike was compared with identical periods in preceding 3 years. 2 later years also examined.	The overall rate during the period was significantly lower than the mean rate for the preceding 3 years. However, for women aged 15-24 and 25-34 the suicide rates during the blackout were the lowest in the 6 years studied.	Wilcoxon matched pairs signed rank test. Male and females considered separately and each age group was used to form matching pairs (3-year mean rate vs. rate during strike). Actual statistics not given.	Yes. Age- and sex-specific

Table 3.

STUDIES EXAMINING MEDIA INFLUENCES ON SUBSEQUENT IMITATIVE SUICIDES*
A. Nonfictional Suicide Stories

Citation	Period and Population Studied	Methodology	Comparison Group/Period	Findings	Statistics	Support of Imitation
Bollen and Phillips, 1981 (36)	Daily Detroit mortality statistics for 1973-1976 Motor vehicle fatalities considered covert suicides.	Compiled a list of all suicide stories appearing on the front pages of the 2 largest daily newspapers in Detroit (9 suicide stories identified). Examined relationship between publicized suicides and motor vehicle fatalities (MVF). Designed as replication of Phillips (1979) study. Quasi-experimental analysis similar to Phillips' study and regression analysis. Ecological study.	In quasi-experimental analysis the experimental period was the third day after the publicized suicide. The control period was 1 week before.	Motor vehicle fatalities increased significantly on the third day after a suicide was publicized in the newspaper. Third day corresponds to peak found in Phillips' (1979) study.	T-test for matched pairs: t=2.77, 8df, p=.012. In regression analysis, variables representing the day of week, month, year, and national holidays were included as explanatory variables. Lagged variables form 0 to 8 days were included to estimate duration of the effect. Controlling for daily, monthly, and yearly effects, increase of 1.83 (regression coefficient, t=2.26) in MVF 3 days after story.	Yes
Bollen and Phillips, 1983 (38)	U.S. daily mortality statistics (suicides), 1972-1976.	The Vanderbilt Television News Index was searched for all stories about specific individual suicides carried on 2 or more network news programs (presented by ABC, CBS, and NBC). Several publicized suicides identified. Examined the relationship between publicized TV suicides and subsequent suicides. Quasi-experimental design as well as regression analysis. Ecological study.	In quasi-experimental analysis the experimental period was the entire week after the publicized suicide. The control period was the week before the experimental period.	Suicides generally increased in the week after publicized suicide story. The effect did not extend beyond 10 days.	T-test for matched pairs: t=1.725, 6df, tailed, p=.068' In regression analysis controlled for day of week, month, year, holidays. Regression coefficients representing effect on the same day and 1, 6, and 7 days were statistically significant. The suicide stories had larger effects than the other variables considered. There was no statistically significantly increment in explained variance beyond a lag of 10 days. To test for spuriousness of results, examined effects before story—no significant increase before story.	Yes

Table 3 continued.

STUDIES EXAMINING MEDIA INFLUENCES ON SUBSEQUENT IMITATIVE SUICIDES*

A. Nonfictional Suicide Stories

Citation	Period and Population Studied	Methodology	Comparison Group/Period	Findings	Statistics	Support of Imitation
Littmann, 1985 (47)	Toronto subway suicides, 1968-1977. Epidemic of subway suicides in 1971 (N=96 subway suicides).	Examined the temporal relationship between subway suicides and all suicide-related reports (reports, articles, features and editorials) in Toronto Star newspaper. Ecological study.	Before and after periods (ranging from 1 to 21 days) for each subway suicide. An annual before and after average was calculated for each interval.	No significant difference between the number of suicide-related newspaper reports before and after subway suicides. However, as author reports, there were overlaps of before periods of some suicides with the after periods of other suicides.	No specifics given	No
Motto, 1967 (58)	Suicide rates in 7 cities that had complete cessation of newspaper publication during newspaper strikes (Baltimore: 48 days in 1965; New York: 109 days in 1963; Detroit: 135 days in 1963; Portland: 25 days in 1949; Seattle: 56 days in 1945; Honolulu: 63 days in 1963). Ecological study.	Compared incidence of suicide during newspaper blackout to incidence during the same months of the 5 years before the newspaper blackout. An imitation hypothesis would predict the reduction of suicides during a newspaper blackout.	Blackout period compared with same months in 5 prior years (Use of prior 5 years as comparison period introduces possible confounding of secular trends.)	No significant difference between the incidence during the blackout and the mean of the prior 5 years. However, there was a trend for the incidence to be lower during the blackout in 5 cities. In Detroit, the previous rising trend of suicide attempts appeared to be interrupted by the blackout. Attempts were examined only in this city.	Wilcoxon matched pairs signed ranks test not significant.	No (although trends in data give some support)
Motto, 1970 (42)	Period of newspaper blackout in Detroit, 11/17/67 through 8/10/68 (268 days).	The age, sex, and method of suicides during the newspaper blackout were determined and the suicide rates of age and sex specific groups were calculated. The same data were obtained for the same period of the preceding 4 years, and the year after the blackout year. Ecological study.	Blackout period compared with same period in 4 prior years and 1 subsequent year.	60% drop in incidence during blackout from women's prior mean. Specific age groups showed consistent decline in incidence during blackout with exception of 55 to 64 year group. Women aged 15 to 24 and 25 to 35 showed the most marked decline.	Wilcoxon matched pairs signed ranks test performed separately for men and women (4-yr. mean compared with blackout mean)--significant difference for women at .01 level.	Yes age- and sex-specific
Phillips, 1974 (33)	Monthly U.S. suicide statistics for 1947 to 1967.	Compiled a list of suicide stories appearing on the front page of the New York Times. The New York Daily News, Chicago Tribune, and London Daily Mirror were used to examine the effect of the amount of publicity. 35 front page suicide stories were identified; 3 pairs shared same dates. Quasi-experimental design. Ecological study.	In quasi-experimental analysis the experimental period was the month of the suicide story. The control period was the average of the same months in the prior and subsequent years. For suicide stories late in a month (after the 23rd), the experimental period was the month after the story. The 23rd was an arbitrary cutoff; however, results were consistent when other cutoffs were used.	Suicides increased after 25 front-page stories. Excess suicides occurred only after stories, not before stories. The more publicity, the large the rise in subsequent suicides. The rise is restricted to the area of publication. Bereavement, effect of prior conditions, and misclassification were ruled out as explanations.	Probability of increase after 26 of 33 front page stories is .00066 (binomial test, p=.5, n=33); rank order or suicide stories according to amount of publicity (0 to 4 days) in precise predicted order (p=.0083 [1/120]); Wilcoxon matched pairs signed rank test on rise in publicized area vs. other area significant (.005).	Yes

Table 3 continued.

STUDIES EXAMINING MEDIA INFLUENCES ON SUBSEQUENT IMITATIVE SUICIDES*

A. Nonfictional Suicide Stories

Citation	Period and Population Studied	Methodology	Comparison Group/Period	Findings	Statistics	Support of Imitation
Phillips, 1979 (34)	Daily motor vehicle fatalities in California 1966-73.	Compiled list of front-page suicide stories from the Los Angeles Times and San Francisco Chronicle. 23 front page suicides identified; 2 and 2 suicides occurred within 1 week of each other and therefore each group treated as 1 story. To examine the effect of publicity, the 5 largest papers in California were examined. Ecological study.	The experimental period was the week after the story. The control period was the same period in remaining (prior and subsequent) years of study. A regression line was fitted to the number of MVF in the control periods to estimate the expected number of deaths in the period. For the analysis of the duration of the effect, the periods varied from 2 days before to 11 days after the story.	The number of MVF increased an average of 9% in the week after each suicide story. The greatest increase occurred 3 days after story (31%). The more publicity, the greater increase in MVF. The age of the drivers was correlated to the age of the person described in the story. Single car accidents increased more than other types. Fatalities more frequent in area where story was publicized. Last, crashes after suicide stories were more lethal than crashes at other times, as indicated by time between crash and death.	Walsh test, p = .010 1 tailed (used for examination of increase). Pearson correlation between amount of publicity and change in MVF = .59, p < .005. Ratio of death of death from single vehicle accidents to other types of death is .88 for experimental period and .43 for control period. The difference between the 2 ratios is significant at .0213 (hypergeometric, 1 tail). Correlation between age of publicized suicide and age of drives is .46 (p = .02, t-test, 1 tailed, 16df).	Yes
Stack, 1983 (45)	Monthly U.S. suicide rates for Jan. 1977–June 1980 and unemployment rates.	Two months of media coverage were set at a score of 1 to be a dummy variable.	Pre- and post-exposure time periods were compared.	There was no relationship between reporting of the Jonestown suicides and U.S. suicide rates. The greater the unemployment rate, though, the greater the suicide rate.	Cochrane-Orcutt time series techniques: beta = -.179, F = 1.45, p > .05 for Jonestown event, and beta = .327, F = 4.83, p < .05 for unemployment rate.	No
Stack, 1984 (46)	Monthly U.S. suicide statistics for 1972 through 1980.	Two indices of television of suicide events were developed. The first index represented the number of events per month on the evening news (ABC, NEC, CBS). The second index was the seconds of coverage per month. The data were taken from the Vanderbilt Television News Archives. Time series analysis to examine the relationship between TV coverage and monthly suicide rate. Additional variables in multi-variate model were monthly divorce rate, unemployment rate, and duration of employment. Ecological study.	Indirect control periods through the use of regression analysis.	Amount of television coverage was unrelated to monthly suicide rate. Duration of unemployment and springtime were related to increase in suicide rate.	Cochrane-Orcutt procedure, a form of generalized least-squares estimation (multivariate time series analysis). Standardized coefficient for index representing number of seconds of TV news coverage was -.01.	No.

Table 3 continued.

STUDIES EXAMINING MEDIA INFLUENCES ON SUBSEQUENT IMITATIVE SUICIDES*

A. Nonfictional Suicide Stories

Citation	Period and Population Studied	Methodology	Comparison Group/Period	Findings	Statistics	Support of Imitation
Wasserman, 1984 (40)	Monthly U.S. suicide rates for 1947 through 1977.	Extended Phillips' (1974) list of front page suicides in the New York Times (N = 46 cases). Also indicated whether the suicides were rational celebrities. Quasi-experimental design as well as multivariate time series analysis. Used months as the unit of analysis. Included duration of unemployment as another explanatory variable, controlling for seasonal effects and wars. Ecological study.	For quasi-experimental analysis the experimental period was the month after the suicide story; the control period was the same month in prior and subsequent years. Indirect control periods time-series analysis.	There was a rise in suicides after 34 of the 46 cases. The increase was due to the celebrity suicides. There was a mean rise of 133.8 suicides after the suicides of entertainment celebrities, a rise of 98 for rational political celebrities, and a rise of 35.8 after the suicide of an international celebrity.	Probability of increase after 34 of 46 cases is .00027 (binomial test). In time series analysis, the slope coefficient representing the celebrity story was .47 (t = 3.66, p < .01).	Yes

*A few studies on "covert suicides" are included (Bollen & Phillips, 1981; Phillips, 1979). A study that examined the impact of murder-suicide stories on subsequent airplane crashes (Phillips, 1980) was not included. The findings from the 1980 study do support a theory of imitation and suggestion.

Table 3 continued.

STUDIES EXAMINING MEDIA INFLUENCES ON SUBSEQUENT IMITATIVE SUICIDES

B. Fictional Suicide Stories

Citation	Period and Population Studied	Methodology	Comparison Group/Period	Findings	Statistics	Support of Imitation
Gould and Shaffer, 1986 (53)	Adolescent suicides and attempted suicides aged 19 years and younger during the period 9/16/84 through 3/9/85 in the Greater New York Metropolitan Area.	The variation in suicide and attempted suicide before and after 4 made-for-television movies broadcast in the fall of 1984 and winter of 1985 was examined. Ecological study.	2-week periods before and after each movie were compared. In addition, observed numbers of suicides and attempts during the 'after' periods were compared with expected numbers derived from the average of all weeks.	The observed number of attempted suicides following the television movies was significantly greater than expected, and a significant excess of completed suicides was found after 3 broadcasts. Referral bias, sensitization of medical examiners, or hospital personnel were unlikely to account for the increase in attempted and completed suicides.	The mean number of attempts after the broadcasts (22, sd = 4.2) was significantly greater than the mean before the broadcasts (14, sd = 3.8) (t = 2.61, df = 5, p.05). The observed proportion of attempted suicides to occur during the 4 2-week periods after the movies, 40% (n = 88) was significantly greater than expected (32%, n = 70) (p = .007, based on the binomial distribution). The mean number of completed suicides after 3 broadcasts (4.33, sd = .58) was significantly greater than the mean before the 3 broadcasts (1, sd = 1) (t = 4.99, df = 4, p.01). The observed number of completed suicides (13) after the 3 broadcasts was significantly greater than the expected number (7.44) (p = .02, based on the binomial distribution).	Yes
Holding, 1974, 1975 (59,60)	Completed suicides and undetermined deaths in Edinburgh during the same 30-week period in 1969-1973.	The variation in deaths before, during, and after 'The Befrienders,' an 11-episode weekly series on BBC in 1972 was examined. As described in Holding (1974), the series dramatized the suicide prevention work of the Samaritans. Corresponding weeks in comparison years (1969-1971, and 1973) were examined. Ecological study.	The 4 weeks before the series broadcast date each year were used as the baselines. Numbers of referrals and suicide attempts during and after the series dates were compared with baseline numbers for each year.	Average weekly suicide attempt admissions increased by 13% during the 'Befrienders' series and by 22% during the following 4 weeks. Samaritan new client referrals increased by 112% during the series and 140% in the next 4 weeks.	None	Yes

Table 3 continued.

STUDIES EXAMINING MEDIA INFLUENCES ON SUBSEQUENT IMITATIVE SUICIDES

B. Fictional Suicide Stories

Citation	Period and Population Studied	Methodology	Comparison Group/Period	Findings	Statistics	Support of Imitation
Kessler and Stripp, 1984 (52)	Same as Phillips (1982).	Designed as a replication and extension of Phillips' (1982) work. Used additional sources of soap opera summaries and found 3 additional suicide stories overlooked by Phillips. A story used in Phillips's work was deleted here because it involved only a discussion of a past suicide attempt. Most noteworthy was the use of the exact date of the story. Phillips' earlier study, by employing weekly summaries, inadvertently misspecified the dates of 8 of the 13 stories. In the present study, the corrected data were reanalyzed with a quasi-experimental analysis and a time-series regression analysis.	In quasi-experimental design, the experimental period was the 4 days including and after the story. The control period was the closest time interval preceding the story that contained the same days of the week as the experimental period and did not contain any holidays, real-life celebrity suicides, or soap-opera suicide stories. In the regression analysis, the control variables were days of the week, months of the year, and 2 celebrity deaths.	Soap-opera suicides had no significant effect on real suicides.	The mean difference (3.55) between the experimental and control periods was not significant (t = -.4, 10df). None of the story coefficients in the time-series equations were significant. Separate time-series equations estimated for subgroups defined by sex and urban-rural location yielded no significant story effects.	No

Table 3 continued.

STUDIES EXAMINING MEDIA INFLUENCES ON SUBSEQUENT IMITATIVE SUICIDES

B. Fictional Suicide Stories

Citation	Period and Population Studied	Methodology	Comparison Group/Period	Findings	Statistics	Support of Imitation
Phillips, 1982 (37)	U.S. suicides and motor-vehicle deaths for 1977. Restricted to persons described as "white" on their death certificates.	Compiled a list of television soap-opera episodes in which a suicide or suicide attempt occurred. The list was derived from a newspaper column, "The Soaps," published in the Los Angeles Times. The plot summaries identified the week in which a soap-opera suicide occurred, but not the specific day. Examined whether suicide and motor vehicle deaths increased after these episodes. 13 soap opera suicide stories were identified. Quasi-experimental design. Ecological study.	A 1-week experimental period was used; this was defined as the week, Monday-Sunday, in which the TV soap opera suicide episode occurred. The control period was 1 week before the experimental period. If an experimental period of a particular episode overlapped with a major holiday, it was deleted from the sample. If the control period overlapped with a major holiday, it was replaced by the nearest available control period that occurred before the holiday. To compensate for a possible linear trend in deaths, the control periods, which by design always preceded the experimental periods, were given an adjustment to reflect the slope of the regression line . . . fit the . . .	White suicides increased significantly on and just after the dates of soap-opera suicide stories. Single-vehicle crash deaths also increased after the suicide stories, whereas multiple-vehicle deaths did not increase. This provides additional support for the belief that single-vehicle crash deaths may be "covert" suicides.	T-test for matched pairs = 2.449, 8df, 1 tailed test, p < .02. Same results for analysis that did not correct for linear trends.	Inconclusive because an inaccurate and nonexhaustive index of TV suicide stories was used. See Kessler and Stripp (1984).

Table 3 concluded.

STRESS AND LIFE EVENTS

E.S. Paykel, M.A., M.D., F.R.C.P., F.R.C. Psych, Professor of Psychiatry, University of Cambridge, Addenbrooke's Hospital, Cambridge, England

RECENT LIFE EVENTS AND SUICIDAL BEHAVIOR

Methodology

This paper reviews studies of suicidal behavior in youth in relation to recent and early stressful life events. By a "recent life event" we mean a change in the external social environment that can be dated approximately. A life event represents a change, in contrast to a chronic difficulty or problem, such as a bad marriage or chronic poverty. The change is external and not just one of perception: increased worry over work is not a life event unless it reflects some actual change in circumstances. One "internal event" is physical illness, which is externally verifiable and carries major implications for change of life pattern.

Adequate study of recent life events has entailed solving a number of methodological problems (1), the most prominent of which is retrospective reporting of events. The ordinary inaccuracies of recall may be magnified in suicidal patients by the effort to give meaning, in terms of life experience, to such a major occurrence as suicide, and by pessimism, quilt, and other misperceptions due to psychiatric disorder.

The technique for data collection is probably crucial. The complexities involved in eliciting information, accurately dating occurrences to the relevant period, and deciding whether the threshold and definition for a specific life event have been met, are of such magnitude as to require a systematic and probing interview, rather than a self-report checklist. Review of reliability studies (1) shows that self-report methods such as the questionnaire used by Holmes and Rahe (2) tend to give low reliabilities; interview methods, usually employing semi-structured format with considerable probing, give moderately high reliabilities. Interview methods also produce better patient-informant concordances of the order of 0.8, and relatively little retrospective fall-off of event recall as time periods extend back.

Psychiatric disorders may produce new events, such as loss of job, which are consequences rather than causes of illness. To eliminate these from study, two approaches have been adopted. One is to confine attention to time periods preceding symptomatic onset. The second is to concentrate on "independent" events (3)--those which, evaluated in terms of their specific circumstances, appear highly unlikely to have been brought about by the patient.

Alternative methods of quantifying the stress in events have included consensus scaling and a summation to total-stress scores (2), individual judgments of contextual threat (3), and categorization of events into groups depending on their qualities (1). The different methods, in practice, produce rather similar findings.

The methodology of chronic stress is less well worked out. Brown and Harris (3) have studies "difficulties"--long-standing rather than recent stresses--and have successfully used methodology parallel to that of life events. There are, however, fewer studies of reliability and validity in this area, or in the closely related area of social support as a protective factor (4). It can be particularly difficult here to be sure that the stress is external: to separate perception and reality. It can also be difficult to make sure that the stress is truly independent of the person. Personal resources influence the creation of social networks and close relationships and the finding of solutions to long term problems, so that social isolating and chronic problems may reflect personal qualities as well as external circumstances.

Additional Problems in Relation to Youth Suicidal Behavior

Some additional problems arise in studies of suicidal behavior in youth. First, the methodology of life events in children has not been as well worked out. Adult life event lists are not appropriate. Some adaptations of scaling to children's life event lists have been described (5,6,7) although they have received only limited application in studies of suicidal behavior (8,9).

Second, the retrospective detailed interviewing method that is usually employed and validated in life stress studies can only be applied to suicide attempts. For completed suicide, the principal witness is no longer available. Other sources of information may be used--interview with relatives or access to various kinds of records--but these are likely only to be reliable in relation to the most major events, namely, bereavement.

Studies are therefore predominately of attempted rather than completed suicide. The differences between these two groups are well known and it cannot be assumed that findings valid for one are valid for the other. Also, most studies are of adults over the age of 25, do not analyze by age group, and when they extend to younger ages, still tend to omit

children and adolescents. The studies that do exist of the young often only look in passing at stress, and with deficient methodology.

An issue that arises in young adults is the extent to which increased numbers of life events may reflect a more generally unstable lifestyle prone to self-induced life change, and itself rooted in personality. A number of papers have hinted at this, and detailed acquaintance with some young suicide attempters does suggest a generally chaotic and impulsive life. The same issues can arise in relation to life events and other disorders. One way to tackle them is by followup studies using recovered patients as their own controls (10) to rule out the possibility that as many events might occur at any other period, irrespective of onset of disorder. Brown's methodology of independence of events (3) should control for this element but it is hard to make the judgment of independence from personality. Interpersonal arguments and separations, which are common in young suicide attempters, often reflect contributions from both sides of the relationship.

Studies of Suicide Attempts and Recent Life Events

The literature on recent life events mainly involves suicide attempts, in samples unselected by age, but usually with large representation of young adults. Studies are summarized in Table 1. (Tables appear at the end of this chapter.) Four studies have made comparisons with general population controls. In one study of adolescents aged 14 to 18, Jacobs (11) compared suicide attempters and normal controls for events over lifetime. The time periods nearer the attempt showed an excess of events, particularly in the weeks or months before the attempt, when there were more break-ups of relationship, illnesses or injuries, and pregnancies.

Among studies of adults, Paykel et al. (12) interviewed suicide attempters for life events in the six months before the attempt. Comparisons were made with matched general population controls and with matched depressives who were interviewed for the six months prior to onset. Suicide attempters reported four times as many events as in the general population and one and a half times as many events as did depressives in the period prior to onset. There was a marked peak of events in the month before the attempt, and often in the week before. The excess over general population controls involved most types of life events.

Cochrane and Robertson (13) used a less satisfactory method, a self-report checklist, and studied only male subjects. This study did undertake separate analysis of subjects under 25. Total stress scores for the year before the attempt and the number of life events were much higher in depressives than matched general population controls, and the excess was equally apparent in the two samples: under 25 and over 40 years of age. It particularly involved unpleasant events and disrupted interpersonal relationships.

Isherwood et al. (14) also used a modified Holmes-Rahe methodology. Suicide attempters showed much higher stress scores than general population controls or a second control group of drivers involved in automobile crashes.

Several studies have made comparisons with patient control groups. Only one study examined life stress and suicidal behavior in children, and life event methodology was limited. Cohen-Sandler et al. (8) compared 20 children admitted to an inpatient psychiatric unit because of suicide attempts and threats with depressed, nonsuicidal children and with nondepressed children admitted to the same unit. Life events over the whole of the life span were ascertained from the case history charts, a method that might be vulnerable to unreliability in the original recording. Mean stress scores increased over developmental periods, particularly in the suicidal sample. In the twelve months prior to admission, the suicidal sample had experienced higher stress scores than either control group. The suicidal group had experienced more death of a grandparent, separation, divorce, remarriage and hospitalization of a parent, psychological trauma, broken homes, and peer acceptance change.

Among studies of adult suicide attempters not restricted in age, Paykel et al. (12) found that suicide attempters had experienced more events than depressive controls, particularly in the month before the attempt. This excess was confined to threatening event categories: Undesirable events, events scoring as more stressful in a scaling study, or events outside the control of the patient. Slater & Depue (15) compared depressives who made moderately serious suicide attempts with other depressives. In the year preceding the attempt, particularly between onset of depression and the attempt, there were higher rates of independent events and of exit events involving departure of someone from the immediate social field of the subject. Luscomb et al. (16) used a self-report inventory to study male suicide attempters admitted to Veterans Administration hospitals and patients with no history of suicide attempts. Using a number of events and scores for perceived stress, frequency-of-events rated high in stress, exit events, desirable events, and undesirable events, the researchers found some differences, with a particularly high rate of exit events. However, differences were confined to subjects over 35 and, most markedly, those over 50; the differences were not present in those 19 to 34 year olds.

O'Brien & Farmer (17) compared life events in the six weeks before interview of suicide attempters who had taken overdoes of medication, compared with young people visiting general practitioners for various complaints. Most life events were much more frequent in the suicide attempters. Patients were followed up at three months and a year. At three months, there was no decrease in life event rates, but at twelve months there was a decrease. This was in the only study in which subjects served as their own controls, confirming that not all the life event elevation before the attempt was due to unchanging life style.

Three studies have been limited to separations, both recent and early. Levi et al. (18) examined actual threatened disruptions of interpersonal relationships in the preceding year among suicide attempters, patients with suicidal thoughts, and nonsuicidal patients. Suicide attempters experienced more separations than the nonsuicidal group, whereas those the patients with suicidal thoughts were intermediate. In a replication study of working class subjects, Stein et al. (10 found more recent separations among suicide attempters than psychiatric controls. Greer et al. (10) found that disrupted interpersonal relationships in the last six months were more common in suicide attempters than in psychiatric or medical controls.

One study (21) using a multiple regression analysis found that life stress on the Holmes-Rahe scale related significantly to suicide intent, but a study in adolescents (22) failed to find this.

In some other relevant, uncontrolled studies, Power et al. (23) found that severe events, ascertained over a six month period, peaked in the month before a suicidal attempt, but non-severe events did not. Suicidal intent, assessed subjectively and objectively, correlated with total life event stress, but lethality of attempt did not. Katschnig (24) found a peak of threatening events in the three weeks before the attempt.

In controlled study, but of a less recent event, Birtchnell (25) found that more psychiatric patients with a recent suicide attempt had experienced death of a parent in the preceding one to five years, than in nonsuicidal psychiatric controls.

In a controlled comparison, Paykel et al. (26) studies suicidal feelings in the general population. Subjects reporting suicidal feelings in the last year experienced more life events, particularly undesirable events.

Studies of Completed Suicide and Recent Life Events

A small number of studies have examined completed suicide, depending usually on interview of relatives. Studies are summarized

in Table 2. None of the studies have specifically addressed youth suicide, and most samples have been over 24 years. Bereavement, of a parent or spouse, is an event which can usually be ascertained accurately. Bunch (27) interviewed informants concerning bereavement in the previous five years in suicides and general population controls. There was a significant excess among suicides in the last two years. The difference particularly involved deaths of mothers and spouses. Men appeared more vulnerable to loss of a mother (especially if unmarried). MacMahon and Pugh (28) used death certificates to compare timing of deaths from suicides and other causes in widows and widowers. Suicides showed a clustering in the few years following death of spouse, and particularly in the first year.

In a third study in general population, Hagnell and Rorsman (29) compared recent events among suicides from the prospective Lundby cohort study, matched nonviolent deaths, and general population controls. Seven of 20 suicides experienced stressful life events in the two weeks before death, compared with none of the people who had natural deaths. Viewed over the year before death, the suicides showed more changes of living conditions, work problems, and object losses than the normal controls, and more object losses than the people with natural deaths, for whom work was not relevant because of the nature of their terminal illness. Some of the events in the suicides appear to have been consequences of psychiatric illness, rather than independent events.

Other studies have used psychiatric patient controls. Humphrey (30) studied male suicides, homicidal offenders, and patients hospitalized with neurotic disorders but with no suicidal or homicidal histories. The study examined losses over a lifetime rather than purely recent ones. Excluding early losses, the suicides had significantly more evidence of student, occupational, marital, and parental loss than did the neurotic patients; homicides tended to be intermediate. Information on neurotic patients was obtained from hospital charts, which might not be comparable with the psychological autopsies on the suicides.

Pokorny & Kaplan (31) interviewed relatives of psychiatric inpatients at a Veterans' Administration hospital, patients who subsequently committed suicide. Suicides were more likely to have had adverse life event between discharge and suicide than patients who, over a comparable time period, did not commit suicide particularly when scores during the hospitalization had been high on a measure of defenselessness, mainly reflecting depressive content.

Borg and Stahl (32) also compared psychiatric patients who committed suicide (in varying time periods up to two years following presentation) with matched psychiatric controls. There were no significant differences for the individual life events analyzed from case notes, and overall, the controls had experienced more events, although the suicide victims had reported more deaths.

Fernando and Storm (33) undertook a similar comparison. They found a significantly greater frequency of losses in the last year; these included divorce, separation, illness or death of a first degree relative or friend, and loss of job.

Murphy et al. (34) in an uncontrolled study also found that alcoholics who committed suicide tended to have recent loss of close interpersonal relationships. Humphrey et al. (35), examining the sequence of events in case histories of former psychiatric patients who committed suicide, identified a characteristic sequence starting with drinking problems, followed by difficulties with family, sex, friends, and work. This sequence was regarded as reflecting the lifestyle of the suicide, suggesting alcohol problems leading to gradual social deterioration.

Magnitude of Effect

It has often been pointed out that the recent life events implicated in psychiatric disorder, although stressful, usually fall short of major catastrophes. Separation, divorce, and death are no uncommon in the general population; together, they form the end of all marriages. Case control studies ignore base rates. In circumstances where the causative event is common and the disorder uncommon it is obvious that most event occurrences are not followed by disorder. Suicide attempts and suicide are rare occurrences in the general population; in children, they are even rarer. Their predictability from any kind of single causative factor is recognized to be low (36).

In studies of life events, conventional estimates of magnitude of effect depend on the time period used, since there is a consistent tendency for differences between subjects and controls to diminish as time periods are extended retrospectively further back. The effects of life events are most marked soon after the event and decay with time. This fact renders difficult comparisons with long-acting factors such as demographic risk factors or early loss. Further problems are the tendency of different studies to use different time periods, different ways of assessing event stress, and analyses that are sometimes categorical and sometimes quantitative. Findings also vary with the type of event analyzed, precluding a single summary index.

One useful epidemiological measure of magnitude (37) is the relative risk of disorder in those exposed to a causative factor and those not exposed. An approximation, the relative odds, can be used in case control studies. Applying this measure to studies of psychiatric disorder (37) suggests values of around 6.0 for the risk of depression in the six months following the more stressful classes of life event, with considerably lower values of 2.0-3.0 for schizophrenia. Values fall off considerably with extension back of the time periods.

Table 3 gives relative odds for suicidal acts, from studies using general population controls which report data in a suitable form for computation. For suicide, values range from 4.6 to 6.5, but for periods of one to two years: for suicide attempts, from 6.0 over 6 months to 10.0 over 1 month. In general, these suggest effects that are higher than for depressive onset.

Overall, these effects are moderate in magnitude, suggesting an important effect but very far from an overwhelming one. A comparison is provided by acute infectious diseases where risks of disorder are high early after exposure then fall off rapidly. Using this comparison, risks are dramatically lower than for disorders such as chickenpox after exposure in those who have not acquired immunity, but comparable to tuberculosis, where there are many modifying factors (38). If effects were summated over a lifetime in suicide, they would be higher for persisting associations, such as demographic variables and, personality, than for recent life events, although in short periods the life event effect can be dominant (39).

There has been considerable study of interactions with potential modifying factors such as social support in depression (3,38), but relatively little similar study in suicidal behavior. Slater and Depue (15) found poorer social support in suicide attempters than controls, but much of this was due to prior exit events. A rich literature relates social isolation to suicidal behavior, although it is not so clear the extent to which some of this association might reflect personality and previous psychiatric illness, and the extent to which it acts specifically as a modifying factor to the consequences of recent life events.

Conclusions Regarding Recent Stressful Life Events

There are few studies of recent life events and youth suicidal behavior that use rigorous methodology. Including all studies irrespective of subject's age, findings are that life events strongly and consistently precede suicide, attempted suicide, and suicidal feelings. For suicide attempts, four studies, one of adolescents, also show stressful life events more common than in the general population; such life events are more common in attempters than in depressives, in mixed psychiatric patients, and in medical patient controls. One of the comparisons with other

psychiatric patients was in children and one in young adults; another found differences only among older and not younger adults. Various stressful events are involved. One flaw in existing studies is that few have considered separately events that are independent, in the sense of not previously being caused by the psychiatric disorders which may precede suicidal behavior. The one study that did so found that effects of events and bereavement, one event involved, is almost always independent. Lifestyle effects are not ruled out, but one study did find a fall-off of events on followup, supporting a clustering at onset. It cannot be excluded that lifestyle contributes to the events even if they do cluster at onset: even if this were the case, the events nevertheless may be pathogenic in their own right. Effects are moderate in magnitude, higher than for other psychiatric disorders, although predominately short term.

Possibilities for prevention are limited by the rarity of suicidal behavior. Many life events, at least in adults, are inevitable consequences of the life cycle and interpersonal relationships, and cannot easily be prevented. However, as will be seen in descriptive studies of children and adolescents reviewed in a later section, some events may be consequences of living in very disturbed family settings and might be preventable. Otherwise, preventive efforts must focus on modifying the consequence of the event. Major events can be used to signal a period of high risk when crisis intervention may be indicated, although in adults, so far, this approach has not proved useful in modifying behavior in adult repeat suicide attempters (40).

EARLY LOSS AND SUICIDAL BEHAVIOR.

Methodology

Studies of early environment and suicidal behavior have mainly concerned loss of a parent in childhood, by death or other causes. Careful controls and matching are required (41).

Rates of childhood bereavement tend to be higher in older subjects, born in earlier decades, as death rates in young adults, who are parents of young children, have declined progressively through this century. Divorce rates, on the other hand, have risen. Death rates also tend to be higher in lower social classes and in certain areas. Higher rates of childhood bereavement will also be found in conditions associated with greater parental age. Reliable information is difficult to obtain. Finlay-Jones et al. (42) found that only parental death and marital breakup were reported reliably in an eight-month test-retest study: these made up only one-third of reported childhood separations.

Childhood bereavement effects are generally assumed to be mediated environmentally, but could indicate common genetic influences on parent and child, such as suicide in affectively disordered parents. For loss in other ways, such as marital separation and divorce, the influence of personality patterns becomes more plausible. Parental chaotic lifestyle may contribute much to early marital breakdown and even early parent death, and could well represent genetically inheritable traits manifested in the next generation both in lifestyle and in suicidal behavior. Tsuang (43) found that, among families of schizophrenic and manic depressives, risk of suicide in relatives was higher when the patient had committed suicide.

Retrospective studies of qualitative aspects of early upbringing are even more difficult, in view of the likely retrospective distortions and the limited possibilities for validation. In an elegant study, Wolkind and Coleman (44) showed that recollections of the quality of relationships between parents in childhood varied with the mood state at the time of the interview, whereas reports of separation from parents in childhood did not.

Completed Suicide

The plentiful literature on early loss and depression suggests a weak association between parental death and later depression, a stronger association with parental loss by separation, and a possible association with severity of depression (45,46). Most studies of suicidal behavior deal with suicide attempts rather than completed suicide.

In one of the few studies of completed suicide, Paffenberger et al. (47) used college records and death records of former students at Harvard and the University of Pennsylvania to examine antecedents of 381 suicides and 652 matched controls over a 17 to 51 year followup. An earlier publication (48) had used a smaller sample included in this later analysis. Maternal loss did not predict suicide, but paternal loss by death did so, with paternal loss by separation showing a trend at 10 percent significance. The effect of paternal death was a relatively small one, with a relative risk of 1.6, only reaching significance by the large sample size, but its specificity and causative importance were reinforced by an absence of any similar effects on accident deaths, another group where familial lifestyle might have been of importance. Roy (49) compared case notes of 30 chronic schizophrenics who committed suicide with 30 chronic schizophrenics who did not. The rates for loss of parent before age 17 by death or separation were closely comparable. Studying patients with recurrent affective disorder, the same author (50) found that more of those who committed suicide had early parental loss than those who did not. Studying 90 psychiatric patient suicides with mixed diagnoses, presumably including some or all of the above (51), he found only a trend at the 10 percent level for parental loss by death or separation before age 17.

Suicide Attempts

Table 4 summarizes a number of studies of suicide attempts and early loss in adults. Only two of these separately analyzed younger subjects under 30. Four studies made comparisons with general population samples. Two of these used medical patient controls. For the purposes of recent life event studies, these are best regarded as a patient control group since there is evidence that life events may precede some medical disorders and hospitalization. For early loss, there is no similar evidence and it is reasonable to regard medical patients as a normal control group.

Greer et al. (20) compared suicide attempters, nonsuicidal psychiatric patients and medical patients and found significantly higher rates of early separation among attempters, particularly for loss of both parents and loss under the age of 4. Analysis confirms that the differences were significant separately for death and for separation or divorce. Crook and Raskin (52) compared depressed inpatients who had histories of suicide attempts, depressives without such histories, and general population controls. They reported a significant excess of loss in the suicidal group by divorce, desertion or separation, but not by death. Detailed figures were not given. Goldney (53) compared female suicide attempters aged 18 to 30 with a small sample of women attending a community health center. There was no difference for parental death but more loss by divorce and separation. Adam et al. (54) studied suicide attempters and general practice controls. Again, there was a slight but not significant difference for deaths, but there was a significant excess of loss due to divorce and separation. Overall, all four studies confirm that parental divorce or separation is a risk factor for suicide attempts in adults but, with one exception, leave doubtful the impact of parental death.

Other studies have made comparisons with psychiatric controls. Many have not distinguished the type of loss. Farberow (55) reported no difference overall in the incidence of separation in small samples of suicide attempters and nonsuicidal patients but more loss before the age of 6. Moss and Hamilton (56) reported separation in 60 percent of seriously suicidal patients as opposed to 15 percent in other patients, both those who were potentially suicidal and nonsuicidal. Walter (57) studies early loss in patients with suicidal threats or attempts, and in nonsuicidal depressed patients. Early loss

was reported in 77 percent of the former and 20 percent of the latter, a remarkably high difference. Bruhn (58) reported more loss in suicidal patients, than in nonsuicidal outpatients or inpatients.

Greer (59) studied patients with neurotic and sociopathic disorder. These with a history of a suicide attempt had more evidence of parental loss for at least 12 months before the age of 18; they had experienced such loss particularly before the age of 55 and more commonly were deprived of both parents. The analyses were significant both in patients under 30 and 30 & over. Reanalyzing Greer's data to examine the nature of loss, loss by death just failed to reach significant (23.5% attempters, 24.3% controls, p = .06), whereas loss by divorce or separation was significant (17.3% vs 8.3% p <.05). Gay and Tonge (60) found significantly more separations before the age of 15 in new consecutive referrals to a psychiatric department with a history of a suicide attempt than in those without it.

Hill (61) examined case notes of depressed patients, comparing those who had made a suicide attempt and those who had not, for early parental deaths. Overall rates were not much different in the two groups but there was some excess of deaths in certain subgroups: patients of both sexes who had lost their fathers when they were aged 10 to 14 and women who had lost their fathers when they were aged 15 to 19.

Birtchnell (25) studies psychiatric patients with a history of attempted suicide. Pooling data about all parental deaths and illegitimacy, he found more such events had occurred in suicide attempters. This was mainly due to parental deaths than occurred when the patients were age 10 to 19, although this difference failed to reach significance. In a later, similar study (62), he found no differences for loss at any age in childhood or adolescence.

Levi et al. (18) studies the effect of parental separation of six months, comparing psychiatric patients who had made a recent suicide attempt, who had had suicidal feelings, or who were nonsuicidal. The first group were significantly more likely to have experienced a separation than the third, with the second group intermediate. The differences were particularly distinct when the separation occurred before the age of 7. Stein et al. (19) replicated this study in working class attempters, analyzed separately by sex and race. There were significant differences for loss up to the age of 7 for all four groups, and for loss up to the age of 17 for all except black males, for whom the differences were suggestive and the sample small.

Both these studies also examined separations in the last year and have been included in Table 2. Both sought to examine whether there was a particular aggregation of patients with the combination of early and recent loss, suggesting that early loss acted to sensitize the patient to recent loss. Brown and Harris (3) have presented evidence that this is the case for depression in women, although not all the evidence is consistent. Interactions in these two studies were tested by partitioning the total chi square; in neither study were they significant, although inspection of frequencies does suggest some interaction in the predicated direction. Greer et al. (20) used a different mode of analysis and found both suicide attempters and nonsuicidal psychiatric patients tended to show this pattern but medical controls did not, which would be consistent with an effect in various psychiatric disorders. Some confirmation of an effect was found in an uncontrolled study (63) in which suicide attempters were interviewed about early separation and recent interpersonal loss. There was an association between early and recent loss for females, but not males.

Pooling these comparisons with psychiatric controls, four studies have found more early parental death in adult suicide attempters than in psychiatric controls, while two have failed to find this association. Three studies have found a difference for parental separation or divorce and none have failed to. Among studies not distinguishing cause of

separations, and usually including temporary separation, all seven have shown an excess in suicide attempters. There is a clear and strong association with loss by other means and a weaker, but probable, association with loss by death.

Suicidal Feelings

Some additional studies have been made of suicidal feelings. Adam et al. (64) found in students attending a student mental health service that suicidal ideation was associated with loss of a parent by death and divorce or separation. Ross et al. (65) studied a mixed sample of students, medical patients, and state employees, and found that those with suicidal feelings more often reported their parents had separated. Goldberg (66) in an epidemiological community study of 18 to 24 year olds found a significant association with loss of mother before the subjects reached age 16.

Retrospective study of qualitative childhood environment is very liable to selective falsification. Ross et al. (65) found that those with suicidal feelings reported parents who favored siblings, were unstimulating, guilt-engendering, rejecting, and unaffectionate, abusing, and punitive. Goldney (53) found that young women attempting suicide were more likely than normal controls to report parental quarrelling, frequent disagreements with their parents, financial problems at home, poor childhood physical health, and various negative parental characteristics. These findings may say something important regarding subjects' perceptions rather than their real environments.

Studies in Children and Adolescents

Few studies of children and adolescents comparing early loss in suicide attempters and control groups have used adequate samples and methods. In the study already shown for recent life events in Table 1, Cohen-Sandler et al. (8) compared children aged 5 to 14, admitted after making suicidal acts of threats with admitted children who were depressed but not suicidal, or not depressed. Data were obtained from case histories. When compared with the two other groups, the suicidal children showed, during infancy and preschool years, a higher incidence of separation from parents; during early childhood, more parental divorce; and, during late childhood, more separation and divorce of parents.

However, Jacobs [11] found only small differences between adolescent suicide attempters and general population controls in the incidence of separation or divorce of parents during childhood, with considerable differences for more recent break up.

Stanley and Barter [67], comparing suicidal and nonsuicidal hospitalized adolescents, found that parental loss through separations and divorce occurred in both groups, although more common before age 12 in suicide attempters.

Conclusions Regarding Early Loss

There are few adequately controlled studies of youth suicidal behavior, with no systematic study of completed suicide in the group under 25. The very few studies in adult groups do suggest that early loss characterizes suicides, when they are compared with psychiatric controls.

Regarding attempted suicide, one study of children does show a considerable increase of separation from and between parents, although methodology was not ideal, and other studies provide less support. Studies of adult suicide attempters show higher rates of early loss by separation and divorce than the general population in all studies, but increased parental death in only one of four.

Comparisons between adult suicide attempters and psychiatric controls consistently show more loss in the former when the study examines separation, divorce or loss not distinguished by nature, although in some studies, the differences are weak and selective to certain groups. Studies of parental death also tend to show an excess, but to a weaker degree and with some negative studies. Studies that specify the child's age at time of loss and sex of parent or patient do not report consistent findings.

More controlled studies of children and adolescents are needed. Stronger effects might have been expected if events decay over time; early childhood events are not far in the past for the child, as they are for the adult. Parental loss is also clearly an event of major salience in general terms for the child.

Effects are moderate in magnitude. In adult comparisons with the general population where relative odds are computable from the data given, the figures are: completed suicide and parental divorce or separation, 1.6 [47]; attempted suicide and parental death 2.5 [20]; attempted suicide and parental divorce or separation, 3.9 [20]; 3.8 [54]. Although lower than relative odds obtained for recent life events computed over six months, they are impressive for effects acting over prolonged times.

Overall, there is an association between early loss and suicide attempts, more marked than for psychiatric disorder in general and more marked for early loss by separation or divorce than by death. The association with death could be due to parental suicide and genetic transmission of suicidal behavior, since parental suicide is not usually excluded from parental death, but this is unlikely to be of sufficient magnitude to account for the differences. A more plausible explanation might be in an associated risk-taking lifestyle, but there is a prima facie case for regarding the death itself as pathogenic.

Loss for reasons other than death, is likely if permanent, to be due to breakup of parents' marriage. Here, conclusions can be less clear. The effect is larger and more consistent than for early parental death. This might reflect familial lifestyle towards acting-out, whether genetically or environmentally based, rather than causation. However, marital strife that precedes breakup and the subsequent uncertainties of having two separated parents may be more persistently harmful than the major loss itself, even by death.

OTHER STUDIES OF SUICIDAL BEHAVIOR IN YOUTH

The studies reported so far have been predominately of adults, reflecting the paucity of good controlled studies in young adults, adolescents, and children. Studies that lack control groups are unsatisfactory in life event collection or other methodological aspects can supplement these. A selection of studies is reviewed rather than a comprehensive survey.

One recent study is reassuring. Rich et al. (68) (in press) compared 133 completed suicides aged 15 to 29, with 150 aged 30 and over. There was no difference in the number of stresses at the time of death, although the older group had more illnesses and the younger group had experienced more unemployment and legal problems, with more separations regarded as suicide precipitants when present. The presence and salience of stresses is likely to be related to the life cycle. Even in this study only 31 of the suicides were under 25.

There have been many uncontrolled descriptive studies, mostly in adolescents rather than younger children. Shaffer (69) made a detailed study of 31 completed suicides aged under 15. Common precipitants were disciplinary crises, fights with peers and disputes with parents or with friends of the opposite sex, bereavements. Only in 10 percent were there no precipitants. Many suicides took place during a period of absence from school. Most children were living with one or both parents and early loss was not common. Amir (70) studied Israeli suicides aged 10 to 18. Common motives recorded were quarrels with parents, with family members and others. In only 3 percent were motives recorded as unknown. Seventy-six percent came from intact families.

Studies of suicide attempters are plentiful. Toolan (71) reviewed 102 admissions to Bellevue Hospital under age 18 but mostly over age 12. There was a high incidence of broken homes; only 32 were living with both parents, with paternal absence common. Jacobziner (72) reported on 597 suicide attempts in subjects aged 12 to 20 in New York City. There was a high incidence of family disorganization. In 21 percent of the cases, the parents were not living together. The author felt that most attempts were sudden, precipitous reactions to stressful situations.

Barter, et al. (73) studied case notes of 45 suicide attempters under 21. Twenty-three had lost one of both natural parents, and of 21 cases where natural parents were living together, 11 had marital problems. School performance was almost uniformly poor. Fifteen of the attempts grew out of an argument with parents and 14 were associated with a break-up of a relationship. Only in 9 cases did the case notes not indicate a precipitant cause.

Rohn et al. (74) studied 65 adolescents who attempted suicide. Fifty-nine percent came from one-parent families, with prolonged absence of a parent in 11 percent more; 25 percent were not living with either parent at the time of the attempt. Seventy-five percent had very poor school records. Tischler et al. (75) studying 108 adolescent suicide attempters, found that most frequently cited precipitants were family problems (52%), problems with the opposite sex (30%) and school problems (30%). Almost 50 percent reported that at least one of their parents had been divorced. Only 49 percent were living at home with both parents at the time of the event.

These studies were American. Similar findings have been obtained in Britain. White (76) studied 50 adolescents admitted to a general hospital following overdose. Seventy percent were experiencing difficulties with important persons in their environment, 8 percent academic worries, 6 percent concern regarding physical illness. In 10 percent no cause was known to the patient. Fifty percent had undergone separation from parents before the age of 15.

Hawton and colleagues (77,78) studies 50 adolescent overdosers. Family backgrounds were disturbed, 36 percent living with a single parent and 12 percent with neither parent, higher than national figures. The common problems identified at the time of the overdoses were arguments with parents, problems with school or work, including unemployment and problems with boy or girl friends. Eleven percent had problems with physical health.

Seiden (79) reviewed the literature on the special case of university student stress and suicidal behavior. Most studies find students to have higher suicide rates than their non-academic peers. The degree to which this is related to academic stress or other self-selection factors is not clear.

Otto (80), in a study of suicidal attempts in children and adolescents related to school problems, concluded that they were of relatively low importance. However, recent suicides in school children in Japan reported in the popular press suggest that findings may be different in a culture in which school children are under considerable academic pressure.

Comparisons with psychiatric controls tend to suggest that these factors are only weakly specific to suicidal behavior, and characterize a variety of disturbed adolescents. Mattson et al. (81) studied 75 suicidal children and adolescents referred as emergencies to a child psychiatry clinic. Only about half came from intact families, 27 having experienced parental divorce or separation, 6 loss of one parent, 8 loss of both. However, this was not different from other children referred to the clinic. The common triggering situations were conflicts with parents and loss of heterosexual love objects, with school problems, sexual conflicts, and pregnancy in a smaller proportion. In the nonsuicidal children these were less common, except for conflict with parents, whereas physical injury and exacerbations in chronic physical illness were more common.

Pfeffer et al. (82) studies 42 children with suicidal ideas, threats or attempts and 16 who were nonsuicidal. There were no differences between the two groups in the type of recent stresses, which were most commonly preoccupations about school failure, disturbed friendships, fears of parental punishment, and school and family crises. Nor were there significant differences in family situations, with high incidences of parental separation, parental absence and abuse home atmospheres in both groups. Comparing delinquent adolescents with and without a previous history of suicide attempts (Miller et al.) (83), found no difference in the incidence of absent parents. However, Garfinkel et al. (84), comparing case record information on 505 suicidal children and adolescents presenting at an emergency room and 505 nonsuicidal cases, found the attempters to show significantly more unemployed fathers, employed mothers, and parents absent form the home.

An English study (85) compared children admitted to a general hospital after overdoses with matched psychiatric outpatient referrals. The suicide attempters showed more family disturbances, with more evidence of poor relationship between child and father or mother, lack of warmth, and discord, but no greater evidence of other stresses such as poor living conditions, migration, stress within the family, stress at school, or other extra familial stress.

Overall, these studies uniformly confirm high rates of early loss, broken homes and precipitant stress in adolescent suicide attempters, but suggest lower rates of broken homes for completed suicides. Stresses particularly center around family problems, break or threat of a break in relationships, and school problems. Physical illness is uncommon as a stressor. The stresses are those which might be expected to loom importantly at this stage of the life cycle.

Controlled comparisons with other psychiatrically disturbed adolescents show similar rates of recent stress and fairly similar rates of family breakdown and early loss, indicating that these phenomena are not highly specific to the suicidal, but characterize the psychiatrically disturbed. The rates are probably above those in the general population, although better studies are needed to confirm that.

One issue does emerge clearly: the precipitant life stresses in adolescents are to some extent bound up with the disturbed family backgrounds: both are facets of disturbed families. A second issue often described is the impulsiveness of the suicide attempts, raising the question of how much personality traits of impulsiveness and acting out contribute to the ultimate consequence.

GENERAL CONCLUSIONS

A number of general conclusions and directions for further studies emerge form this overview.

1. There is a dearth of studies that assess the impact of employing careful methodology and controlled comparisons of recent life events in the role of youth suicidal behavior.

2. There are more studies of early parental loss, but even here, there are not many controlled comparisons or attempts to date the family break-up to examine the extent to which the associations depend on recent or earlier family break-up.

3. There are few studies involving completed suicides, rather than suicide attempts. The former is more difficult to study, but the many differences in demographic and epidemiological characteristics of the two populations mandate separate studies.

4. Studies of recent life events in older populations consistently indicate increased rates before suicide attempts and suggest the same for major events, before completed suicides. In terms of relative risks, effects are moderate in magnitude, but tend to be short term, with rates of events in suicide attempters (and other psychiatric patients) converging with those in control groups as time periods are extended retrospectively beyond a year. Suicide attempts probably bear the strongest and most immediate relationship in time to recent life events of any

psychiatric disturbances; in particular, they often rapidly follow interpersonal disruptions.

5. Studies of early loss in older suicides and suicide attempters consistently show rates higher than in normal control groups or other psychiatric disorders because of break-up of parental marriage. Relative risks are moderate in magnitude; less than for recent events but apparently long-enduring. For parental death, the effects are less marked; rates are probably raised but only a little.

6. Uncontrolled studies of adolescent suicide attempters and the few comparisons with general population controls suggest particularly high rates both of recent life stress and of earlier family disruptions. Precipitant stresses particularly involve family problems, break-ups of relationships, and school problems. Physical illness as a stressor is uncommon. Recent stresses often appear to arise out of disturbed family settings.

7. Comparisons of adolescent suicide attempters with other psychiatrically disturbed adolescents show only small differences, suggesting that the early losses and disturbed families are relatively nonspecific, and the recent stresses only partly specific.

8. Interpretations of these associations are not fully clear cut. In careful studies of recent life events, it is clear that much of the excess in events is independent of causation by the patients and represents a genuine clustering of external stress before the suicidal act, rather than simply an enduring aspect of lifestyle that would be found at any other time. Nevertheless, generally disturbed lifestyles and, for adolescents, family settings not in their control, do put subjects more at risk of major events.

9. For early loss, the small differences in parental death and considerably larger differences in loss by marital break-up are susceptible to two alternative explana-

tions, both of which suggest that something other than the loss itself is pathogenic. One interpretation is that the findings to some degree reflect a tendency to an acting-out personality and life style, genetically or environmentally transmitted down the generations. The second is that the preceding marital strife and arguments are more disruptive to the child, on a long term basis, than is the loss of a parent itself.

10. Neither recent nor early environment can be regarded as sufficient causes by themselves. They, particularly recent events, clearly interact with other personality variables related to acting-out and impulsive behavior.

11. Implications for prevention are not easy. Partly, this is a general problem in relation to the occurrence of rare consequences, so that most occurrences of a cause will not be followed by disorder. In addition, most of the recent or early events are not preventable. At best, the recent events might serve as signals for high-risk periods when crisis interventions might be attempted.

REFERENCES

1. Paykel ES: Methodological aspects of life events research. J. Psychosom. Res. 1983; 27:341-352.

2. Holmes TH, Rahe RH: The social readjustment rating scale. J. Psychosom. Res. 1967; 11:213-218.

3. Brown GW, Harris T: Social Origins of Depression. 1978; London:Tavistock Publications.

4. Paykel ES: Life events, social support and clinical psychiatric disorder, in Sarason IG, Sarason BR (eds): Social support: theory research and application. Martinus Nijhiff, The Hague, Netherlands, 1985, pp 321-347.

5. Coddington DR: The significance of life events as aetiologic factors in diseases of children. J. Psychosom. Res. 1971; 16:205-213.

6. Monaghan J, Robinson J, Doge J: The children's life event inventory. J. Psychosom. Res. 1979; 23:63-68.

7. Yeaworth R, York J. Hussey M, Ingle M, Goddwen T: The development of an adolescent life change event scale. Adolescence 1980; 15:91-97.

8. Cohen-Sandler R, Berman AL, King RA: Life stress and symptomatology: determinants of suicidal behavior in children. J. Am. Acad. Child Psychiat. 1982; 21:178-186.

9. Ferguson WE: Gifted adolescents, stress, and life changes. Adolescence 1981; 16:974-985.

10. Paykel ES: Recent life events and clinical depression, in Gunderson EKE, Rahe RH (eds) Life Stress and Illness. Springfield, Illinois, Charles C. Thomas 1974, pp 134-163.

11. Jacobs J (ed) Adolescent suicide. Wiley-Interscience New York 1971.

12. Paykel ES, Prusoff BA, Myers JK: Suicide attempts and recent life events: A controlled comparison. Arch. Gen. Psychiat. 1975; 32:327-337.

13. Cochrane R, Robertson A: Stress in the lives of parasuicides. Social Psychiat. 1975; 10:161-171.

14. Isherwood J, Adam KS, Hornblow AR: Life event stress, psychosocial factors, suicide attempt and auto-accident proclivity. J. Psychosom. Res. 1982; 26:371-383.

15. Slater J. Depue RA: The contribution of environmental events and social support to serious suicide attempts in primary depressive disorder. J. Abnormal Psychol. 1981; 90:275-285.

16. Luscomb RL, George AC, Patsiokas AT: Mediating factors in the relationship between life stress and suicide attempting. J. Nervous and Mental Diseases 198; 168:644-650.

17. O'Brien SEM, Farmer RDT: The role of life events in the aetiology of episodes of self poisoning, in Farmer R, Hirsch S (eds): The suicide syndrome. London, Croom Helm 1980, pp 124-130.

18. Levi ID, Fales CH, Stein M, Sharp VH: Separation and attempted suicide. Arch. Gen. Psychiat. 1966; 15:158-164.

19. Stein M, Levy MT, Glasberg HM: Separations in black and white suicide attempters. Arch. Gen. Psychiat. 1975; 31:815-821.

20. Greer S, Gunn JC, Koller KM: Aetiological factors in attempted suicide. B.M.J. 1966; 2:1352-1357.

21. Papa LL: Responses to life events as predictors of suicidal behavior. Nursing Res. 1979; 29:362-369.

22. Friedrich W, Reams R, Jacobs J: Depression nd suicidal ideation in early adolescents. J. Youth & Adolescence 1982; 11:403-407.

23. Power KG, Cooke DJ, Brooks DN: Life stress, medical lethality, and suicidal intent. Br. J. Psychiat. 1985; 147:655-659.

24. Katschnig H: Measuring life stress: a comparison of two methods, in Farmer R, Hirsch S (eds) The Suicide Syndrome, London, Croom Helm 1980, pp 116-123.

25. Birtchnell J: The relationship between attempted suicide, depression and parent death. Br. J. Psychiat. 1970; 116:307-313.

26. Paykel ES, Myers JK, Lindenthal JJ, Tanner J: Suicidal feeling in the general population: A prevalence study. Br. J. Psychiat. 1974; 30:771-778.

27. Bunch J: Recent bereavement in relation to suicide. J. Psychosom. Res. 1972; 16:361-366.

28. MacMahon BR, Pugh TF: Suicide in the widowed. Am. J. Epidemiology 1965; 81:23-31.

29. Hagnell O, Rorsman B: Suicide in the Lundby study: a controlled prospective investigation of stressful life events. Neuropsychobiology 1980; 6:319-332.

30. Humphrey JA: Social loss: A comparison of suicide victims, homicide offenders and non-violent individuals. Dis. Nerv. System 1977; 38:157-160.

31. Pokorny AD, Kaplan HB: Suicide following psychiatric hospitalization. The interaction effects of defenselessness and adverse life events. J. Nerv. Ment. Dis. 1976; 162:119-125.

32. Borg SE, Stahl M: Prediction of Suicide. A prospective study of suicides and controls among psychiatric patients. Acta Psychiat. Scand. 1982; 65:221-232.

33. Fernando s, Storm V: Suicide among psychiatric patients of a district general hospital Psychol. Med. 1984; 14:661-672.

34. Murphy GE, Armstrong JW, Hermele SL, Fischer JR, Clendenin WW: Suicide and Alcoholism. Interper-

sonal loss confirmed as a predictor. Arch. Gen. Psychiat. 1979; 36:65-69.

35. Humphrey JA, Puccio D, Niswander GD, Casey TM: An analysis of the sequence of selected events in the lives of a suicidal population: A preliminary report. J. Nerv. Ment. Dis. 1972; 154:137-140.

36. Rosen A: Detection of suicidal patients: an example of some limitations in the prediction of infrequent events. J. Consul. Psychol. 1954; 18:397-403.

37. Paykel ES: Contribution of life events to causation of psychiatric illness. Psychol. Med. 1978; 8:245-253.

38. Paykel ES: Recent life events in the development of depressive disorders, in Depue RA (ed). The psychobiology of depressive disorders: Implications for the effects of stress. New York Academic Press 1979, pp 245-262.

39. Paykel ES, Hollyman JA: Life events and depression: a psychiatric view. Trends in Neurosciences 1984; 478-481.

40. Hirsch SR, Walsh C, Draper R: Parasuicide: A review of treatment interventions. J. Affect. Dis. 1982; 4:299-311.

41. Granville-Grossman KL: The early environment in affective disorder, in Coppen A, Walk A (eds). Recent Developments in Affective Disorders, Royal Medico-Psychological Association 1968.

42. Finlay-Jones R, Scott R, Duncan-Jones P, Byrne D, Henderson S: The reliability of reports of early separations. Aust. N.Z., J. Psychiat. 1981; 15:27-31.

43. Tsuang MT: Risk of suicide in the relatives of schizophrenics, manics, depressives, and controls. J. Clin. Psychiat. 1983; 44:396-400.

44. Wolkind S, Coleman E: Adult psychiatric disorder and childhood experiences. The validity of retrospective data. Br. J. Psychiat. 1983; 143:188-191.

45. Paykel ES: Life events and early environment, in Paykel ES (ed) Handbook of Affective Disorders. Edinburgh, Churchill Livingstone 1982, pp 146-161.

46. Lloyd C: Life Events and Depressive Disorder Reviewed. I. Events as predisposing factors. Arch. Gen. Psychiat. 1980; 37:529-535.

47. Paffenbarger RS, King SH, Wing AL: Chronic disease in former college students. IX. Characteristics in youth that predispose to suicide and accidental death in later life. Am. J. Pub. Health 1969; 59:900-908.

48. Paffenbarger RS, Asnes DP: Chronic diseases in former college students: III precursors of suicide in early and middle life. Am. J. Pub. Health 1966; 5:1026-1036.

49. Roy A: Suicide in chronic schizophrenia. Br. J. Psychiat. 1982a; 141:171-177.

50. Roy A. Suicide in recurrent affective disorder patients. Can J Psychiat 1984; 29:319-322.

51. Roy A: Risk factors for suicide in psychiatric patients. Arch Gen Psychiat 1982; 39:1089-1095.

52. Crook T, Raskin A: Association of childhood parental loss with attempted suicide and depression. J. Consul Clin Psychol 1975; 43:277.

53. Goldney RD: Parental loss and reported childhood stress in young women who attempt suicide. Acta Psychiat Scan 1981; 64:34-59.

54. Adam KS, Bouckoms A, Streiner D: Parental loss and family stability in attempted suicide. Arch Gen Psychiat 1982; 39:1081-1085.

55. Farberow NL: Personality patterns of suicidal mental hospital patients. Gent Psychol Monogr 1950; 42:3.

56. Moss LM, Hamilton DM: The psychotherapy of the suicidal patient. Am J Psychiat 1955; 112:814-819.

57. Walton JH: Suicidal behavior in depressive illness: A study of aetiological factors in suicide. J Ment Sci 1958; 104:884-891.

58. Bruhn JG: Broken homes among attempted suicides and psychiatric outpatients: A comparative study. J Men Sci 1962; 108:772-779.

59. Greer S: Parental loss and attempted suicide: A further report. Br J Psychiat 1966; 112:465-470.

60. Gay MJ, Tonge WL: The late effects of loss of parents in childhood. Br J Psychiat 1967; 113:753-759.

61. Hill DW: The association of childhood bereavement with suicidal attempt in depressive illness. Br J Psychiat 1969; 115:301-304.

62. Birtchnell J: Some familial and clinical characteristics of female suicidal psychiatric patients. Br J Psychiat 1981; 138:381-390.

63. Lester D, Beck AT: Early loss as a possible "sensitizer" to later loss in attempted suicides. Psychol Rep 1976; 39:121-122.

64. Adam KS, Lohrenz JG, Harper D: Suicidal ideation and parental loss. A preliminary research report. 1973; 18:95-100.

65. Ross MW, Clayer JR, Campbell RL: Parental rearing patterns and suicidal thoughts. Acta Psychiat Scand 183; 67:429-433.

66. Goldbery EL: Depression and suicide ideation in the young adult. Am J Psychiat 1981; 138:35-40.

67. Stanley ES, Barter JT: Adolescent suicidal behavior. Am J Orthopsychiatry 1970; 40:87-96.

68. Rich CL, Young D, Fowler RD: San Diego suicide study: I. Young vs Old Cases Arch. Gen. Psychiat. (In press).

70. Amir M: Suicide among minors in Israel. Israel Ann. Psychiat. and Related Disciplines 1973; 11:219-268.

71. +Toolan JM: Suicide and suicidal attempts in children and adolescents. Am. J. Psychiat. 1962; 118:719-724.

72. Jacobziner H: Attempted suicides in adolescence. JAMA 1965; 191:101-105.

73. +Barter JT, Swaback DO, Todd D: Adolescent suicide attempts. A follow-up study of hospitalized patients. Arch. Gen. Psychiat. 1968; 19:523-527.

74. Ronn RD, Sarles RM, Kenny TJ, Reynolds BJ, Heald +FP: Adolescents who attempt suicide. J. Pediatrics 1977; 90:636-638.

75. Tischler CL, McKenry PC, Morgan KC: Adolescent suicide attempts: Some significant factors. Suicide and Life Threatening Behavior 1981; 11:86-92.

76. White HC: Self Poisoning in Adolescents. Br. J. Psychiat. 1974; 124:24-35.

77. Hawton K, O, Grady J, Osborn M, Cole D: Adolescents who take overdoses: Their characteristics, problems and contacts with helping agencies. Br. J. Psychiat. 1982; 140:118-123.

78. Hawton K, Osborn M, O'Grady J, Cole D: Classification of adolescents who take overdoses. Br. J. Psychiat. 1982; 140:124-131.

79. Seiden RH; Suicide among youth: A review of the literature 1900-1967. Supplement to the Bulletin of Suicidology. U.S. Gov't. Printing Office, Washington, D.C., 1969.

80. Otto U: Suicidal attempts made by children and adolescents because of school problems. Acta Paediatrica Scan. 1965; 54:348-356.

81. Mattsson A, Hawkins JW: Suicidal behavior as a child psychiatric emergency. Arch. Gen. Psychiat. 1969; 20:100-108.

82. Pfeffer CR, Conte HR, Plutchik R, Jerrett I: Suicidal behavior in latency-age children, Am. Acad Child Psychiat. 1979; 18:679-692.

83. Miller ML, Chiles JA, Barnes VE: Suicide attempters within a delinquent population. J. Consul. Clin.

Psychol. 1982; 50:491-498.

84. Garfinkel BD, Froese A, Hood J: Suicide attempts in children and adolescents. Am. J. Psychiat. 1982; 139:1257-1261.

85. Taylor EA, Stansfield SA: Children who poison themselves: I. A clinical comparison with psychiatric controls. Br. J. Psychiat. 1984; 145:127-135.

CONTROLLED COMPARISON OF LIFE EVENTS AND SUICIDE ATTEMPTS

Controls	Sample Size	Method	Findings
1. General Population Controls			
a) Studies of Children			
Jacobs (1971)	Adolescent attempters N = 31 Control adolescents N = 31	Interview	Excess of events in weeks/months before attempt, particularly break of relationship, physical illness, injury, pregnancy
b) Studies of Adults			
Paykel et al (1975)	Attempters N = 53 Controls N = 53	Interview for recent life events	Excess of life events over six months. Especially last month. Most types of event.
Cochrane & Robertson (1975)	Attempters N = 100 Controls N = 100	Self report checklist scores	Higher stress scores and number of life events over 1 year. Especially unpleasant events, disrupted interpersonal relationships. Equally for under 25, over 40.
Isherwood et al (1982)	Attempters = 150 Controls = 200 Automobile accident drivers = 100	Self report Total stress scores	Higher stress than both control groups. Time not stated.
2. Other Patients			
a) Studies of Children			
Cohen Sandler et al (1982)	Suicidal children N = 20 Depressed N = 21 Other psychiatric N = 35	From case records	Higher mean stress scores separation, divorce remarriage, hospitalization of parent, broken homes, other illness.
b) Studies of Adults			
Paykel et al (1975)	Attempters = 53 Depressives = 53	Interview for recent life events	Attempters experienced more events in threatening classes: undesirable; higher rated stress, uncontrolled.
Slater & Depue (1981)	Primary depressive Attempters N = 14 Depressive N = 14	Interview	Attempters experienced more independent events exits in year before attempt, particularly between onset of depression and attempt.

Table 1.

Controlled Comparison of Life Events and Suicide Attempts (continued)

Controls	Sample Size	Method	Findings
Luscomb et al (1980)	Male attempters N = 47 Psychiatric patients N = 51	Self report Checklist	More events, perceived stress, high stress events exits, desirable, undesirable events. In previous year, no attempter-control differences under age 35.
O'Brien & Farmer (1980)	Overdosers N = 197 General practice attenders N = 152	Interview	Higher rates in previous 6 weeks for most events. Fall off on one year follow-up.
Levi et al (1966)	Suicide attempters N = 40 Suicidal feelings N = 40 Non-suicidal N = 40	Interview Separations only	Attempters experienced more separations in last year. Suicidal feelings intermediate.
Stein et al (1974)	Suicide attempters N = 165 Other psychiatric N = 165	Interview Separations only	Attempters experienced more separations in last year. Significant except for black women where suggestive.
Greer et al (1966)	Suicide attempters N = 146 Other psychiatric N = 148 Medical controls N = 148	Interview only disrupted interpersonal relationships	Attempters experienced more disruption in last 6 months than either groups. Psychiatric controls intermediate.

Table 1 concluded.

111

STUDIES OF RECENT LIFE EVENTS AND COMPLETED SUICIDE

Study	Sample	Comparison Group	Method	Findings
General Population Controls				
Bunch (1972)	Suicides N = 75	General Population N = 75	Interview of informants. Bereavement only	More loss of parents spouse in previous 2 years. Males, especially unmarried more vulnerable to loss of mother.
MacMahon & Pugh (1985)	Suicides N = 320	Non-suicidal deaths N = 320	Death Certificates of spouses	Clustering of subject death by suicide in 4 years following spouse death, especially previous year.
Hagnell & Rosman (1980)	Suicides N = 28	Natural deaths N = 25 General population controls N = 50	Sources unclear	More changes of living conditions, work problems and object loss than general population in last year: more object loss than natural death.
Psychiatric Patient Controls				
Humphrey (1977)	Psychiatric patient suicides on followup N = 98 (Males only)	Homicidal offenders N = 62 Neurotic patients N = 76	Psychological autopsy, life histories and hospital charts	More losses, not all recent, than in neurotics. Homicides intermediate.
Pokorny & Kaplan (1976)	Male psychiatric patient suicides N = 20	Patients who did not commit suicide N = 20	Interview with relative relative	More adverse events after discharge, particularly where higher defenseless, probably reflecting depression, during hospitalization.
Borg & Stahl (1982)	Psychiatric patient suicides N = 34	Patients who did not commit suicide N = 34	Case records	No significant difference although tendency to more deaths.
Fernando & Storm (1984)	Patient suicides N = 22	Non-suicide patients N = 22	Case records	More losses.

Table 2.

RELATIVE RISKS IN COMPARISONS OF LIFE EVENTS IN SUICIDAL AND GENERAL POPULATION SAMPLES

Author	Time Period	Event	Event Rates Patient	Event Rates Controls	Relative Odds
Suicide					
Bunch (1972)	2 years	Bereavement	7/95	7/150	6.5
Hagnell & Rorsman (1980)	1 year	Work problems	14/28	10/56	4.6
		Object loss	11/28	4/56	8.4
Suicide Attempts					
Paykel et al (1975)	6 months	Undesirable events	32/53	21/53	6.0
	1 month	Any event	37/53	10/53	10.0

Table 3.

113

Studies of Early Loss in Adult Suicide Attempters

Study	Sample	Comparison Sample	Type of Loss	Findings
General Population Controls				
Greer et al (1966)	Suicide attempters N = 156	Non-suicidal psychiatric patients N = 156 Medical patients N = 156	Death of parent under 15 Separation, divorce under 15	Greater incidence than both comparison groups. Greater incidence than both comparison groups. Particularly under 4, and loss of both parents.
Crook & Raskin (1975)	Depressives with history of suicide attempt N = 115	Non-suicidal depressives N = 115 General population controls N = 285	Death of parent under 12. Loss for at least one year due to separation, divorce, desertion.	No difference. Higher incidence in suicidal.
Goldney (1981)	Female suicide attempters aged 18-30 N = 110	Women attending a community health centre (N = 25)	Death under 16 Divorce, separation	No significant difference. More loss in suicidal.
Adam (1982)	Suicide attempters N = 98	General practice controls (N = 102)	Deaths under 25 Divorce, separation	No significant difference. Significantly higher in suicidal.
Psychiatric Patients Controls				
Farberow (1950)	Suicide attempters N = 32 Suicide threat (N = 32)	Non-suicidal patients (N = 32)	Permanent loss under 19	No significant difference overall. More loss before 6.
Moss & Hamilton (1955)	Seriously suicidal inpatients (N = 50)	Potentially suicidal inpatients N = 50 Non-suicidal patients N = 50	Permanent loss in early life	60% in seriously suicidal vs 15% in each comparison group.
Walton (1958)	Psychiatric patients with suicide attempt or threat N = 60	Non-suicidal patients N = 60	Temporary loss under 15	Significantly more.
Bruhn (1962)	Suicide attempters N = 91	Psychiatric outpatients N = 91 Non-suicidal psychiatric inpatients N = 50	Temporary loss under 15	More loss in suicidal.
Greer (1966)	Neurotic or sociopathic patients with history of attempt N = 81	Other neurotic or sociopathic patients N = 385	All loss for 1 year under 15. Death	More loss.. Both over 30 and under 30. More loss (p < .06)
Gay & Tonge (1967)	Psychiatric patients with history of suicide attempts N = 111	Non-suicidal psychiatric patients N = 382	Separation for at least six months prior to 15	More loss in suicide attempters.

Table 4.

SEXUAL IDENTITY ISSUES

Joseph Harry, Ph.D., Associate Professor, Department of Sociology, Northern Illinois University, De Kalb, Illinois

Study Selection Criteria

In this literature review, it was necessary to create several criteria for selection of studies and for emphasis of certain types of studies.

1. Since much of the literature dealing with sexuality and suicide does not specifically focus on adolescent or youthful populations, it was decided to include all studies dealing with the relationship between suicide and a particular aspect of sexuality. Whereas this decision increased the number of studies to be reviewed, the final result was largely a study of youth suicide. This arose because many studies of sexuality are also studies of the young.

2. Those studies with control groups have been given greatest emphasis. However, single-group studies are also included.

3. Primary emphasis was given to studies of attempted and completed suicide with less attention to suicidal gestures, suicidal ideation, or self-mutilation.

4. Little attention has been given to clinical observations, interpretations, and studies reporting one or two cases.

Homosexuality

The literature clearly and consistently shows that homosexuals of both sexes attempt suicide much more often than do heterosexuals. Saghir and Robins found that 7 percent of their 89 homosexual males and none of the 35 heterosexual controls had attempted suicide (1). The respective percent-ages among the female groups were 12 (N=57) and 5 (N=43). All four groups generally studied young people in their twenties or thirties. In a much larger study in which the four comparison groups were matched on age, race, and education, Bell and Weinberg found the following percentages of subjects who had ever attempted suicide: homosexual men, 18 percent (N=686); heterosexual men, 3 percent (N=337); lesbians, 23 percent (N=293); heterosexual women, 14 percent (N=140) (2). Similar significant (ANOVA) differences in their histories of suicide attempts have been found in comparing lesbian and nonlesbian female prisoners, although means or percentages were not presented (3).

Turning to studies of clinical populations, one study of 500 psychiatric outpatients found that 50 percent of 12 homosexuals compared with 13 percent of 488 non-homosexual patients had attempted suicide (4). A 6 to 12 year followup study of these patients reported that two of the homosexuals had committed suicide (5). This suicide rate was 17 times greater than the age- and sex-specific death rate for that State. Another study of 60 homosexual men with a mean age of 20 found that 32 percent had attempted suicide at least once (6). As might be expected, the percentages who had attempted suicide are higher among the clinical than among the nonclinical populations.

The literature also speaks clearly to the nature of suicide attempts by homosexuals, although that differs by gender. Five of the six homosexual male attempters reported by Saghir and Robins had made their attempts before the age of 20 during conflict with family members or within themselves over their incipient homosexuality (1). Five of the seven lesbian attempters had made their attempts during their twenties during a depression following the break-up of a relationship. Bell and Weinberg similarly report that homosexual men in their study generally attempted suicide at an earlier age than the lesbians (2). The homosexual men were more likely to report that their attempts were related to trying to deal with their homosexuality than was the case for the lesbians, whose attempts were more related to the break-ups of relationships.

The above data indicate that the period of coming to an acceptance of one's homosexuality--"coming out"--is a period that may be accompanied by a heightened risk of suicide attempts. The average age of coming out among homosexual men has been found to be 18 or 19; (7,8,9) this seems to coincide with the time when homosexual men are at risk of attempts. Two studies of large nonclinical populations of homosexuals have reported that just under half of the respondents agreed with the item: "Before I came out, the idea that I might be homosexual troubled me a lot" (8,10). In a recent study more intensively analyzing the Bell and Weinberg data, Harry found that, among the homosexual men, being troubled over one's homosexuality during adolescence was related to subsequent suicide attempts (11). Among the men of both sexual orientations, childhood cross-gender behaviors were related to attempts. Among all four study groups, being a loner during adolescence and general adolescent unhappiness were related to attempts. It thus seems that a number of the pre-adult characteristics and experiences of homosexuals may create special difficulties for them and that, for some, suicide may seem preferable to other solutions. Studies suggest that trying to grow up homosexual in a culture organized for heterosexuality likely contributes to many of the problems of these troubled youths.

Confusion Over Sexual Identity

The topic of confusion over sexual identity has been here interpreted to mean transsexuals. Although it could also refer to the case of young homosexuals attempting to accommodate themselves to their sexual orientation, that has been dealt with in the previous section. All except one of the studies dealing with transsexuals and suicide are single-group studies lacking a control group. In the one exception, male transsexuals still living as males had made significantly more suicide attempts than male transsexuals living as females, homosexual psychiatric patients, homosexual non-patients, and heterosexual nonpatients (12). Also, the two transsexual groups were significantly higher in suicidal thoughts than were the other three groups. The sample sizes in this study ranged from 19 to 25.

Turning to the single-group studies, Walinder reported that 20 percent of 30 Swedish male transsexuals and 8 percent of 13 female transsexuals had made attempts (13). These percentages should be considered minimum estimates because the author only reported attempts documented in hospital records, thereby excluding those not leaving such records. Another study of 72 English transsexuals (55 men and 17 women) reported that 53 percent had made attempts. Four (5.7 percent) had completed suicide (14). Person and Ovesey reported that six of ten male transsexual patients were preoccupied with suicidal thoughts and two had made attempts (15).

Although these studies dealing with transsexuals either lack a control group or do not report means or percentages of those who had made attempts, the percentages available indicate that transsexuals may be at higher risk for suicide attempts than other groups at risk, e.g., homosexuals, and much higher than the general population. As a matter of caution when discussing the attempts of transsexuals, it is important to distinguish between past attempts and threats, attempts, and self-mutilation to induce a therapist to undertake desired medical actions. Such threats and acts seem to be fairly common among clinical transsexuals. However, as far as possible, such attempts have not been included in the percentages cited above.

Acquired Immune Deficiency Syndrome (AIDS), AIDS-Related Complex (ARC)

Since the phenomenon of AIDS is quite new and since the associated medical prospects are frequently changing, little can be said about the relationship of AIDS to suicide attempts or completions. Approximately 70 to 75 percent of persons with AIDS or ARC are male homosexuals. However, there have been cases reported of both attempts and completions (16,17,18). Also, one homosexual man who had been unsuccessful with suicide attempts devised an interesting–and successful–means: having sex with persons known to have AIDS (19).

With our current medical knowledge of AIDS as a classical terminal illness, one might expect suicide and attempts. If attempts and completions are not directly due to the medical aspects of AIDS, they may also be the indirect result of societal reaction to the individual with AIDS. For example, one homosexual man with AIDS attempted suicide after his employer fired him for having the illness (18). Similarly, AIDS can result in evictions, loss of a lover, and loss of a sex life. AIDS can also effect an involuntary disclosure of an individual's homosexuality to others. Hence, these indirect effects of the illness potentially could enhance the possibility of suicide. No information is currently available on any link between ARC and suicide.

Sexual Inhibition or Promiscuity

Computer searches of the SIEC data base, Psychological Abstracts, and Medline facilities produced nothing on this topic. One study suggested a relationship between promiscuity and suicide attempts in a population of 105 adolescents who were pregnant (20). The 14 (13 percent) who had attempted suicide during the two years following pregnancy were more likely to have had a venereal disease. While the presence of venereal disease indirectly suggests promiscuity, the 14 attempters were also significantly more likely to be single and have a number of other problems. Hence, isolating these girls' sexual activity as a contributory factor in their attempts should be viewed with extreme caution.

Victims of Physical and Sexual Assault

The strongest relationship between suicide attempts and physical abuse was reported in an Australian study comparing 20 suicidal and 50 nonsuicidal children under 14 from a child psychiatric hospital (21). Sixty percent of the suicidal children versus 4 percent of the nonsuicidal had been subjected to parental physical abuse; 65 percent versus 4 percent had also witnessed physical fights between their parents. However since one is more likely to be interested in predicting from abuse to attempts, rather than the reverse, these percentages should be made in the other direction. In that case, the percentage among the abused who were suicidal was 86 versus 14 among the nonabused. Viewed in this way, these data appear to show a massive and significant association between abuse and suicidality. However, this association is very likely an artifact of the clinical populations studied. Suicidal children are probably much more likely than nonsuicidal ones to come to clinical attention with problems. Also, abused children are probably more likely to come to clinical attention than are nonabused children with problems. Children who are both abused and suicidal are thus more likely to come to clinical attention than either the simply abused, the simply suicidal, or children who are neither. Hence, abused **and** suicidal children will be far over-represented in clinical populations and thus suggest an apparent association even when none may exist in the general population. These data suggest that clinical populations may be very inappropriate for studying the association between two phenomena when **both** of those phenomena are major correlates of, or criteria for, admission to a clinical population.

Another study compared 60 abused children, 30 neglected ones, and 30 nonclinical children (22). Their respective rates of self-destructive behaviors were 41 percent, 17 percent, and 7 percent. The percentage among the abused who had made attempts was 8.5 (figures for the other two groups were not given). Again, since both self-destructive behaviors and abuse are both likely to be brought to either clinical or official attention, the reported associations may well overstate the strengths of the true associations.

The studies of sexual abuse and suicidal behaviors are also from clinical populations. Herman and Hirschman compared 40 women who had had incestual relationships with their fathers, with 20 women who had had seductive, but not incestual, relationships with their fathers (23). The women in both groups were private psychiatric patients. The researchers found that 38 percent of the former and 5 percent of the latter had attempted suicide; the difference was statistically significant. A single-group study of sexually abused girls from 201 families served by a protective service agency found that eight girls (4 percent) from these families had also attempted suicide (24). All attempts occurred when the girls were 14 to 16 years old. Since the families of these girls were generally chaotic and conflictful, it is difficult to attribute direct causality to the abusive behaviors of their fathers. Also, the percentages of attempts in this study and the one previously mentioned (22) are not particularly high when compared with groups discussed earlier. Although there may be a relationship between sexual abuse and suicide attempts, these studies cannot show one.

A study comparing 25 women who had been raped several times with 92 women who had been raped once indicates a possible relationship between suicide attempts and being multiply raped (25). All subjects were from a hospital rape center. The multiply raped women were significantly more likely to have attempted suicide (52 percent vs 16 percent), to be younger, poorer, loners, immigrants to the city, and to have had more psychiatric treatment. Although there may be an association between multiple rape and attempts, attribution of causality here is clouded because of the apparently disorganized histories of the multiply raped victims. Both their suicides and rapes may be symptoms of disorganized personal histories. A suggestive study of 13 young (18 to 23 years) military servicemen who had been raped by other military personnel found that two (15 percent) had made subsequent suicide attempts out of feelings of deflation of their manhood (26). A study of prison sexual violence in New York State men's prisons found that 38 percent of 107 inmates who had received verbal threats to physical assault for sex had made suicidal gestures (27). This percentage was more than twice that among 45 sexual aggressors recorded in inmate files and 17 times that among nonharrassed prisoners. These data provide some presumptive evidence that, at least among young males, being subjected to same-sex sexual harrassment or abuse in situations where there is little escape may precipitate suicide attempts. However, it is possible that those prone to suicide may also be subjected to more threats and assaults.

Pregnancy-Related Suicidality

It is very difficult to conclude anything about the association between suicide and pregnancy because of the diverse types of studies, the varying definitions of the term "pregnancy-related," the lack of adequate controls for age, and the small sample sizes.

1. Types of Studies. The studies divide into those that show the percentage of pregnancies among attempters, those that show the percentage of attempters among the pregnant, those with adequate control

groups, and those of completed suicides.

2. Definitions of "Pregnancy-Related." The definitions include pregnant during a suicide or attempt, postpartum attempts or suicides, belief that the attempter was pregnant, and overdue menstuation. These varying definitions make any conclusions from this literature almost impossible.

3. Controls for Age. Since suicide completers are generally middle-aged to old and both attempters and pregnant women are generally young, controls for age--and fairly precise ones--are mandatory.

The above-listed problems occur in the scientific literature about pregnancy and suicide in many, if not all, possible combinations. Below, we proceed through the most common groupings.

Attempts Among the Pregnant. One study of 105 pregnant girls under 18 at an urban hospital found that 14 (13.3 percent) had attempted suicide at least once during a 2-year followup (20). Clearly, these attempts are postpartum and beyond. The attempters were significantly more likely to be single, Catholic, to have had venereal disease, and to have come from higher socioeconomic areas. This study lacks a control group of adolescent nonpregnant girls.

Pregnancies Among Attempters. Comparing 30 pregnant attempters with 453 non-pregnant attempters from Australia, Whitlock and Edwards concluded that since 6 percent of suicidal women are pregnant compared with 7 percent of women who are pregnant in the population at any given time, pregnancy is not a predictor or inhibitor of suicide attempts (28). In their study, the pregnant women were less likely to be married than the nonpregnant (53 percent vs 41 percent). Teicher found that "Twenty-two percent of all suicide-attempting girls compared to zero percent of control girls were either pregnant or believed themselves to be pregnant" (29,30). It is difficult to determine the sample size on which this 22 percent figure is based because the various publications describing this study leave it unclear as to whether the number in the sample, which was three-quarters female, was 20, 48, or 68.

Pregnancies Among Attempters and Controls. It seems that in only two studies did the researchers bother to obtain a nonclinical control group matched for age with the attempters. Jacobs compared 50 adolescent attempters, of whom 38 were female, with 22 female age-matched adolescent nonattempters (22). Matches were made on age, race, sex, and maternal education. The data showed that 21 percent of the attempters were either pregnant or believed themselves to be at the time of the attempt compared with none of the controls. Since the figure of 21 percent is very close to Teicher's figure of 22 percent in the previous study and since the two authors worked together, it is unclear if they are actually describing different sets of respondents. The 22 or 21 percent figures of these studies are much higher than the figure of 6 percent of attempters who are pregnant reported by Whitlock and Edwards. However, since the former studies include both real and suspected pregnancies while the Whitlock and Edwards study includes only real pregnancies, no conclusions can be drawn.

Birtchell and Floyd compared 107 female attempters with 110 female nonattempters with a control for age (32). Of the attempters, 12.1 percent compared with 2.7 percent among the nonattempters, were either pregnant or overdue in their menstrual cycles. Ten (77 percent) of the 13 pregnant attempters were unmarried. Because the definition of "pregnancy-related" employed in this study includes being menstrually overdue, comparison with the immediately preceding three studies is, once again, impossible.

Studies of Completed Suicide. A study of completed suicides in Minnesota for the years 1950-1965 found that 1 percent (14/1019) of female suicides were pregnant (33). The study reported that suicides per 100,000 population were 16 for men and 4 for women during this period. For pregnant women, suicides were close to 1 per 100,000 live births (14/92,982). None of these 14 pregnant women were unmarried. The author concluded that pregnancies during suicide were extremely low and that pregnancy served as a protector against suicide. Ten of the 14 pregnancy-related suicides in this study occurred postpartum. While this further reinforces the author's conclusion, it also suggests that the postpartum period may be the time of greatest, although still extremely low, risk. It should be noted from this study that using live births as a proxy for the number of pregnant women is a more accurate denominator than using the total universe of women in the reproductive age range (15 to 45).

A later study disputing the conclusion that pregnancy is an inhibitor of suicide presented data on 8 pregnancy-related suicides among a total of 47 suicides in New Mexico (34). Twelve and a half percent (4/32) of female suicides of ages 15 to 34 were pregnant. This age range was provided by the authors to coincide better with the principal years of childbearing. While the 12.5 percent figure is considerably higher than that from the Minnesota study, the numerator (four) is so low that the percentage is extremely unstable from a sampling viewpoint. It should be noted that all of the eight women who completed suicides were married and that their means of suicide were principally guns and hanging.

Despite the dreary inconclusiveness of the various studies on pregnancy-related suicides, one finding does emerge. Most pregnant attempters are single, whereas most pregnant completers are married (20,29,32,33,34). Also, the means of suicide for the single attempters are drugs primarily whereas the means for the completers are mainly guns and hanging. These data suggest that the two groups are different populations, although with some overlap. Hence, being in a pregnant population at risk of attempt may only marginally affect the risk of completing suicide.

Conclusions

Homosexuality. Homosexuals of both sexes are two to six times more likely to attempt suicide than are heterosexuals. Data on completed suicide do not exist. Kinsey et al. estimated that 10 percent of all males and 1/3 to 1/2 that of females are predominantly homosexual (35,36). However, because Kinsey's data included large numbers of prisoners, Gebhard later revised Kinsey's estimates to 4 percent of white males with at least some college education and 1 to 2 percent among all adult females (37). The data show that these two populations are markedly at risk of attempted suicide during late adolescence and early adulthood.

Confusion Over Sexual Identity. Whereas studies with adequate control groups are lacking, the percentages from the single-group studies strongly suggest that transsexuals may be an extremely high risk group for attempted suicide. Adequate data do not exist for completed suicide.

AIDS. Only case reports exist. However, there are strong reasons to suspect that suicidal behavior may be very common among AIDS sufferers.

Sexual Inhibition or Promiscuity. There has been no research on this topic. If research is undertaken, it is important to attend to the sexual behaviors of both men and women to prevent continued bias on labeling of promiscuous behavior in reference to women only.

Victims of Physical or Sexual Abuse. Although the data on this topic come mainly from single-group studies, there does not appear to be a markedly high rate of attempts among abuse victims. The two groups of abuse victims in which there might be an elevated rate are women who have been raped on several occasions and men who have been raped, or sexually assaulted by other men.

Pregnancy-Related Suicide. The literature on this topic is too conflicting in its findings to conclude anything. However, the two subgroups who may be at risk are single pregnant women and married postpartum women. The former group may be at risk of attempts, while the latter group may be at risk of completing.

Recommendations for Future Research

Control Groups. We need control groups to determine whether a given population has a high or low risk for suicide.

Nonclinical Control Groups. While comparing suicidal with nonsuicidal patients is convenient, it can only show that one specially defined population may differ from another specially defined population.

In the case discussed earlier where one examines the association between attempts and some other clinical characteristic, both of which serve as criteria for becoming a clinical patient, it is likely that one may find totally false associations. When introduced to the clinical literature, such associations can mislead others into pursuing, or funding, lines of research that may be ultimately unprofitable, especially if pursued in clinical settings.

Nonclinical Experimental Groups. It would be most desirable to obtain both experimental and control groups from nonclinical populations through conventional methods of survey research. For example, it has been possible to profitably study family violence through survey methods, including even telephone surveys (38,39). Such research was an immense advance over earlier research of family violence based largely on clinical samples. Two major hurdles to conducting survey research on attempted or completed suicide come to mind. First, there is the intrinsic sensitivity of asking persons about the suicidal behaviors of themselves or of other family members. However, since it has proven possible to ask people in survey situations about the crimes they have committed, deviant sexual activities, and family violence, it should also prove possible to ask about suicide. Second, since attempted and completed suicide are infrequent-to-rare

events, the difficulty arises of obtaining sufficient numbers of such persons in a general survey to analyze. This difficulty can be overcome by focusing the survey on limited segments of the general population such as high school students or pregnant women. Also, the numbers for analysis can be increased by asking about suicidal behaviors not only of the respondent but also of a limited set of close relatives. This recommendation of survey research does not extend to possible research on AIDS or ARC and suicide since, given the infrequency of both of these phenomena, survey research on this topic without massive and expensive samples becomes impossible. However, given the considerable potential of AIDS as both a direct and indirect cause of suicidal behavior, one would hope that research on the relationship be soon undertaken.

As a concrete example of my proposed form of research, I suggest a survey of the general population which includes a question on sexual orientation. To date this has not been done. Until the 1960s, and especially the 1970s, homosexuality was a topic studied largely by clinicians. Beginning with the works of Evelyn Hooker, there began a continuing stream of studies based on nonclinical samples of homosexuals, the results of which differed much from those reported by clinicians (40). However, all studies of homosexuals to date still involve non-probability samples, hence, estimates of rates of suicide can only be approximate (41). The time may be ripe for a survey of the general population that includes a question, possibly placed among the demographic items, on sexual orientation. This would permit more accurate, if still imperfect, estimates of the true risk of suicidal behaviors among such populations.

REFERENCES

1. Saghir M, Robins E: Male and female homosexuality. Baltimore: Williams and Wilkins, 1973; 118-, 276-277.

2. Bell A, Weinberg M: Homosexualities. New York: Simon and Schuster, 1978:450.

3. Clermont C, Ervin F, Rollins A, Plutchik R, Batinelli C: Epidemiological studies of female prisoners: Homosexual behaviors. J. Nerv. Ment. Dis. 1977; 164:25-29.

4. Woodruff R, Clayton P, Guze S: Suicide attempts and psychiatric diagnoses. Dis. Nerv. Syst. 1972; 33:617-629.

5. Martin R, Cloninger R, Guze S, Clayton P: Mortality in a follow-up of 500 psychiatric outpatients. Arch. Gen. Psychiatry 1985; 42:58-66.

6. Roesler T, Deisher R: Youthful male homosexuality. JAMA 1972; 219:1018-1023.

7. Dank B: Coming out in the gay world. Psychiatry 1971; 34:180-197.

8. Harry J, DeVall W: The social organization of gay males. New York: Praeger 1978:64.

9. Troiden R: Becoming gay. (Dissertation). Stonybrook, NY: State University of New York, 1977. p. 183.

10. Harry J: Gay children grown up. New York: Praeger, 1982:134.

11. Harry J: Parasuicide, gender, and gender deviance. J. Hlth. and Social Behav. 1983; 24:350-361.

12. Langevin R, Paitich D, Steiner B: The clinical profile of male transsexuals living as females vs those living as males. Arch. Sex Behav. 1977; 6:143-154.

13. Walinder J: Transsexualism. Goteberg, Sweden: Scandinavian University Books, 1967.

14. Huxley J, Brandon S: Partnership in transsexualism, part I: Paired and non-paired groups. Arch. Sex Behav. 1981; 10:133-141.

15. Person, E, Ovesey L: The transsexual syndrome in males: I primary transsexualism. Am. J. Psychotherapy 1974; 28:4-21.

16. Anonymous: AIDS likely motive for double suicide. Edmonton Journal, Oct. 25, 1985 (Reuters).

17. Anonymous: Suicidal AIDS victim saved. San Francisco Chronicle, May 8, 1985.

18. Anonymous: Gay man with AIDS attempts suicide after being fired. Advocate, Jan. 21, 1986, Issue #438.

19. Frances R, Wikstrom T, Alcena V: Contracting AIDS as a means of committing suicide. Am. J. Psychiatry 1985; 142:656.

20. Gabrielson I, Klerman L, Currie J, Tyler N, Jekel J: Suicide attempts in a population pregnant as teenagers. Am. J. Public Health 1970; 60:2289-2301.

21. Kosky R: Childhood suicidal behavior in battered children. Am. J. Psychiatry 1983; 24:457-468.

22. Green A: Self-destructive behavior in battered children. Am. J. Psychiatry 1978; 135:579-582.

23. Herman J, Hirschman L: Families at risk for father-daughter incest. Am. J. Psychiatry 1981; 138:967-970.

24. Goodwin J: Suicide attempts in sexual abuse victims and their mothers. Child Abuse and Neglect 1981; 5:217-221.

25. Ellis E, Atkeson B, Calhoun K: An examination of differences between multiple- and single-incident victims of sexual assault. J. Abn. Psychol. 1982; 91:221-224.

26. Goyer P, Eddleman H: Same-sex rape of non-incarcerated men. Am. J. Psychiatry 1984; 141:576-579.

27. Lockwood D: Prison sexual violence. New York: Elsevier, 1980:66-70.

28. Whitlock F, Edwards E: Pregnancy and attempted suicide. Comprehensive Psychiatry 1968; 9:1-12.

29. Teicher J: A solution to the chronic problem of living: Adolescent attempted suicide. In: Schoolar J, ed. Current issues in adolescent psychiatry. New York: Brunner-Mazel, 1973:129-147.

30. Teicher J, Jacobs J: Adolescents who attempt suicide. Am. J. Psychiatry 1966; 122:1248-1257.

31. Jacobs J: Adolescent suicide. New York: Wiley, 1971:67-68.

32. Birtchnell J, Floyd S: Further menstrual chracteristics of suicide attempters. J. Psychosom. Res. 1975; 19:81-85.

33. Barno A: Criminal abortion deaths, illegitimate pregnancy deaths, and suicides in pregnancy. J. Obst. Gyn. 1967; 98:356-367.

34. Goodwin J, Harris D: Suicide in pregnancy: The Hedda Gabler syndrome. Suicide and Life-Threatening Behav. 1979; 9:105-115.

35. Kinsey A, Pomeroy W, Martin C: Sexual behaviors in the human male. Philadelphia: W.B. Saunders, 1948:651.

36. Kinsey A, Pomeroy W, Martin C, Gebhard P: Sexual behavior in the human female. Philadelphia: W.B. Saunders, 1953:473-474.

37. Gebhard P: Incidence of overt homosexuality in the United States and Western Europe. In: Livingood, J., ed. National Institute of Mental Health Task Force on Homosexuality, Final Report and Background Papers. Washington, DC:GPO, 1972:22-29.

38. Straus M, Gelles R, Steinmetz S: Behind closed doors. Garden City, NY: Doubleday, 1980.

39. Schulman M: A survey of spousal abuse against women in Kentucky. New York: Lou Harris Associates, 1979.

40. Hooker E: The adjustment of the male overt homosexual. J. Proj. Techniques 1957, 21:17-31.

41. Harry J: Sampling gay men. J. Sex Res. 1986; 22:21-34.

Risk Factors Potentially Associated with Adolescent Suicide or Attempted Suicide

Risk Factor	Citation	Outcome Variable	Experimental Group	Control Group	Results	Significance Tests*
Homosexuality	Bell, A., Weinberg, M. Homosexualities. New York, 1978, Simon & Schuster, p. 450	suicide attempts	686 gay males, 293 lesbians	337 straight males, 140 straight females	gay men, 18% straight men, 3%; lesbians, 23%; straight females, 14%	X^2
	Clement, C., Ervin, F., Rollins, A., Plutchik, R., Batinelli, C. Epidemiological studies of female prisoners: homosexual behaviors. J. Nerv Mental Dis 1977; 164:25-29.	suicide attempts	27 self-reported lesbians, 27 staff-identified lesbians in prison	27 straight women in prison	lesbians more, but figures not provided	ANOVA
	Harry, J. Parasuicide, gender, & gender deviance. J Health & Soc Behav 1983; 24:350-361.	suicide attempts	Same as Bell & Weinberg above	Same as Bell & Weinberg above	adolescent guilt over sexual feelings related to later attempts	Log-linear analyses
	Martin, R., Cleninger, R., Guze, S., Clayton, P., Mortality in a follow-up of 500 psychiatric outpatients. Arch Gen Psychiatry 1985; 42:58-66.	completed suicides	11 gay male outpatients	488 other outpatients	gays complete more suicides than other patients	X^2, Poisson
	Roesler, T., Deisher, R., Youthful male homosexuality. JAMA 1972; 219:1018-1023.	suicide attempts	60 young (16-22) gay males	none	32% made attempts	none
	Saghir, M., Robins, E., Male and female homosexuality. Baltimore: Williams & Wilkins, 1973; 118:276-277.	suicide attempts	89 gay men; 57 lesbians	35 straight men; 43 straight fem.s	gay men, 7%; straight men, 0%; lesbians, 12%; straight fem.s, 5%	X^2
	Woodruff, R., Clayton, P., Guze, S. Suicide attempts and psychiatric diagnoses. Dis of Nerv Sys 1972; 33:617-619.	suicide attempts	12 gay male outpatients	488 non-gay outpatients	gay men, 50%; others, 13%	none

Table 1.

Risk Factors Potentially Associated with Adolescent Suicide or Attempted Suicide

Risk Factor	Citation	Outcome Variable	Experimental Group	Control Group	Results	Significance Tests*
Transsexuals	Huxley, P., Kenna, J., Brandon, S. Partnerships in transsexualism, part I. Arch Sex Behav 1981; 10:133-141.	suicide attempts	72 English transsexuals	none	53% had attempted; 4 had completed	none
	Langevin, Paitich, D., Steiner, B. The clinical profile of male transsexuals living as males vs those living as females. Arch Sex Behav 1977; 6:143-154.	suicide attempts	25 transsexuals living as males; 19 transsexuals living as females; 20 gay patients	19 gay non-patients; 24 straight non-patients	both transsexual groups made more attempts than other groups; means, % not given	F-tests
	Wallinder, J. Transsexualism. Goteborg, Sweden: Scan University Books, 1967.	suicide attempts	30 male and 13 female transsexuals, all patients	none	males, 20%; females, 8% as recorded in Swedish hospitals	none
	Person, E. Ovesey, L. The transsexual syndrome: primary transsexualism. Am J Psychotherapy 1974; 28:4-21.	suicide attempts	10 male patient transsexuals	none	2 had made attempts	none
	Lockwood, D. Prison sexual violence. New York: Elsevier, 1980.	suicide gestures	107 targets of sexual harassment in men's prisons	45 sexual aggressors in men's prisons	targets more than twice as likely as aggressors to make suicidal gestures	none

Table 1 continued.

Risk Factors Potentially Associated with Adolescent Suicide or Attempted Suicide

Risk Factor	Citation	Outcome Variable	Experimental Group	Control Group	Results	Significance Tests*
Pregnancy-Related	Barno, A. Criminal abortion deaths, illegitimate Pregnancy in pregnancy. J Obst and Gyn 1967; 98:356-367.	completed suicide	14 pregnant suicides in Minn., 1950-1965	92,982 live births in Minn., 1950-1965	suicide rate of pregnant women is about 1/100,000	none
	Birtchnell, J., Floyd, S. Further menstrual characteristics of suicide attempters. J Psychosom Res 1975; 19:81-85.	suicide attempts	107 female attempters	110 female non-attempters matched for age	13% vs 3% of controls were pregnant or menstrually overdue	none
	Gabrielson, I., Klerman, L., Currie, J., Tyler, N., Jekel, J. Suicide attempts in a population pregnant as teenagers. Am J Public Health 1970; 60:2289-2301.	subsequent suicide attempts	105 under 18 pregnant patients	none	13.3% made attempts in 2 years after giving birth	none
	Goodwin, J., Harris, D. Suicide in pregnancy. Suicide and Life-Threatening Behav., 1979; 9:105-115.	completed suicide during pregnancy or postpartum	8 pregnant or postpartum suicides in New Mexico	47 female suicides in New Mexico	17% female suicides are pregnant or postpartum	none
	Jacobs, J. Adolescent suicide. New York: Wiley, 1971; 87-88.	pregnant or believed self to be	38 adolescent female attempters	22 female age-matched controls	21% vs 0% of female controls were pregnant or believed self to be	none
	Teicher, J. A solution to the chronic problem of living: adolescent attempted suicide. In: Schooler, J. Current issues in adolescent psychiatry. New York: Brunner-Mazel, 1973: 129-147.	pregnant or believed self to be	female adolescent attempters; N = 20 or 48 or 68	22 female adolescents	22% versus 0% of controls were pregnant	none
	Whitlock, F., Edwards, E. Pregnancy and attempted suicide. Comprehensive Psychiatry 1968; 9:1-12.	being pregnant	30 pregnant attempters in Australia	453 nonpregnant attempters in Australia	6% of attempters are pregnant vs 7% of all women in Australia aged 15-45	none

Table 1 continued.

Risk Factors Potentially Associated with Adolescent Suicide or Attempted Suicide

Risk Factor	Citation	Outcome Variable	Experimental Group	Control Group	Results	Significance Tests*
Physical and Sexual Abuse	Ellis, E., Atkeson, B., Calhoun, K. An examination of differences between multiple- and single-incident victims of sexual assault. J Abn Psychol 1982; 91:221-224.	suicide attempts	25 women raped more than once; hospital patients at rape center	92 women raped once; also patients at rape center	52% earlier attempts vs 16% in control group	x^2
	Goodwin, J. Suicide attempts in sexual abuse victims. Child Abuse & Neglect 1981; 5:217-221.	suicide attempts	8 children from 201 families with sexually abused daughters	none	4% had made attempts after abuse	none
	Goyer, P., Eddleman, H. Same-sex rape of non-incarcerated men. Am J Psychiatry 1984; 141:576-579.	subsequent suicide attempts	13 young (18-23) servicemen raped by other servicemen	none	15% made subsequent attempts	none
	Green, A., Self-destructive behavior in battered children. Am J Psychiatry 1978; 135:579-582.	suicide attempts	60 battered children	30 neglected children; 30 normal children	8.5% of battered made attempts; sign. difference, but data on other groups not given	ANOVA
	Herman, J., Hirschman, L. Families at risk for father-daughter incest. Am J Psychiatry 1981; 138:967-970.	suicide attempts	40 female patients with paternal incest	20 female patients with seductive fathers	38% vs 5% of controls and attempted suicide	none
	Kosky, R. Childhood suicidal behavior. J Child Psychol & Psychia & Allied Disciplines 1983; 24:457-468.	physical abuse	20 "suicidal" children patients under 14 in Australia	50 other child patients under 14 in Australia	60% had been abused vs 4% of controls; significant	x^2

*Where significant tests are indicated differences were significant at the .05 level.
However, in studies involving more than 2 groups, not all differences among all groups are necessarily significant.

Table 1 concluded.

"MAJOR PSYCHIATRIC DISORDERS" AS RISK FACTORS IN YOUTH SUICIDE

Maria Kovacs, Ph.D., Department of Psychiatry, Western Psychiatric Institute and Clinic, University of Pittsburgh School of Medicine, Pittsburgh, Pennsylvania

Joaquim Puig-Antich, M.D., Department of Psychiatry, Western Psychiatric Institute and Clinic, University of Pittsburgh School of Medicine, Pittsburgh, Pennsylvania

The aim of this review is to assess whether major psychiatric disorders constitute risk factors in youth suicide. As the data on this matter are limited, we have chosen to present succinct reviews of three different sources of information that can illuminate this relationship, namely: (1) the types of psychiatric diagnoses found among youths who have completed suicide, (2) psychiatric diagnoses among youth who attempted suicide, and (3) the relationship between familial aggregation of suicidal behaviors and familial aggregation of major psychiatric disorders. The limitations of each data source and of each group of studies will be discussed in each section.

Psychiatric disorders and youth suicide

The strongest evidence about the suicide risk posed by psychiatric illness would have to come from **prospective** studies of clearly defined psychiatric cohorts. Ideally, such a study would entail at least two different diagnostic samples; a suitable, psychiatrically unaffected group of controls; and a period of followup sufficient for the outcome of interest (suicide) to occur. Alternatively, a **retrospective** study of a consecutive, unselected sample of young people who had died by suicide could provide data about the incidence of various psychiatric disorders among them. But, the resultant figures are best interpreted against base rates derived from demographically comparable populations. Finally, the retrospective, case-controlled study of select samples of youth suicides could shed light on the contributing role of mental illness. Strictly speaking, however, both the latter approaches identify correlates or associated features of suicide.

Although there has been increasing concern about youth suicide in the United States and other countries (1-5), the evidence about its association with specific psychiatric diagnoses is neither scientifically unassailable nor unequivocal. The scarcity of conclusive data is partly a reflection of the enormous technical, practical, and ethical problems that are inherent in the study of suicide, including the extremely low base rate of its occurrence. Additionally, data from earlier publications cannot be readily interpreted because, in the last 15 years, there have been substantial changes in the use of psychiatric diagnoses in juvenile cohorts. Nonetheless, the available findings are clinically alarming and suggest that major psychiatric disorders play an important role in youth suicide.

Suicide among psychiatrically ill youth: Prospective studies

The mere fact of "patienthood" is apparently

associated with a higher than expected rate of suicide across the age span. Morrison (6), whose database consisted of 12,104 patients (age range not given) treated over an 8-year interval (1972-1980) by a San Diego-based private practice group, computed the cohorts suicide rate by age and sex (controlling for years of followup). As shown in Table 1, the patients had a consistently higher suicide rate than similarly aged males and females in the general county population. This higher rate was most marked for patients aged 19 or younger, who committed suicide at roughly 40 times the expected rate.

There is evidence that suicide among youths is associated with certain major psychiatric disorders more than with others. Welner et al (7) reported on the 8 to 10 year followup status of 77 psychiatric inpatients whose index hospitalization occurred between 1965 and 1968, at a mean age of 16. On followup, a comprehensive interview verified initial diagnoses, according to the Feighner criteria. The data were gathered from the patients, significant others, or records of rehospitalizations. The authors provided the number of cases in each diagnostic group who committed suicide over the followup interval. Using these figures, we computed the number of suicides in a followup year, and then, the portion of each diagnostic group who committed suicide in a year. Then, we multiplied the resultant figure by 100,000 to estimate the **rough suicide rate** per 100,000 diagnostic population per year. Please note that these rates are only "rough estimates" in part, because inpatients may not represent the entire population of cases with a given diagnosis. We realize the shortcomings of this method, but the rates are easier to compare this way.

As Table 2 indicates, schizophrenia, bipolar affective illness, and primary unipolar depression in adolescence were associated with astonishingly high rates of suicide (the table does **not** include the "alcoholism only" diagnosis, because there were only two such cases, nor six others who had a variety of different diagnoses). It is of interest here that

there were no suicides among the "antisocial personality" cases, although each had concomitant alcohol and drug abuse and most (7 out of 9) were hospitalized because of "depressive symptoms and suicide attempts."

We used the same computational procedure on data from King and Pittman (8) data who determined the 6-year followup status of 65 consecutively admitted patients (aged 12 to 19). This group was an earlier cohort from the same university hospital that provided cases in the study of Welner et al., with index admissions from mid-1959 to mid-1960. Followup status was ascertained via structured interviews with the patients themselves, adult informants, and/or hospital records. The diagnoses (listed in Table 3) were derived according to symptomatic criteria specified by the authors. On followup, all available data were used to determine the diagnoses. However, the findings were presently only for 51 cases who fell into two general categories: affective disorders (n = 26) and "other" disorders (n = 25). The one case of suicide was a patient whose diagnosis was "organic brain syndrome." This study is notable because it illustrates changes in diagnostic practices and/or in the actual manifestations of psychopathology. For example, the authors specifically stated that none of the patient met criteria for "addiction and alcoholism." In contrast, in a current inpatient adolescent sample, one is far more likely to

Suicide Rates in a Sample of Psychiatrically Hospitalized Adolescents at 6-Year Follow-up (Adapted from King & Pittman, 1970)			
		Suicide/Year	
Diagnosis/n	n	No.	Rate
Affective disorder (depression/mania)	26	–	–
Schizophrenia/ schizophreniform syndrome	5	–	–
Organic syndromes (OBS, convulsive disorder, Sydenham's chorea)	12	.166	1,388/ 100,000
Sociopathic personality	4	–	–
Other	4	–	–

Table 3.

128

Suicide Rates in a Sample of Private Practice Patients and in the Corresponding General San Diego County Population
(Adapted from Morrison, 1984)

| Age/Sex | Rate/100,000/Year | |
	Patients	County Pop.
0-19		
Female	63.05	1.66
Male	173.01	3.99
20-24		
Female	80.61	10.71
Male	205.66	23.17

Table 1.

Suicide Rates in a Sample of Psychiatrically Hospitalized Adolescents
(Adapted from Welner et al., 1979)

Diagnosis at Follow-up (n; $\bar{X}$ age at onset)	Follow-up Length ($\bar{X}$)	Suicide/Year No.*	Rate/100,000
Schizophrenia (13; 14.5 yrs)	8.5 yrs		
Female (7)		.00	—
Male (6)		.235	3,921
Bipolar Affective (12; 15 yrs)	9.0 yrs		
Female (3)		.00	—
Male (9)		.333	3,700
Unipolar, Primary Depression (16; 15 yrs)	10.0 yrs		
Female (10)		.01	1,000
Male (6)		.00	—
Antisocial Personality (9; ?)	?		
Female (4)		.00	—
Male (6)		.00	—
No Mental Illness (8; ?)	?		
Female (6)		.00	—
Male (2)		.00	—
Undiagnosed Illness (8; ?) (probably adjustment reaction)	?		
Female (?)		.00	—
Male (?)		.00	—

? = data not given; *rounded to nearest digit

Table 2.

find the latter conditions than "organic syndromes."

Based on an average of 3 years of followup (up to June 1970) of 227 drug-using adolescent girls who had been admitted to a remand home in London during 1966-1968, Noble et al. (9) assessed the outcome and correlates of this condition. Using those data, Miles (10) computed the cohorts suicide rate as 3,500/100,000/year. However, a careful reading of the original publication reveals this rate to be suspect because the suicides were cited for all admissions commencing in 1964—which was 2 years before the study sample's admission date--and included deaths up to one year after the cut-off date for the study samples followup (p .501). Moreover, the number of all admitted cases was not provided.

We will close this section by noting three other studies which underscore that the likelihood of suicide being detected varies with the length of followup and the nature of sample, including the type of diagnosis. For example, Annesley (11) who described the 2 to 5 year followup status of 362 previously hospitalized adolescents (aged 7 to 18), reported no suicides among them. This was particularly notable because the admission diagnoses were wide-ranging, covering various psychotic disorders, sociopathy (i.e., "behavior disorders"), neuroses, and obsessional states. Likewise, Strober and Carlson (12), who conducted a 3 to 4 year followup of 60, hospitalized, depressed adolescents (diagnosed according to RDC), aged 13 to 16 years, found no suicide among them.

On the other hand, in a highly select sample, followed for a period ranging from 1 to 14 years, 2 out of 28 patients were found to have died by suicide (13). The patients, who had a diagnosis of manic-depressive illness, were specifically examined because their first attack occurred before age 19 at the mean age of 15 (range: 13-18). The patients entered the study as a result of having been hospitalized at a particular institution; the followup took place after the index the admission (mean age at followup: 41 years, range: 23 to 69 years). Again, using our rough computations, and taking the maximal followup interval (14 years), we obtain a frequency of .143 suicides/year in this group of 28, which then yields a suicide rate of 510/100,000/year.

Studies of youth suicides in the general population

The retrospective method of identifying psychiatric risk factors for suicide suffers from numerous constraints, including ascertainment and interviewer bias, incomplete databases, and probable distortions of historic information because of the informants' "need" to explain the suicidal act. Nonetheless, the findings do deserve consideration, although for youth suicides, estimated rates of mental illness are extremely variable, ranging from 92 percent (14) to 12 percent (15). All things considered, psychiatric disturbance seemed more likely to be detected if study investigators used more extensive or systematic information sources.

According to Rich and associates (14), "psychiatric illness is a necessary (but insufficient) condition for suicide." Using the San Diego Coroner's list for the period of November 1981 to June 1983, they located 133 consecutive cases of suicide under 30 years of age. These cases were compared with 150 consecutive cases aged 30 and older, sampled from November 1981 to September 1982. Multiple information sources were used (92% of the sample) to determine the most valid responses to an extensive, structured interview; then, consensual, DSM-III diagnoses were derived. Subsequently examined toxicology reports might be appended to the diagnoses. For our purposes, the interpretation of the findings were constrained because the data were grouped by cases aged "under 30" versus "over 30" and the exact age range was not reported. Although the second paper on this cohort (16), provided an age distribution by 5 and revealed that 44 percent ($\underline{n}$ = 59) of the 133 suicides were in the 25 to 29 age range, diagnosis data by age were not included. This is problematic because, for example, a particular diagnosis such as cocaine abuse may be more prevalent among persons 25 to 30 than under 25. Without more specific age by diagnosis data, the exact prevalence of a diagnosis among early adolescent suicides cannot be determined.

Nonetheless, as Table 4 indicates, 92 percent of those "under 30" had psychiatric diagnoses (comparable to 91% of the older cases), and substance abuse was very prevalent (much more so than among the older suicides). According to a subsequent report (16), altogether 53 percent of the younger cases had a diagnosis of substance abuse. Affective disorders were relatively frequent ($n = 47$), but less than in the contrast group ($n = 78$), and 52 percent of the "under 30" cases had a past history of psychiatric care. It should be pointed out, however, that the high overall rate of disturbance in this study's cohort included "minor" DSM-III conditions, such as "adjustment disorders" or dysthymia (which has been viewed as a form of "minor" depression). Moreover, the use of multiple diagnoses per case accounts for the large, absolute frequencies in Table 4.

Psychiatric Characteristics of 133 Younger Suicides (aged <30) in San Diego County (Adapted from Rich et al., 1986).	
Post-Mortem Diagnoses-DSM-III	N cases with Diagnoses*
Substance Use Disorder	?
Drug Use	88
Alcohol Use	72
Affective Disorders	47
Atypical Depression	32
Major Depression	9
Schizophrenic Disorder	6
Other Psychoses	16
Antisocial Personality	12
Any Diagnosis (92%)	122
Psychiatric Care (%)	
Past	52
At time of suicide	23

*Table does not include all the diagnoses that were listed.

Table 4.

Another methodologically complete study reported a very high rate of "psychiatric symptoms" and a notable incidence of psychiatric contacts among children who killed themselves; unfortunately, no diagnoses were provided (17). In this total population survey of suicides in England and Wales during 1962-1968, there were 30 unequivocal youth suicides (aged 12 to 14). Using coroner, school, psychiatric, and social service records, Shaffer (17) found that 30 percent of the victims ($n = 9$) had been in contact with a psychiatrist; 20 percent more ($n = 6$), although not referred to a psychiatrist, were recognized as having "conduct or emotional problems"; and all but 13 percent had "psychiatric symptoms" of the "antisocial," "emotional, affective," or "mixed" (emotional plus conduct) kind.

The foregoing findings were echoed by a recent study that combined the total population survey and case control methods (18). The Jefferson County (KY) coroner's office was used to locate all cases of youth suicides (aged ≤ 19 years) from January 1980 through June 1983; 24 cases (aged 12 to 19) were found, and their families were then contacted. The families of 20 (83%) agreed to cooperate. Extensive questionnaires, checklists, and inventories were used with families, friends, and relatives to determine the victim's psychologic profile. Similar data were collected on matched-pair controls (friends of the deceased). The 20 suicides differed from the 17 controls on the following variables of interest to us: frequent use of nonprescribed drugs or alcohol (70% vs. 29%, p <.02); having exhibited "antisocial behavior," including shoplifting, physical fights, or disciplinary problems in school (70% vs. 24%, p <.003); and having had previous psychiatric treatment (45% vs. 24%, p <.04). However, despite the high rate (65%) among the suicide cases of inhibited/withdrawn/overly sensitive "personality," they did not differ from the case-controls (25%) in this regard.

Although Bourque and associates (19) focused on long-term trends in suicides among females only, the data are useful to us because they are analyzed by age. In this methodologically careful study, the authors examined the coroner's records in Sacramento County (CA) over a 55-year period; both case ascertainment and data retrieval accuracy were verified. In the final tabulation, data on Asian and Black women were excluded because of the small sizes of these subsamples. The authors appeared confident in their findings particularly because, since the 1950s, the county coroner's staff has been trained to systematically gather data on several psychosocial variables. The variables of interest to this paper included: "despondency," "emotional problems," "alcoholism," or "drinking problem," and prior psychiatric treatments. The data for the most recent 10-year period (1970-1979) are the most pertinent. During that time, 40 females, aged 15 to 24, were identified as suicides, of whom 85 percent had shown evidence of despondency; 45 percent had emotional problems or "unbalance;" 5 percent had recent arrests; 25 percent had prior psychiatric treatment; none had evidenced problems with alcohol.

In contrast, Sathyavathi (15) found a low rate of "mental illness" among children who killed themselves in Bangalore, India, during the years of 1967-1973. In this total population survey of suicides reported to the police ($n = 1834$), the author found 45 cases aged 14 years old or younger and 351 cases aged 15 to 19; only the findings on the younger aged group were summarized. The records were scrutinized for the presumed "causes" or "motives" of the fatal act. In 10 cases, the cause was "unknown." Categorization of the remaining records showed that in 12 percent, "mental illness was reported as the cause of suicide." Unfortunately, the author had no details as to the nature of the mental disturbances.

Another suggestive set of findings was reported by Marek et al. (20), based on their survey of all documented suicides in Cracow, Poland, for the period 1960-1974. There were 76 cases of youth suicides (aged 8 to 18). Although note is made of "mental disease such as schizophrenia, epilepsy, and characteropathy" ($n = 3$), as well as drug addiction

($n = 3$) in the cohort, the manner in which these diagnoses were ascertained and the exact meaning of the terms are ambiguous.

The final total population survey we summarize was conducted in Upper Austria, for the years 1977 to 1979 (21). The families of all 47 "adolescents" (age criteria not given) who committed suicide in the 3-year period were contacted; 29 families were finally interviewed within two to four years of the suicide. Based on a multi-item questionnaire, the deceased youths (aged 9 to 20) had the following attributes: 14\percent ($n = 4$) had a history of psychiatric treatment ("including two psychoses"); "2/3 had shown behavior disturbances;" 7 percent ($n = 2$) were "beginning stage" drinkers; and 10 percent ($n = 3$) were "unmistakably drug addicts."

Unfortunately, an extensive exposition of another cohort (aged 17 or younger) is uninterpretable for our purposes (22). For reasons best known only to the author, the psychosocial data on all official cases of suicidal acts by youths in Israel (for 1963-1966) were combined for the fatal-outcome and nonfatal-outcome cases ($n = 21$ and $n = 343$, respectively). We must also take note of a widely cited, mostly narrative-report by Jan-Tausch (23) on suicide among school children in the New Jersey public school system during 1960-1963. Although it was probably the first U.S. survey of its kind, its description of 41 child suicides (aged 7 to 19), did not include information on psychiatric or mental illness. Additionally, the study did use a preselected sample (rather than the general population), although the specific method by which cases were ascertained was not well described.

Table 5 summarizes some of the salient data from the studies we just reviewed. Findings on psychiatric variables (diagnoses, conditions, symptoms) are extremely difficult to synthesize because of the range of linguistic labels used, the lack of definitions, differences in data retrieval methods, and significant changes in "diagnostic habits" across the years.

Suicide Attempts and Psychiatric Diagnoses

Given the scant diagnostic information on completed youth suicides, we decided to examine also the evidence available on the relationship between psychiatric diagnoses and attempted suicide in the same age group. This strategy has been criticized because many attempters never complete suicide (24), and because systematic differences in demographics and diagnosis have been found between attempters and completers in both youth and adults (24 to 27). Nevertheless, it is also true that there is overlap between the two groups. For example, from a prospective viewpoint, suicide attempts among adults also represent a risk factor for completed suicide (28). It is known that up to 75 percent of adults who committed suicide had made previous attempts or threats (29). Attempts also predict future attempts; thus, about one quarter of adults who attempt suicide had at least one previous attempt (30).

The data for youth are similar. As in adults, sex ratios are different for completed and for attempted suicides. For every completed suicide in children and adolescents, there are at least 3 to 4 attempts in boys and 25 to 30 in girls (31). Among adolescent attempters, the male/female ratio is approximately 1:4, but in preadolescence it is 1:1 (31-33). In approximately 9/10 cases, drug ingestion was the method of choice (31,32,34). In two large studies of youth attempters 16 percent and 37 percent of their subjects had made at least one previous attempt, and 6 percent and 17 percent of the samples, respectively, had

	Prevalence of Psychiatric Variables Reported in Total or Partial–Population Surveys of Youth Suicides						
	Study (by Reference List Number)						
Variable	**14 16**	**17**	**19**	**18**	**15**	**20**	**21**
Location	U.S.	U.K.	U.S.	U.S.	India	Poland	Austria
Years: 19_	81-83	62-68	70-79	80-83	67-73	60-74	77-79
N described	133	30	40	20	45	76	29
Age range	"<30"	12-14	15-24	12-19	"≤14"	8-18	9-20
Psych. data source:							
records-coroner	X	X	X		X	X	
records-other	X	X		X			
interviews	X			X			X
Psych Rx (%)							
Past	52		25	45			14
Current	23	30					
Mental/emotional problems/illness (%)	92 +	50 +	45 +		12	4	*
Behavior/conduct disturbances (%)		*		70			67
Psych symptoms (%)		87	85	65			
Drinking problem (%)	53 + +		0	70			7
Drug problem (%)						4	10

Table 5.

made two or more attempts (31,32). More important for this review, in Otto's study (31), child and adolescent attempters who ultimately killed themselves in the 10 to 15 year followup period were more likely to commit suicide in the first two years after the attempt, but the risk continued all through the followup, and repeated attempts constituted a major predictor of suicide in the boys in this sample. The suicide rate on followup in male attempters was 11.3 percent, a 7-fold increase over the control group. In the female attempters, the suicide rate was 3.9 percent, a 2-fold increase over the control group. Followup showed that about 19 percent of the male repeated attempters at intake, versus only 8 percent of those without prior attempts, subsequently completed suicide. The predictive power of early attempts for future suicidal acts has also been reported by Stanley and Barter (35) and by Cohen-Sandler et al. (36) in youth and by Tefft et al. (37) in adults, among others.

There is some evidence that suicidal attempts in childhood and early adolescence may be particularly associated with later suicide. In Otto's study (31), besides the history of repeated attempts for boys, other factors associated with later completed suicide among these attempters were male sex, length of prior functional impairment (which was, in turn, associated with attempts under age 13 years, and with major psychiatric disorders like manic depression and schizophrenia, in both boys and girls), and the use of active (violent) methods. Girls who used active methods in their attempts accounted for only 7 percent of all girl attempters, but appeared unique in that they were also over-represented among those whose first suicidal attempt occurred before the age of 13; they were more likely to have left a note and to have attempted suicide by hanging than by overdose. This divergence between intent and lethality has also been found among suicidal prepubertal children with major depression (38). It is apparent that pre- or peripubertal attempts may carry the highest risk for future suicide completion. Unfortunately, good prospective diagnostic studies

focusing on very young attempters cannot be found in the literature.

Psychiatric characteristics of youth who attempt suicide

Bergstrang and Otto (39) collected charts on 1727 patients under the age of 21 years who had presented to all hospitals in Sweden between 1955-1959 for attempted suicide. Evidence of parental mental illness (28%), parental alcoholism (15%), and father's absence (44%) were characteristics of the group. Otto (40) reexamined a probably representative subsample of 484 cases that yielded enough information to make a psychiatric diagnosis. Neurotic-depressive reaction was diagnosed in 30 percent of cases, neurosis in 23 percent, schizophrenia in 12 percent (19% in boys and 9% in girls), manic depression in 5 percent, and psychopathy in 13 percent (18% of boys and 11% of girls). Only primary diagnoses were considered. In an attempt to delineate a presuicidal syndrome in children and adolescents, Otto (41) could only ascertain that during the 3 months before the attempt, the symptoms of some mental disorders--namely, anxious and depressive neurosis, schizophrenia, and manic depression--had worsened considerably in about 50 percent of patients with these diagnoses. Personality characteristics showed much less change during the preattempt period. In a 10 to 15 year followup of the original sample (31), the investigators selected a control group matched for age, sex, and geographical birth site. Attrition rate of the attempter sample was only 10.4 percent. The attempters on followup had committed more legal offenses. Mental conditions in military health classifications were 10-fold higher (53%) in the attempters. Unfortunately, no systematic analysis of the predictive power of psychiatric diagnosis for suicide outcome was provided.

In a cross-sectional study based on chart reviews from a pediatric emergency room (ER), Garfinkel et al (32) identified 505 children and adolescents who had made 605 suicide attempts, and compared them with

505 nonsuicidal patients who had come to the same ER at the same time. Prior substance abuse, past history of psychotherapy, and current (not specified) psychiatric diagnoses (most frequent symptoms were dysphoric affect (55%) and aggressiveness and hostility (41%)) were significantly more common in the attempters. The families of the attempters had significantly higher rates of history of mental illness (especially drug and alcohol abuse), suicide, paternal unemployment, group or foster placement, and absence of father. Only 36 percent of the attempts were judged to have carried a moderate or high danger (criteria not provided). These were associated with family history of suicide and current psychiatric symptoms, although this analysis included 100 patients twice and it is therefore flawed. After a followup for up to 9 years, 8 of the 505 attempters had died by hanging, overdose, or motor vehicle accident, while the 5 deaths in the control group were due to medical disease.

Brent et al. (34) also used chart reviews to study the characteristics of 131 consecutive suicide attempts by 126 children and adolescents presenting in a pediatric emergency room between 1978-1983. The median age was 14 years. A bimodal distribution was noted, with approximately one-third of attempts noted to be medically serious, which usually involved a high degree of planning and use of a psychotropic agent (rather than an over-the-counter agent) (34). The following variables were associated with a medically serious attempt: male sex, family history of affective disorder, high suicidal intent, and a diagnosis of affective disorder, either in isolation or associated with substance abuse. The following distribution of diagnoses were found: affective disorder (39%), conduct disorder (26%), substance abuse (23%), and adjustment disorder (26%). Many of the patients had multiple diagnoses. Multivariate analysis of these data suggests the existence of two groups of attempters: **a dysphoric, affectively disturbed, hopeless group** whose lethality is very much a function of intent, and **an impulsive group** whose

lethality is very unpredictable. In fact, the class of agent ingested was the most important variable to predict the medical seriousness of the attempt in this impulsive group.

Strober (42) compared 250 suicidal inpatient youths aged 10 to 18 years with an equal number of nonsuicidal inpatient controls matched for age, socioeconomic status, and sex. From a diagnostic point of view, emotional, neurotic and conduct disorders (depression was "hidden" within these two categories, according to the author) were more prevalent in the suicidal group, although statistical significance levels are not reported. Alcoholism was only present in the suicidal group (5%). But Carlson and Cantwell (43), in a sample of 102 clinically referred children and adolescents, found that suicide attempts occurred with and without the syndrome of depression. Attempters did not differ from nonattempters in any particular diagnostic category.

Several studies have included only adolescents. In such studies, "neurotic" depression, conduct or personality disorders, and alcoholism, are the most common psychiatric diagnoses (44,45). As new assessment methods become more generally used, several reports have emphasized the relationship between suicidal attempts and major depression in adolescents (34,46-48). All these papers have also emphasized the increase in alcohol and drug abuse as an associated diagnosis to major depression, and also as a precipitant to the attempt. A similar point has been made by McKenry et al. (49) and by O'Brien (50). One study found a 5-fold excess of patients with epilepsy among attempters, of whom 60 percent were under 30 years old. Phenobarbital was the most frequent overdose (51). Brent (52) replicated this finding recently in adolescents, indicating further that 8/9 epileptic attempters were receiving phenobarbital as their main anticonvulsant. Studies of adolescent delinquents show similar agreement. Depressive symptomatology and suicidal behavior were found to be associated among 48 delinquent girls aged 13 to 18 years. All 23 girls with history of suicidal attempts were rated as moderately or severely depressed. In turn, depression and suicidality were mainly associated with antisocial and neurotic personality patterns. Some of the girls showed no suicidality in spite of marked depressive symptomatology (53). Alessi et al. (54) reported similar findings with a sample of incarcerated adolescent delinquents of both sexes. Those with major affective disorders or borderline personality disorders presented the highest suicidality and committed the most serious attempts. But there also is substantial evidence that various other characteristics (i.e., externalizing symptoms, impulsivity and borderline personality) may also be related to suicidality in the absence of an affective syndrome (34,55-57,17).

Studies of only preadolescents with suicidal behavior had to address suicidal threats and ideation, especially those with a definite plan, because actual attempts in this age group are rare. Evidence suggests that suicidality before 13 years may constitute a very high risk for later suicide (31). Myers et al. (58) compared chart reviews of 61 suicidal and 287 nonsuicidal preadolescent inpatient children. Depressive disorders were present in 30 percent of suicidal children and only 3 percent of the controls. This was the only diagnosis for which the rate significantly differed between the two groups. Other variables that differentiated the groups were family history of suicidal behavior and abuse of the mother (usually by the father). In a series of uncontrolled studies, Pfeffer et al. (59,60,61) have repeatedly found that prepubertal children with suicidal ideation, threats or acts, frequently present symptoms of depression, hopelessness and low self-esteem, psychomotor activity, conduct disorder, and that the parents present suicidal behaviors and/or depression. Ryan et al. (38) found that among prepubertal major depressive children, 46 percent present with persistent and severe suicidal ideation involving at least a concrete suicidal plan. Kazdin et al. (62) found that hopelessness related more closely than depression to suicidal intent in prepubertal inpatients, a finding similar to

that for adults, whereas hopelessness has been shown to be the key link between depression and suicidal behavior (63) and also predicts later suicide in samples of depressive patients (64).

Therefore, it appears that affective disorders, alcoholism, and other drug abuse play the same central role in regard to suicidal attempts among youth, as they do in completed suicide in youth and in the rest of the age spectrum. Schizophrenia appears more related to suicide than to attempts, whereas personality diagnoses may relate more to attempts. The primacy of unipolar and bipolar affective disorders and alcoholism, as well as schizophrenia and schizoaffective disorder, as the diagnosis most often associated with adult suicide has been known since the 1960's (65–70). But there appears to be no doubt that there is also a prominent component of irritability, aggression, impulsivity, borderline features, and conduct disorder among seriously suicidal young people, which is similar to findings in adults (71-73). It should be noted that many of these symptoms are by no means inconsistent with the diagnosis of an affective disorder (74) and especially bipolarity (75). Further refinement of diagnostic instruments and improvements in clinical skills to diagnose mixed bipolar illness in adolescents, which probably is the commonest presentation of bipolarity in adolescents, are likely to bring about further advances in the clinical characterization of this aggressive-impulsive subgroup. Nevertheless, it is also likely that a subgroup of impulsive suicidal adolescents will remain outside the major classical diagnostic categories. Their nosology and biology will require further study.

Familial patterns of suicidality and psychiatric disorders

It is clear that suicidality cuts across several psychiatric diagnoses, the most frequent being bipolarity, nonbipolar MDD, alcoholism and substance abuse, schizophrenia, and perhaps some personality disorders including, borderline and antisocial. In addition, several of the studies previously cited have noted the frequency of suicidal behaviors in the relatives of suicide attempters and victims. Another way to study the relationships between specific psychiatric diagnoses and suicidality is to review their patterns of association in families, to determine if the familial transmission of suicidality overlaps with, or is independent from, the psychiatric disorders just mentioned. This strategy is possible because most of the diagnoses involved, as well as suicidality, have been shown to aggregate in certain families. Although most of the data come from adult studies of affective disorders, the findings are relevant to this review because there is increasing evidence of diagnostic continuity between youth and adults in most of the diagnoses involved, as well as in suicide, and because young adult, probands and relatives, were also included in many of the studies.

Most of the evidence indicates that although some diagnoses (i.e., major affective disorders) and suicide may be associated within families, familial transmission for suicidality and for psychiatric diagnoses are separate and probably independent. Overall, the data suggest that, given a positive family history of suicide, a superimposed major psychiatric disorder constitutes a serious risk factor for suicide.

In a study of adult primary major depressive probands, only age of onset of affective illness and the secondary diagnoses of alcoholism or an anxiety disorder in the proband were independently related to higher familial aggregation for major depression in relatives. On the other hand, suicidality or the presence of any of the following clinical characteristics during major depressive episodes in the proband showed no independent relationship to familial aggregation for affective illness: any of the Research Diagnostic Criteria depressive subtypes, recurrent depression, or hospitalization (76). A chart review of 243 inpatients with a definite family history of suicide in a first or second degree relative, and 5602 inpatients without such family history found that almost half of the index group had attempted suicide, and that more than half had an affective disorder. A family history of suicide increased the risk for suicidal attempts across the following diagnostic categories: schizophrenia, unipolar and bipolar affective illness, dysthymia, and personality disorders (77). Similar findings were reported by Tsuang (78) comparing suicide rates among adult schizophrenics, manics, depressives, and surgical controls. Suicide rates were high for all psychiatric patient groups, and the relatives of patients who had committed suicide had higher risk of suicide than the remaining relatives.

Egeland et al. (79) reported that, among the Amish, 78 percent of all suicides in the last century were accounted for by four extended pedigrees with high density for major unipolar and bipolar affective disorders, which together account for only 16 percent of the Amish population. Nevertheless, other Amish pedigrees with heavy loading for affective illness present no suicidal acts among their members. Similarly, Linkowski et al. (80) in a study of 713 major depressive inpatients found that a family history of violent suicidal behavior was associated with the same in the proband, and the effect was more marked in bipolar women. In a sample of 50 bipolar patients, those with a family history of suicidality also had suicidal attempts, and associated alcoholism in the parents or in the probands increased the risk (81). From another viewpoint, the findings of Murphy and Wetzel (82) point to the possibility that in the presence of a similar family history of suicidal behavior, the presence of affective disorder or alcoholism, or both, in the proband will substantially increase the person's risk of completing suicide compared to cases with other or no psychiatric diagnoses.

CONCLUSIONS

The available figures suggest that the condition of psychiatric "patienthood" in the adolescent and young adult years is associated with an alarmingly high mortality risk via suicide. This conclusion is inescapable in light of the general population base rates for death-by-suicide for these age groups (83), and in comparison with the suicide mortalities associated with most psychiatric disorders among adults. Using very global and "rough" estimates, psychiatrically disturbed youths may be running a risk of suicide about 200-fold (or more) the rate of their general population counterparts. And psychiatric illness in the young also seems to pose a suicide risk that may be up to five times higher than the rates reported for adult patients (see below).

Although changes in diagnostic practices in child psychiatry and in the use, definition, and meaning of psychiatric labels make it exceedingly difficult to compare the risk value of various conditions, tentative conclusions can be made. The "classic" mood and thinking disorders, namely, affective illness and schizophrenia, are prognosticators of suicide mortality. Because much of the supporting evidence derives from studies of youths with a history of inpatient hospitalization, the implication is that the major factor could be the presence of psychosis. Among the affective disorders, this would further imply that bipolarity in this age groups is likely to be a major factor (12). The addictive disorders may also carry a high risk value, although the study of these conditions has been constrained by the fact that their incidence and prevalence may be far more subject to societal factors than seems to be the case for affective disorders and schizophrenia. Finally, data are scant on the prognostic value of "neurosis" or personality disorders for suicide in the preadult years. In no small measure, the relative absence of such evidence probably reflects long-standing debates about the diagnostic validity of these conditions in juveniles.

Our conclusions about the risk value of psychiatric illness for suicide in the younger years is underscored by the data on the prognostic value of these conditions among adults. This body of information also suggests that "patienthood" is associated with elevated suicide rates; that the risk is probably higher for previous inpatients than outpatients; and that, although the mortality figures even within diagnostic groups vary, affective illness, schizophrenia, alcoholism, and disorders involving drug addiction probably carry the highest relative risk in this regard.

For example, in this recent 5-year followup report of 4,800 consecutive, first-admission VA psychiatric inpatients, Porkorny (84) found a suicide rate of 279/100,000 patients/year. In a similarly recent study, Morrison (85) estimated the suicide mortality among outpatients, using a large private practice sample (n = 12,500); the overall rate was found to be 120/100,000/year.

The rates for particular psychiatric conditions are difficult to interpret because of their variability. The variability is especially evident with data that were presented in percentages or frequencies without adjusting for the length of the followup. Miles (10), who, in his comprehensive review of this body of literature estimated the overall risk for several conditions, arrived at 230/100,000/year suicides for depressives; 270/100,000/year for alcoholics; and up to a 3-fold higher suicide rate for adult opiate addicts. However, the variable data bases with which Miles (10) had to contend can be readily illustrated in reference to schizophrenia. Recently reported suicide figures for this diagnosis yield rates ranging from a low of 203/100,000/year (86) to a high of 456/100,000/year (87).

Given the available evidence, therefore, it is difficult to say whether affective illness in adults is associated with a lower, higher, or equivalent suicide risk than schizophrenia, for instance. However, the two most recent studies of unselected adult patient samples give every indication that different conditions make differential contributions to the cohort's overall suicide rates. In Pokorny's (87) sample, for example, diagnosis-specific

138

suicide rates varied from a high of 695/100,000/year for affective disorder to a low of 71/100,000/year for organic brain syndrome, with other conditions occupying the middle ranges (e.g., 187/100,000 for alcoholism). Likewise, in Morrison's adult outpatient series (85), the suicide rates ranged from 42/100,000/year for "unipolar' affective disorder, through 318/100,000/year for bipolar illness, to the peak of 411/100,000/year for schizophrenia. Suicide rates for "personality disorders" as well as for the "neurosis" have been also estimated. The overall trends suggest that these diagnoses are also associated with elevated risk rates, although by no means as high as those cited above (e.g.,10,85).

In light of the available information on the various disorders in adults, it is more than likely that the major psychiatric illnesses also contribute differentially to the overall rate of suicide among children and adolescents. Furthermore, the diagnostic findings in attempted suicide in youth point in the same diagnostic directions as those for completed suicide, except for a larger overall proportion of cases with "personality disorders." Given the diagnostic problems associated with these conditions, not the least of which is that mixed bipolar illness can be easily missed, even when the patient can be interviewed, it is not unthinkable that this could also occur with post-suicide diagnoses. Thus, identifying a group of child and adolescent suicide attempters who resemble suicide completers may be very useful, not only for therapeutic and preventive purposes, but also because this population may most closely approximate suicide completers. Moreover, from these attempters, we could learn the most about the affective, cognitive, and biological process that characterize the young patients who actually do commit suicide.

Some have proposed focusing on patients who have engaged in suicidal behavior of high lethality and intent, on the assumption that only chance circumstances allowed their survival; however, in adolescent and adult subjects, such "chance" survival may represent lower intent. Although cluster analyses of data on adult suicidal attempters reveals a group who used more violent methods, with more intent to succeed (71), nevertheless, adolescents and adults with the highest intent are still much more likely to kill themselves, thereby removing themselves from prospective scrutiny (64,88,89). However, in prepubertal children, there is a discrepancy between intent and lethality which makes the situation quite different. While suicidal ideation with a plan occurs among prepubertal children with MDD almost as frequently as in their post-pubertal counterparts (46% vs. 49%) (38), the suicide rate among prepubertal children remains quite low (3,17), in spite of its secular increase among adolescents and young adults. Prepubertal children's lack of cognitive maturity and skills necessary to complete suicide probably accounts for the low rates (3,17). Therefore, this age group provides the opportunity to study suicidality naturally untruncated by suicide completion. The findings reviewed earlier, showing that attempts before age 13 seem to carry a bleak prognosis for later suicide, also suggest that prepubertal suicidality may be much more representative of completed suicides and deserve special study. Suicidality of very early onset may enable the selection for future studies of those attempters who are most at risk, as the closest approximation to completed suicides.

This approach would be consistent with the findings by one of us regarding differences in GH responses and REM latency, and in their patterns of association, among suicidal and among nonsuicidal prepubertal children with major depression, both during the episode and in the recovery drug-free state. Such findings may relate to the evidence for the association of a functional CNS serotonin deficit in adult suicides (90-103), which may be familial (102). Furthermore, the evidence for familial aggregation of suicidality is also consistent with higher risk with earlier age of onset, especially if genetic factors are at least partially responsible for such familial transmission (104-106).

It is difficult to integrate the pertinent data on youths who have killed themselves with the information on the prognostic value of psychiatric illness in juveniles. In part, this is a consequence of the methodologic problems posed by the use of coroner's records and "psychologic autopsies." In this ex post facto database, probably the most "hard core" indicator of psychiatric illness is a positive history of mental health care. However, even those figures can be only approximations of the prevalence of mental illness in the cohorts because treatment is mediated by a variety of factors including recognition that a disorder exists, the availability of mental health treatment resources, awareness of such resources, and social influences that determine referral patterns. With the above caveat in mind, we used known rates of treatment referrals for pediatric cohorts to interpret the pertinent data on completed suicide among youth.

In their review of epidemiologic studies, Gould and associates (89) noted that "almost all psychotic children and adolescents are known to some treatment facilitiy." But only approximately 1 percent to 49 percent of "maladjusted" children receive mental health care. If we eliminate figures that included treatment by general medical personnel (e.g., pediatricians), 30 percent is about the upper limit of treated cases among "maladjusted" youths. Turning to information about rates of referral, Costello (107) found that, from about 2 percent to 5 percent of youngsters seen by primary health care providers (pediatricians, family practitioners) are referred to mental health specialists. She also estimated that 50 percent is the modal referral rate for youths who had been definitively identified by their health care providers as having a psychiatric problem.

The reported rates of psychiatric treatment or contact among youths who have committed suicide in the United States and Britain (see Table 5) therefore suggest that these youths were unlike normal pediatric populations, but similar to maladjusted or disturbed juveniles. That is, the portions of youth suicides with known histories of psychiatric care--from one-third to about one-half of the samples--are far higher than the mental health referral rates in the general youth population. But the figures on the suicides are comparable in this regard both to the portion of psychiatrically identified cases who have been referred for treatment and the portion of maladjusted youths who actually received mental health care.

Our conclusions must be viewed in light of the "methodologic" problems that confound a review of this body of literature. First, using conventional referencing methods, it is not possible to access every study of mentally ill youths that may have found suicide among the sample (e.g., 7), because of the way in which the studies were apparently indexed. Second, in some of the available prospective studies of psychiatrically ill juveniles, the absence of data on suicide could mean either that this outcome was **not** observed or that the investigators did not look for it (e.g., 11,108,109). Third, some of the published data are inconsistent, which is most evident in multiple publications regarding the same cohort. For example, the followup time intervals and the sample sizes may be discrepant (6,74) or case frequencies with certain diagnoses may not exactly correspond (14,16). Should it be desirable to conduct a meta-analysis on the reported findings, such methodologic issues need to be taken into account.

In summary, there is significant evidence that major psychiatric disorders constitute an important risk factor for completed and attempted suicides in children and adolescents. The efficacious treatment and care of psychiatrically ill youths may be the most feasible way to alter their risk of suicide.

BIBLIOGRAPHY

1. Rushforth NB, Ford AB, Sudak HS, et al: Increasing suicide rates in adolescents and young adults in an urban community (1958-1982). Tests of hypotheses from national data. In Suicide in the Young. Edited by Hudak HS. Littleton, MA, John Wright, 1984, pp. 45-68.

2. Maris R: The adolescent suicide problem. Suicide Life Threat Behav 15:91-1099, 1985.

3. Shaffer D, Fisher P: The epidemiology of suicide in children and young adolescents. J Am Acad Child Psychiatry 20:545-565, 1981.

4. McClure GMG: Recent trends in suicide amongst the young. Br J Psychiatry 144:134-138, 1984.

5. Rubinstein DH: Epidemic suicide among Micronesian adolescents. Soc Sc Med 17:657-665, 1983.

6. Morrison J: Suicide in psychiatric patients: Age distribution. Suicide Life Threat Behav 14:52-58, 1984.

7. Welner A, Welner Z, Fishman R: Psychiatric adolescent inpatients. Eight-to-ten-year follow-up. Arch Gen Psychiatry 36:698-700, 1979.

8. King LJ, Pittman GD: A six-year follow-up study of 65 adolescent patients. Natural history of affective disorders in adolescence. Arch Gen Psychiatry 22:230-236, 1970.

9. Noble P, Hart T, Nation R: Correlates and outcome of illicit drug use by adolescent girls. Br J Psychiatry 120:497-504, 1972.

10. Miles CP: Conditions predisposing to suicide: A review. J Nerv Ment Dis 164:231-246, 1977.

11. Annesley PT: Psychiatric illness in adolescence: Presentation and prognosis. J Ment Sc 107:268-278, 1961.

12. Strober M, Carlson G: Bipolar illness in adolescents with major depression. Clinical, genetic, and psychopharmacologic predictors in a three- to four-year prospective follow-up investigation. Arch Gen Psychiatry 39:549-555, 1982.

13. Olsen T: Follow-up study of manic-depressive patients whose first attack occurred before the age of 19. Acta Psychiatr Scand (Suppl 162) 37:45-51, 1961.

14. Rich CL, Young D, Fowler RC: San Diego suicide study: I. Young vs old cases. Arch Gen Psychiat 43:577-582, 1986.

15. Sathyavathi K: Suicide among children in Bangalore. Indian J Pediatr 42:149-157, 1975.

16. Fowler RC, Rich CL, Young D: San Diego suicide study: II. Substance abuse in young cases. Arch Gen Psychiat 43:962-965, 1986.

17. Shaffer D: Suicide in childhood and early adolescence. J Child Psychol Psychiatry 15:275-291, 1974.

18. Shafii M, Carrigan S, Whitinghill JR, et al: Psychological autopsy of completed suicide in children and adolescents. Am J Psychiatry 142:1061-1064, 1985.

19. Bourque LB, Kraus JF, Cosand BJ: Attributes of suicide in females. Suicide Life Threat Behav 13:123-138, 1983.

20. Marek Z, Widacki J, Zwarysiewicz W: Suicides committed by minors. Forensic Sci 7:103-108, 1976.

21. Leblhuber F, Schony W, Fisher F, et al: Study on suicides committed by adolescents in Upper Austria covering a period of three years. Depression et Suicide 652-655, 1981.

22. Amir M: Suicide among minors in Israel. Isr Ann Psychiatry 11:219-269, 1973.

23. Jan-Tausch J: Suicide of children 1960-63. New Jersey public school students. Unpublished manuscript, undated, Department of Education, Trenton, NJ.

24. Clayton PJ: Epidemiologic and risk factors in suicide. In Psychiatry Update, American Psychiatric Press, Washington, D.C., 1983, pp.406-428.

25. Shaffer D: Depression, mania and suicidal acts in child and adolescent psychiatry: Modern Approaches, Ed. by M Rutter and L Hersov. London, Blackwell, 1985.

26. Robins E, Schmidt EH, O'Neal P: Some interrelations of social factors and clinical diagnosis in attempted suicide: A study of 109 patients. Amer J Psychiat, 114-221-231, 1957.

27. Stangel E: Suicide and attempted suicide, MacGibbon & Kee, Bristol UK, 1965.

28. Wan AG, Nielsen B, Bille-Brahe U, Hansen W, Kolmos L: Attempted suicide in Denmark III. Assessment of repeated suicidal behaviour. Acta Psychiatr Scand 72:389-394, 1985.

29. Schneidman ES, Faberow NL: Clues to suicide. Pub Health Rep 71:109, 1956.

30. Schmidt EH, O'Neal P, Robins E: Evaluation of suicide attempts as a guide to therapy. J Am Med Assoc 155:549, 1954.

31. Otto U: Suicidal acts by children and adolescents, a follow-up study. Acta Psychiatrica Scandinavica, Supplementum 233, 7-123, 1972.

32. Garfinkel BD, Froese A, Hood J: Suicide attempts in children and adolescents. Am J Psychiatry, 139-141, 1972.

33. Nichol H, Guichon D: Attempted suicide among children and adolescents in 1966. B C Med J 14:139-141, 1972.

34. Brent D: Correlates of medical lethality of suicidal attempts in children and adolescents. J Amer Acad Child Psychiat, in press.

35. Stanley EJ, Barter JT: A Adolescent suicidal behavior. Am J Orthopsychiat 40:87-96, 1970.

36. Cohen-Sandler R, Berman AL, King RA: A follow-up study of hospitalized suicidal children. J Acad Child Psychiat 21:398-403, 1982.

37. Tefft BM, Pederson AM, Babigian HM: Patterns of death among suicide attempters, a psychiatric population, and a general population. Arch Gen Psychiat 34:1155-1161, 1977.

38. Ryan ND, Puig-Antich J, Rabinovich H, Robinson D, Ambrosini PJ, Nelson B, Iyengar S: The clinical picture of major depression in children and adolescents. (Submitted).

39. Bergstrand OG, Otto U: Suicidal attempts in adolescence and childhood. Acta Paediatrica, 51:17-26, 1962.

40. Otto U: Suicidal attempts in adolescence and childhood. States of mental illness and personality variables. Acta Paedopsychiatrica, 31:397-411, 1964.

41. Otto U: Changes in the behaviour of children and adolescents preceding suicidal attempts. Acta Psychiatrica Scandinavica, 40:386-400, 1964.

42. Stober B: Social environment and suicidal children and adolescents: A comparative study, in Depression et Suicide, pp. 608-615, Pergamon Press, 1981.

43. Carlson GA, Cantwell DP: Suicidal behavior and depression in children and adolescents. J Amer Acad, 21:361-368, 1982.

44. White HC: Self-poisoning in adolescents. Brit J Psychiat 134-24-35, 1974.

45. Hawton K, Osborn M, Grady J, Cole D: Brit J Psychiat 40:124-131, 1982.

46. Crumley FE: Adolescent suicide attempts. J Am Med Assoc 241:2404-2407, 1979.

47. Crumley FE: Adolescent suicide attempts and melancholia. Texas Med 78:62-65, 1982.

48. Robbins RR, Alessi, NE. Depressive symptoms and suicidal behavior in adolescents. Amer J Psychiat 142:588-592, 1985.

49. McKenry PC, Tishler CL, Kelley C: The role of drugs in adolescent suicide attempts. Suicide and Life-Threatening Behavior 13:166-175, 1983.

50. O'Brien JP: Increase in suicide attempts by drug ingestion: The Boston experience, 1964-1974. Arch Gen Psychiat 34:1165-1169, 1977.

51. Hawton K, Fagg J, Marsack P: Association between epilepsy and attempted suicide. J Neurol Neurosurg Psychiat 43:168-170, 1980.

52. Brent D: Overrepresentation of epileptics in a consecutive series of suicide attempters at a children's hospital, 1978-1983. J Amer Acad Child Psychiat 25:242-246, 1986.

53. Gibbs JT: Depression and suicidal behavior among delinquent females. J Youth Adoles 10:159-167, 1981.

54. Alessi NE: McManus M, Brickman A, Grapentine L: Suicidal behavior among serious juvenile offenders. Am J Psychiat 141:286-287, 1984.

55. Chiles JA, Miller ML, Cox GB: Depression in an adolescent delinquent population. Arch Gen Psychiat 37:1179-1186, 1980.

56. Crumley FE: Adolescent suicide attempts and borderline personality disorder: clinical features. Southern Med J 74-564-549, 1981.

57. Connell PH: Drug addiction: Adolescent drug taking. Proc Roy Soc Med 58:409-412, 1965.

58. Myers KM, Burke P, McCauley E: Suicidal behavior by hospitalized preadolescent children on a psychiatric unit. J Amer Acad Child Psychiat 24:474-480, 1985.

59. Pfeffer CR, Conte HR, Plutchik R, Jerrett I: Suicidal behavior in latency-age children: An empirical study. J Amer Acad Child Psychiat 18:679-692, 1979.

60. Pfeffer CR, Conte HR, Plutchik R, Jerrett I: Suicidal behavior in latency age children: An outpatient population. J Amer Acad Child Psychiat 19:703-710, 1980.

61. Pfeffer CR, Zuckerman S, Plutchik R, Mizruchi MS: Suicidal behavior in normal school children: A comparison with child psychiatric inpatients. J Amer Acad Child Psychiat 23:416-423, 1984.

62. Kazdin AE, French NH, Unis AS, Esveldt-Dawson K, Sherick RB: Hopelessness, depression, and suicidal intent among psychiatrically disturbed inpatient children. J Consult Clin Psychol 504-510, 1983.

63. Beck AT, Kovacs M, Weissman A: Hopelessness and suicidal behavior: An overview. J Am Med Assoc 234:1146-1149, 1975.

64. Beck AT, Steer RA, Kovacs M, Garrison B: Hopelessness and eventual suicide: A 10-year prospective study of patients hospitalized with suicidal ideation. Am J Psychiat 142:559-563, 1985.

65. Dorpat TL, Ripley HS: A study of suicide in the Seattle area. Compr Psychiat 1:349-359, 1960.

66. Robin E, Murphy E, Wilkinson RH, Gardner S, Kayes J: Some clinical considerations in the prevention of suicide based on a study of 134 successful suicides. Amer J Pub Health 49:888-898, 1959.

67. Guze SB, Robins E: Suicide and primary affective disorders. Br J Psychiat 117:437-438, 1970.

68. Barraclough B, Burch J, Nelson B, Sainsbury P: A hundred cases of suicide: Clinical aspects. Brit J Psychiat 125:355-373, 1974.

69. Tsuang MT: Suicide in schizophrenics, manic depressives, and surgical controls. Arch Gen Psychiat 35:153-155, 1978.

70. Tsuang MT, Dempsey GM, Fleming JA: Can ECT prevent premature death and suicide in 'schizoaffective' patients? J Affect Disord 1:167-171, 11979.

71. Paykel ES, Rassaby: Classification of suicide attempters by cluster analysis. Brit J Psychiat 133:45-52, 1978.

72. Crook T, Raskin A, Davis D: Factors associated with attempted suicide among hospitalized depressed patients. Psychol Med 5:381-388, 1975.

73. Weissman M, Fox K, Klerman G: Hostility and depression associated with suicide attempts. Am J Psychiat 130:560-455, 1973.

74. Puig-Antich J: Major depression and conduct disorder in prepuberty. J Amer Acad Child Psychiat 21:392-397, 1982.

75. Akiskal HS, Downs J, Jordan P, Watson S, Daugherty D, Pruitt DB: Affective disorders in referred children and younger siblings of manic-depressives. Arch Gen Psychiatr 42:996-1003, 1985.

76. Weissman MM, Merikangas KR, Wickramaratne P, Kidd KK: Understanding the clinical heterogeneity of major depression using family data. Arch Gen Psychiat 43:430-434, 1986.

77. Roy A: Family history of suicide. Arch Gen Psychiat 40:971-974, 1983.

78. Tsuang MT: Risk of suicide in the relatives of shizophrenics, manics, depressives, and controls. J Clin Psychiat 44:396-400, 1983.

79. Egeland JA, Sussex JN: Suicide and family loading for affective disorders. J Am Med Assoc 254:915-918, 1985.

80. Linkowski P, deMaertelaer V, Mendlewicz J: Suicidal behaviour in major depressive illness. Acta Psychiatr Scand 72:233-238, 1985.

81. Johnson GF, Hunt G: Suicidal behavior in bipolar manic-depressive patients and their families. Comprehensive Psychiat 20:159-164, 1979.

82. Murphy GE, Wetzel RK: Family history of suicidal behavior among suicide attempters. J Nerv Ment Dis 170:86-90, 1982.

83. U.S. Bureau of the Census: Statistical Abstract of the United States: 1979 (100th Edition). Washington, DC, U.S. Government Printing Office, 1979.

84. Pokorny AD: Prediction of suicide in psychiatric patients. Report of a prospective study. Arch Gen Psychiatry 40:249-257, 1983.

85. Morrison J: Suicide in a psychiatric practice populations. J Clin Psychiatry 43:348-352, 1982.

86. Black DW, Winokur G, Warrack G: Suicide in schizophrenia: The Iowa record linkage study. J Clin Psychiatry 46:14-17, 1985.

87. Pokorny AD: A follow-up study of 618 suicidal patients. Am J Psychiat 122:1109-1116, 1966.

88. Pierce DW: A predictive validation of a suicide intent scale: A five-year follow-up. Brit J Psychiat 139:391-396, 1981.

89. Gould MS, Wunsch-Hitzig R, Dohrenwend BP: Formulation of hypotheses about the prevalence, treatment, and prognostic significance of psychiatric disorders in children in the United States, in Mental Illness in the United States: Epidemiologic Estimates. Edited by Dohrenwend BP, Gould MS, Link B, et al. New York: Praeger, 1980, pp. 9-44.

90. Agren H: Symptom patterns in unipolar and bipolar depression correlating with monoamine metabolites in the cerebrospinal fluid: II. Suicide. Psychiat Res 3:225-236-1980.

91. Asberg M, Traskman L, Thoren P: 5-HIAA in the cerebrospinal fluid. A biochemical suicide predictor? Arch Gen Psychiat 33:1193-1197, 1976.

92. Banki C, Molnar G, Feliete I: Correlation of individual symptoms and other clinical variables with cerebrospinal fluid amine metabolites and tryptophan in depression. Arch Psychiatr Nerv 229:345-353, 1981.

93. Banki C, Arato M, Papp Z, Kurcz M: Biochemical markers in suicidal patients. Investigations with cerebrospinal fluid amine metabolites and neuroendocrine tests. J Affect Dis 6:341-350, 1984.

94. Oreland L, Wiberg A, Asberg M, Traskman L, Sjostrand L, Thoren P, Bertilsson L, Tylring G: Platelet MAO activity and monoamine metabolites in cerebrospinal fluid in depressed and suicidal patients and

in healthy controls. Psychiatry Res 1:21-29, 1981.

95. Traskman L, Tybry G, Asbert M, Bertilsson L, Lantto O, Schalling D: Cortisol in the CSF of depressed and suicidal patients. Arch Gen Psychiat 37:761-767, 1980.

96. van Praag HM: Depression, suicide and the metabolism of serotonin in the brain. J Affect Dis 4:275-290, 1982.

97. Brown G, Goodwin F, Ballenger J, Goyer P, Major L: Aggression in human correlates with cerebrospinal fluid amino metabolites. Psychiat Res 1:131-139, 1979.

98. Brown G, Ebert M, Goyer P, Jimerson D, Klein W, Bunney W, Goodwin F: Aggression, suicide, and serotonin: Relationships to CSF metabolites. Am J Psychiat 139:741-746, 1982.

99. Linnoila M, Roy A, Guthne S: Indices of serotonin metabolism in violent offenders, arsonists, and alcoholics. Presented at The New York Academy of Sciences. Conference on Psychobiology of Suicidal Behavior, New York, NY, September 19, 1985.

100. Traskman-Bendz L, Asberg M, Schalling D: Serotonergic function and suicidal behavior in personality disorders and neuroses. Presented at The New York Academy of Sciences, Conference on Psychobiology of Suicidal Behavior, New York, NY, September 19, 1985.

101. Lidberg L, Tuck JR, Asberg M, Scalia-Tomba GB, Bertilsson L: Homocide, suicide and CSF 5-HIAA. Acta Psychiatr Scand 71:230-236, 1985.

102. Sedvall G, Fyro B, Gullberg B, Nybadi H, Weisal FA, Wode-Helgodt B: Relationships in healthy volunteers between concentrations of monoamine metabolites in cerebrospinal fluid and family history of psychiatric morbidity. Brit J Psychiat 136:366-374, 1980.

103. van Praag HM: Significance of biochemical parameters in the diagnosis, treatment and prevention of depressives. Biol Psychiat 12:101-131, 1977.

104. Juel-Nielsen N, Videbech T: A twin study of suicide. Acta Genet Med Gemellol 19:307-310, 1970.

105. Tsuang MT: Genetic factors in suicide. Dis Nerv Sys 38:498-501, 1977.

106. Wender PH, Kety SS, Rosenthal D, Schulsinger F, Ortmann J, Lunde I: Psychiatric disorders in the biological and adoptive families of adopted individuals with affective disorders. Arch Gen Psychiat 43:923-929, 1986.

107. Costello EJ: Primary care pediatrics and child psychopathology: A review of diagnostic, treatment, and referral practices. Pediatrics, in press.

108. Kivowitz J, Forgotson J, Goldstein G, et al: A follow-up study of hospitalized adolescents. Comp Psychiatry 15:35-42, 1974.

109. Warren W: A study of adolescent psychiatric inpatients and the outcome six or more years later. II. The follow-up study. J Child Psychol Psychiatry 6:141-160, 1965.

PERSONALITY AS A PREDICTOR OF YOUTHFUL SUICIDE

Allen Frances, M.D., Professor of Psychiatry, Cornell University Medical Center, New York Hospital, New York, New York

Susan Blumenthal, M.D., Chief, Behavioral Medicine Program, Health and Behavior Research Branch, Division of Basic Sciences, National Institute of Mental Health, Rockville, Maryland

INTRODUCTION

This paper will summarize the limited available literature on the personality risk factors associated with youth suicide and will outline the methodological difficulties inherent in this line of investigation. Personality disorder research has recently flourished greatly because the Diagnostic and Statistical Manual III (DSM III) provided a separate axis for personality diagnosis and specified explicit criteria defining each of the personality disorders. This has led to the development of reliable semistructured interview instruments to assess personality disorders in adults. Preliminary findings also suggest that personality disorders may influence, in important ways, the presentation, course, biological test results, and treatment response of various Axis I conditions. Thus far, however, there has been very little systematic research on personality assessment in children and adolescents, and there are many inherent conceptual and practical obstacles to any precise determination of the personality risk factors for youth suicide.

We will briefly review personality variables associated with suicide in adults, summarize research on the personality variables associated with youth suicide, and outline a number of the pertinent methodological problems and some of their possible solutions. We will conclude with suggestions for future research, current clinical practice, and prevention. The most interesting question that emerges from this review is the degree to which the personality factors that predict youth suicide are equivalent to factors that also pertain to adult suicide. This question has important theoretical, clinical, and prevention implications.

Personality Predictors of Adult Suicide Behavior

The two DSM III personality disorders most clearly associated with adult suicides, both completed and attempted, are the borderline (BPD) and the antisocial (APD) (1). Suicide rates for several-year followup studies of BPD patients are reported at 4 percent (2) and 7 percent (3); on a 15-year followup, the rate was 7.5 percent (4). Several studies suggest that the comorbidity of BPD with affective and/or substance abuse disorders results in particularly lethal combinations (5-7). Although most self-destructive behavior in BPD patients is probably nonlethal in intent, a substantial portion of BPD patients do eventually die by suicide, usually in young adulthood.

Reported rates of suicide attempts in APD individuals vary considerably (11%-46%), perhaps because of differences in underlying base rates of APD and of suicide attempts in the samples studied and the fact that most studies did not use DSM III criteria (8-10). It is thus difficult to generalize the findings across studies. It is estimated that 5 percent of APD individuals eventually die by suicide (8-11). APD may also predict for frequent and recurrent attempts (12-14). These may occur in response to anger and frustration in interpersonal relationships and in order to manipulate others (15,16). The comorbidity of APD with affective and/or substance abuse disorders may, as with BPD, result in more frequent and more lethal attempts (6,17,18).

The psychology literature has employed a different strategy to determine the personality predictors of suicide. Rather than assessing the presence of a categorical personality disorder in suicidal individuals or the rate of suicide in those with personality disorder, many psychology studies have measured specific personality dimensions or traits in suicide attempters and/or completers. Attempters and completers appear to be different in their personality and in other characteristics. Attempters have the more disturbed personality profiles and are also more likely to be young, female, to lack an Axis I diagnosis, and to commit public, impulsive, suicidal acts using less serious means (19). Most of the personality dimensions that have been studied apply only to suicide attempters and may not generalize to completers.

The following personality traits seem to be particularly characteristic of suicide attempters: aggression or hostility (20-29), impulsivity (30), social withdrawal or interpersonal difficulties (31-37), low self-esteem (38-45), dependency (21,26,27,46), hopelessness (47-49), external locus of control, rigid cognitive style, and poor problem solving (54). The many studies that have tested the ability of the MMPI to differentiate suicidal patients have been inconsistent (55), and the same is true for studies of the association of hysterical traits and suicide

(24,25,56,57,58). Studies using the Eysenck Personality Inventory fairly consistently find high neuroticism, psychoticism, and introversion scores (59-62). The major limitation of available personality dimension studies is that each has tended to assess in isolation only one or a small number of dimensions so that we don't know the degree and direction of convariation among them and the amount of total variance they explain. Dimensional personality trait measures may also be difficult to obtain in ordinary clinical situations.

Recently, a particularly fascinating connection has emerged between the personality dimension of aggressive impulsivity in suicidal and violent individuals and the biological finding of low central nervous system serotonin turnover (63-67). The association holds up in patients with impulsive personality disorder, even in the absence of an Axis I diagnosis of affective disorder (68,69). The serotonin dysfunction appears to represent more a trait than a state condition (70). It has been postulated that a central problem in serotonergic metabolism may contribute to the individual's impulsivity, aggressiveness, and suicidal potential, which then may be released in the presence of clinical depression.

Personality Predictors of Youthful Suicide

This paper reviews the available research literature on personality traits and disorders in adolescent suicide attempters and completers. Most of the literature on personality applies to suicide attempters and may not generalize to completers. The four studies on completed suicides in youth are retrospective and do not utilize standardized personality measures. In studies of attempted suicide, assessments frequently are brief and often are made in crisis settings. Patients in these studies who are not admitted to the hospital are difficult to follow and frequently do not want to discuss their suicide attempt. Assessment of personality occurs at variable time intervals from the attempt and may be confounded by the presence of an Axis I diagnosis and by stress.

Very few of the studies reviewed have used systematic and rigorous diagnoses of personality disorder since the focus of attention has usually been on Axis I disorders. A variety of different control groups have been used in some studies but not in others. Because suicide is an event with relatively low frequency, there are few prospective studies in the literature. Furthermore, there are extremely few studies of suicide attempters in a population with identified personality disorders. This review focuses on studies using standardized personality measures and assessments with appropriate control groups. The most frequently used method of assessment has been the questionnaire, but issues of reliability and validity are infrequently addressed, and the findings and measures have not been replicated in other studies (11).

Conduct Disorder: Strictly speaking, childhood conduct disorders cannot be considered the exact equivalent of personality disorder since the majority of children who qualify for this diagnosis do not go on to display a pattern of adult categorical disorder (71). Nonetheless, we discuss conduct disorders here because they tend to be relatively stable and are, by far, the sturdiest predictors of adult antisocial personality. The fact that conduct disorder is a major risk factor for both youth suicide and for adult antisocial personality disorder (which itself predicts for adult suicide) suggests that this diagnosis deserves special treatment and preventive attention.

Conduct disorder appears to be strongly associated with both suicide (72-74) and with suicide attempts (75-77). Conduct disorder is much more common among male suicide victims, and the precipitating event for the episode is often a disciplinary crisis. There is a frequent comorbidity of conduct disorder with affective, substance abuse, and borderline personality disorders, and the frequency and lethality of attempts increases with the degree of comorbidity. The few studies reviewed here that have systematically assessed for conduct disorder in suicidal youngsters are supported by the additional studies to be reviewed soon that have found aggressive, impulsive, and irritable personality traits to be more generally associated with suicide.

Borderline Personality Disorder (BPD): Although the construct of borderline personality disorder has not yet been carefully investigated or validated in adolescent patients, there are several interesting preliminary studies suggesting that it is often present and can be reliably diagnosed in adolescent suicide attempters (78-81). It also appears that the comorbidity of BPD and other disorders in adolescents is particularly likely to predict for more frequent and more lethal suicide attempts. Friedman et al. (82) found that among 76 adolescent inpatients, those who met criteria for both BPD and for major affective disorder were the most suicidal. In this same sample, Clarkin et al. (78) found that adolescent suicidal patients were equivalent to their adult counterparts in the prevalence of personality disorders (defined by a duration criterion of one year). Crumley found that BPD was the most common personality disorder in a group of hospitalized adolescents and that this diagnosis usually coexisted with major depression (67%) and/or substance abuse (77%). Alessi et al. (81) found a high prevalence (35%) of BPD in a sample of incarcerated juvenile offenders who would presumably also meet criteria for conduct disorder. The BPD diagnosis strongly predicted for greater frequency, seriousness, and lethality of suicide attempts. The association between BPD and suicide held up in both the Friedman (82) and the Alessi (81) studies even when the suicide item was itself eliminated as a criterion for making the BPD diagnosis, thus removing the risk that the association was merely a tautological artifact resulting from the fact that the DSM III definition of BPD includes one criterion devoted to suicidal behavior. Pfeffer (76) and colleagues found that BPD was the most frequent diagnosis among 48 preadolescent inpatients who were both assaultive and suicidal.

The place of the BPD diagnosis remains controversial in adult psychiatry and this is even more the case for adolescent patients who have received less systematic personality disorder assessment. Nonetheless, it seems likely that a diagnostic construct tapping characterological instability usefully predicts for suicidal behavior and this can be reliably assessed fairly early in life.

It is of great theoretical interest, and also of practical importance, that antisocial and borderline personality disorders that are most associated with adult suicidal behavior are also, in their adolescent form, (that is, conduct disorder substituting for antisocial) the most common personality disorders predicting adolescent suicidal behavior. Moreover, the personality trait measures associated with suicide are similar in adults and adolescents.

Personality Traits: In contrast to the relative paucity of studies having systematic psychiatric diagnosis, a number of studies have focused on personality traits in suicidal youngsters. The personality traits most commonly found in suicidal adolescents are equivalent to those found in adults and include aggressiveness (83-87), irritability (89-92), low frustration tolerance (83,84), social isolation (83,87,92-98), hopelessness and helplessness (91,104), poor self-concept (90,91,99-101), sexual conflicts (93,101,102), poor problem solving (100,103), resentfulness (88), and external locus control (105). It is of interest that these personality traits (especially aggressiveness, irritability, low frustration tolerance, and resentfulness) are fully consistent with the personality diagnostic categories (i.e., conduct disorder, borderline personality disorder) most often found in youthful suicides.

As is the case in studies of personality dimensions in adults, there have been several major problems in studies of such dimensions in adolescents. Generally, a given study focuses on only a small number of possibly important

dimensions so it is impossible to determine the degree to which the various dimensions can vary. Predictors are reported to be significantly different in large groups of suicidal individuals compared with nonsuicidal individuals, but the absolute and comparative predictive powers of the variables for the individual patient are not calculated. Studies of personality traits are usually not coordinated with studies of personality disorders so it is impossible to determine the degree to which these are correlated. Finally, there is the problem of comparison groups. Many studies of personality traits of suicidal individuals compared them to normal controls. Unless subjects are equivalent in their psychiatric diagnosis, it is impossible to determine the degree to which a given finding in the suicidal group is specific to suicide or whether it represents a trait more generally characteristic of psychiatric patients.

METHODOLOGICAL ISSUES

The Ability to Assess Personality in Youth: Before we can confidently determine whether particular personality disorders or personality traits are useful predictors of suicide, we must address the more fundamental question about the degree to which personality assessment is meaningful in the younger age groups. How does personality diagnosis in children approximate that in adults?

The DSM III definition of personality disorder requires an age of onset that occurs by adolescence or earlier and a continuous course throughout most of adult life. The relationship of personality disorder diagnosis in children and adolescents to that in adults is addressed specifically, and in some detail, in the introduction to the DSM III personality disorders section. It is proposed (without any great empirical support) that certain diagnostic categories from the DSM III Infancy, Childhood, and Adolescence section correspond to, and in effect eventually develop into, certain personality disorders (e.g. Schizoid Disorder of Childhood or Adolescence into Schizoid Personality Disorder; Avoidant Disorder of Childhood or Adolescence into Avoidant Personality Disorder; Conduct Disorder into Antisocial Personality Disorder; Oppositional Disorder into Passive Aggressive Personality Disorder; and Identity Disorder into Borderline Personality Disorder). The presumption is that the childhood or adolescent condition will be diagnosed if the individual is under age 18 whenever the personality psychopathology has persisted at an intensity sufficient to meet disorder criteria. Adult personality disorders without a corresponding childhood or adolescent category (e.g., hystrionic or paranoid) can be applied in childhood or in adolescence "in those unusual instances in which the particular traits appear to be stable. When this is done there is obviously less certainty that the personality disorder will persist unchanged over time."

Indeed, there are a number of reasons to be concerned that personality assessment may be less stable over time and predictive of future behavior in younger individuals. Since the past is the best predictor of the future in most things, including behavior, it makes sense to assume that the more of the past one has available, the more accurate the prediction will be. One is on statistically safer ground predicting that an individual with 30 previous criminal offenses by age 30 will soon commit more crimes than that a first offense at age 16 will be repeated over and over again. This general threat to the stability of personality assessment in early life is enhanced even further by three more specific confounds (personality/state; personality/role; and personality/developmental) which are also inherent problems in adult personality diagnoses but become especially problematic in assessing youths. We will discuss each of these in turn.

It is well documented that current state factors in adults (particularly the presence of accompanying mood disorder) greatly influence personality ratings by causing retrospectively distorted reporting of previous behaviors. State conditions, especially those that are chronic, may also interact in complicated ways with personality functioning; they may cause personality dysfunction or, conversely, personality dysfunction may predispose to state conditions, or, in many instances each may influence the other. The Axis I/Axis II confound presents major problems in adult personality disorder diagnosis, but there are several reasons to suppose that it is an even more difficult problem in childhood and adolescence. First, the various Axis I conditions have been less clearly and definitively described in younger patients and, in this age group, may be more likely to present in atypical or individual ways (perhaps influenced by developmental factors). Second, children have a less extensive track record on which to decide whether the problems are more state- or more trait-related. This combination of atypical Axis I presentations and a limited Axis II data base makes it doubly difficult to determine with any certainty whether a particular symptom or behavior (say irritability and/or poor conduct) arises from an Axis I syndrome (e.g., depression) or instead represents the early onset of stable personality features that may become manifest, for example, as conduct disorder or, ultimately, as antisocial personality.

The confounding of situational factors and personality disorders is also a problem in adult personality diagnosis but may be even more difficult in childhood because children tend to be more influenced by their social environment and its role expectations. For example, when a youngster presents with a conduct disturbance, it is difficult to determine whether he is responding to a disturbed family environment or to peer pressure or whether this is the beginning of what will become an antisocial personality disorder. In the first two instances, the appropriate diagnosis would be adjustment disorder with disturbance of conduct, with the expectation that the conduct problems will be self-limited if the precipitating stressors are removed. A diagnosis of conduct disorder or personality disorder implies that the behavior is more specific to the individual and likely to be stable and manifest across different social situations and role expectations.

Developmental changes constitute the third specific confound complicating personality assessment in children and adolescents. It is often difficult to predict prospectively whether a given behavior represents a stage-specific manifestation that the child is likely to "grow out of" or whether it is the beginning of a stable and lifelong pattern of personality functioning. For example, as a group, adolescents in our society are probably more narcissistic, troubled by identity problems, and prone to conduct disturbances than they will be as adults. The diagnoses of narcissistic, borderline, or antisocial personality disorder therefore will be applied prematurely and too liberally if these are based on a small slice of developmentally influenced adolescent behavior. Rather, such diagnosis should be based on a longer and wider strip of life experience beyond the confines of the developmental epoch in which such behaviors are less pathologic and specific to the individual.

Despite all these methodological cautions concerning personality diagnosis in childhood, there is evidence that some personality characteristics consistent across time can be detected fairly early in life. A number of studies indicate that marked individual differences in aggression become manifest early in life (certainly by age 3) and remain stable to a degree that approximates the stability of the I.Q. There is also abundant evidence that the presence of conduct disorders in childhood is uniformly obtained in the histories of individuals who go on to exhibit adult antisocial personality. (Note, however, that the majority of childhood conduct disorder youngsters do not grow up to be antisocial.) (106-111). These data suggest that although many children with conduct disorders "grow out" of them, many others do not. A childhood diagnosis of conduct disorder predicts both for childhood suicide and also for adult antisocial personality. Thus, in the personality areas that most reliably predict youthful and adult suicide, the pertinent personality variables have demonstrated suffi-cient stability to suggest the value of early detection, treatment, and prevention.

The best, although partial, solution to the methodological problem raised in this section is to develop semistructured personality disorder interviews adapted for children and adolescents. This is analogous to the fairly recent development of specialized Axis I interviews adapted especially for children (KIDDIE SADS). It will be necessary to define more specifically the behavioral criteria for childhood personality disorder as this is not handled with sufficient clarity in DSM III. Personality assessment in children will always be more difficult and less predictive than in adults, but such assessment will improve as it becomes more systematic and as empirical data accumulate.

Possible Relationships Between Personality Variables and Suicide: Establishing a correlational relationship between personality variables and suicide does not alone establish the direction of causality. We will discuss the several possible relationships that may be involved:

a. Definitional overlap: suicidal behavior may form an inherent part of the personality disorder definition, just as suicidal behavior is included within the definition for major depression. For example, DSM III includes reference to suicide within the criteria sets for both the borderline and hystrionic personality disorders. Whenever suicidal behavior is included within the definitional set for a disorder, it is inevitable that there will be some connection between that disorder and suicide. To establish that the relationship is real and not just definitional, one must demonstrate empirically that the criteria set for the personality disorder predicts for suicide even when the suicide item is omitted.

b. Personality disorder directly predisposes to suicidal behavior or to a form of suicide attempt (e.g., if one considers the impulsivity and aggressivity of BPD as a direct cause of suicidal behavior).

c. Personality disorders may predispose to Axis I disorders (e.g., depression), which then independently increase the risk for suicide.

d. Personality disorders may exert an influence on the expression of the Axis I condition so that the suicide risk is increased (e.g., most depressed patients do not suicide; the presence of personality disorder may increase the vulnerability to suicide in depressed patients.

e. Axis I conditions (e.g., depression), especially in chronic presentations, may predispose to behaviors that are indistinguishable from personality disorders or may exacerbate personality characteristics so that they present at the disorder level and/or the combination may interact to increase risk for suicide.

f. Personality traits (e.g., impulsivity or aggressivity) that cut across the categorical Axis II personality disorders may predispose to suicidal behavior.

g. The covariation between suicide and personality disorders may be based on chance or on the covariation of each with some other underlying factor.

A number of different types of studies and analyses are necessary to establish the nature of causality. The first step is to document that the prevalence of personality disorders is higher in suicidal patients compared with nonsuicidal patients, controlling for Axis I diagnosis. This would establish that there is a greater than baseline or chance comorbidity. The degree of independent specific contribution to suicide of the pertinent personality disorders (BPD and APD) can be determined by comparing their rates of suicide with those that occur in other kinds of personality disorder and also comparing the rates that obtain for them with and without comorbid Axis I disorders. Studies should also compare that predictive power of the categorical DSM III disorder system with dimensional measures of pertinent personality traits (e.g., aggressivity).

Attempters vs. Completers: In adults, suicide attempters and suicide completers seem to constitute two separate, but overlapping populations. A previous attempt carries an increased risk of eventual suicide (2% in one year and 10% lifetime), but attempters do not greatly resemble completers in demographic, diagnostic, or personality variables. The relationship of attempters to completers needs to be defined for the child and adolescent populations. The degree to which data on attempters (who are much easier to study) can be extrapolated to completers remains unclear. Moreover, the data gathered after a suicide attempt may not accurately reflect the individual's presuicidal functioning. Studies on personality characteristics in successfully completed suicides will have to depend upon informant methods of data gathering that are now being developed for adult personality assessment. Informant methods also may be very useful for childhood attempters who are not very reliable reporters of their own personality characteristics.

Comparison Group Selection: Many studies attempting to isolate the characteristics of suicidal patients compare them with normal controls. This is a serious methodological limitation, given that factors in the suicidal patients may be secondary to their psychiatric disturbance and not be particularly specific to, or predictive of, suicide. To relate a risk factor specifically to suicide, it is necessary to use a comparison group that is matched on diagnosis (as well as other possibly pertinent variables) so that suicide is the only uncontrolled variable in the comparison. Risk factors may vary by sex and age groups.

Interactions with Environmental Variables: Personality variables usually have been considered in isolation from the environmental variables with which they may interact in important ways. Future studies will have to redress this simplification. It will be necessary not only to tap the personality variables and the environmental variables associated with suicide but also to determine the specific interactions between these variables that heighten risk (e.g., angry impulsivity in a borderline personality disorder interacting with the loss of love object or the conduct disorder individual who has been caught in a misdemeanor).

Predictive Power: Suicide is a rare event, is associated with many correlates, and may result from heterogeneous causes. It seems unlikely that any variable, or grouping of variables, will ever have a high predictive power for suicide, especially in cross-sectional evaluation. By isolating personality variables associated with suicide, we can probably improve our ability to identify a group of youngsters at high suicide risk who deserve extra treatment and preventive efforts. Assessment is unlikely ever to be very successful in predicting which specific youth is at high risk to attempt suicide in the very near future.

DISCUSSION

Thanks largely to the increased reliability afforded by DSM III, personality disorder research in adults has recently been flourishing and promises to provide increasing clarity on the relationship of Axis I and Axis II disorders and in the interaction of these with suicidal behavior. However, the technical innovations in personality assessment developed for adults have not yet been translated into improved assessments of childhood personality features. Although the diagnosis of personality in youngsters is inherently problematic in the many ways we have outlined, it is likely to improve greatly as research attention turns in this direction. The results of this literature review suggest that the personality features that predict youthful suicide are very closely related to those that are associated with suicide in adults (borderline personality, conduct disorder/antisocial personality, impulsivity, aggression, social withdrawal). This would seem to confirm the continuity of personality factors throughout the life cycle as possible contributors to suicide risk.

Suggestions for Current Clinical Practice: Youngsters who present with conduct disorders and/or the impulsivity associated with borderline personality disorder deserve an especially thorough diagnostic evaluation that specifically assesses for the possible presence of Axis I conditions (e.g., affective disorder and substance abuse). Suicide risk and lethality appear to be highest for patients who present with comorbid combinations of Axis I and personality disorders so that aggressive treatment of the depression and/or substance abuse is crucial in this group. The presence of specific stressors (trouble with the law, loss of love object) that are particularly associated with suicide in personality-disordered youngsters should alert the clinician to increased risk and provide a target for immediate education and intervention. Although effective treatments for conduct and borderline disorders have yet to be documented, certain promising leads deserve further clinical and research attention.

Suggestions for Prevention: Robins and Earls (112) have suggested a promising research design to test the ability of a special prevention strategy to reduce the incidence of conduct disorder. They would select a group of children who have at least a 50 percent morbid risk of developing conduct disorder (i.e., those who have at least one antisocial parent). Since some of the origins of conduct disorder may occur early (prenatal exposure to neurotoxins and distress, postnatal trauma and illness, and parental deprivation) and since the earliest manifestation may occur during the preschool years, the preventive intervention would be designed for early delivery. The sample would be selected from pregnant women with antisocial disorder. The intervention aim to offset known risks for conduct disorder by providing adequate prenatal and pediatric care, offering high risk infants a special curriculum to increase language and social skills, and providing training and support of the parents. The research design would include randomization to a special developmental center or to a no-intervention control group. If the intervention were successful, Robins and Earls would expect significant differences to be evident by age 3 and that these would be substantial through age 10. Positive results detected at this point would presumably reduce the longer term risk of antisocial personality and also of youthful adult suicide, although such determination would require additional longitudinal study. This strategy for studying the effects of primary prevention for conduct disorders would appear to be feasible, cost-effective, and likely to have an impact on youthful suicide rates.

Suggestions for Future Research: The most immediate need is to develop methods to assess childhood personality disorders and personality traits. Available personality definitions and assessment instruments designed for adults have been developed only recently and must now be adapted for use in youngsters. The stability and predictive power of childhood personality measures and their relation to Axis I conditions must be determined empirically. Once assessment problems have been addressed, it will be important to evaluate treatment and prevention programs.

CONCLUSIONS

Personality disorder diagnosis has only recently achieved reliability, and empirical studies have only just begun to demonstrate the predictive power of personality variables. Thus far, almost all the available research has been conducted among adults, and we must recognize that personality assessment in childhood and adolescence is difficult and subject to inherent limitations. Nonetheless, it is fascinating that the very same personality variables that are associated with adult suicide are also associated with youth suicide, suggesting that preventive efforts focused on personality variables should be targeted to early identification, treatment and prevention, in high risk populations. Interventions that are effective in reducing personality risk factors are likely to reduce the suicide rates, not only in youthful populations but also in these same populations as they grow older.

It seems crucial to develop programs of prevention and treatment to counteract the disturbing cohort effect for conduct and affective disorder that may be responsible for the increasing rate of suicide in younger age groups.

Specific conclusions derived from our review include:

- The personality predictors of youthful suicide are equivalent to the personality predictors of adult suicide.

- There is stability of adolescent personality diagnoses into adulthood.

- Conduct disorder and borderline personality disorder are the most important personality disorder risk factors for adolescent suicide.

- Certain dimensional personality and cognitive traits (e.g., aggressivity, impulsivity, hopelessness, social isolation) may be important predictors, perhaps cutting across categorical personality disorder diagnosis.

- The comorbidity of Axis I and personality diagnosis increases the frequency and lethality of attempts.

- There may be a contributory role of a family history of antisocial behavior, substance abuse, and/or affective disorders to suicidal behavior.

- Comorbidity plus family history may increase lethality (both through genetics and environmental reinforcers).

- There is a need for better personality measures and assessments for children and adolescents.

- There is a need to establish whether the biological (particularly serotonergic) correlates of personality and suicidal behavior found in adults also apply to adolescents.

- It is necessary to determine how personality disorder/traits interact with other risk factors (i.e., family history, biological abnormalities, lack of social supports, other psychosocial risk factors, presence or affective disorder) to increase risk for suicidal behavior.

- Perhaps most important of all is the possibility that programs of primary and secondary prevention that succeed in reducing the morbidity of personality disorders in the young may thereby reduce not only the youthful suicide rate, but also the rates of adult personality disorders and the rates of adult suicide.

REFERENCES ···························

I. Frances A, Fyer M, Clarkin J: Personality and Suicide in Psychobiology of Suicidal Behavior (ed. J. Mann, M. Stanley) New York Academy of Science, New York; in press.

2. Akiskal HS, Chen SE, Davis GC, et al: 1985 Borderline: An adjective in search of a noun. J. Clin. Psych. 45:42-48.

3. Pope HG, Jr., Jonas JM, Hudson, JI, et al: 1983. The validity of DSM-III Borderline personality disorder. Arch. Gen. Psych. 40:23-30.

4. Stone, MH: 1986. Long Term follow-up of Borderline Personality Disorder. Journal of Personality Disorders (in press).

5. Fyer M, Frances A, Sullivan T, et al: (unpublished). Borderline personality disorder and affective disorder: Impact of comorbidity on suicide.

6. Rounsaville BJ, Weissman MM, Kleber H & Wilber C: 1982. Heterogeneity of psychiatric diagnosis in treated opiate addicts. Arch. Gen. Psych. 39:161-166.

7. Friedman RC, Aronoff MS, Clarkin JF, et al: 1983. History of suicidal behavior in depressed borderline inpatients. Am. J. Psych. 140:1023-1026.

8. Maddocks RD: 1970. A five year followup of untreated psychopaths. Br. J. Psych. 116:511-515.

9. Robins LN: 1966. Deviant Children Grown Up. Williams & Wilkins, Baltimore.

10. Woodruff RA, Jr., Clayton PJ & Guze SB: Suicide attempts and psychiatric diagnosis. Dis. Ner. Syst. 33:617-621.

11. Miles A: 1977. Conditions predisposing to suicide: A review. J. Nerv. Ment. Dis. 164:231-245.

12. Garvey MJ & Sooden F: 1980. Suicide attempts in antisocial personality disorder. Compre. Psychiatr. 21 (2):146-149.

13. Morgan HG, Borton J, Poffle LS, et al: 1976. Deliberate self-harm: A followup study of 279 patients. Br. J. Psych. 128:361-368.

14. Buglass P & Horton J: 1974. The repetition of parasuicide: A comparison of three cohorts. Br. J. Psych. 125:168-174.

15. Robins E, Schmidt EH & O'Neal P: 1957. Some interrelations of social factors and clinical diagnosis in attempted suicide: A study of 109 patients. Am. J. Psych. 114:221-231.

16. Batchelor, IRC: 1954. Psychopathic states and attempted suicide. Br. Med. J. 1:1342-1347.

17. Robins, LN, Murphy GE, Wilkinson RH, et al: 1959. Some clinical consideratiaons in the prevention of suicide based on a study of 134 successful suicides. Am. J. Public Health. 49:888-889.

18. Ward NG, Bonuowit MA: 1980. Factors associated with suicidal behavior in polydrug abusers. J. Clin. Psych. 41(11):379-385.

19. Clayton PJ: 1985. Suicide. Psych. Clin. N. Amer. 8(2):203-214.

20. Crook T, Raskin A & David D: 1975. Factors associated with attempted suicide among hospitalized depressed patients. Psychol. Med. 5:381-388.

21. Paykel ES, Dienelt M: 1971. Suicide attempts following acute depression. J. Nerv. Met. Dis. 153:234-243.

22. Henderson AS, Hartigan J, Davidson J, et al: 1977. A typology of parasuicide. Br. J. Psych. 131:631-641.

23. Conte HR & Plutchik R: 1974. Personality and background characteristics of suicidal mental patients. J. Psych. Res. 10:181-188.

24. Vinoda KS: 1966. Personality characteristics of attempted suicides. Br. J. Psych. 112:1143-1150.

25. Murthy VN: 1969. Personality and the nature of suicidal attempts. Br. J. Psych. 115:791-795.

26. Birtchnell J: 1981. Some familial and clinical characteristics of female suicidal psychiatric patients. Br. J. Psych. 138:381-390.

27. Pallis DJ & Birtchnell J: 1977. Serious of suicide attempt in relation to personality. Br. J. Psych. 130:253-259.

28. Weissman MM, Fox K & Klerman GL: 1973. Hostility and depression associated with suicide attempts. Am. J. Psych. 130(4):450-454.

29. Philip A: 1970. Traits, attitudes and symptoms in a group of attempted suicides. Br. J. Psych. 116:475-482.

30. Cantor, PC: 1976. Personality characteristics found among youthful female suicide attempters. J. Abnormal Psychol. 85(3):324-392.

31. Topol P & Reznikoff M: 1982. Perceived peer and family relationships, hopelessness and locus of control as factors in adolescent suicide attempts.

32. Nelson, NL, Nielsen EC & Obecketts MT: 1977. Interpersonal attitudes of suicidal individuals. Psychological Reports 40:983-989.

33. Farberow N, Devries AG: 1967. An item differentiation analysis of MMPIs of suicideal neuropsychiatric hospital patients. Psychological Reports 20:607-617.

34. Yusin A, Sinai R & Nihira K: 1972. Adolescents in crises: evaluation of questionnaire. Am. J. Psych. 129:574-577.

35. Rushing: 1969. Deviance, interpersonal relations and suicide. Human Relations 22(1):61-76.

36. Meyhryar AH, Hekmat H & Khajavi F: 1977. Some personality correlates of contemplated suicide. Psychol. Rep. 40:(3 of 2):1291-1294.

37. Flood R & Seager C: 1968. A retrospective examination of psychiatric case records of patients who subsequently committed suicide. Br. J. Psych. 114:443-452.

38. Ross MW, Clayer JR & Campbell RL: 1983. Parental rearing patterns and suicidal thoughts. Acta. Psychiatr. Scand. 67:429-433.

39. Wetzel RD: 1975. Self concept and suicidal intent. Psychological Reports 36:279-282.

40. Farberow NL & McEvoy YL: 1966. Suicide among patients with diagnoses of anxiety reaction or depressive reaction in general medical and surgical hospitals. J. Abnormal Psychol. 71:287-299.

41. Spalt L & Weisbauch JB: 1972. Suicide: an epidemiological study. Dis. Nerv. Syst. 33:23-29.

42. Kamano DK & Crawford CS: 1966. Self-evaluations of suicidal mental health patients. J. Clin. Psychol. 2:278-279.

43. Wilson LM, Brtaught JN, Miskimins RW, Berry KL: 1971. The severe suicide attempter and self-concept. J. Clin. Psychol. 27:307-309.

44. Neuringer C: 1973. Attitude toward self in suicidal individuals. Life-threatening Behavior. 4:86-106.

45. Neuringer C: 1974. Self-and-other-appraisals by suicidal, psychosomatic and normal hospitalized patients. J. Consult. Clin. Psychol. 42:306.

46. Braaten, LJ & Darling CD: 1962. Suicidal tendencies among college students. Psych. Quarterly 36:665-698.

47. Bedrosian RC & Beck AT: 1979. Cognitive aspects of suicidal behavior. Suicide and Life-Threatening Behavior. 9(2):87-96.

48. Beck AT: 1963. Thinking and depressional idiosyncratic content and cognitive distortions. Arch. Gen. Psych. 9:324.

49. Minkoff R, Bergman E, Beck AT & Beck R: 1973. Hopelessness, depression and attempted suicide. Am. J. Psych. 130(4):455-459.

50. Wenz FV: 1977. Subjective powerlessness, sex, and suicide potential. Psychological Reports 40:927-928.

51. Boor M: 1976. Relationship of internal-external control and United States suicide rates. 1966-73. J. Clin. Psychol. 38(4):795-797.

52. Patsiokas AT, Clum GA & Luscomb RL: 1979. Cognitive characteristics of suicide attempters. J. Consult. & Clin. Psychol. 47(3):478-484.

53. Neuringer O: 1964. Rigid thinking in suicidal individuals. J. Consult. Psychol. 88:54-58.

54. Echette DB & Clum SA: 1982. Suicide ideation in a college population: A test of a model. J. Consult. & Clin. Psychol. 50(5):690-696.

55. Eastwood MR, Henderson RS & Montgomery IM: 1978. Personality and parasuicidal methodological problems. Med. J. Aust. 1:170-175.

56. Goldney RD: 1981. Are young women who attempt suicide hysterical? Br. J. Psych. 138:41-146.

57. Farberow NL: 1950. Personality patterns of suicidal mental hospital patients. Gen. Psychol. Monograms 42:3-79.

58. Clooton J, Post R, Larce J: 1983. Identification of suicide attempters by means of MMPI profiles. J. Clin. Psychol. 38(8):868-871.

59. Roy A: 1978. Selfmutilation. Br. J. Med. Psychol. 51:201-203.

60. Infani S: 1978. Personality correlates of suicidal tendency among Iranian and Turkish students. J. of Psychol. 99:151-153.

61. Colson CE: 1978. Neuroticism, extraversion and repression-sensitization in suicidal college students. Brit. J. Soc. & Clin. Psychol. 11:88-89.

62. Pallis DJ & Jenkins JS: 1977. Extraversion, neuroticism and intent in attempted suicides. Psychological Reports 41:19-22.

63. Traskman L, Asberg M, Bertilsson L & Sjostrand L: 1981. Monamine metabolites in cerebrospinal fluidand suicidal behavior. Arch. Gen. Psych. 38:631-636.

64. van Praag H: 1982. Depression, suicide and metabolism of serotonin in the brain. J. Aff. Dis. 4:275-290.

65. Asbert M, Traskman L & Thoren P: 1976. 5 HIAA in the cerebrospinal fluid: A biochemical suicide prediction? Arch. Gen. Psych. 33:1193-1197.

66. Agren H: 1980. Symptom patterns in unipolar and bipolar depression correlating with monamine metabolites in the cerebrospinal fluid: Suicide. Psych. Res. 3:225-236.

67. Bankicm, Vojnik M, Papp Z, et al: Cerebrospinal fluid magnesium and calcium related to amine metabolites, diagnosis and suicide attempt. Biol. Psych. 980:163-171.

68. Brown GL, Goodwin FK, Ballinger JC, et al: 1979. Aggression in humans correlates with CSF metabolites. Psych. Res. 1:131.

69. Brown GL, Ebert ME, Goyer PF, et al: 1982. Aggression, suicide and serotonin: Relationships to CSF amine metabolites. Am. J. Psych. 139:631-636.

70. Agren H: 1983. Life at risk: Markers of suicidality and depression. Psych. Devel. 1:87.

71. Robins LN: Study childhood predictors of adult antisocial behavior. Psychological Medicine 8:611-622, 1978.

72. Shaffer D: Suicide in childhood and early adolescence. J. Child Psychol. Psychiat. 15:275-291, 1974.

73. Pfeffer CR: Self-destructive behavior in children and adolescents. Psychiatr. Clin. of North America, Vol. 8, No. 2, 1985.

74. Shaffer D: Diagnostic Considerations in suicidal behavior in children and adolescents. J. Am. Acad. Child Psych. 21:414-415, 1982.

75. Carlson GA, Cantwell DP: Suicidal behavior and depression in children and adolescents. J. Am. Acad. of Child Psychiatry 21:361-368, 1982.

76. Pfeffer CR, Plutchik R, Mizouchi MS: Suicidal and assaultive behavior in children: classification, measurement and interrelations. Am. J. Psychiatry.

77. Cohen-Sandler R, Berman AL, King RA: Life Stress and symptomatology. Determinants of Suicidal behavior in children. J. Am. Acad. Child Psych. 21:178-186, 1982.

78. Clarkin T, Friedman R, Hurt S, Corn R & Arnonoff M: Affective and character pathology of suicidal adolescent and young adult inpatients. Psychiatr. 45:19-22, 1984.

79. Crumley FE: Adolescent suicide attempts and borderline personality disorder: clinical features. Southern Medical Journal 74:546-549, 1981.

80. Crumley FE: The adolescent suicide attempt: A cardinal symptom of a serious psychiatric disorder. Am. J. Psychotherapy 36:158-165, 1982.

81. Alessi NE, McManus M, Brikman A & Grapetine L: Suicidal behavior among serious juvenile offenders. Am. J. Psychiatr. 141:2, 1984.

82. Friedman RL, Clarkin JF, Corn R: DSM III and affective pathology in hospitalized adolescents. J. Nerv. Ment. Dis. 170:511-521, 1982.

83. Petzel SV & Riddle M: Adolescent suicide: Psychosocial and cognitive aspects. Adol. 9:343-398, 1981.

84. Cantor PC: Personality characteristics found among youthful female suicide attempters. J. Abnormal Psychol. 85:324-329, 1976.

85. Goldberg EL: Depression and suicide ideation in the young adult. Am. J. Psychiatr. 138:1, 1981.

86. Tishler CL & McKenry PC: Intrapyschic symptom dimensions of adolescent suicide attempters.

87. Hawton K, Cole D, O'Grady & Osborn M: Motivational aspects of deliberate self-poisoning in adolescents. Brit. J. Psychiat. 141:286-291, 1982.

88. Lester D: Suicide as an aggressive act: A replication with a control for neuroticism. J. Gen. Psychol. 79:83-86.

89. Haider L: Suicidal attempts in children and adolescents. Brit. J. of Psychiat. 114:1113-1134, 1968.

90. Toolan JM: Suicide and suicidal attempts in children and adolescents. Am. J. of Psychiat. 118:719-724, 1962.

91. Marks PA & Haller DL: Now I lay me down for keeps: A study of adolescent suicide attempts. J. Clin. Psychol. 33:390-400.

92. Jacobs J: Adolescent Suicide. New York: Wiley-Interscience.

93. Peck ML & Schrut A: Suicidal behavior among college students. HSMHA Health Reports 86:149-156.

94. Lukianowicz N: Attempted suicide in children. Acta Psych. Scandinavica 44:415-435.

95. Schrut A: Some typical patterns in the behavior and background of adolescent girls who attempt suicide. Am. J. Psychiat. 125:107-112.

96. Barter JT, Swaback DO & Todd D: Adolescent suicide attempts: a follow-up study of hospitalized patients. Arch. Gen. Psychiatr. 19:523-527, 1968.

97. Yusin A, Sinay R & Nihira K: Adolescents in crisis: evaluation of a questionnaire. Am. J. Psychiatr. 129:574-577.

98. Weitzel WD, Nerviano V & Hatcher: Adolescent failure during secondary socialization: A study of army trainee casualties. J. Psychiatr. Res. 13:125-135, 1977.

99. Mcintire MS, Angle CR, Wikoff RL & Schlicht ML: Recurrent adolescent suicidal behavior. Pediatrics 60:605-608, 1977.

100. Levenson M & Neuringer C: Intropunitiveness in suicidal adolescents. J. of Projective Tech. and Personality Assessment 34:409-411.

101. Senseman LA: Attempted suicide in adolescents: A suicide prevention center in Rhode Island is in urgent need. Rhode Island Medical Journal 52:449-451,1969.

102. Sabbath JC: The suicidal adolescent - the expendable child. J. of Am. Acad. Child Psychiatry 8:272-285, 1969.

103. Maxman JS & Tucker GJ: No exit: The persistently suicidal patient. Comprehensive Psychiatry 14:71-79, 1973.

104. Melges FT & Weisz AE: The personal future and suicidal ideation. J. of Nerv. and Mental Dis. 153:244-250, 1971.

105. Goldney RD: Locus of control in young women who have attempted suicide. J. of Nerc. and Ment. Disease 70:4.

106. Farrington DP: The family backgrounds of aggressive youths. In L. Hersov, M. Berger & D Shaffer (eds.) Aggression and antisocial disorders in children. Oxford, England: Pergamon Press, 1978.

107. Moore, DR & Arthur JL: Juvenile delinquency. In T.H. Ollendick & M. Hersen (eds.), Handbook of Child Psychopathology. New York. Plenum Press, 1983.

108. Olweus D: Aggression and peer acceptance in adolescent boys: Two short-term longitudinal studies of ratings. Child Development, 1977, 48:1301-1313.

109. Olweus D: Stability of aggressive reaction patterns in males: A review. Psychological Bulletin, 1979, 86:852-875.

110. Roff M: Childhood social interactions and young adult bad conduct. Journal of Abnormal and Social Psychology, 1963, 63:333-337.

111. Roff, JD & Wirt RD: Childhood aggression and social adjustment as antecedents of delinquency. Journal of Abnormal Child Psychology, 1984, 12:111-126.

112. Earls F: Towards the Prevention of Psychiatric Disorders. In: The Annual Review of Psychiatry (ed. R. Hales & A. Frances) American Psychiatric Press, Washington, D.C. 1987.

SUBSTANCE USE AND ABUSE: A RISK FACTOR IN YOUTH SUICIDE

Marc A. Schuckit, M.D., Professor of Psychiatry, University of California Medical School, and Director, Alcohol Research Center, San Diego Veterans Administration Medical Center, San Diego, California

Judith J. Schuckit, San Diego, California

INTRODUCTION

This paper reviews the relationship between the use and abuse of substances and adolescent suicidal behaviors. Before presenting the actual data, it is important to address some relevant problems of definition.

For purposes of this overview, childhood and adolescence extend to age 24, although the majority of studies have focused on people 19 years old or less. Suicidal behavior can include intense thoughts of wishing to be dead; attempts or "gestures" can relate to any level of deliberate self harm; while completion of suicide requires documentation through a coroner's report or interviews with "significant others."

Alcohol and substance **use** connote intake of these drugs without associated major life problems (1,2). Information about use is distinct from data on alcoholism or drug abuse which relate to heavy intake of drugs or alcohol and documentation of serious and persistent related life problems (1,5). Unfortunately, in many studies specific criteria are not clearly stated.

Also of central importance to this discussion is the definition of psychiatric disorders. Many of the earlier studies set forth no rigorous criteria for the syndromes being described. The more recent investigations often use the Research Diagnostic Criteria (RDC) or the Third Diagnostic and Statistical Manual of the American Psychiatric Association (DSM III) (4,5). Reflecting these more rigorous and reliable classifications, whenever possible emphasis is placed on findings from current studies.

Discussions of behavior associated with substance abuse, however, must go a step further in classifying subjects. In the course of misuse of drugs or alcohol almost all types of behavioral aberrations can develop, including severe states of anxiety, depression, acute psychoses, and severe confusion (1,2,6). Using diagnosis to indicate prognosis and to help in selection of treatment, it is important to attempt to establish a hierarchy of problems. One approach is to differentiate between primary and secondary illness (3,7). A primary psychiatric label is assigned when an individual fulfills criteria for that disorder and has no major preexisting psychiatric problem. An example would be an adolescent who met the requirements for drug abuse and who had no antisocial personality disorder (ASPD), major depressive disorders, schizophrenia, etc., prior to the onset of severe drug related difficulties. A secondary label is assigned when an individual meets criteria for a disorder only after another major psychiatric illness was present. An example of this phenomenon is the man or woman with an ASPD (e.g. the onset prior to the age of 15 of pervasive antisocial difficulties) who, at age 18, went on to develop severe alcohol-related life problems; this is a case of primary ASPD and secondary alcoholism and the prognosis is likely to be that of the personality disorder, not alcoholism (6,8-10).

With these caveats in mind, we turn to a discussion of some risk factors associated with adolescent suicidal behavior. Section II briefly reviews the prevalence of suicide attempts and completions among young people in order to place into perspective the data that follow. Section III reviews the direct relationship between substance use or abuse and suicidal behavior, emphasizing the application to adolescents. Section IV looks at indirect associations between substance use or abuse and suicidal behavior as they relate to other primary diagnoses including ASPD, borderline personality, affective or depressive disorders and schizophrenia. This includes brief comments on the ties between suicidal behavior and substance abuse in adolescents and family environment or family history of psychiatric disorders. Finally, Section V synthesizes the information and offers some clinical and research implications.

THE EPIDEMIOLOGY OF SUICIDE ATTEMPTS AND COMPLETIONS

The following discussion distinguishes between the prevalence of suicide attempts and completions. Within each section, information is first given regarding rates in the general population, and this is followed by figures among adolescents. Each section concludes with data on changes in the rate of these phenomena over the years.

Attempts

About 10 percent (10,000/100,000/yr) or more of people in the general population reported suicidal feelings over the prior year, including 2.5 percent who had more intense thoughts (11-13). Counting all age groups, actual suicide attempts are observed at a rate between 100 and 800/100,000/yr, with women age 15 to 24 years standing out with the high figures shown in Table 1 (12,14,16). In men, the 15 to 24 year olds also predominate, but in each age group the actual rates are about half those seen in women (12,14,15,17-22).

Since the peak age for suicide attempts is between 15 and 24 years old (14-19), it is not surprising that a number of studies have focused specifically on the attempt rate for

Suicidal Behavior by Sex and Age per 100,000/yr (12-15,17,19,22,30,31)

Age	ATTEMPTS Male	ATTEMPTS Female	COMPLETIONS Male	COMPLETIONS Female
< 15	26	92	< 1	< 1
15-24	423	786	16	4
25-44	267	598	24	10
45-64	152	257	26	14
65 +	70	41	33	11

Table 1.

children and adolescents. Looking first at more anecdotal data on children who have sought help, it has been estimated that 3 percent of a consecutive series of young people coming to private practice or psychiatric outpatient settings had ever attempted suicide. The same is true for 10 percent to 30 percent of adolescents coming to emergency rooms, and the rate of attempts increases to between 10 percent and 50 percent among young psychiatric inpatients (18,20-22). These figures are probably inflated because of the troubled nature of the populations observed.

The high prevalence of suicide attempts in any age group, including adolescents, is not a new phenomenon (13,16,17,23-25). Most of the literature focuses on more anecdotal reports; between 1972 and 1980 there was a 5-fold increase in adolescents seen for suicide attempts in a Louisville, Kentucky psychiatric hospital (26), and an almost doubling of adolescent suicidal behavior was seen between 1970 and 1975 in a New Haven, Connecticut emergency room (14).

Suicide Completions

Suicide completion is a much rarer phenomenon than suicide attempt. The ratio between the two depends upon the definitions used, but is at least 10 to 1 (17,27), and could be as high as 100 or more to 1 in some groups (28,29). There is, however, an important connection between attempts and completions, because as many as 50 percent or more of completers have attempted suicide in the past (27).

As shown in Table 1, overall about 15 people per 100,000 of the general population died by suicide in 1980, with a male preponderance of between 2 or 3 to 1, and a peak rate for men age 65 or older (15,30-33). As infrequent as completed suicide is in the general population, it is even less common among adolescents. However, self-inflicted death has long rated as the third leading cause of mortality in this otherwise healthy group, especially for youth with histories of psychiatric care (18,21,34,35). Despite isolated cases of apparent short-term

"epidemics" of suicidal behavior among young people (36), completed suicide is especially rare for children under age 15 (15,30,35).

The prevalence of suicides in the United States and Canada appears to have been stable during the 1950s (20,32). However, as reported for attempts, suicidal death began to increase in the 1960s. The overall rate in 1961 was 5/100,000/yr for men and 1 for women in Alberta, Canada; almost double the figures from 1951 (32). Self-inflicted death rose to 25 and 5 for the two sexes by 1971, on to approximately 32 and 5 by 1976 (32). In general, the U.S. suicide rate rose from 5.2 to 13.3/100,000/yr from 1960 to 1980 (31). Other investigators have also documented an increase of at least two- to threefold between 1960 and 1980 (18,30,31,37,38).

SUBSTANCE USE/MISUSE AND SUICIDE RISK: A DIRECT ASSOCIATION

Alcohol and drug use and violent death (accidents, homicide, and suicide) are potentially related in a number of ways (39-41). Drugs of abuse, especially brain depressants (e.g. barbiturates, antianxiety drugs, and alcohol) and brain stimulants (e.g. amphetamines, cocaine, weight reducing products) can impair judgment, increase levels of impulsivity, and are capable of producing severe mood disturbances, including temporary, intense and suicidal depressions (1,6,42). Any substance of abuse can also exacerbate a preexisting state of psychopathology, including increasing the level of hallucinations or delusions in psychoses, enhancing anxiety, and increasing levels of depression (1,6,43-45). The following sections briefly review information on the association between substances and suicide attempts or completions in general (Section A), as well as in adolescents (Section B).

Alcohol, Drugs, and Suicide Attempts: A General Discussion

One obvious association between substances

and suicide is the use of alcohol or drugs as vehicles for the suicidal act. Historically, drug overdoses of prescription or over-the-counter drugs have been a favored mechanism in suicide attempts, especially overdoses with brain depressants in women (14,46). The use of drugs as the mechanism of attempt by young people is equally strong. In one consecutive series of 505 adolescents and children seen in a pediatric emergency room for a suicide attempt, 88 percent had used drug overdose, as had 78 percent to 100 percent of suicide attempting youth reported in other samples (1,22,47-49), although some authors have reported lower rates (30,31).

In any age group, intoxication with alcohol or drugs often immediately precedes suicidal behavior (17,39,50-52). In some instances, this relates to suicide attempts among alcohol or drug abusers, but in others it reflects the use of substances as part of the attempt itself or in an effort to "screw up enough courage" to carry it out. In any event, one study reported as many as 70 percent of male and 40 percent of female suicide attempters had consumed heavy doses of ethanol before the act, with average resulting blood alcohol concentrations (BACs) of almost 150 milligrams per deciliter (mg/dL) for the men and over 100 mg/dL for the women (12). Alcohol was found to have "contributed to the death," through perhaps impaired judgment or exaggerated mood swings as well as through effects on vital systems, in more than half the autopsied cases in one study in Washington, D.C., and more than two-thirds of the suicides in another study in New York City (61,62).

There is ample documentation of a high suicide rate among substance abusers themselves. At entrance into an alcohol treatment program, at least 20 percent of alcoholics report histories of suicide attempts (53). Prospective followup of identified alcoholics have revealed a three-fold or higher increased rate of suicide completion (41,54,55), with Miles estimating a lifetime rate as high as 15 percent (56).

The association with violent death extends to

drug abusers as well, with at least 15 percent admitting to past suicide attempts. The estimated lifetime suicide completion rate among some types of drug abusers exceeds 10 percent (1,53,56-59), including a four-fold increased rate over the general population among amphetamine abusers, as well as a high of suicide among cocaine and heroin addicts. Drug abusers who express extreme feelings of depression or hopelessness may be at exceptionally high risk (60).

Considering the lifetime rate of suicide completion among substance abusers, it is not surprising that studies of patients who have committed suicide have noted that a high proportion have a history of substance misuse. Using rigorous criteria, 20 percent to 50 percent of suicide attempters or completers were found to be drug abusers, while between 15 percent and 50 percent of completed suicides in several studies were alcoholics (27,33,63-68).

In summary, from the studies in the general population and focusing on all ages there appears to be a close relationship between alcohol and drug use or abuse and suicide. The association is supported by followup studies of alcoholics or drug abusers, evaluations of the characteristics of suicide victims, and followup evaluations of psychiatric patients.

Alcohol, Drugs, and Suicidal Behavior Among Adolescents

Analyses of data for adolescents also document a close association between substances and suicide, as outlined in Table 2 (35,69,70). This conclusion is supported by studies of suicidal youth, evaluations of substance abusers, and through observation of young psychiatric patients.

Adolescents who fulfill criteria for drug abuse or who have relatively heavy drug intake patterns have an increased rate of death overall, including high rates of suicide. A 10-year followup of two groups of teenagers (one from the general population and the second identified because of prior drug use) revealed a two- to seven-fold increased death rate among boys with histories of drug misuse, and an almost two-fold to eight-fold increased death rate among girls (71). Approximately half of this increase in death rate was from suicide.

The relationship between drugs, alcohol, and suicide in young people is corroborated when populations identified because of suicidal behavior are evaluated. Patel reported that among suicide attempters age 12 to 19 years old, 41 percent of the boys and 19 percent of the girls had been drinking immediately before the attempt (13), and Garfinkel found a ten-fold higher rate of recent alcohol or drug use in 505 adolescent attempters than for controls (22). Shafii noted "frequent use of nonprescription drugs or alcohol" among 70 percent of the 20 teenagers who committed suicide in the Louisville area between 1980 and 1983 (26), while almost half of the suicides aged 15 to 19 in Erie County, New York, had alcohol in their blood (50). The study of suicides under age 30 in San Diego found that more than 75 percent abused drugs or alcohol, including between a third and a half for whom these diagnoses were the primary illnesses (31). Among those with drug problems in the San Diego sample, 79 percent had abused marijuana, 45 percent cocaine, 34 percent amphetamines, and about 25 percent each had abused opiates, sedatives/ hypnotics, or hallucinogens. There was an average of three to five substances abused per individual.

The association between suicidal behavior and drugs is just as strong among adolescent psychiatric patients. Robbins and Alessi studied 33 teenage psychiatric inpatients who had histories of prior suicide attempts, looking for the relationship between alcohol or drug use and suicidal behavioral (18). They used an analysis of correlation that evaluates the degree to which two factors change at the same time (the higher the correlation, the greater the similarity in change). A history of alcohol abuse correlated with the number of past suicidal "gestures" at a 0.42 level (p<.001), accounting for 25 percent of the variance or range of the number of gestures in this group. Similarly, the correlation between alcohol abuse and the seriousness of past attempts was 0.35 (p<.01), and alcohol problems correlated with the level of medical seriousness at 0.36 (p<.01). Overall, the association between a history of alcohol abuse and the occurrence of a suicide attempt was 0.28 (p<.05). A history of drug abuse correlated with the number of suicide "gestures" at 0.32 (p<.05), and with the medical seriousness at 0.26 (p<.05). Those authors conclude that "substance abuse in depressed adolescents appears both to increase the risk of multiple attempts and to add to the medical seriousness of the attempt."

Suicidal Behavior and Substance Abuse in Adolescents are Linked	
(13,18,22,26,30,31,50,71)	
Among heavy substance users:	Four fold increased suicidal death rate
Among adolescent suicide attempters:	Ten fold increased substance use 30 percent drank before attempt
Among adolescent suicide completers:	70 percent used drugs frequently 50 percent had alcohol in blood 75 percent fit criteria for drug or alcohol use disorders
Among young psychiatric patients:	Suicidal behavior and substance abuse correlate

Table 2.

Several factors complicate the interpretation of these data. First, adolescence and early adulthood are ages of maximal alcohol and drug use (1,72-74). Second, as discussed by Weissman (75) people with multiple problems are more likely to seek care than those with one problem alone. Therefore, substance users who also have depressive symptoms and multiple life crises are the ones most likely to be identified and to be a part of studies. The apparent close association between substance use and suicidal behavior in treated groups might not completely generalize to substance users in the general population.

In summary, there is much evidence connecting alcohol and drug use with suicide attempts and completions in both adults and adolescents. This includes an increased prevalence of alcohol and drug use prior to suicide attempts, a marked increase in risk for suicide attempts and completions among drug and alcohol abusers, an overrepresentation of drug and alcohol abusers among suicide attempters, and a correlation between suicide attempts and a history of drug or alcohol abuse among psychiatric patients.

MORE INDIRECT EVIDENCE CONNECTING DRUGS AND ALCOHOL WITH SUICIDAL BEHAVIOR

Section I described how careful psychiatric diagnostic labels can give important clinical information on a patient's probable prognosis and treatment needs (1,3). To meet these goals, however, it is necessary to distinguish between primary disorders and those illnesses that develop only after another preexisting psychiatric problem was established (secondary illness). This is especially important for alcohol and drug abuse, because the prognosis and rehabilitation needs can be quite different for primary and secondary misusers (1,6,9,45).

This section highlights a number of primary psychiatric disorders in which both suicidal behavior and substance abuse are common problems. Thus, an important association between substance abuse and suicidal behavior is mediated through personality disorders and psychiatric illnesses that can be seen in adolescents and that sometimes run in families.

Personality Disorders

Over the years, attempts have been made to use clear-cut criteria to outline psychiatric disorders for which good followup data are available (3-5). Unfortunately, with one or two exceptions, the progress for personality labels has been less impressive than for the other categories of the DSM III.

Personality disorders in general are likely to be associated with suicidal behavior. Anecdotally, character and behavior (or personality) disorders are among the most frequent diagnoses for soldiers or sailors with suicide attempts (17,19,29,76). Among psychiatric patients with histories of self-harm, between 35 percent and 80 percent are noted to have some type of personality disorder (21,77-79), although few studies used objective criteria to identify the personality problem involved.

It is probable that the specific label of the antisocial personality disorder (ASPD) is closely tied to suicidal behavior. The diagnostic framework for this problem has changed over the years, evolving from the psychodynamic concept presented by Cleckley (80) to a more precise constellation of symptoms outlined by Robins and colleagues and adopted (with some modifications) by the DSM III (5,81,82). As presently used in most studies, the label of ASPD connotes an individual with antisocial problems in multiple life areas beginning prior to the age of 15 and continuing into adulthood; these are problems that cannot be explained solely by alcohol or drug use histories. Subjectively, these individuals are likely to be impulsive, have difficulty conforming to the expectations of others and learning from mistakes, and show impairment in establishing long-term relationships.

Approximately 80 percent of ASPD patients

have a history of alcohol abuse and associated serious problems (6,83,84), and these men and women carry an elevated risk for drug related pathology as well (82-86). ASPD patients are also more likely than the general population to attempt and complete suicide (1,35,68,83). One in four have history of suicide attempts, and during a 5- to 6-year followup, 5 percent had died by suicide (53,87).

Two other personality disorders appear to be associated with both substance abuse and suicidal behavior. First is the DSM III syndrome of somatization disorder that grew out of a concept of hysteria and Briquet's disease (3,5,88,89). Patients with this disorder are usually women who at an early age develop somatic complaints in multiple body system, including numerous conversion symptoms (neurological symptoms other than pain with no known medical basis). Severe mood swings are common and suicide attempts occur at a much higher rate than in the general population (3,89,90). Women with this disorder may have a 15 percent prevalence of concomitant use of substances for "recreation" or use outside of normal prescribing practices (89). Therefore, considering the relatively early age of onset, this may be a second example where substance misuse and suicidal behavior are tied together through a separate primary illness.

Finally, an early onset personality disorder characterized by severe mood swings and an inability to handle life stress has been described as the "borderline personality" (91,99). Subjectively, these patients share many characteristics with individuals with ASPD or somatization disorder, demonstrating impulsiveness and frequent mood swings. In addition to an increased rate of suicide attempts, these men and women are also more likely than the general population to misuse alcohol or other drugs (93,94).

Major Psychiatric Disorders

The most frequently reported diagnoses associated with suicidal behavior are affective illnesses, usually unipolar or bipolar major depressive disorders or, in the earlier studies, "depressive neurosis." An affective disorder is seen in 50 percent to 65 percent of adult suicide attempters (19,20,53,100,103), as well as in between 55 percent and 95 percent of suicide attempting adolescents and children (18,22,93,104). The association between suicide completion and depressive illness is also high for all ages, with about half of suicide completers noted retrospectively to have had major depressive disorders (64,101,105). Synthesizing this information, Miles projects that the life-time risk for completed suicide among major affective disorder patients is at least 15 percent (56).

Another psychiatric illness with an elevated risk for suicide attempt and completion appears to be schizophrenia. This diagnosis is especially important in young people because the onset of the process is usually in the teens or twenties (3). While definitive conclusions are jeopardized by the marked variation in diagnostic criteria utilized in different studies, it appears that 12 percent to 15 percent of adolescent or adult suicide attempters have schizophrenia (20,21), while 3 percent to 10 percent of suicide completers fulfill criteria for this disorder (64,101,105).

This section is included both because each of these problems is a risk factor in suicidal behavior, and because secondary substance abuse during the course of these disorders can exacerbate symptoms (1,6). As many as two-thirds of manics and one-third of severe depressives escalate their drinking while ill, a problem that could intensify depressed feelings and impulsiveness and might increase suicidal behavior (45). Similarly, schizophrenics who increase intake of brain depressants or stimulants are likely to experience a worsening of their poor judgment and psychotic thinking (107,108). Finally, it is possible that heavy drinking or drug use might exacerbate mood swings or intensify almost any major medical disorder (1,109).

Substance Misuse, Suicidal Behavior and the Family

The previous subsections have documented

that few adolescents who attempt or complete suicide are free of major psychopathology. This finding impacts on two other observations: the high prevalence of family instability and the high rate of psychiatrically ill relatives among suicidal young people.

During the 1970s it was common for authors to emphasize the observation of broken or chaotic homes among suicidal youth (19,101,105). Interpersonal difficulties were often named as an immediate precipitant for suicide attempts in adolescents (19), and many of these young people were reported to have observed suicidal behavior within their immediate families. Indeed, there is evidence that self-destructive acts run in families (111). For example, one evaluation of 243 psychiatric inpatients concluded that those with a family history of suicide were more likely than their coevals to have themselves attempted suicide (50 percent vs 22 percent, p<.0001) (110).

Few clinicians doubt the interaction between suicidal behavior, chaotic homes, and a family history of suicide attempts or completions. The causal nature of the relationship is, however, less obvious. Not only are most children raised by their parents, but they also get their genetic material from them. Considering the close relationship between suicidal behavior and psychiatric illness described in the prior sections, if the major psychiatric disorders associated with suicide are themselves genetically influenced, then part of the familial nature of suicidal behavior could relate to genetic factors increasing the predisposition towards similar illness in parents and children.

Three of the disorders carrying the highest lifetime risk for suicide attempts and completions do each appear to be genetically influenced. The importance of biological, genetic factors in alcoholism is supported by the familial nature of this disorder, the 60 percent to 80 percent rate of concordance for alcoholism in identical twins of alcoholics compared to a risk of approximately 30 percent for the fraternal twins, as well as the four-fold increased risk for alcoholism in

sons and daughters of alcoholics adopted away close to birth and raised without knowledge of the biological parent's problem (112-114). Similarly, family, twin and adoption studies indicate that major depressive disorders (especially bipolar, manic depressive disease) are also genetically influenced (115,116), and the data supporting the probable importance of genetic factors in schizophrenia are equally impressive (116). For at least one of these disorders (alcoholism), the greater the number of alcoholic relatives and the more severe their problem, the greater the probability of an earlier onset and more intense course for those children who develop the disorder (117,118).

Thus, there is another level of association between substance misuse, psychiatric disorders, and suicidal behavior in children and adolescents. Alcoholism or other illness in parents are relatively common findings among suicidal children and teenagers (110), it is possible that substance abuse or psychiatric disorders in these parents might have contributed to the increased rate of broken homes and chaotic childhood lifestyles for young people; these children may have a high risk for early onset of the disorder itself (117,118). Therefore, the suicidal behavior in these children may sometimes reflect their own early onset of illness associated with disordered mood or judgment.

In summary, substance abuse or psychiatric disorders in parents could contribute to the suicidal behavior in young people in at least two ways. First, some of the self-destructive problems in these children could have been influenced by the models set by the rearing parents, as well as the child's reaction to the anger and frustration engendered by the behavior of the ill parent. Second, some of the suicidal behavior observed in the children may reflect the inheritance of a predisposition towards the genetically influenced illness itself, with concomitant suicidal risk associated with the disorder and not just the specific childhood environment.

SUMMARY AND CONCLUSIONS

This paper has presented data and also attempted to stimulate thought and discussion. The emphasis has been on the potential contribution of alcohol and drugs to suicidal behavior in children and teenagers.

There is an important relationship between substance use or misuse and violent behavior in adults. Controlled substances and/or alcohol are frequently used as the means of attempting self-harm (especially among younger women), and alcohol is often taken as a prelude to the suicidal act, thus contributing to impaired judgment and impulsivity. Also, the lifetime risk for completed suicide appears to be 15 percent among alcoholics and about 10 percent for drug abusers.

It is not surprising, therefore, that the association between substance intake or abuse and suicidal behavior is also observed in adolescents. Whether studied in the general population or among groups in treatment, substance abusing young people have a significantly increased rate of self-inflicted death; youth identified because of their suicidal behavior frequently use and abuse nonprescription drugs and alcohol; and there is a close relationship between substance misuse patterns and the number and severity of suicide attempts.

Suicidal behavior early in life is also associated with substance problems in more indirect ways. Diagnoses such as the ASPD and "borderline personality" carry high risks for both self-harm and substance misuse. It is also probable that heavy drinking or drug use during major depressive episodes or in the midst of other psychiatric problems can exacerbate problems and might contribute to a suicide attempt or completion in these high risk individuals. A third indirect association between substance abuse and self-harm relates to the probable importance of genetic factors in the development of alcoholism and early onset psychiatric disorders. Thus, for example, children of alcoholics are more likely than the general population to observe suicidal behavior in their parents, more likely to suffer chaotic homes during childhood, and themselves have a genetically increased risk for both suicidal behavior and substance misuse.

From this review it is appropriate to conclude that, through both direct and indirect mechanisms, intake and abuse of substances is a potentially important risk factor in suicidal behavior early in life. The relationships between these substances and self-harm is rather complex, and careful data collection will be required if we are to understand more about this clinically relevant association.

It is possible to speculate about some of the clinical implications of the data reviewed in this paper. First, through numerous direct and indirect mechanisms, adolescent alcohol and drug abusers have an elevated risk for suicide attempts and completions. Second, whatever the mechanism, children of alcoholics and of patients with depressive or schizophrenic disorders may themselves be at elevated risk for suicide attempts and completions. The same may be true for children of drug abusers, although less data is available to substantiate that conclusion. In working with these families the potential dangers for self-harm in children should be recognized. A third clinical implication of the data comes from the recognition that almost all substances of abuse are likely to exacerbate preexisting emotional or psychiatric disturbances. Therefore, heavy intake of any of these controlled substances or alcohol may be important risk factors increasing the suicidal propensity of young people in crises, as well as those with major psychiatric disorders or personality disturbances. Efforts aimed at minimizing the risk for suicide should include educating young people and their families about the need to refrain from intake of all substances of abuse during times of mood swings or anger. Finally, physicians must learn to be careful in prescribing psychotropic agents or drugs of potential abuse to teenagers with emotional or psychiatric disturbances because there is evidence that in many instances the suicidal overdoses involve prescribed drugs (119).

The research implications of this review are also apparent. Studies of suicidal behavior in adolescents should rigorously document drug and alcohol use patterns in the recent past, evaluate individuals for major primary and secondary psychiatric disorders including those related to substance abuse, and document the presence of these problems in first-degree relatives. Investigators must also take care to not assume that an association between two factors (e.g., a suicide attempt in a child and alcoholism in a parent) proves that it is the disturbance in the home environment that caused the attempt. While the environmental stressors probably contribute greatly, other important avenues of influence must also be considered. For example, it is possible that children of alcoholics may themselves have inherited (or acquired through *in utero* damage) problems of impulsivity, hyperactivity, or a propensity to misuse substances with subsequent mood swings, anger, and frustration in their own lives.

REFERENCES

1. Schuckit MA: Drug and alcohol abuse: A clinical guide to diagnosis and treatment. 2nd ed. New York: Plenum Publishing Corporation, 1984.

2. Schuckit MA: Alcohol and Alcoholism. In: Petersdorf, R.G., Adams, R.D., Braunwald, E. eds., Harrison's principles of internal medicine, 11th ed. New York: McGraw-Hill Co., in press.

3. Goodwin DW, Guze SB: Psychiatric diagnosis. New York: Oxford University Press, 1984.

4. Spitzer RL, Endicott S, Robins E: Research diagnostic criteria. Arch Gen. Psychiat. 1978; 35:773-82.

5. Diagnostic and Statistical Manual of Mental Disorders, 3rd ed. Washington, D.C.; American Psychiatric Association, 1980.

6. Schuckit MA: Alcoholism and other psychiatric disorders. Hospital and Community Psychiatry 1983; 34:1022-7.

7. Guze SB: The need for tough mindedness in psychiatric thinking. So. Med. Journal 1970; 63:662-71.

8. Schuckit MA, Winokur G: A short-term follow-up of women alcoholics. Diseases of the Nervous System 1972; 33:672-78.

9. Schuckit MA: The clinical implications of primary diagnostic groups among alcoholics. Arch. Gen. Psychiat. 1985; 42:1043-9.

10. Vaillant G: Natural history of male alcoholism: Is alcoholism the cart to sociopathy? Presented at the American Psychiatric Association Annual Meeting, Toronto, Ontario, May 5, 1982.

11. Lukianowicz N: Attempted suicide in children. Acta Psychiat. Scand. 1968; 44:415-35.

12. Paykel ES, Myers JK, Lindenthal JJ, Tanner J: Suicidal feelings in the general population: A prevalence study. Brit. J. Psychiat. 1974; 124:460-9.

13. Patel AR, Roy M, Wilson, GM: Self-poisoning and alcohol. The Lancet 1972; 2:1099-102.

14. Wexler L, Weissman MM, Kasl SV: Suicide attempts 1970-75: Updating a United States study and comparisons with international trends. Brit. J. Psychiat. 1978; 132:180-5.

15. Jarvis GK, Ferrence RG, Johnson FG, Whitehead PC: Sex and age patterns in self-injury. J. Hlth. Soc. Behav. 1976; 17:145-55.

16. O'Brien JP: Increase in suicide attempts by drug ingestion. Arch. Gen. Psychiat. 1977; 34:1165-9.

17. Weissman MM: The epidemiology of suicide attempts. 1960-1971. Arch. Gen. Psychiat. 1974; 30:737-46.

18. Robbins DR, Alessi NE: Depressive symptoms and suicidal behavior in adolescents. Am. J. Psychiat. 1985; 142:588-92.

19. White HC: Self-poisoning in adolescents. Brit. J. Psychiat. 1974; 124:24-35.

20. Balser BH, Masterson JF: Suicide in adolescents. Am. J. Psychiat. 1957; 116:400-4.

21. Toolan JM: Suicide and suicidal attempts in children and adolescents. Am. J. Psychiat. 1962; 118:719-24.

22. Garfinkel BD, Froese A, Hood J: Suicide attempts in children and adolescents. Am. J. Psychiat. 1982; 139:1257-61.

23. Rygnestad TK: Prospective study of social and psychiatric aspects in self-poisoned patients. Acta Psychiat. Scan. 1982; 66:139-53.

24. Kreitman N, Schreiber M: Parasuicide in young Edinburgh women, 1968-75. Psychol. Med. 1979; 9:469-79.

25. Holding TA, Buglass D, Duffy JC, Kreitman N: Parasuicide in Edinburgh--a seven-year review, 1968-74. Brit. J. Psychiat. 1977; 130:534-43.

26. Shafii M, Carrigan S, Whittinghill JR, Derrick A: Psychological autopsy of completed suicide in children and adolescents. Am. J. Psychiat. 1985; 142:1061-4.

27. Ovenstone IM: Spectrum of suicidal behaviors in Edinburgh. Brit. J. Prevent. Soc. Med. 1973; 27:27-35.

28. Bakwin R: Teenage suicides. U.S. Medicine 1973; Oct. I:4.

29. Hoiberg A, Garfein AD: Predicting suicide gestures in a Naval recruit population. Military Medicine 1976; 141:327-31.

30. Rich CL, Young D, Fowler RC: San Diego suicide study: I. Young vs old cases. Arch. Gen. Psychiat. (in press).

31. Statistical Abstract of the United States: 1984 (104th edition). Washington, D.C., U.S. Bureau of the Census, 1983; 78-86.

32. Solomon MI, Hellon CP: Suicide and age in Alberta, Canada, 1951 to 1977. Arch. Gen. Psychiat. 1980; 37:511-3.

33. Murphy GE: Clinical identification of suicidal risk. Arch. Gen. Psychiat. 1972; 27:356-9.

34. Rydelius PA: Deaths among child and adolescent psychiatric patients. Acta Psychiat. Scand. 1984; 70:119-26.

35. Holinger PC: Violent deaths among the young: Recent trends in suicide, homicide, and accidents. Am. J. Psychiat. 1979; 136:1144-7.

36. Curry B: Suicides of young Indians called epidemic. Times. Part 1, 1985 Oct. 12:4.

37. Meares R, Kraijuhin C, Benfield J: Adolescent suicide. Aust. Fam. Physician 1983; 12:614-6.

38. Weiss NS: Recent trends in violent deaths among young adults in the United States. Am. J. Epidemio. 1976; 103:4l6-22.

39. Lester D: Alcohol and suicide and homicide. J. Stud. Alc. 1980; 41:1220-3.

40. Wolfgang M: Patterns in criminal homicide. Philadelphia; University of Pennsylvania Press, 1958.

41. Schuckit MA, Gunderson EKE: Suicide in naval service. Am. J. Psychiat. 1974; 131:l328-31.

42. Wetli CV: Changing patterns of methaqualone abuse. A survey of 246 fatalities. J.A.M.A. 1983; 4:62l-6.

43. Langevin R, Paitich D, Orchard B, Handy L, Russon A: The role of alcohol, drugs, suicide attempts and situational strains in homicide committed by offenders seen for psychiatric assessment. A controlled study. Acta Psychiat. Scand. 1982; 66:229-42.

44. Schuckit MA: The history of psychotic symptoms in alcoholics. J. Clin. Psychiat. 1982; 43:53-7.

45. Schuckit MA: Alcoholism and affective disorder: Genetic and clinical implications. Am. J. Psychiat. (in press).

46. Whitlock FA: Suicide in Brisbane, 1956-1973. The drug-death epidemic. Med. J. Aust. 1975; 14:737-43.

47. Connell HM: Attempted suicide in schoolchildren. Med. J. Austr. 1972; 1:686-90.

48. Haider I: Suicidal attempts in children and adolescents. Brit. J. Psychiat. 1968; 114:1133-4.

49. Ghodse AH: Deliberate self-poisoning: a study in London casualty departments. Br. Med. J. 1977; 26:805-8.

50. Abel EL, Zeidenberg P: Age, alcohol and violent death: A postmortem study. J. Stud. Alcohol 1985; 46:228-3l.

51. Haberman PW, Baden MM: Alcoholism and violent death. Quart. J. Stud. Alc. 1974; 35:221-31.

52. Mayfield D, Montgomery D: Alcoholism, alcohol intoxication and suicide attempts. Arch. Gen. Psychiat. 1972; 27:349-53.

53. Woodruff RA, Clayton PJ, Guze SB: Suicide attempts and psychiatric diagnosis. Dis. Nerv. Sys. 1972; 33:617-21.

54. Thorarinsson AA: Mortality among men alcoholics in Iceland, 1951-74. J. Stud. Alc. 1979; 40:704-l8.

55. Berglund M: Suicide in alcoholism. Arch. Gen. Psychiat. 41:888-891, 1984.

56. Miles CP: Conditions predisposing to suicide: A review. J.Nerv. Ment. Dis. 1977; 164:231-46.

57. Mollhoff G, Schmidt G: Deaths resulting from drugs of abuse. Forensic Sci. 1976; 7:31-40.

58. Kalant H, Kalant OJ: Death in amphetamine users: Causes and rates. Can. Med. Assoc. J. 1975; 8:299-304.

59. Lundberg GD, Garriott JC, Reynolds PC, Cravey RH, Shaw RF: Cocaine-related death. J. Forensic Sci. 1977; 22:402-8.

60. Watson JM: Glue sniffing. Two case reports. Int. J. Addict. 1979; 14:451-64.

61. Riddick L, Luke JL: Alcohol-associated deaths in the District of Columbia--a postmortem study. J. Forensic Sci. 1978; 23:493-502.

62. Novick LF, Remmlinger E: A study of 128 deaths in New York City correctional facilities (1971-1976): Implications for prisoner health care. Med. Care 1978; 16:749-756.

63. Beskow J: Suicide in mental disorder in Swedish men. Acta Psychiat. Scand. 1979; 227:131-138.

64. Robins E: The final months: A study of the lives of 134 persons who committed suicide. New Eng. J. Med. 1982; 306:1117.

65. Murphy GE, Armstrong JW, Hermele SL, Fischer JR, Clendenin WW: Suicide and alcoholism. Arch. Gen. Psychiat. 1979; 36:65-9.

66. Crawshaw R, Bruce JA, Eraker PL, Greenbaum M, Lindemann JE, Schmidt DE: An epidemic of suicide among physicians on probation, J.A.M.A. 1980; 243:1915-7.

67. Borg SE, Stahl M: Prediction of suicide. A prospective study of suicides and controls among psychiatric patients. Acta Psychiat. Scand. 1982; 65:221-32.

68. Morrison JR: Suicide in a psychiatric practice population. J. Clin. Psychiat. 1982; 43:348-52.

69. McKenry PC, Tishler CL, Kelley C: The role of drugs in adolescent suicide attempts. Suicide Life Threat Behav. 1983; 13:166-75.

70. Goldney RD: Alcohol in association with suicide and attempted suicide in young women. Med. J. Aust. 1981; 22:195-7.

71. Benson G, Holmberg MB: Drug-related mortality in young people. Acta Psychiat. Scand. 1984; 70:525-34.

72. Ryser PE: Students and drug abuse, 1974 and 1980. J. School Health 1983; 53:435-6.

73. Schuckit MA: Overview: Epidemiology of Alcoholism. In: Schuckit, M.A., ed. Alcohol patterns and problems. New Brunswick, NJ; Rutgers University Press, 1985:1-42, (Series in psychosocial epidemiology, Vol. 5).

74. Smart RG, Goodstadt MS, Adlaf EM, Sheppard MA, Chan GC: Trends in the prevalence of alcohol and other drug use among Ontario students: 1977-1983. Canadian J. Public Hlth. 1985; 76:157-62.

75. Weissman MM: Alcoholism and depression: Separate entities? Presented at the seventh annual Alcoholism Symposium: "Diagnosis and Treatment: Current Developments," sponsored by the Department of Psychiatry, The Cambridge Hospital. Boston Park Plaza, March 3, 1984.

76. Schuckit MA, Gunderson EKE: The clinical characteristics of personality subtypes in Naval service. J. Clin. Psychiat. 1979; 40:175-9.

77. Yessler PG, Gibbs JJ, Becker HA: On the communication of suicide ideas. Arch. Gen. Psychiat. 1960; 3:612-31.

78. Leese SM: Suicide behavior in twenty adolescents. Brit. J. Psychiat. 1969; 115:479-80.

79. Dizmang LH, Watson J, May PA, Bopp J: Adolescent suicide at an Indian reservation. Am. J. Orthopsychiat. 1974; 44:43-9.

80. Cleckley H: The mask of sanity. St. Louis, C.V. Mosby, 1955.

8l. Robins LN: Deviant children grown up. Baltimore: Williams and Williams Co. 1966.

82. Robins LN: Sturdy childhood predictors of adult antisocial behavior: Replications from longitudinal studies. Psychological Medicine 1978; 8:611-22.

83. Schuckit MA: Alcoholism and sociopathy: Diagnostic confusion. Quart J. Stud. Alc. 1973; 34:157-64.

84. Virkkunen M: Alcoholism and antisocial personality. Acta Psychiat. Scand. 1979; 59:493-501.

85. Fowler RC, Liskow B, Tanna VL: Psychiatric illness and alcoholism. Presented at the National Council on Alcoholism convention. Washington, D.C., May 1976.

86. Cadoret R, Widmer RN, Troughton E: Clinical differences between antisocial and primary alcoholics. Presented at the National Council on Alcoholism annual meeting. Washington, D.C., May 1982.

87. Maddocks PD: A five year follow-up of untreated psychopaths. Brit. J. Psychiat. 1970; 116:511-5.

88. Bibb RC, Guze SB: Hysteria in a psychiatric hospital. Am. J. Psychiat. 1972; 129:224-8.

89. Lewis CE, Helzer J, Cloninger CR, Croughan J, Whitman BY: Psychiatric diagnostic predispositions to alcoholism. Comprehensive Psychiatry 1982; 23:451-61.

90. Guze SB, Woodruff RA, Clayton PJ: Hysteria and antisocial behavior. Am. J. Psychiat. 1971; 127:957-60.

91. Gunderson JG, Kolb JE: Discriminating features of borderline patients. Am. J. Psychiat. 1978; 135:792-6.

92. Gunderson JG, Elliott GR: The interface between borderline personality disorder and affective disorder. Am. J. Psychiat. 1985; 142:277-88.

93. Crumley FE: Adolescent suicide attempts and borderline personality disorder: Clinical Features. South. Med. J. 1981; 74:546-549.

94. Akiskal HS, Chen SE, Davis GC, Puzantian VR, Kashgarian M, Bolinger JM: Borderline: An adjective in search of a noun. J. Clin. Psychiat. 1985; 6:41-48.

95. Frances A, Clarkin JF, Gilmore M, Hurt SW, Brown R: Reliability of criteria for borderline personality disorder: A comparison of DSM-III and the diagnostic interview for borderline patients. Am. J. Psychiat. 1984; 141:1080-4.

96. Pope HG, Jonas JM, Hudson JI, Cohen BM, Gunderson JG: The validity of DSM-III borderline personality disorder. Arch. Gen. Psychiat. 1983; 40:23-30.

97. Schultz SC, Goldberg SC: Borderline personality disorder: New Findings on Pharmacotherapy. Psychopharmacology Bulletin 1984; 20:554-60.

98. Akiskal HS, Yerevanian BI, Davis GC, King D, Lemmi H: The nosologic status of borderline personality clinical and polysomnographic study. Am. J. Psychiat. 1985; 142:192-8.

99. McManus M, Lerner H, Barbour C: Assessment of borderline symptomatology in hospitalized adolescents. J. Am. Acad. Child Psychiat. 1984; 23:685-94.

100. Urwin P, Gibbons JL: Psychiatric diagnosis in self-poisoning patients. Psychol. Med. 1979; 9:501-7.

101. Barraclough B, Bunch J, Nelson B: A hundred cases of suicide. Brit. J. Psychiat. 1974; 125:355-73.

102. Porot M, Coudert A, Collett M: Suicidal behavior of adolescents. Psychiatric de l'Enfant 1968; 11:317-69.

103. Reeves JC, Large RG, Honeyman H: Parasuicide and depression: A comparison of clinical and questionnaire diagnoses. Aust. NZ J. Psychiat. 1985; 19:30-3.

104. Friedman RC, Clarkin J, Corn R: DSM-III and affective pathology in hospitalized adolescents. J. Nerv. Ment. Dis. 1982; 170:511-21.

105. Dorpat TL, Jackson JK, Ripley HS: Broken homes and attempted and completed suicides. Arch. Gen. Psychiat. 1965; 12:213-216.

106. Weinberg S: Suicidal intent in adolescence: A hypothesis about the role of physical illness. Journal of Pediatrics 1970; 77:579-86.

107. Schuckit MA, Winokur G: Alcoholic hallucinosis and schizophrenia: A negative study. Brit. J. Psychiat. 1971; 119:549-550.

108. Segal DS, Schuckit MA: Animal models of stimulant induced psychosis. In: Creese I, (ed). Stimulants: neurochemical, behavioral, and clinical perspectives. New York; Ravan Press, 1982; 131-68.

109. Saghir MT, Robins E, Walbran B, Gentry KA: Homosexuality: III. Psychiatric disorders and disability in the male homosexual. Amer. J. Psychiat. 1970; 126:1079-86.

110. Roy A: Family history of suicide. Arch. Gen. Psychiat. 1983; 40:971-4.

111. Murphy GE, Wetzel RD: Family history of suicidal behavior among suicide attempters. J. Nerv. Ment. Dis. 1982; 170:86-90.

112. Schuckit MA: Genetics and the risk for alcoholism. J.A.M.A., 1985; 254: 2614-7.

113. Goodwin DW: Alcoholism and genetics. Arch. Gen. Psychiat. 1985; 42:171-4.

114. Schuckit MA: Studies of populations at high risk for alcoholism. Psychiatric Developments 1985; 3:31-63.

115. Gershon ES, Bunney WE, Leckman JF, Van Eerdewegh M, DeBauche BA: The inheritance of affective disorders: A review of data and of hypotheses. Behavior Genetics 1976; 6:227-261.

116. Schuckit MA: Trait (and state) markers of a predisposition to psychopathology. In: Michael, R., Judd, L.L., Groves, P., eds. Physiological foundations of clinical psychiatry, Vol. 3. Philadelphia: J.P. Lippincott, 1985: 1-19.

117. Schuckit MA: Relationship between the course of primary alcoholism in men and family history. J. Stud. Alc. 1984; 45:1-8.

118. Frances RJ, Timm S, Bucky S: Studies of familial and nonfamilial alcoholism. Arch. Gen. Psychiat. 1980; 37:564-6.

119. Prescott LF, Highley MS: Drugs prescribed for self poisoners. Br. Med. J. 1985; 1:1633-6.

METHODS AS A RISK FACTOR IN YOUTH SUICIDE

J. William Worden, Ph.D., Assistant Professor of Psychiatry, Harvard Medical School, Boston, Massachusetts

In this paper we will consider methods of suicide as a risk factor. Although other risk factors already discussed in this conference may be more important than methods as precipitants and precursors of suicidal behavior, none is more important than methods when it comes to the risk of death. Some methods lead to almost certain death while other methods are more uncertain as to outcome and they portend more reversibility and rescuability. We have seen a recent rise in youth suicide, especially with regards to completed suicide. Is this increase in completed suicide due to an overall increase in suicidal behavior or is it due to the fact that youths who engage in suicidal behavior are using more lethal means of self-destruction? A better understanding of methods may provide us with an answer to this question, as well as providing us further insights into the dynamics of youth suicide and possibly offering some clues for prevention.

How do adolescents and young adults kill themselves? Overall, those in the 10 to 24 age range most frequently kill themselves by firearms and explosives, with guns being the most prominent means. The second most frequently used method of suicide is by hanging, strangulation, or suffocation. Self-poisoning by ingesting solid and liquid substances is the third most frequent method of self-destruction. (Holinger, 1978). Although there are few major differences in choice of method between black and white youths, there are some distinctives. Proportionately more black males than white males hang themselves or die by jumping from high places or drowning, whereas relatively more white males use firearms or die utilizing carbon monoxide. White females are more likely to hang themselves than black females. Overall, a higher proportion of females to males poison themselves irrespective of race. (Fredrick, 1984). It is interesting to note that suicide statistics in the United States are not kept for children under 10 years of age. This implies that suicide is not seen as an option for young children by those collecting such information.

Paulson at UCLA disputes this fact. Studying children who were seen at the UCLA Neuropsychiatric Institute from 1970 to 1974, Paulson found 34 children ages 4 to 12 who demonstrated suicidal behavior--mostly suicide threats and attempts. The mean age of his sample was 8.2 years. Suicidal behavior in this age group involved more self-abuse and bodily mutilation than self-poisoning. Examples of self-abuse were cutting, stabbing, burning, and jumping either from high places or in front of moving vehicles. Children exhibiting the most mutilating assaults on themselves frequently came from highly disorganized families and were also the children with the highest ideational violence. It is interesting to note that Paulson did not find significant gender differences in ideational violence among his young subjects. (Paulson et al., 1978).

Pfeffer also studied suicidal behavior among younger children. In investigating children ages 6 to 12 who were inpatients in the child psychiatry unit of the Bronx Municipal Hospital and who demonstrated some type of suicidal behavior, she found that jumping was the most frequent choice of these young attempters. Out of the 42 subjects in her study, jumping was chosen by 38 percent of the children. Of those remaining, 25 percent chose self-poisoning, 19 percent burned themselves, 13 percent cut themselves, and 6 percent ran into oncoming traffic. (Pfeffer et al., 1979). In a subsequent study of 65 children admitted to the child psychiatry unit of New York Hospital Westchester she also found jumping from high places to be the most frequent method and this was found in 25 percent of the cases. (Pfeffer et al., 1982).

Although jumping is a frequent method for these very young attempters, self-poisoning should not be overlooked. McIntire and Angle discovered an interesting phenomenon when investigating reports from 50 poison control centers in the United States and the United Kingdom. In the 6 to 10 age range, self-poisoning was more frequently found among males (63%) than females (37%). This is the opposite of what they found in their older group of children, 11 to 18 where self-poisoning by females far exceeded that by males. This same gender differences can be also found among adult self-poisoners where the number of females exceeds males. McIntire and Angle offered no explanation for the difference they found, but they did conclude from their study that self-poisoning in a child over the age of 6 is rarely accidental. (McIntire & Angle, 1971b). It should also be noted, however, that completed suicide for these very young children is rare.

Hawton & Goldacre studied cases of self-poisoning in a population of young people ages 12 to 20 years who were admitted to hospitals in the Oxford area of England. They also noted that self-poisoning was higher for females than for males at all of these ages. (Hawton & Goldacre, 1982). It would have been useful if the investigators had included the younger children from ages 6 to 12 in their study to see if the reverse male to female phenomenon that McIntire found could have been replicated in such a large sample and in another country.

There is general agreement that incidents of self-poisoning become more frequent as children increase in age. There is less agreement as to what substances they ingest. Hawton compared adolescent self-poisoners to adults and found that adolescents more frequently ingested non-opiate analgesics and less frequently took psychotropic drugs. The use of alcohol as an adjunct factor in an overdose was found less frequently among adolescents than among adults. This was especially true in the younger groups of children. Most young children tended to ingest drugs found around the house rather than drugs specifically prescribed for them. (Hawton, 1982). Hawton also found that the ingestion of psychotropic drugs increased as the females in his study became older, but the same was not true for the males studied. Fredrick (1984) reported that barbiturates and tranquilizers were the most frequently ingested substances for completed suicides among 15 to 24 year olds in 1979. Goldney in looking only at female self-poisoners ages 18 to 30 found that anti-depressant medications were often ingested as overdoses. This was especially true for attempts judged to be highly serious both from the standpoint of medical lethality and the ratings from the Beck Intent to Die Scale which was given to these 109 women in the study. (Goldney, 1981). One might conjecture that younger children are more likely to ingest substances found around the home. As children grow older they may be in psychiatric treatment and receiving medication which is available to them if they decide to overdose.

The reasons given for choice of method are always of interest. Some suicide behavior is well thought out and the methods selected well in advance. Other suicides are impulsive and the person may turn to the nearest perceived lethal substance at hand. To the extent that the choice is rational, there was an interesting study conducted by Marks with approximately 700 college students. The mean age of his respondents was 19.5 years. He asked the students to rank order nine means of self-destruction according to their acceptability and to suggest which methods they thought were used most often by males, by females, and why. Both males and females in his study ranked self-poisoning as the most acceptable. Firearms were ranked higher by men than by women. Women were more likely than men to cite "lack of pain" as the reason for their choice. In citing additional reasons, "availability" and "knowledgeability" were associated with self-poisoning for females; with firearms for males. Similarly, "efficiency" was related to self-poisoning for females and to firearms for males. (Marks, 1977).

Although self-poisoning is the frequent choice of the adolescent suicide attempter, it ranks third in the causes of suicidal deaths in the 10 to 24 year old population. Most young people who succeed in taking their own lives do so with guns and explosives. For young people ages 15 to 24 the rate of suicide by firearms increased 97.1 percent from 1966 to 1975 while the rate of suicide by other means increased 72.4 percent for the same period. The significantly large increase in death by firearms may reflect the 14.5 percent increase in the availability of legal handguns during that same time period (Seiden & Freitas, 1980, Boyd, 1983).

To what extent, then, is availability a determining factor in the choice of a method of self-destruction? There has been considerable discussion as to the availability of a method, both as a determinant for choice and as a possible way to reduce suicidal behavior, such as gun control. Marks and Abernathy (1974) minimize physical availability as a determinant. The most available methods are not those most frequently employed. For example, rope with which to hang oneself is more readily available than firearms, yet firearms are more frequently used. Obviously, however, availability is a necessary precondition in the choice of a method.

There is evidence that when a certain method becomes unavailable some persons wishing to suicide will switch to another means. Lester and Murell (1982) found that States with stricter gun-control laws had lower rates of suicide by firearms but higher rates of suicide by other means. However, in an earlier report, Lester and Murell (1980) found that the total suicide rate was lower in States with stricter gun-control laws. Thus it is possible that when firearms are less available, persons turn to other methods which may leave more time for intervention.

Marks and Abernathy (1974), in trying to explain both gender and individual differences in choice of method, have posited a sociocultural perspective of differential socialization which takes into account not only availability but several other factors which also influence such a choice. Marks and Abernathy respond negatively to what they term the "psychological perspective"--a perspective which suggests that the difference in choice of method solely reflects a difference in intent to die. This perspective implies that the higher incidence of handgun use in male suicides indicates that males are more intent on killing themselves.

Marks and Abernathy argue against this psychological perspective on several grounds. For instance, if it were correct, then we would expect to find different methods employed by female attempters than female completers. However, the use of poisons is high in both groups. Furthermore, one would expect those areas of the country in which the more deadly methods, e.g. firearms, are preferred to also have the highest suicide rates. However, such is not the case.

Marks and Abernathy have identified at least three factors beyond availability which may influence the choice of a suicide method. The first of these is the sociocultural acceptability of the method. Certain methods have greater or lesser acceptability within the internalized social and cultural norms of the individual, and this will be reflected in the choice of a method. Examples of this may be reflected in the distinctives mentioned earlier between young black and white males and between young black and white females. The second factor is the person's knowledge of the methods. A person is more likely to employ a method with which he or she is knowledgeable and familiar. The third factor is personal or social accessibility. For example, heroin may be physically available from a street supplier but socially inaccessible because of the person's social standing as a police officer. In this example heroin would be a less likely method for an overdose.

Research by McIntosh & Santos (1982) also supports the idea that selection of a method is dependent upon a constellation of sociocultural factors. They found that no generalization could accurately describe the range of suicidal behavior displayed by various sex, racial, or ethnic groups. Although they did not specifically study youth suicide or break down their sample by age, their point is most applicable to our discussions of youth suicide in this conference. We must be careful not to draw overgeneralized conclusions about youth suicide methods without more closely examining the various sociocultural influences on these young men and women and how these influences might differ by age, sex, social position, cultural background, geographical location and personal history. Much more research is needed to understand the selection of suicide methods by youth.

One important factor influencing gender preferences for suicide methods may be "anticipatory socialization." (Marks & Abernathy 1974). Traditionally boys have been exposed to and encouraged to participate in violent games and activities to a greater degree than their female counterparts. An example would be the game of cops and robbers. This may account, in part, for the greater incidence of firearm use by males. One could speculate that changing role definitions for women may account for the increase in the use of firearms in female suicides. It is interesting to note that the majority of young women in the U.S. Army who suicide (73%) do so predominantly with firearms (Datel & Jones, 1982). Taylor & Wicks (1980), while supporting the sociocultural perspective, find no evidence that cer-

tain groups of women who prefer firearms to other methods are any more "liberated" than those women who prefer poison or some other means of self-destruction. Liberation is probably a poor choice of terms. Changing role definitions does not necessarily imply liberation. Location within the social structure is a better term than liberation and fits within the sociocultural perspective. Changes in traditional role expectations are pervasive in our society and its culture and this needs to be taken into consideration when explaining gender changes in patterns of suicidal behavior.

There are important implications to be drawn from the sociocultural perspective with regard to suicide methods and youth. The most important is the need to determine what sociocultural factors differentiate youths and adolescents from the adult population. Are different methods more or less available to youths than to adults? Are certain methods more culturally acceptable to youths? How do these sociocultural factors vary by age within the youth population? There is no specific research in this area though it is clearly needed. We recommend research which will clearly differentiate between adults and youth and carefully examine the influence of sex, age, geography, cultural values, social status, intent to die, familiarity and availability of methods, and how these factors relate to the choice of self-destructive methods in these populations.

Some suicidal methods obviously carry more risk of death than others. Because of this, clinicians are apt to use nominal classifications when they discuss the relative lethality of a suicidal act. Words like "gesture," "moderate lethality," and "serious suicide attempt" are still used when talking about a person's suicidal behavior. However there are many suicide attempts of intermediate lethality which cannot be dichotomized easily into "gestures" and "serious" attempts. This is especially true in the area of self-poisoning.

In 1972, Weisman and Worden developed a scale known as the Risk-Rescue Rating Scale in an attempt to describe and quantify lethality in suicide attempts. (Weisman & Worden, 1972). This scale is based on the assumption that the probability of death is substantially influenced by what a person does to himself and the context in which he does it. Any suicide attempt entails a calculated risk. But because any attempt must also take place in a psychosocial context or within a specific set of circumstances, survival may depend upon the resources for rescue as well as upon the specific form of the attempt. Jumping off a high bridge into the river beneath has similar risk to physical damage whether it is done at 3 p.m. or 3 a.m. However, rescue factors are different in the early morning hours when it is dark and there are fewer people around. The Risk-Rescue Rating Scale assesses five factors of risk and five factors of rescue and enables the clinician or researcher to quantify the lethality of implementation in any suicide attempt.

There are other scales similar to the Risk-Rescue that look at the relative seriousness of methods. Recently, Smith, Conroy, and Ehler at the Menninger Foundation created a nine-point interval scale for assessing the relative lethality of a suicide attempt. (Smith et al., 1984). This is a well developed scale and their updated toxicity chart is an improvement over the older one developed by Sterling-Smith and used by Weisman and Worden.

The ability to quantify a suicidal act by looking at methods in context is valuable from several standpoints. First, you can compare one group of suicide attempters with another. We know for example that young females more frequently use self-poisoning than young men, but young men do poison themselves. Even though there is less self-poisoning among males, is the lethal level of their attempts higher than for females? Using a scale like the Risk-Rescue Rating could help answer this. We presently know the types of methods used by youth in different age categories and the percentage of use for various methods varies widely for different age groups and possibly for youth in various social sub-cultures and geographic locations. Being able to rate methods within their context and to be able to scale the observations would clearly aid in our attempt to understand youth suicide across the age cohorts.

Second, such a rating scale also helps one to assess relative lethality for a person who has made multiple attempts. It is well known that those who have made previous attempts are at higher risk for completed suicide. Rating each attempt with the same scale enables one to see whether lethality is ascending, decending, remaining the same, or forming some other pattern. In one study Worden found that one could predict the lethal level of subsequent attempts in adults by rating previous attempts in combination with various other demographic information. (Worden & Sterling-Smith, 1973).

A third use for a lethality rating scale is to better understand the complex issue of intent to die. Measuring intent is often very difficult. Patients do not always give an accurate account of their intent to die from an attempt. There are both conscious and unconscious factors that lead to distortion. Patients may say one thing when taken to the emergency room and have a totally different story a day later. Also, ambivalence is present in most people trying to hurt themselves. On the extreme ends of the spectrum intent to die is rather easy to discern. The young girl who ingests 25 aspirin and immediately tells her mother is clearly in the low lethal range. The young man who takes a gun into the remote woods and shoots himself in the head is obviously in the high lethal range. These are obvious. But there is a whole range of behaviors that fall into the middle ranges of lethality and using a rating scale that looks at methods in context would be very useful in future studies of youth suicide to better understand the issues of intent especially in those falling into the middle ranges of lethality.

In any discussion of youth suicide methods one should not overlook automobile accidents as suicide equivalents. In the 1970s we did a study of automobile fatalities in the greater Boston area under a grant from the Department of Transportation. One part of the study investigated the human factors associated with these accidents. A number of these fatal accidents involved young drivers from 18 to 25 years of age. Our retrospective analysis, fashioned after the psychological autopsy, revealed a number of probable suicides especially in cases involving young men who died in single car accidents. (Sterling-Smith, 1976).

What are the implications and recommendations from our investigation into youth suicide methods? There are several:

- Although the numbers may be few, suicide statistics should be gathered on children under 10 years of age.

- In the U.S. Vital Statistics we were able to find methods by age and methods by sex but not methods by age by sex. We recommend that statistics be made available in this fashion.

- The extant literature on youth suicide with regards to method has several shortcomings. There is a lack of control studies. These are necessary so that we might determine more accurately to what extent youth suicide differs by age and from the adult population.

  For example, are different methods available to youth than adults? If so, at what ages and how does this discrepancy arise?

- We believe that the selection of a self-destructive method depends upon a constellation of sociocultural factors. However, just what and how these factors are has not been well documented. There is a need for well developed studies that will identify what social factors are influencing the choice of method for the youth population and how these factors might differ by sex, by age, and from the adult population. It is also important, once these factors have been isolated to know how they might be

changing. This would have implications both for prevention and for prediction of future trends.

- We also believe that methods should be studied in context. If those who are collecting data on youth suicide methods would use one of the existing scales that accounts for the context of the event, we would have a better grasp on the relative lethality for various age, sex, and ethnic groups as well as important distinctives between methods chosen by youth as compared to adults. This would greatly enhance our understanding and take us beyond our current state of listing methods only in the grossest of forms.

REFERENCES

1. Card, J.J: Lethality of suicidal methods and suicide risk: Two distinct concepts. Omega 1977; 5:37-45.

2. Boyd, J.H: The increasing rate of suicide by firearms. New England Journal of Medicine 1983; 308:872-874.

3. Datel, W.E., Jones, F.D: Suicide in United States Army personnel. Military Medicine 1982; 147:843-847.

4. Fredrick, C.J: Suicide in young minority group persons, in Sudak, H.S., et al. Suicide and the Young. Boston: John Wright, 1984; pp. 31-44.

5. Goldney, R.D: Attempted suicide in young women: Correlates of lethality. British Journal of Psychiatry 1981; 13:497-503.

6. Hawton, K: Attempted suicide in children and adolescents. Journal of Child Psychiatry 1982; 23:497-503.

7. Hawton, K., Catalan, J: Attempted Suicide. Oxford: Oxford University Press, 1982.

8. Hawton, K., Goldacre, M: Hospital admissions for adverse effects of medicinal agents (mainly self-poisoning) among adolescents in the Oxford region. British Journal of Psychiatry 1982; 141:166-170.

9. Hawton, K., et al: Adolescents who take overdoses: Characteristics, problems, and contacts with helping agencies. British Journal of Psychiatry 1982; 140:118-123.

10. Holinger, P.C: Adolescent suicide: An epidemiological study of recent trends. American Journal of Psychiatry 1978; 135:754-756.

11. Klagsbrun, F: Too young to die: Youth and suicide. Boston: Houghton Mifflin, 1976.

12. Lester, D., Murrell, M.E: The preventive effect of strict gun control laws on suicide and homicide. Suicide and Life Threatening Behavior 1982; 12:131-140.

13. Marks, A., Abernathy, T: Toward a sociocultural perspective on means of self-destruction. Life-Threatening Behavior 1974; 4:3-17.

14. Marks, A: Sex differences and their effect upon cultural evaluation of methods of self-destruction. Omega 1977; 8:65-70.

15. McIntire, M.S., Angle, C.R: Suicide as seen in poison-control centers. Pediatrics 1971; 45:914-922.

16. McIntire, M.S., Angle, C.R: Is the poisoning accidental?: An ever present question beyond the early childhood years. Clinical Pediatrics 1971; 10:414-417.

17. McIntosh, J.L., Santos, J.F: Changing patterns in methods of suicide by race and sex. Suicide and Life-Threatening Behavior 1982; 12:221-233.

18. Pallis, D.J., Barraclough, B.M: Seriousness of suicide attempt and future risk of suicide: A comment on Card's paper. Omega 1977; 8:141-149.

19. Paulson, M.J., Stone, D., Sposto, M.A: Suicidal potential and behavior in children ages 4 to 12. Suicide and Life-Threatening Behavior 1978; 8:225-242.

20. Pfeffer, C., et al: Suicidal behavior in latency-age children: An outpatient population. Journal of the American Academy of Child Psychiatry 1980; 19:703-710.

21. Pfeffer, C., et al: Suicidal behavior in latency-age children: An empirical study. Journal of the American Academy of Child Psychiatry 1979; 18:679-692.

22. Pfeffer, C., et al: Suicidal behavior in latency age psychiatric inpatients: A replication and cross validation. Journal of the American Academy of Child Psychiatry 1982; 21:564-569.

23. Rustford, N.B., et al: Increasing suicide rates in adolescents and young adults in an urban community. in Sudak, H.S., et al. Suicide and the Young. Boston: John Wright, 1984; pp. 45-68.

24. Seiden, R.H., Freitas, R.P: Shifting patterns of deadly violence. Suicide and Life-Threatening Behavior 1980; 10:195-209.

25. Shaffer, D: Suicide in childhood and early adolescence. Journal of Child Psychology and Psychiatry 1974; 15:275-291.

26. Smith, D., Conroy, R.W., Ehler, B.D: Lethality of suicide attempt rating scale. Suicide and Life-Threatening Behavior 1984; 14:215-242.

27. Sterling-Smith, R.S: An analysis of drivers most responsible for fatal accidents versus a control sample. Springfield, VA: National Technical Information Service, 1976.

28. Taylor, M.C., Wicks, J.W: The choice of weapons: A study of methods of suicide by sex, race, and region. Suicide and Life-Threatening Behavior 1980; 10:142-149.

29. Weisman, A.D., Worden, J.W: Risk-rescue rating in suicide assessment. Archives of General Psychiatry 1972; 26:553-560.

30. Worden, J.W., Sterling-Smith, R.S: Lethality patterns in multiple suicide attempts. Life-Threatening Behavior 1973; 3:95-104.

31. Worden, J.W: Lethality factors and the suicide attempt. In Shneidman, E.S. Suicidology: Contemporary Developments. New York: Grune and Stratton, 1976.

ACKNOWLEDGEMENT ····················-

The author is grateful to Michael S. Worden for assistance in preparing this paper.

STUDY	N	AGES	POPULATION	FINDINGS
Goldney 1981	109 Females	18-30	Women admitted to large city general hospital for self-poisoning.	— There was no significant correlation between age and intent to die. (Beck Scale) — There was a significant correlation between intent to die and seriousness of the attempt. — Many of the serious attempts involved anti-depressant medications.
Hawton	50	13-18	Admissions to Oxford General Hospitals.	Compared to adult self-poisoners, adolescents more frequently took non-opiate analgesics and less frequently took psychotropic drugs. Alcohol was less related to overdoses among adolescents than in adults, especially in the younger groups. Most of the drugs used were found around the house and not prescribed specifically for the patient.
Hawton & Goldacre 1982	682	12-20	General Hospital admissions, Oxfordshire 1974-79	Self-poisoning was higher for females then for males. Of frequent use were analgesics and anti-pyretics, the use of which increased by age for males and decreased by age for females. The use of psychotropic drugs increased as the women got older but such was not true for the males.
Hollinger 1978	unknown	10-24	U.S. vital statistics completed	
Mcintyre & Angle 1971 (A)	1,103 35% M 65% F	6-18	Reports from 50 poison centers in U.S. and U.K., 1968-1969.	— 75% of the poisonings were suicide related. — Self-poisoning was higher among males than females in the younger ages (6-10) but the order was reversed in the older group (11-13). — Self-poisoning among blacks decreased with age while it increased with age for caucasians. There is speculation that the older blacks may have looked to other means than poison.
Mcintrye & Angle 1971 (B)	1,103	6-18	Reports from 50 poison control centers in U.S. and U.K.	
Marks 1977	600 M = 268 F = 332	Mean age was 19.5 yrs.	College Students from South and Non-South	In ranking preference for method of suicide, both sexes ranked self-poisoning the most desirable. Firearms were ranked higher by men than women. Women were more likely than men to cite painlessness for their choice of method. Men were more likely to choose methods because of their accessibility or efficiency.

Hollinger 1978 findings:

	Poison	Gas	Hanging	Firearms	Other
10-14	5%	0%	46%	47%	3%
15-18	13%	7%	19%	55%	3%
20-24	13%	8%	16%	55%	0

— The smaller number of self-poisoning in the 10-14 age may be due to listing such behavior as "accidental."
— Firearms, Gas, and Hanging were used most frequently by males; self-poisoning was not frequently used by females.

Mcintyre & Angle 1971 (B) findings:

	Male%'	Female%
6-10	63%	37%
1-13	31%	69%
14-16	28%	72%
17-18	39%	61%

— As in adults, self-poisoners are more frequently female.
— Self-poisoning in a child over 6 years of age is rarely accidental.
— Sedatives (barbiturates, non-barbiturates, & Tranquilizers) were used most frequently by all age groups. The next most used drug was aspirin which was used in a quarter of all cases.

Table 1.

STUDY	N	AGES	POPULATION	FINDINGS
Paulson 1978	34 M = 23 F = 11	Mean age = 8.2 yrs.	Seen at UCLA Neuropsychiatric Institute 1970-1974	Documented suicide attempts involved more self-abuse and bodily mutilation than self-poisoning. Self-abuse involved cutting, stabbing, burning and jumping in front of moving vehicles or from high places. Although there were no sex significant differences in ideational violence, there was a significant relationship between family disorganization, violent ideation, and a mutilating assault.
Pfeffer 1979	42	6-12 Mean age = 9.0	Bronx Municipal Hospital, Child Psyc. In-patient.	Jumping was the most frequent choice of attempters (38%), followed by self-poisoning (25%), burning (19%), cutting (13%), and running into traffic (6%).
Pfeffer et al. 1980	13	6-12		Although jumping was the most frequent ideation or threat, only one jumped in front of traffic. Of the remaining 12, there was 1 self-poisoning, 1 stabbing, 2 hangings, and ??
Pfeffer	65 M = 48 F = 17	6-12	Children admitted to the child psychiatry unit of New York Hospital, Westchester March 1979–June 1981	Jumping from high places was the most frequent method used and it was used in 25% of all cases.
Shaffer 1974	30	12-14	Completed suicides in England & Wales 1962-1968.	– Most frequent method used was carbon monoxide. – More males than females hanged themselves. – More females than males used self-poisoning.
Seiden & 1980	unknown	15-24	National statistics??	The rate of suicide by firearms increased 97.1% from 1966-1975 while the rate of suicide by other means increased 72.4% for the same period. The significantly large increase in death by firearms may reflect the 14.5% increase in the availability of legal handguns during the same time period.

Table 1 concluded.

NEUROTRANSMITTER MONOAMINE METABOLITES IN THE CEREBROSPINAL FLUID AS RISK FACTORS FOR SUICIDAL BEHAVIOR

Marie Asberg, M.D., Professor, Department of Psychiatry and Psychology, Karolinska Hospital, Stockholm, Sweden

Introduction

The idea that brain biochemistry may contribute to a person's decision to take his own life is fairly recent. In a bibliography (1) of research on suicide published between 1958 and 1967, only five out of 1267 titles deal with biochemical subjects. Suicide has been conceived of as an exclusively human behavior, which presupposes intentionality and a concept of death, and whose biological background is remote and irrelevant.

Recently, however, two lines of study have suggested that some instances of suicidal behavior may indeed have biological correlates, which obtain not only in conjunction with depression, but even perhaps when no depressive disorder is apparent. Two clusters of biological factors have emerged that tend to correlate with suicidal behavior, namely variables associated with a neurotransmitter, the monoamine serotonin (5-hydroxytryptamine, 5-HT), and variables associated with certain neuroendocrine functions. This paper will review the evidence for a relationship between serotonin and suicide attempts or completed suicide.

Biochemical Methods

The biochemical investigation techniques used in the field almost entirely derive from studies of depressive illness. They include studies of brain tissue obtained at autopsy, and measurements in cerebrospinal fluid (CSF), blood platelets and plasma, and urine. Monoamines and their precursors, catabolizing enzymes, and degradation products have all been measured; and hormonal processes thought to be controlled by monoamine neurons, and the reaction of the various systems to challenge, have been studied. This review will focus on measurements of CSF concentrations of monoamine metabolites, particularly the serotonin metabolite, 5-hydroxyindoleacetic acid (5-HIAA) and the dopamine metabolite, homovanillic acid (HVA).

Cerebrospinal Fluid Measurements as an Indicator of Brain Events

CSF metabolite concentrations have been widely studied to clarify the turnover of the monoamines in the brain. The advantage of the CSF studies is that spinal fluid is comparatively easily obtained with little discomfort to the patient--usually by means of a lumbar puncture (LP), a routine procedure in neurological investigations.

There are disadvantages as well. The concentration of the metabolites of serotonin and dopamine, 5-HIAA and HVA, depend, *inter alia*, on the subject's sex and age (2-4),

177

and on body height (5-7). The dependence on body height is presumably due to an active removal from the CSF of the acid metabolites as they flow from the brain ventricles down to the lumbar sac where the CSF is sampled. The concentrations of 5-HIAA and HVA decrease along the route of the CSF from the cerebral ventricles to the lumbar sac (8-9). A concentration gradient is seen even within the small volume usually drawn at lumbar puncture (10-12).

Metabolite concentrations also vary seasonally (7,13), and with the time of the day (14). Most important for clinical studies, the concentrations of 5-HIAA and HVA are drastically altered by treatment with certain psychotropic drugs. Many antidepressant treatments lower CSF 5-HIAA (4,15-19), and neuroleptic drugs usually increase HVA (20-23). Some factors of importance for the concentrations of 5-HIAA and HVA in lumbar CSF are summarized in Table 1. (Tables begin on page 207.)

Clearly, when groups of subjects are compared, confounding factors must be controlled or taken into account, as their influence is sometimes substantial and may lead to erroneous conclusions. Thus, if consistently more CSF is drawn from one group than from another in a comparative study, the average concentration of 5-HIAA and HVA will naturally be lower in the group from whom less CSF was taken. On the other hand, a true difference in concentration may be hidden if, for instance, control subjects are taller on the average than experimental subjects. The difference in average CSF 5-HIAA between depressed patients and healthy controls of equal stature, is numerically smaller than the difference between tall (>180 cm) and short (>160 cm) subjects, irrespective of whether they are healthy or depressed (7).

The concentration of a transmitter metabolite in the CSF is at best an indirect measure of the turnover of the parent amine in the brain, and it has been argued that, for example, 5-HIAA concentrations reflect events in the spinal cord, rather than in the brain (24). However, the recent finding by Stanley and coworkers (25) of a strong correlation between 5-HIAA concentrations measured *post mortem* in the frontal brain cortex, and in the lumbar spinal fluid, supports the contention that CSF 5-HIAA indeed reflects brain events; interestingly, the correlation between HVA in brain and in CSF was lower and was not statistically significant.

The concentration of the acid monoamine metabolites in the CSF is a function not only of their production rate, but also of their removal by an active transport mechanism from the cerebrospinal space. That the transport mechanism can be blocked by means of probenecid, has been taken advantage of in attempts to obtain more valid estimates of transmitter turnover (26). The probenecid technique has been described in detail by van Praag et al. (28). The probenecid technique, while removing one source of error, introduces other problems, however. With lower concentrations of probenecid, the blockade of the transport mechanism is incomplete, and may vary within individuals because of differences in probenecid metabolism. Higher probenecid concentrations often cause nausea and vomiting, and may also alter central neurotransmitter turnover.

One of the advantages with the probenecid technique is that concentrations of the monoamine metabolites are increased, which places less heavy demands on the analytical methods. With the very sensitive methods available today, concentrations in the nanomole range can be measured with satisfactory precision, and most investigators rely on baseline measures of the metabolites rather than on probenecid-induced accumulation.

Measures of Suicidal Behavior

In comparison with the advanced biochemical methods used in the studies to be reviewed, the approach to measuring suicidal behavior has been much less sophisticated. The reason for this is probably that, rather

178

than being designed to deal with suicidal behavior, most studies were focused on depressive illness and relied on procedures developed for measuring severity of depression. Diagnostic inventories and depression rating scales often contain an item dealing with suicidal ideation and tendencies, and such ratings have been used in some studies.

In other studies, the occurrence of 'suicide attempts' has been related to the biological variables. While some studies use more or less explicit, operational definitions of the term **suicide attempt**, others do not even attempt a definition. Although, in very few studies, ratings have been made of intent and lethality of a suicide attempt, heuristically the most useful classification seems to be according to the method used in the attempt (active, violent, or passive, nonviolent)-- perhaps because of its high reliability.

The time span involved also varies from one study to another. Some investigators have considered the incidence of any suicide attempts in the patient's history, while others have focussed on attempts during the current illness episode. In the former approach, the biological measures are assumed to be stable over time, a controversial assumption which will be discussed later.

Only a very few investigators have examined the possible predictive value of biological variables for ultimate suicide--understandably so, considering the low base rate of suicide and the time and cost of the investigation.

None of the available studies has dealt with the question of youth suicide. Although there seems to be little reason to believe *a priori* that a correlation between a biological variable and suicidal behavior would be limited to a certain age group, the issue remains to be empirically examined.

CSF 5-hydroxyindoleacetic acid (5-HIAA)

In a study of possible clinical correlates of CSF 5-HIAA in depressed patients, Asberg

et al. (29) unexpectedly found patients with low concentrations of the serotonin metabolite to represent an increased incidence of suicide attempts (defined as any deliberate, self-inflicted injury, regardless of the lethality risk involved, that the patient had thought to entail a death risk).

The findings of previous research by van Praag and Korf (30) and Asberg and coworkers (4,31) (see also Gibbons and Davis (32)) had indicated that the concentrations of the metabolite were bimodally distributed in depressed patients, suggesting the existence of a biochemical subgroup of depressive illness characterized by disturbed serotonin turnover. In the study by Asberg et al. (29), 40 percent of the patients with low CSF 5-HIAA concentration had attempted suicide during their current illness, as compared with 15 percent in patients with normal 5-HIAA. Moreover, the attempts were of a more determined nature with a preference for active, violent methods in the low 5-HIAA patients, whereas those in the high 5-HIAA groups were confined to drug overdoses. Two deaths from suicide occurred during the study period, both in low 5-HIAA patients.

The relationship between CSF 5-HIAA and suicidal behavior was confirmed by Agren (33), who studied depressed patients and measured suicidal behavior by means of the suicide behavior scales in the Schedule for Affective Disorder and Schizophrenia (SADS). These scales do not differentiate suicidal ideation and suicidal acts. In the Asberg et al. (29) study, low CSF 5-HIAA was not correlated to suicidal ideation, only to suicidal acts. Argren's choice of method may thus have weakened the correlation, which nonetheless was statistically significant.

These early studies did not take into account the relationship between CSF 5-HIAA and such interference factors as sex and body height. Men tend to have lower CSF 5-HIAA concentrations than women, and they are also more prone to use violent methods if they attempt suicide. The sex factor could, however, be ruled out in a subsequent confirmatory study by Traskman et al. (34), who adjusted for interference factors by analysis of covariance (ANCOVA).

More recently, the relationship between 5-HIAA and suicide has been confirmed in Dutch depressed patients studied by van Praag (35), who found a highly significant increased incidence of suicide attempts in patients with low probenecid-induced accumulation of 5-HIAA. The association between 5-HIAA and a violent mode of the attempt was not confirmed, however.

In a British study of depressed patients, Montgomery and Montgomery (36) also found more suicide attempts in patients with low CSF 5-HIAA concentrations (using the cut-off point between "low" and "normal" 5-HIAA suggested by Asberg and coworkers (31)).

Among depressed patients in India, Palaniappan and coworkers (37) found a significant correlation between CSF 5-HIAA concentrations and suicidal tendencies estimated by scores on the item Suicide in the Hamilton Rating Scale. A rating scale index of suicidal tendencies was also used by Leckman et al. (38), who found an association with 5-HIAA which was confined to patients with disturbed reality testing.

Banki and coworkers (39) found a relationship between low CSF 5-HIAA and suicide attempts in Hungarian female patients, a relationship that was confined to those who had used active methods. Lopez-Ibor et al. (4) (1985) reported a relationship between suicide attempts and low CSF 5-HIAA in Spanish patients, irrespective of the method used in the attempt. A further confirmation in Swedish patients was provided by Edman and coworkers (41), using the same methods as in the original Asberg et al. (29) study.

There are also, however, some nonconfirmatory studies. Vestergaard and coworkers (42) mention that among depressed patients studied by them, suicide and suicide attempts were equally frequent in individuals with low and high CSF 5-HIAA. Since they do not provide any further information, their data

have not been included in Table 2, which summarized the relevant studies.

A well-designed, nonconfirmatory study was performed by Roy-Byrne and coworkers (43), who studied American patients, most of them more or less treatment-resistant, referred to a research center specializing in the study of depressive disorders. No significant relationship was found between CSF 5-HIAA and suicide attempts (over the individual's lifetime), possibly owing to the high proportion of bipolar (manic depressive) patients in the group. Suicidal unipolar patients tended to have lower CSF 5-HIAA than had nonsuicidal unipolars, but the number of such patients was too small for statistical analysis. The biological correlates of suicidal behavior may thus differ between bipolar and unipolar disorders, a conclusion also reached by Agren (44).

Another difference between the study of Roy-Byrne et al. (43) and those of Asberg et al. (29) and Traskman et al. (34), is that the former considered suicidal behavior over the patient's entire life span. In the Asberg et al. (29) study, the significant association with CSF 5-HIAA was restricted to suicidal behavior during the index illness episode. The discrepancy suggests that CSF-HIAA values may not be stable over time in suicidal individuals, a possibility that will be discussed in further detail below.

Only about half of those who commit suicide are retrospectively diagnosed as having suffered from a depressive syndrome, as suggested from the thorough psychological autopsies performed by Beskow (45) and Asgard (in preparation). Several groups have studied the relationship between suicide attempts and CSF 5-HIAA in other diagnostic categories. Traskman et al. (34) found CSF 5-HIAA concentrations to be lower in **nondepressed** suicide attempters (mainly patients with personality disorders and minor affective disorders). Brown et al. (46-47), studying two groups of men with **personality disorders**, found more subjects who had made a suicide attempt at some point in life among those with low CSF 5-HIAA.

van Praag (48), and Ninan and coworkers (49), found a similar association in **schizophrenia**. This finding is somewhat against the odds, considering the report by Sedvall and Wode-Helgodt (5) that a subgroup of schizophrenic patients (those with a family history of the disorder) have abnormally high concentrations of the metabolite. Both suicide studies are well-designed with carefully selected, matched controls. Patients with a depressive disorder superimposed on their schizophrenia were deliberately excluded from van Praag's (48) study. Roy et al. (51), however, found no difference in CSF 5-HIAA concentrations between chronic schizophrenic subjects who had attempted suicide at some time during their life, and those who had not made such attempts. Lower CSF 5-HIAA concentrations were, however, reported in suicidal patients with schizophrenia than in nonmatched controls by Banki et al. (39), who also found similar relationships in **alcoholism** and **adjustment disorder**. The bulk of the evidence would thus seem to support the notion that potential for suicidal behavior is reflected in low concentrations of CSF 5-HIAA-- even when no major affective disorder is apparent.

CSF Concentrations of Homovanillic Acid (HVA)

The average concentration of the dopamine metabolite, HVA, in CSF is reduced in depression (52-53), and more consistently so than is CSF 5-HIAA, to which HVA is nevertheless strongly correlated. Whether the correlation between the two metabolites is due to their sharing the same transport mechanism, or to a functional connection between the parent amines is not known. A functional connection would seem to be indicated because of the consistent finding that, in addition to reducing 5-HIAA, drugs that interfere with serotonin turnover--such as the antidepressants clomipramine (54), zimeldine (19), and citalopram (55)--change HVA concentrations in CSF, while having no known direct effects on dopamine neurons.

Low concentrations of HVA in suicidal depressed patients have been reported by Traskman et al. (34), by Montgomery and Montgomery (36), by Palianappan (37), and by Roy et al. (56). In the Roy et al. (56) study of 27 depressed patients, the association between low HVA and suicidal behavior was much stronger than that between 5-HIAA and suicide, which did not reach statistical significance. In his 1980 study, Agren (33) found no association between HVA and any of the SADS suicide scales. In Agren's later (44) and larger patient group, he reports an association between low HVA and the lethality of suicide attempts made prior to the current episode.

Banki et al. (39), on the other hand, found suicide attempts to be less clearly related to HVA than to 5-HIAA. In particular, their depressed patients who had taken drug overdoses had significantly higher HVA than had nonsuicidal patients, whereas HVA was low in attempters who had used violent methods.

The studies of HVA in CSF in relation to suicidal behavior are summarized in Table 3. Interestingly, none of those who have studied nondepressed groups have reported any association between CSF HVA and suicidal behavior. Thus, Brown et al. (47) found no association in their patients with personality disorders. Leckman et al. (38) report no association in their diagnostically heterogeneous group, and Traskman et\al. (34) found an association only in those of their patients who fulfilled research criteria for a diagnosis of depressive illness. Ninan et al. (57) found no association in their schizophrenic subjects. A possible interpretation of the findings would be that CSF concentrations of HVA are related to suicidal tendencies, but only in conjunction with a depressive illness. Studies of patients with bipolar depressive illness would seem to be particularly interesting in the context.

Noradrenaline and 4-hydroxy-3-methoxy-phenylglycol (HMPG)

In contrast to the evidence relating suicide to serotonin, the relationship with noradrenaline is less clear. In depressed patients, Agren (33) reported a negative correlation between suicidal tendencies and the CSF concentration of the noradrenaline metabolite, 4-hydroxy-3-methoxy-phenylglycol (HMPG). Brown and coworkers (46) found a positive correlation in subjects with personality disorders, which was not reproduced in their study (47) of borderline patients.

In two studies of mixed diagnostic groups, Ostroff and associates (58-59) measured the ratio between noradrenaline and adrenaline (the NA:A ratio) in urine and found a relationship between a low ratio and suicidal behavior. Within a group of suicide attempters, Prasad (60) found the NA:A ratio to be significantly lower in those who used violent methods in the attempt.

Other Substances in the CSF: Cortisol and Magnesium

The relative robustness of the association between CSF 5-HIAA and suicide tendencies has inspired investigators to examine the correlations with other biological markers than the amine metabolites. Traskman et\al. (61) thus measured cortisol concentrations, but found no abnormality in suicide attempters. Depressed patients, on the other hand, had significantly higher CSF cortisol than had healthy control subjects.

Banki and coworkers (62) found a relationship between suicide attempts and low CSF concentrations of magnesium. There was a strong positive correlation between CSF magnesium and CSF 5-HIAA. Interestingly, magnesium concentrations in CSF are strongly correlated to CSF melatonin concentrations (63). Melatonin in plasma may in turn be related to suicidal tendencies. Beck-Friis and coworkers (64) reported that nocturnal serum melatonin concentrations, known to be decreased in depression (65-66),

were closer to normal in suicidal, than in non-suicidal depressed patients. Melatonin production is dependent on prevalent lighting conditions and thought to be regulated by beta-adrenergic neurotransmission. Serotonin is a precursor of melatonin, although little is known of any correlation between the concentrations of the two compounds in humans.

Post Mortem CSF Measurements in Suicide Victims

The concentrations of monoamines (serotonin, dopamine, noradrenaline and adrenaline) after death by suicide were measured in suboccipital CSF by Kauert et al. (67), who somewhat unexpectedly found increased serotonin concentrations in the suicide victims. Their finding has, however, received support from preliminary findings by Arato et al. (68), who report significantly higher concentrations of 5-HIAA in lumbar and suboccipital CSF obtained post mortem from suicide victims.

The CSF autopsy studies are summarized in Table 4, which also contains summaries of some studies of monoamines and metabolites in brain tissue from suicide victims. The post mortem CSF findings may prove crucial for our understanding of how alterations in serotonin transmission predispose to suicidal behavior--that is, if they can be confirmed and are not due to any of the sources of error that mar autopsy studies of suicide victims (such as delay between death and discovery of the body, the influence of drugs, mode of dying and agonal state).

Prediction of Suicide from CSF Measures

Those who commit suicide and those who merely attempt it differ notoriously in many important respects, even if there is an overlap between the two populations (69). In several studies, subsequent mortality from suicide among suicide attempters has amounted to about 2 percent within a year after the attempt (70). Although this is a considerable increase in suicide frequency over that of the general population, suicide is a rare event even in this group.

Estimating suicide risk so as to be able to take appropriate precautions is one of the most difficult tasks of the practicing psychiatrist, and many attempts have been made to create rating scales and inventories for the purpose. Most of these have not been very successful (71-72), which may be due, at least partly, to the low base rate of suicide and other statistical problems (73).

Among a well-known risk group for suicide, namely patients who have made a suicide attempt, those with low CSF 5-HIAA were 10 times more likely to die from suicide than the remainder (34) (see also Table 5). Roy et al. (56) reported a relationship to exist between low concentrations of HVA in the CSF and subsequent suicide in depressed patients, regardless of whether previous attempts have been made. These findings suggest that inclusion of biological variables in the clinical assessment of suicide risk might increase its precision.

To judge from the studies published so far, there is fairly consistent evidence that low concentrations of CSF 5-HIAA are associated with an increased rate of suicide attempts, and may be a risk factor for suicide in individuals with a psychiatric history. There is also evidence relating low HVA concentrations in the CSF to suicide, although so far only in depressed individuals.

Among the many questions raised by these findings, a few will be discussed here: how do the CSF risk factors correlate with other potential biological risk markers; what can be inferred about the processes whereby a disturbed serotonin system may predispose to suicide; and how this knowledge can be applied in preventing suicide.

Correlations Between Possible Biological Risk Factors

Apart from the 5-HIAA concentrations in CSF, a series of biological markers related to

serotonin have been reported to be disturbed in depressive illness. Among them are the concentrations of the precursor, tryptophan, in serum and its ration to other amino acids transported by the same mechanism (74), the binding of the antidepressant drug imipramine to specific sites in blood platelets (75-76), the uptake of serotonin by the platelets (77-78), and the concentrations of serotonin in platelets and plasma. The urinary output of 5-HIAA, on the other hand, is of little interest since it is strongly influenced by diet, varies from day to day, and is uncorrelated to CSF 5-HIAA (79).

So far, there are very few studies of other serotonin-related markers in relation to suicidal behavior, and little is known of the interrelations between them. These relationships need to be clarified, both with a view to understanding their physiological significance and for practical diagnostic purposes.

Interestingly, there are no clear-cut relationships between imipramine binding and serotonin uptake in depressed patients (80). These two possible serotonin markers may thus reflect different aspects of serotonin function. The relationships reported between CSF 5-HIAA and platelet MAO activity have not been consistent (81-82).

Monoaminergic neurons are known to be involved in the chain of events resulting in the release of many hormones, including cortisol. The details of this have not yet been worked out, but the data from the Meltzer et al. (83) study of 5-hydroxytryptophan-induced release of cortisol strongly suggest a functional connection between the serotonin system and HPA axis.

The available human data do not, however, show any negative correlations between markers of the serotonin system and the hypothalamus-pituitary-adrenal axis, such as might be expected if they reflect an identical risk factor for suicide. Thus, CSF concentrations of cortisol and of 5-HIAA have been shown to correlate positively, though weakly (61), or not at all (62,84). Both Carroll et al.

(85), and Banki and Arato (86), found a positive correlation between postdexamethasone cortisol and 5-HIAA. Interpretation of the results of Carroll et al. (85) is, however, complicated by the fact that spinal fluid was drawn after the administration of dexamethasone, which raises CSF 5-HIAA concentrations (87).

Among other potential markers of serotonin, the ratio of l-tryptophan to other neutral amino acids was positively correlated to postdexamethasone cortisol (88), whereas vmax of serotonin uptake into platelets (which is reduce in depression) tended to be negatively correlated to an abnormal DST (89). Preliminary reports suggest that the 5 hydroxytryptophan-induced cortisol release may be related to CSF 5-HIAA (90).

Gold and coworkers (91) report an inverse correlation between CSF 5-HIAA concentrations and the magnitude of the increase in thyroid stimulating hormone (TSH) reaction to administration of thyrotropin releasing hormone (TRH). The negative correlation between CSF 5-HIAA and the TRH/TSH-test also appears in a study by Banki and coworkers (39), where it is compatible with their finding of more normal TRH/TSH- responses in suicidal than in non-suicidal patients.

Stability of CSF Concentrations of 5-HIAA over Time

Related to the question of the usefulness of biological markers as risk factors for suicide, is their stability over extended periods.

Unfortunately, CSF studies of recovered depressives are rare. Such patients are often maintained on drugs for extended periods, and those who are not, even if available for lumbar puncture studies, may well be non-representative of the depressed population.

A further complication in followup studies is that most serotonin-related variables also seem to vary seasonally. Seasonal rhythms have been shown for the serotonin concentration in the human hypothalamus (92),

for the platelet serotonin uptake (93-94), and for the platelet 3H-imipramine binding (95-96). There is some evidence that a seasonal rhythm, very similar to that observed for serotonin in the hypothalamus, may also exist for CSF 5-HIAA (7).

The evidence from four published followup studies of depressed patients (52,97-99) is summarized in Table 6. 5-HIAA concentrations in CSF appear to remain fairly stable over limited periods in normal subjects, and in depressed patients re-admitted for relapse of depression (99). Recovered depressives, whose concentrations are normal during illness, also remain stable over prolonged periods, whereas in depressives with low 5-HIAA during illness the concentration sometimes increases with recovery, though it remains in the low range in most cases.

A possible interpretation of available data is that there is a subgroup of depressed patients, characterized by concentrations of CSF 5-HIAA that are not only low but also less stable over time. If this type of unstable serotonin system is associated with an increased vulnerability to illness, and with a further decrease in release during illness, the emergence of bimodal distributions in diseased populations is easily explained.

In line with the 'instability' hypothesis, are findings from two patients in whom repeated lumbar punctures were made, and who subsequently committed suicide (Asberg and coworkers, in preparation). In both cases, there was a substantial reduction in CSF 5-HIAA from one puncture to the next. The above-mentioned finding by Arato et al. (68), of higher CSF 5-HIAA in CSF from suicide victims than in controls may also be in line with an instability hypothesis.

Low CSF 5-HIAA - a Vulnerability Marker?

Low concentrations of 5-HIAA in CSF occur not only in depressed and suicidal people, but also in perfectly healthy subjects (53). This suggests that low CSF 5-HIAA is not a marker of the state of depression, but rather an indicator of vulnerability. Supporting the vulnerability hypothesis, van Praag and de Haan (100) found an increased incidence of depressive illness in relatives of patients with low CSF 5-HIAA, compared with those of patients with normal 5-HIAA concentrations. This finding is reminiscent of the observation by Sedvall and coworkers (101) that CSF 5-HIAA concentrations were lower in healthy subjects with a family history of depressive illness than in healthy subjects without such antecedents. Preliminary data from twin studies by Sedvall and coworkers (102) further support familial involvement in CSF concentrations of the monoamine metabolites.

Serotonin, Aggression and Suicide

If serotonin transmission is permanently low or unstable, it is conceivable that this may be manifested in other ways than in suicidal tendencies. The often quite unpremeditated, impulsive and violent character of may of the suicide attempts in low 5-HIAA patients gave rise to the suggestion (29) that they might have difficulties in controlling aggressive impulses. The hypothesis was supported by the association known to exist between aggression in animals, and serotonin turnover (summarized by Valzelli (103)), as well as the links between anger and suicide proposed by classic psychoanalytical theory (104-105).

'Aggression' is a somewhat nebulous concept. The word has many meanings, and some aspects of aggression are hardly amenable to empirical study. Aggression, in the sense of verbal threats or violent acts aimed at causing injury to others or to oneself, has, however, been studied in suicidal individuals. Thus, Weissman et al. (106), found that excessive hostility was characteristic of suicidal depressed patients, and Brown et al. (47), found more overt aggressive behavior in subjects who had made suicide attempts.

One of the strongest predictors of suicide is murder. In Great Britain, a 30 percent suicide rate is reported among murderers after the act. The risk of suicide is greatest

in those cases where the victim is a spouse (107). (In the United States, the suicide rate among murderers is lower, around 4 percent according to Wolfgang (108).)

Several investigators have tested the hypothesis that aggression dyscontrol is the link between serotonin turnover and suicidal behavior. Brown and associates (46) found a life pattern of aggressive behavior in subjects with personality disorder and low CSF 5-HIAA.

Further support for a relationship between serotonin and violence came from three studies of murderers. Linnoila and coworkers (109), found lower CSF 5-HIAA in violent offenders whose crimes were unpremeditated. Lidberg et al. (110), found lower CSF 5-HIAA in homicide offenders who had killed a spouse or a lover than in those who had killed someone of less emotional significance (usually a drinking buddy). Lidberg and coworkers (111) also found very low CSF 5-HIAA concentrations in three cases, where suicide attempters had killed, or attempted to kill, their children.

A relationship between serotonin and aggressive behavior in alcoholics was also found by Branchey et al. (112), who studied the ratio of tryptophan to other neutral amino acids in serum. They found significantly lower ratios, compatible with a deficiency of brain serotonin, in those subjects who had been arrested for assaultive behavior than in other alcoholics or in nonalcoholic controls.

Suicide and the Biology of Personality

Interestingly, some personality features that seem to be prominent in patients who attempt suicide, are also associated with CSF concentrations of 5-HIAA. These personality features often reflect impulsivity and problems in the handling of anger. In normal people, low CSF 5-HIAA appears to be associated with vitality, social dominance and easily aroused anger, as shown by Zuckerman et al. (82), and Schalling et al. (in preparation). In psychiatric patients, low

CSF 5-HIAA has also been associated with high vitality, self-reported impulsivity and psychopathy- related features (47,113-114), and with high hostility and anxiety in ratings based on Rorschach protocols (115). Correlations with HVA, when reported, are generally parallel those with 5-HIAA, but are weaker.

Implications for Suicide Prevention

Their association with a heightened risk of suicide suggests that markers of serotonin may be valuable in a clinical context. Low concentrations of CSF 5-HIAA in suicide attempters, for instance, were connected with a 20 percent mortality from suicide within a year, which suggests that the combination may be one of the strongest suicide predictors hitherto identified. The number of false positives is, however, still very large.

Although it seems likely that CSF determinations might help in the assessment of suicide risk, there are problems in applying the technique in a clinical setting. Owing to the many factors that influence CSF concentrations of 5-HIAA and HVA, the spinal tap procedure must be standardized to an extent that is rarely practical in a busy clinic. Furthermore, the patients must be hospitalized overnight, and most difficult of all, they must have been off antidepressant and neuroleptic drugs, and lithium, for several weeks prior to the puncture.

Usually, the spinal tap is easily tolerated by the patient, and the post LP headache that afflicts about a third of the subjects is not a major problem. The procedure sometimes appears to pose greater problems for the psychiatric staff, who may feel that it is too "medical" and out of tune with the type of therapeutic relationship they wish to establish with the patient.

Thus, though there is an obvious need for new, more easily accessible markers of the state of the serotonin system, in centers with access to the relevant analytical procedures, routine spinal taps may nevertheless be a real help in clinical management.

A better understanding of the biological and psychological links between serotonin turnover and suicidal behavior might also open up new approaches to the prevention of suicide. Serotonin transmission can be controlled, with drugs or amino acid precursors, and possibly by dietary changes, and it would seem important to test such treatment regimens in patients with a high suicide potential. It is also possible that an increased understanding of the psychological processes that are controlled by serotonin neurons could be used to develop more specific psychotherapeutic techniques than has hitherto been possible.

CONCLUSIONS

In a number of studies, a relationship has been shown to exist between low CSF concentrations of the serotonin metabolite 5-HIAA and an increased incidence of suicide attempts in psychiatric patients. Although most studies deal with depressed patients, there is fairly strong evidence that this relationship exists in other disorders as well, particularly in personality disorders and possibly also in schizophrenia. Some reports suggest that bipolar (manic-depressive) disorder may be an exception.

Low concentrations of the dopamine metabolite HVA may also be associated with suicide attempts. Although this may to some extent be accounted for by its correlation with 5-HIAA, there is probably more to it, since unlike 5-HIAA, the association may be confined to depressive disorder.

Both markers have been associated with an increased frequency of ultimate suicide, but there is a need for further prospective studies.

Low CSF concentrations of 5-HIAA may reflect a low serotonin output, or possibly a low stability serotonin system, which may in turn be a vulnerability factor. In most individuals with low CSF 5-HIAA, this vulnerability will never be manifested in a suicide attempt. A suicide attempt is unlikely to occur unless the individual finds himself in a situation which he conceives of as desperate, or when he is without hope for the future. Adverse events may have created this situation, or the individual's perception of the situation may be colored by depressive illness. Previous experience of adverse events (e.g., during childhood) is liable to render the interpretation of current adversity more ominous. Whether this state of affairs leads to a suicide attempt, is to some extent determined by the quality of the person's social support network, which may attenuate the effect of adverse events, or render the sufferings of depressive illness more tolerable.

A low-output serotonin system (or perhaps even more likely, a low-stability one) might render an individual more vulnerable to self-destructive or impulsive action in time of crisis. This characteristic of the serotonin system may have a genetic basis, or it may be acquired.

Although little is known of the processes linking serotonin with suicidal behavior, there is some evidence that personality features such as impulsivity and difficulties in handling aggression may be important intervening variables.

CSF measures are currently used as an aid to suicide risk prediction in some highly specialized clinical settings. They appear less likely to be useful on a larger scale, because of the need for strict standardization of the procedure. An important research task would seem to be to identify other markers of the serotonin system that can be measured repeatedly over time in large groups of subjects.

The potential for treatment and prevention of suicide remains to be explored.

REFERENCES

1. Farberow NL. Bibliography on suicide and suicide prevention 1897-1957 1958-1967. Washington DC: National Institute of Mental Health, 1969; DHEW publication no. (PHS) 1979.

2. Bowers MB Jr, Gerbode FA. The relationship of monoamine metabolites in human cerebrospinal fluid to age. Nature 1968; 219:1256-1257.

3. Gottfries CG, Gottfries I, Johansson B, Olsson R, Persson T, Roos B-E, Sjostrom R. Acid monoamine metabolites in human cerebrospinal fluid and their relations to age and sex. Neuropharmacology 1971; 10:665-672.

4. Asberg M, Bertilsson L, Tuck D, Cronholm B, Sjoqvist F. Indoleamine metabolites in the cerebrospinal fluid of depressed patients before and during treatment with nortriptyline. Clinical Pharmacology and Therapeutics 1973; 14:277-286.

5. Wode-Helgodt B, Sedvall G. Correlations between height of subject and concentrations of monoamine metabolites in cerebrospinal fluid from psychotic men and women. Communications in Psychopharmacology 1978;2:177-183.

6. Asbert M, Bertilsson L. Serotonin in depressive illness - Studies of CSF 5-HIAA. In: Saletu B et al., eds. Neuro- psychopharmacology. Oxford-New York: Pergamon Press, 1979:105-115.

7. Asberg M, Bertilsson L, Rydin E, Schalling D, Thoren P, Traskman-Bendz L. Monoamine metabolites in cerebrospinal fluid in relation to depressive illness, suicidal behavior and personality. In: Angrist B, Burrows G, Lader M, Lingjaerde O, Sedvall G, Wheatley D, eds. Recent Advances in Neuro-psychopharmacology. Oxford and New York: Pergamon Press, 1981:257-271.

8. Guldberg HC, Ashcroft GW, Crawford TBB. Concentrations of 5-hydroxyindoleacetic acid and homovanillic acid in the cerebrospinal fluid of the dog before and during treatment with probenecid. Life Sciences 1966;5:1571-1575.

9. Moir ATB, Ashcroft GW, Crawford TBB, Eccleston D, Guldberg HC. Cerebral metabolites in cerebrospinal fluid as a biochemical approach to the brain. Brain 1970;93:357-368.

10. Siever L, Kraemer H, Sack R, et al. Gradients of biogenic amine metabolites in cerebrospinal fluid. Diseases of the Nervous System 1975;36:13-16.

11. Jacupcevic M, Lackovic Z, Stefoski D, Bulat M. Nonhomogeneous distribution of 5-hydroxyindoleacetic acid and homovanillic acid in the lumbar cerebrospinal fluid of man. Journal of the Neurological Sciences 1977;31:165-171.

12. Bertilsson L, Asberg M, Lantto O, Scalia-Tomba G-P, Traskman-Bendz L, Tybring G. Gradients of monoamine metabolites and cortisol in cerebrospinal fluid of psychiatric patients and healthy controls. Psychiatry Research 1982;6:77-83.

13. Losonczy MF, Mohs RC, Davis KL. Seasonal variations of human lumbar CSF neurotransmitter metabolite concentrations. Psychiatry Research 1984;12:79-87.

14. Nicoletti F, Raffaele R, Falsaperla A, Paci R. Circadian variation in 5-hydroxyindoleacetic acid levels in human cerebrospinal fluid. European Neurology 1981;20:834-838.

15. Bowers MB Jr. Cerebrospinal fluid 5-hydroxindoleacetic acid (5-HIAA) and homovanillic acid (HVA) following probenecid in unipolar depressives treated with amitriptyline. Psychopharmacologia 1972;23:26-33.

16. Post RM, Goodwin FK. Effects of amitriptyline and imipramine on amine metabolites in the cerebrospinal fluid of depressed patients. Archives of General Psychiatry 1974;30:234-239.

17. Muscettola G, Goodwin FK, Potter WZ, Claeys MM, Markey SP. Imipramine and desipramine in plasma and spinal fluid. Relationship to clinical responses and serotonin metabolism. Archives of General Psychiatry 1978;35:621-625.

18. Traskman L, Asberg M, Bertilsson L, et al. Plasma levels of chlorimipramine and its demethyl metabolite during treatment of depression. Differential biochemical and clinical effects of the two compounds. Clinical Pharmacology and Therapeutics 1979;26:600-610.

19. Bertilsson L, Tuck JR, Siwers B. Biochemical effects of zimelidine in man. European Journal of Clinical Pharmacology 1980;18:483-487.

20. Persson T, Roos B-E. Acid metabolites from monoamines in cerebrospinal fluid of chronic schizophrenics. British Journal of Psychiatry 1969;115:95-98.

21. Chase TN, Schnur JA, Gordon EK. Cerebrospinal fluid monoamine catabolites in drug-induced etrapyramidal disorders. Neuro- psychopharmacology 1970;9:265-268.

22. Bowers MB Jr: 5-hydroxyindolacetic acid (5-HIAA) and homovanillic acid (HVA) following probenecid in acute psychotic patients treated with phenothiazines. Psychopharmacologia 1973;28:309-318.

23. Fyro B, Wode-Helgodt B, Borg S, Sedvall G. The effect of chlorpromazine on homovanillic acid levels in cerebrospinal fluid of schizophrenic patients. Psychopharmacologia (Berl.) 1974;35:287-294.

24. Bulat M, ZivkovicB. Origin of 5-hydroxyin-doleacetic acid in the spinal fluid. Science 1971;173:738-740.

25. Stanley M, Traskman-Bendz L, Dorovini-Zis K. Correlations between aminergic metabolites simul-taneously obtained from human CSF and brain. Life Sciences 1985;37:1279-1286.

26. Roos BE, Sjostrom R. 5-hydroxyindoleacetic acid (and homovanillic acid) levels in the cerebrospinal fluid after probenecid application in patients with manic-depressive psychosis. Pharmacologia Clinica 1969;1:153-155.

27. van Praag HM, Korf J, Schut D. Cerebral monoamines and depression. An investigation with the probenecid technique. Archives of General Psychiatry 1973;28:827-831.

28. Goodwin FK, Post RM, Dunner DL, Gordon EK. Cerebrospinal fluid amine metabolites in affective illness: The probenecid technique. American Journal of Psychiatry 1973;130:73-79.

29. Asberg M, Traskman L, Thoren P. 5-HIAA in the cerebrospinal fluid: A biochemical suicide predictor? Archives of General Psychiatry 1976;33:1193-1197.

30. van Praag HM, Korf J. Endogenous depressions with and without disturbances in the 5-hydroxytryptamine metabolism: A biochemical classification? Psychophar-macologia (Berl.) 1971;19:148-152.

31. Asberg M, Thoren P, Traskman L, Bertilsson L, Ringberger V. "Serotonin depression" - A biochemical sub-group within the affective disorders? Science 1976;191:478-480.

32. Gibbons RD, Davis JM. A note on the distribution-al form of the Asberg et al. CSF monoamine data. Acta psychiatrica scandinavica (in press).

33. Agren H. Symptom patterns in unipolar and bipolar depression correlating with monoamine metabo-lites in the cerebrospinal fluid: II. Suicide. Psychiatry Research 1980;3:225-236.

34. Traskman L, Asberg M, Bertilsson L, Sjostrand L. Monoamine metabolites in CSF and suicidal behavior. Ar-chives of General Psychiatry 1981;38:631-636.

35. van Praag HM. Depression, suicide and the meta-bolism of serotonin in the brain. Journal of Affective Dis-orders 1982;4:275-290.

36. Montgomery SA, Montgomery D. Pharmacologi-cal prevention of suicidal behavior. Journal of Affective Disorders 1982;4:291-298.

37. Palaniappan V, Ramachandran V, Somasundaram O. Suicidal ideation and biogenic amines in depression. Indian Journal of Psychiatry 1983;25:286-292.

38. Leckman JF, Charney DS, Nelson CR, Heninger GR, Bowers MB Jr. CSF tryptophan, 5-HIAA and HVA in 132 patients characterized by diagnosis and clinical state. Recent Advances in Neuropsychopharmacology 1981;31:289-297.

39. Banki CM, Arato M, Papp Z, Kurcz M. Biochemical markers in suicidal patients. Investigations with cerebrospinal fluid amine metabolites and neuroen-docrine tests. Journal of Affective Disorders 1984;6:341-350.

40. Lopez-Ibor JJ Jr, Saiz-Ruiz J, Perez do los Cobos JC. Biological correlations of suicide and aggressivity in major depressions (with melancholia): 5-hydroxyin-doleacetic acid and cortisol in cerebral spinal fluid, dexamethasone suppression test and therapeutic response to 5-hydroxytryptophan. Neuropsychobiology 1985;14:67-74.

41. Edman G, Asberg M, Levander S, Schalling D. Skin conductance habituation and cerebrospinal fluid 5-hydroxyindoleacetic acid in suicidal patients. Archives of General Psychiatry (in press).

42. Vestergaard P, Sorensen T, Hoppe E, Rafaelsen OJ, Yates CM, Nicolaou N. Biogenic amine metabolites in cerebrospinal fluid of patients with affective disorders. Acta psychiatrica scandinavica 1978;58:88-96.

43. Roy-Byrne P, Post RM, Rubinow DR, Linnoila M, Savard R, Davis D. CSF 5HIAA and personal and family history of suicide in affectively ill patients: A negative study. Psychiatry Research 1983;10:263-274.

44. Agren H. Life at risk: Markers of suicidality in depression. Psychiatric Developments 1983;1:87-104.

45. Beskow J: Suicide and mental disorder in Swedish men. Acta psychiatrica scandinavica 1979;Suppl.277.

46. Brown GL, Goodwin FK, Ballenger JC, Goyer PF, Major LF: Aggression in humans correlates with cerebrospinal fuid amine metabolites. Psychiatry Research 1979;1:131-139.

47. Brown GL, Ebert MH, Goyer PF, et al. Aggression, suicide, and serotonin: Relationships to CSF amine me-tabolites. American Journal of Psychiatry 1982;139:741-746.

48. van Praag HM. CSF 5-HIAA and suicide in non-depressed schizophrenics. Lancet 1983;2:977-978.

49. Ninan PT, van Kammen DP, Scheinin M, Linnoila M, Bunney WE Jr, Goodwin FK. CSF 5-hydroxyin-doleacetic acid in suicidal schizophrenic patients. American Journal of Psychiatry 1984;141:566-569.

50. Sedvall G, Wode-Helgodt B. Aberrant monoamine metabolite levels in CSF and family history of schizophrenia. Their relationships in schizophrenic patients. Archives of General Psychiatry 1980;37:1113-1116.

51. Roy A, Ninan P, Mazonson A, et al. CSF monoamine metabolites in chronic schizophrenic patients who attempt suicide. Psychological Medicine 1985;15:335k-340.

52. Post RM, Ballenger JC, Goodwin FK. Cerebrospinal fluid studies of neurotransmitter function in manic and depressive illness. In: Wood JH, ed. Neurobiology of cerebrospinal fluid. I. New York: Plenum Press, 1980:685-717.

53. Asberg M, Bertilsson L, Martensson B, Scalia-Tomba G-P, Thoren P, Traskman-Bedz L CSF monoamine metabolites in melancholia. Acta psychiatrica scandinavica 1984;69:201-219.

54. Asberg M, Ringberger V-A, Sjoqvist F, Thoren P, Traskman L, Tuck JR. Monoamine metabolites in cerebrospinal fluid and serotonin uptake inhibition during treatment with chlorimipramine. Clinical Pharmacology and Therapeutics 1977;21:201-207.

55. Bjerkenstedt L, Edman G, Flyckt L, Hagenfeldt L, Sedvall G, Wiesel FA. Clinical and biochemical effects of citalopram, a selective 5-HT reuptake inhibitor - A dose-response study in depressed patients. Psychopharmacol-ogy 1985;87:253-259.

56. Roy A, Agren H, Pickar D, et al. Reduced cerebrospinal fluid concentrations of homovanillic acid and homovanillic acid to 5-hydroxyindoleacetic acid ratios in depressed patients: relationship to suicidality and dexamethasone nonsuppression. American Journal of Psychiatry (in press).

57. Ninan PT, van Kammen DP, Linnoila M. Letter to the Editor. American Journal of Psychiatry 1985;142:148.

58. Ostroff RB, Giller E, Bonese K, Ebersole E, Harkness L, Mason J. Neuroendocrine risk factors of suicidal behavior. American Journal of Psychiatry 1982;139:1323-1325.

59. Ostroff RB, Giller E, Harkness L, Mason J. The norepinephrine- to-epinephrine ratio in patients with a history of suicide attempts. American Journal of Psychiatry 1985;142:224-227.

60. Prasad AJ. Neuroendocrine differences between violent and non-violent para-suicides. Neuropsychobiology 1985;13:157-159.

61. Traskman L, Tybring G, Asberg M, Bertilsson L, Lantto O, Schalling D. Cortisol in the CSF of depressed and suicidal patients. Archives of General Psychiatry1980;37:761-767.

62. Banki CM, Vojnik M, Papp Z, Balla KZ, Arato M. Cerebrospinal fluid magnesium and calcium related to amine metabolites, diagnosis and suicide attempts. Biological Psychiatry 1985;20:163-171.

63. Beckmann H, Wetterberg L, Gattaz WF. Melatonin immunoreactivity in cerebrospinal fluid of schizophrenic patients and healthy controls. Psychiatry Research 1984;11:107-110.

64. Beck-Friis J, Kjellman BF, Aperia B, et al. Serum melatonin in relation to clinical variables in patients with major depressive disorder and a hypothesis of a low melatonin syndrome. Acta psychiatrica scandinavica 1985;71:319-330.

65. Wetterberg L, Beck-Friis L, Aperia B, Pettersson U. Melatonin/cortisol ratio in depression. Lancet 1979;1:1361.

66. Claustrat B, Chazot G, Brun J, Jordan D, Sassolas G. A chronobiological study of melatonin and cortisol secretion in depressed subjects: Plasma melatonin, a biochemical marker in major depression. Biological Psychiatry 1984;19:1215-1228.

67. Kauert G, Gilg T, Eisenmenger W, Spann W. Postmortem biogenic amines in CSF of suicides and controls. Poster, 14th Congress of the Collegium Internationale Neuro-Psychopharmacologicum, Florence 1984.

68. Arato M, Falus A,Sotonyi P, Somogyi E,Tothfalusi L, Magyar K. Postmorten neurochemical investigation of suicidal behavior. Abstract, First European Symposiumon Empirical Research of Suicidal Behavior, March 19-22, 1986, Munich FRG.

69. Stenge E, Cook NC. Attempted suicide. London: Chapman & Hall, 1958.

70. Ettlinger R. Evaluation of suicide prevention after attempted suicide. Acta psychiatrica scandinavica. 1975; Suppl. 260.

71. Pokorny AD. Prediction of suicide in psychiatric patients. Archives of General Psychiatry 1983;40:249-257.

72. Burk F, Kurz A, Moller H-J. Suicide risk scales: do they help to predict suicidal behavior? European Archives of Psychiatry and Neurological Sciences 1985;235:153-157.

73. Cohen J. Statistical approaches to suicidal risk-factor analysis. Proceedings of the New York Academy of Sciences (in press).

74. Wood K, Coppen A. Biochemical abnormalities in depressive illness: tryptophan and 5-hydroxytryptamine. In: Curzon G, ed. The biochemistry of psychiatric disturbances. Chichester: John Wiley & Sons Ltd., 1980:13-33.

75. Briley MS, Langer SZ, Raisman R, Sechter D, Zarifian E. Tritiated imipramine binding sites are decreased in platelets of untreated depressed patients. Science 1980;209:303-305.

76. Paul SM, Rehavi M, Skolnick P, Ballenger JC, Goodwin FK. Depressed patients have decreased binding of tritiated imipramine to platelet serotonin 'transporter'. Archives of General Psychiatry 1981;38:1315-1317.

77. Tuomisto J, Tukiainen E. Decreased uptake of 5-hydroxytryptamine in blood platelets from depressed patients. Nature 1976;262:596-598.

78. Coppen A, Swade C, Wood K. Plataelet 5-hydroxytryptamine accumulation in depressive illness. Clinica Chimica Acta 1978;87:165-168.

79. Bertilsson L, Tybring G, Braithwaite R, Traskman-Bendz L, Asberg M. Urinary excretion of 5-hydroxyindoleacetic acid - no relationship to the level of cerebrospinal fluid. Acta psychiatrica scandinavica 1982;66:190-198.

80. Raisman R, Briley MS, Bouchami F, Sechter D, Zarifian E, Langer SZ. 3H-imipramine binding and serotonin uptake in platelets from depressed patients and control volunteers. Psychopharmacology 1982;77:332-335.

81. Oreland L, Wiberg A, Asberg M, et al. Platelet MAO activity and monoamine metabolites in cerebrospinal fluid in depressed and suicidal patients and in healthy controls. Psychiatry Research 1981;4:21-29.

82. Zuckerman M, Ballenger JC, Jimerson DC, Murphy DL, Post RM. A correlational test in humans of the biological models of sensation seeking, impulsivity, and anxiety. In: Zuckerman M, ed. Biological Bases of Sensation Seeking, Impulsivity and Anxiety. Hillsdale New Jersey: Laurence Erlbaum Associates, 1983:229-248.

83. Meltzer HY, Perline R, Tricou BJ, Lowy M, Robertson A. Effect of 5-hydroxytryptophan on serum cortisol levels in major affective disorders. II. Relation to suicide, psychosis, and depressive symptoms. Archives of General Psychiatry 1984;41:379-387.

84. Aminoff A-K, Asberg M, Bertilsson L, Eneroth P, Martensson B, Traskman-Bendz L. CSF monoamine metabolites and the dexamethasone suppression test. Manuscript 1986.

85. Carroll BJ, Greden JF, Haskett R, et al. Neurotransmitter studies of neuroendocrine pathology in depression. In: Svensson TH, Carlsson A, eds. Biogenic amines and affective disorder. Acta psychiatrica scandinavica 1980;61(Suppl 280):183-198.

86. Banki CM, Arato M. Amine metabolites and neuroendocrine responses related to depression and suicide. Journal of Affective Disorders 1983;5:223-232.

87. Banki CM, Arato M, Papp Z, Kurcz M. The influence of dexamethasone on cerebrospinal fluid monoamine metabolites and cortisol in psychiatric patients. Pharmacopsychiatria 1981;16:77-81.

88. Joseph MS, Brewerton TD, Reus VI, Stebbins GT. Plasma L-tryptophan/ neutral amino acid ratio and dexamethasone suppression in depression. Psychiatry Research 1984;11:185-192.

89. Meltzer HY, Arora RC, Tricou BJ, Fang VS. Serotonin uptake in blood platelets and the dexamethasone suppression test in depressed patients. Psychiatry Research 1983;8:41-47.

90. Meltzer HY, Koenig JI, Lowy M, Koyama T, Robertson AG. Serotonergic neuroendocrine challenges in affective disorders. Abstract, IVth World Congress of Biological Psychiatry, Philadelphia, Penn. USA, Sept 8-13, 1985.

91. Gold PW, Goodwin FK, Wehr T, Rebar R. Pituitary thyrotropin response to thyrotropin-releasing hormone in affective illness: Relationship to spinal fluid amine metabolites. American Journal of Psychiatry 1977;134:1028-1031.

92. Carlsson A, Svennerholm L, Winblad B. Seasonal and circadian monoamine variations in human brains examined post mortem. In: Svensson TH, Carlsson A, eds. Biogenic amines and affective disorders. Acta psychiatrica scandinavica 1980;61(Suppl 280):75-83.

93. Wirz-Justice A, Richter R. Seasonality in biochemical determinations: a source of variance and a clue to the temporal incidence of affective illness. Psychiatry Research 1979;1:53-60.

94. Arora RC, Kregel L, Meltzer HY. Seasonal variation of serotonin uptake in normal controls and depressed patients. Biological Psychiatry 1984;19:795-804.

95. Egrise D, Desmedt D, Shoutens A, Mendlewica J. Circannual variations in the density of tritiated imipramine binding sites on blood platelets in man. Neuropsychobiology 1983;10:101-102.

96. Whitaker PM, Warsh JJ, Stancer HC, Persad E, Vint CK. Seasonal variation in platelet 3H-imipramine binding: comparable values in control and depressed populations. Psychiatry Research 1984;11:127-131.

97. Coppen A, Prange AJ Jr, Whybrow PC, Noguera R. Abnormalities of indoleamines in affective disorders. Archives of General Psychiatry 1972;26:474-478.

98. van Praag HM. Significance of biochemical parameters in the diagnosis, treatment, and prevention of depressive disorders. Biological Psychiatry 1977;12:101-131.

99. Traskman-Bendz L, Asbrg M, Bertilsson L, Thoren P. CSF monoamine metabolites of depressed patients during illness and after recovery. Acta psychiatrica scandinavica 1984;69:333-342.

100. van Praag HM, de Haan S. Central serotonin metabolism and the frequency of depression. Psychiatry Research 1979;1:219-224.

101. Sedvall G. Fyro B, Gullberg B, Nyback H, Wiesel FA, Wode-Helgodt B. Relationships in healthy volunteers between concentrations of monoamine metabolites in cerebrospinal fluid and family history of psychiatric morbidity. British Journal of Psychiatry 1980;136:366-374.

102. Sedvall G, Iselius L, Nyback H, et al. Genetic studies of CSF monoamine metabolites. IN: Usdin E, et al., eds. Frontiers in biochemical and pharmacological research in depression. New York: Raven Press 1984:79-85. (Advances in Biochemical Psychopaharmacology; vol. 39).

103. Valzelli L. Psychobiology of aggression and violence. New York, Raven Press 1981.

104. Freud S. Trauer und Melancholie(1917). In: Freud A, Bibring E, Hoffer W, et al., eds. Sigmund Freud - Gesammelte Werke. Vol. 10. 67th Ed. Frankfurt am Main: Fischer, 1973:428-446.

105. Abraham K. Versuch einer Entwicklungsgeschichte der Libido auf Grund der Psychoanalyse seelischer Storungen. Leipzig: Internationaler Psychoanalytischer Verlag 1927. (Freud S, ed. Neue Arbeiten zur arztlichen Psychoanalyse; vol. 2).

106. Weissman M, Fox K, Klerman GL. Hostility and depression associated with suicide attempts. American Journal of Psychiatry 1973;130:450-455.

107. West DJ. Murder followed by suicide. London: Heinemann 1965.

108. Wolfgang ME. Patterns in criminal homicide. London: Oxford University Press, 1958.

109. Linnoila M, Virkkunen M, Scheinin M, Nuutila A, Rimon R, Goodwin FK. Low cerebrospinal fluid 5-hydroxyindoleacetic acid concentration differentiates impulsive from nonimpulsive violent behavior. Life Sciences 1983;33:2609-2614.

110. Lidberg L, Tuck JR, Asberg M, Scalia-Tomba G-P, Bertilsson L. Homicide, suicide and CSF 5-HIAA. Acta psychiatrica scandinavica 1985;71:230-236.

111. Lidberg L, Asberg M, Sudnqvist-Stensman UB: 5-hydroxyindoleacetic acid levels in attempted suicides who have killed their children. Lancet 1984;2:928.

112. Branchey L, Branchey M, Shaw S, Lieber CS. Depression, suicide, and aggression in alcoholics and their relationship to plasma amino acids. Psychiatry Research 1984;12:219-226.

113. Banki CM, Arato M. Relationship between cerebrospinal fluid amine metabolites, neuroendocrine findings and personality dimensions (Marke-Nyman scale factors) in psychiatric patients. Acta psychiatrica scandinavica 1983;67:272-280.

114. Schalling D, Asberg M, Edman G, Levander S. Impulsivity, nonconformity and sensation seeking as related to biological markers for vulnerability. Clinical Neuropharmacology 1984;7(Suppl. 1):746-747.

115. Rydin E, Schalling D, Asberg M. Rorschach ratings in depressed and suicidal patients with low levels of 5-hydroxyindoleacetic acid in cerebrospinal fluid. Psychiatry Research 1982;7:229-243.

116. Johansson B, Roos B-E. 5-hydroxyindoleacetic and homovanillic acid levels in the cerebrospinal fluid of healthy volunteers and patients with Parkinson's syndrome. Life Sciences 1967;6:1449-1454.

117. Andersen O, Johansson BB, Svennerholm L. Monoamine metabolites in successive samples of spinal fluid. A comparison between healthy volunteers and patients with multiple sclerosis. Acta neurologica scandinavica 1981;63:247-254.

118. Hallert C, Astrom J, Sedvall G. Psychic disturbances in adult coeliac diseases. III. Reduced central monoamine metabolites and signs of depression. Scandinavian Journal of Gastroenterology 1982;17:25-28.

119. Andersson H, Roos B-E. Increased level of 5-hydroxyindoleacetic acid in cerebrospinal fluid from infantile hydrocephalus. Experientia 1966;22:539-541.

120. Post RM, Kotin J, Goodwin FK, Gordon E. Psychomotor activity and cerebrospinal fluid amine metabolites in affective illness. American Journal of Psychiatry 1973;130:67-72.

121. Nordin C, Siwers B, Bertilsson L: Site of lumbar puncture influences levels of monoamine metabolites. Letter to the Editor. Archives of General Psychiatry 1982;39:1445.

122. Traskman-Bendz L. Depression and suicidal behavior - a biochemical and pharmacological study (Dissertation). Stockholm: Karolinska institute, 1980. 61 p.

123. Sjoquist B, Johansson B. A comparison between fluoremetric and mass fragmentographic determinations of homovanillic acid and 5-hydroxyindoleacetic acid in human cerebrospinal fluid. Journal of Neurochemistry 1978;31:621-625.

124. Muskiet FAJ, Jeuring HJ, Korf J, et al. Correlations between a fluorimetric and mass fragmentographic method for the determination of 3-methoxy-4-hydroxyphenylacetic acid and two mass fragmentographic methods for the determination of 3 methoxy-4-hydroxyphenylethylene glycol in cerebrospinal fluid. Journal of Neurochemistry 1979;32:191-194.

125. Major LF, Murphy DL, Lipper S, Gordon E. Effects of clorgyline and pargyline on deaminated metabolites of norepinephrine, dopamine and serotonin in human cerebrospinal fluid. Journal of Neurochemistry 1979;32:229-231.

126. Kaye WH, Ebert MH, Raleigh M, Lake R. Abnormalities in CNS monoamine metabolism in anorexia nervosa. Archives of General Psychiatry 1984;41:350-355.

127. Gateless D. Stanley M, Traskman-Bendz L, Gilroy J. The influence of the lying and sitting positions on the gradients of 5-HIAA and HVA in lumbar cerebrospinal fluid. Biological Psychiatry 1984;19:1585-1589.

128. Shaw DN, Camps FE, Eccleston EG. 5-hydroxytryptamie in the hind-brain of depressive suicides. British Journal of Psychiatry 1967;113:1407-1411.

129. Bourne HR, Bunney WE Jr, Colburn RW, et al. Noradrenaline, 5-hydroxytryptamine, and 5-hydroxyindoleacetic acid in hindbrains of suicidal patients. Lancet 1968;2:805-808.

130. Pare CMB, Yeung DPH, Price K, Stacey RS. 5-hydroxytryptamine, noradrenaline and dopamine in brainstem, hypothalamus, and caudate nucleus of controls and of patients committing suicide by coal-gas poisoning. Lancet 1969;2:133-135.

131. Lloyd KG, Farley IJ, Deck JHN, Hornykiewicz O. Serotonin and 5-hydroxyindoleacetic acid in discrete areas of the brainstem of suicide victims and control patients. In: Costa E, Gessa GL, Sandler M, eds. Serotonin: New vistas. New York, Raven Press 1974:387-397. (Advances in Biochemical Psychopharmacology; vol. 11).

132. Cochran E, Robins E, Grote S. Regional serotonin levels in brain: A comparison of depressive suicides and alcoholic suicides with controls. Biological Psychiatry 1976;11:283-294.

133. Beskow J, Gottfries CG, Roos BE, Winblad B. Determination of monoamine and monamine metabolites in the human brain: post mortem studies in a group of suicides and in a control group. Acta Psychiatrica Scandinavica 1976;53:7-20.

134. Owen F, Cross AJ, Crow TJ, et al. Brain 5-HT2 receptors and suicide. Lancet 1983;2:1256.

135. Korpi ER, Kleinman JE, Goodman SI, et al. Serotonin and 5-hydroxyindoleacetic acid concentrations in different brain regions of suicide victims: comparison in chronic schizophrenic patients with suicide as cause of death. Archives of General Psychiatry (in press).

Some factors of importance for the concentrations of 5-HIAA and HVA measured in lumbar spinal fluid samples.

Factor	Possible control measure
Subject's age and sex (2-3,6)	Matched controls or ANCOVA
Subject's body height (5,6)	Idem
Physical illness, e.g. Parkinson's disease (116), multiple sclerosis (117), adult coeliac disease (118) and hydrocephalus (119)	Physically healthy subjects
Drug treatment (4, 15-23)	Drug-free subjects
Time of day (14)	Samples always drawn at the same time
Time of year (7,13)	Patients and controls matched for season
Diet a	Fasting subjects or controlled diet
Physical movement (120)	Bed rest prior to lumbar puncture
Subject's position at lumbar puncture b	Same position always used
Amount of CSF drawn (122)	Same amount always drawn
Handling and storage of samples	Identification procedures for all samples
Analytical method (123-125)	Best available method

a. It cannot be excluded that a diet particularly rich (or poor) in monoamine precursors might influence the metabolic concentrations. Thus underweight anorexia nervosa patients have significantly lower CSF 5-HIAA than weight-recovered and long-term weight-recovered anorectics. (126)

b. Siever et al. (10) report that the concentration gradient of CSF 5-HIAA was cost in the decubitus position. Gateless et al. (127), on the other hand, found similar gradients in sitting and lying patients.

Table 1.

Studies of CSF 5-HIAA in Relation to Suicidal Behavior

Author	Subjects	CSF sampling and analysis	Confounding factors	Measure of suicidality	Result
Asberg et al. 1976 (29)	88 hospitalized depressed patients	standardized; GC-MS	not controlled	attempted or completed suicide within index illness episode	low 5-HIAA in the 15 attempters, particularly those using violent methods
Brown et al. 1979 (46)	22 men with personality disorder	standardized; fluorometry	not controlled	lifetime history of suicide attempt	lower 5-HIAA in the 11 suicide attempters
Agren 1980 (33)	33 depressed patients	standardized; GC-MS	not controlled	SADS suicidality scales	negative correlation between 5-HIAA and suicidality scores
Traskman et al. 1981 (34)	30 suicide attempters (8 major depressive, 22 other psychiatric disorders excluding schizophrenia and alcoholism), 45 healthy controls	standardized; GC-MS	controlled by ANCOVA for age, sex and body height	recent attempted or completed suicide	5-HIAA lower in both categories of attempters than in healthy controls
Leckman et al. 1981 (38)	132 psychiatric patients, several diagnoses	standardized, after probenecid; fluorometry	not controlled	item suicidal ideation or nurse rating scale	negative correlation with suicidal ideation in the 76 psychotic patients
Brown et al. 1982 (47)	12 patients with borderline personality disorder	standardized; GC-MS	not controlled	life time history of suicide attempt	lower 5-HIAA in the 5 attempters
Montgomery and Montgomery 1982 (36)	49 patients with endogenous depression	not reported	not controlled	history of suicidal act	more attempters among patients with low CSF 5-HIAA
van Praag 1982 (35)	203 depressed patients	standardized, after probenecid; fluorometry	not controlled	recent suicide attempt	significantly more suicide attempters among patients with low CSF 5-HIAA
Palaniappan et al. 1983 (37)	40 hospitalized depressed patients	LP procedure not fully described; fluorometry	not controlled	suicide item in the Hamilton Rating Scale	negative correlation between CSF et 5-HIAA and suicide score
Agren 1983 (44)	110 depressed patients	standardized; GC-MS	not controlled	SADS suicidality scales	low 5-HIAA associated with recent or current suicidal ideation

Table 2.

Studies of CSF 5-HIAA in Relation to Suicidal Behavior

Author	Subjects	CSF sampling and analysis	Confounding factors	Measure of suicidality	Result
Roy-Byrne et al. 1983 (43)	32 bipolar, 13 unipolar patients in different phases of illness	standardized; fluorometry or HPLC	not controlled	lifetime history of suicide attempt	no association with 5-HIAA in bipolar patients
van Praag 1983 (48)	10 nondepressed schizophrenics who attempted suicide in response to imperative hallucinations, 10 nonsuicidal schizophrenics, 10 controls	standardized, after probenecid; fluorometry	matched for age and sex	recent suicide attempt	lower CSF 5-HIAA after probenecid in suicide attempters
Banki et al. 1984 (39)	141 female inpatients (36 depressed, 46 schizophrenic, 35 alcoholic, 24 with adjustment disorder; 45 previously reported)	standardized; fluorometry	adjusted for age and body height by ANCOVA	recent suicide attempt	negative correlation with 5-HIAA in all diagnostic groups, particularly with violent attempts
Ninan et al. 1984 (49)	8 suicidal, 8 nonsuicidal schizophrenic patients	standardized; HPLC	matched for age, sex, and physical characteristics	lifetime history of suicide attempt	lower 5-HIAA in suicide attempters
Lopez-Ibor et al. 1984 (40)	21 depressed patients	standardized; fluorometry	controlled	suicide attempt, suicidal ideation rated on the Hamilton Scale and the AMDP system	more attempts and higher suicidality scores in patients with low 5-HIAA
Roy et al. 1985 (51)	54 patients with chronic schizophrenia	standardized; HPLC	adjusted for age and body height by AN-COVA	lifetime history of suicide attempt	no difference in 5-HIAA between 27 attempters and 27 non-attempters
Edman et al. 1986 (41)	7 suicide attempters with various psychiatric disorders, 7 healthy controls	standardized; GC-MS	matched for sex, age and body height	recent suicide attempt	lower 5-HIAA in attempters
Roy et al. 1986 (56)	27 depressed patients, 22 healthy controls	standardized; HPLC	adjusted for sex and age by ANCOVA	lifetime history of suicide attempt	lower HVA in the 19 attempters

Table 2 concluded.

193

Studies of CSF HVA in relation to suicidal behavior

Author	Subjects	CSF sampling and analysis	Confounding factors	Measure of suicidality	Result
Brown et al. 1979 (46)	22 men with personality disorder	standardized; fluorometry	not controlled	lifetime history of suicide attempt	no correlation reported
Agren 1980 (33)	33 depressed patients	standardized; GC-MS	not controlled	SADS suicidality scales	no significant correlations
Traskman et al. 1981 (34)	30 suicide attempters (8 major depressive, 22 other psychiatric disorders excluding schizophrenia and alcoholism), 45 healthy controls	standardized GC-MS	controlled by ANCOVA for age, sex and body height	recent attempted or completed suicide	lower than controls in depressed attempters, nondepressed attempters similar to controls
Leckman et al. 1981 (38)	132 psychiatric patients, several diagnoses	standardized after probenecid; fluorometry	not controlled	item suicidal ideation on nurse rating scale	no correlation reported
Brown et al. 1982 (47)	12 patients with borderline personality disorder	standardized; GC-MS	not controlled	lifetime history of suicide attempt	no correlation
Montgomery and Montgomery 1982 (36)	49 patients with endogenous depression	not reported	not controlled	history of suicidal act	more attempters among patients with low CSF HVA
Palaniappan et al. 1983 (37)	40 hospitalized depressed patients	LP procedure not fully described; fluorometry	not controlled	suicide item in the Hamilton Rating Scale	negative correlation between CSF ef HVA and suicide score
Agren 1983 (44)	110 depressed patients	standardized; GC-MS	not controlled	SADS suicidality scales	low HVA associated with high lethality of suicide attempts prior to present episode
Banki et al. 1984 (39)	141 female inpatients (36 depressed, 46 schizophrenic, 35 alcoholic, 24 with adjustment disorder; 45 previously reported)	standardized; fluorometry	adjusted for age and body height by ANCOVA	recent suicide attempt	higher HVA for drug overdose case within the depression subgroup, otherwise no clear cut association
Ninan et al. 1985 (57)	8 suicidal, 8 nonsuicidal schizophrenic patients, matched for age and sex	standardized; HPLC	matched for sex, age and physical condition	lifetime history of suicide attempt	no difference in HVA between the two subject groups
Roy et al. 1985 (51)	54 patients with chronic schizophrenia	standardized; HPLC	adjusted for age and body height by ANCOVA	lifetime history of suicide attempt	no difference in HVA between 27 attempters and 27 non-attempters
Roy et al. 1986 (56)	27 depressed patients, 22 healthy controls	standardized; HPLC	adjusted for sex and age by ANCOVA	lifetime history of suicide attempt	lower 5-HIAA in the 19 attempters, although the difference was not statistically significant

Table 3.

Some Controlled Studies of Monoamines and Their Metabolites in Brain Tissue and Cerebrospinal Fluid from Suicide Victims

Author	Subjects	Tissue	Result (concentrations in suicide victims compared to controls)
Shaw et al. 1967 (128)	22 suicides, 17 controls	Hindbrain	5-HT lower
Bourne et al. 1968 (129)	23 suicides, 28 controls	Hindbrain	5-HT similar, 5-HIAA reduced, NA similar
Pare et al. 1969 (130)	26 suicides, 15 controls	Brainstem, caudate, hypothalamus	5-HT reduced, NA and DA similar
Lloyd et al. 1976 (131)	7 suicides, 5 controls	Six raphe nuclei	5-HT lower in nuclei raphe dorsalis and centralis inferior, 5-HIAA similar
Cochran et al. 1976 (132)	18 suicides, 12 controls	Several brain areas	5-HT similar
Beskow et al. 1976 (133)	23 suicides, 82 controls	Several brain areas	5-HT similar after adjustment for difference in postmortem delay; NA, DA, 5-HIAA and HVA similar
Owen et al. 1983 (134)	7 suicides, 18 controls	Frontal cortex	5-HIAA similar
Korpi et al. 1983 (135)	30 schizophrenics (50 % dead from suicide), 14 nonschizophrenic suicides, 29 controls	Several brain areas	5-HT lower in hypothalamus in non-schizophrenic suicide victims 5-HIAA and TRY similar
Kauert et al. 1984 (67)	60 suicides and controls	Cerebrospinal fluid	5 HT, NA, NM higher, DA and A similar
Arato et al. 1986 (68)	Not stated	Cerebrospinal fluid	5-HIAA higher

Abbreviations: 5-HIAA = 5 hydroxyindoleacetic acid, 5-HT = 5 hydroxytryptamine (serotonin), A = adrenaline, DA = dopamine, HVA = homovanillic acid, NA = noradrenaline, NM = normetanephrine, TRY = tryptophan.

Table 4.

Mortality from Suicide within One Year after Admission to Hospital in Some High Risk Groups

Patient category	Number	Percentage suicides
Patients admitted to intensive care unit after suicide attempt	45	2%
Patients admitted to a psychiatric clinic after a suicide attempt, CSF 5-HIAA above 90 nanomol/L	42	2%
Ditto, CSF 5-HIAA below 90 nanomol/L	34	21%

Data on suicide attempters admitted to the psychiatric department of the Karolinska Hospital derive from the studies by Asberg et al. (29), Traskman et al. (34), and Edman et al. (41). Data on patients admitted to the intensive care unit of the same hospital after a drug overdose are given for comparison.

Table 5.

Changes in CSF 5-HIAA after Recovery from Depression

Author	Type of 5-HIAA measure	N	Interval between examinations	Results
Coppen et al. 1972 (97)	Baseline 5-HIAA	8	3-59 w	Stable over time
van Praag 1977 (98)	5-HIAA after probenecid	50	6 mo	2 % of patients with low CSF 5-HIAA during illness normalized; the rest remained stable
Post et al. 1980 (52)	5-HIAA after probenecid	11	several months	Stable over time
Traskman-Bendz et al. 1984 (99)	Baseline 5-HIAA	11	2-7 yr	Increased concentrations at follow-up in patients whose levels were low during illness; stable in the remainder

Table 6.

POST MORTEM STUDIES OF SUICIDE

Michael Stanley, Ph.D., Departments of Psychiatry and Pharmacology, Columbia University and New York State Psychiatric Institute, New York, New York

Suicide is a major cause of death in the United States for the adolescent and young adult population. In the 13- to 24-year age range, it ranks as the second leading cause of death. Furthermore, a dramatic increase in the adolescent suicide rate has occurred in the last 15 years. In an effort to counteract this growing rate, recent research has begun to focus on the identification of youths "at risk" for suicide and prevention of suicide. These studies, which are few in number, have principally investigated personality, psychosocial and diagnostic factors. However, suicide research on adults, focusing on the same factors has had limited success and the suicide rates have not been significantly reduced. Predictors are typically overinclusive and identify many individuals as "at risk" who never commit suicide. Furthermore, the association of these predictors with suicide is too weak to have much utility in the clinical setting. Thus, the traditional approaches to identifying suicide risk have been inadequate. Therefore, while psychosocial and diagnostic factors are important to examine in the adolescent and young adult population, the study of suicide in this age group may benefit from an alternative approach that takes into account neurochemical factors. To date, there have been no studies of the neurochemistry of suicide in adolescents.

The purpose of this paper will be to review the post mortem biological findings in the field of suicide. This review will include critiques of studies that have examined enzymatic findings, concentrations of biogenic amines and their metabolites, and the findings from studies that have employed the more recently developed technology of receptor binding.

The advantages of human post mortem neurochemical studies must be balanced against those disadvantages inherent in these investigations. In post mortem research numerous confounding variables may contribute to inconsistencies within a study or across studies. In this review, we will assess the impact of some of these variables (e.g., age, post mortem interval, and regional brain dissection) and describe their impact on several of the neurochemical measures described.

There are several lines of evidence that suggest an association between serotonin and suicidal behavior (2).

Because of the involvement of 5-HT in suicide and because 5-HT is a substrate for monoamineoxidase (MAO-A), Mann and Stanley (6) thought it would be of interest to conduct a post mortem study of this enzyme in a series of suicide victims.

Two previous studies had examined post mortem MAO activity in suicide victims. One study reported no differences in MAO activity compared with controls (7). A second study found reduced MAO activity in patients where the suicide was associated with alcoholism (8). Both these studies, in contrast to the study of Mann and Stanley (6), included a significant proportion of patients who had died by carbon monoxide or drug overdose that may have altered neurochemistry and employed a single substrate concentration, a method that is less informative and less sensitive than enzyme kinetic studies.

Mann and Stanley (6) assayed MAO-A and B in the frontal cortex of 13 suicides and 13 controls using labeled 5-HT and phenylethylamine (PEA) as substrates for MAO-A and B, respectively. The suicide victims we studied generally died by determined and violent means, with the exception of one overdose. There were no significant differences between the suicide and control group with respect to factors such as age, sex and post mortem interval.

The results of this kinetic study show no significant difference between the groups for either substrate (5-HT or PEA). There was a significant positive correlation between age and MAO-B Vmax for both groups. There was no correlation between post mortem interval and MAO enzyme kinetics.

The series of suicide victims included in this study are distinguishable from those of other studies of brain MAO in as much as those who died by overdose were largely excluded, thereby avoiding the potential problem of drug effects contaminating the results. Other studies have suggested that MAO activity was reduced in alcoholic suicides but not in non-alcoholic suicides (8). The data suggest that the reported lowered brain MAO activity in alcoholic suicides, if confirmed, may be related primarily to alcoholism rather than to suicidal behavior.

In many of the post mortem studies, which have measured the concentration of 5-HT or its principal metabolite, 5-Hydroxyindoleacetic acid (5-HIAA), it is important to point out that some diagnostic information was available for the suicide victims. These data indicate that approximately 50 percent of the suicide victims were diagnosed as endogenously depressed: the remaining cases carried a variety of diagnoses including schizophrenia, personality disorders, alcoholism, and reactive depression. These diagnostic groupings are consistent with a number of studies that have made a retrospective diagnostic analysis of individuals who have committed suicide (9-11). In general, these studies found that in addition to the diagnosis of depression, individuals classified as schizophrenic, alcoholic, and having personality disorders were also represented. Thus, it is of both theoretical and practical importance to note that suicide victims typically represent a diagnostically heterogenous group of individuals. With regard to biochemical findings within this population, the diagnostic heterogeneity suggests that differences in neurochemistry may be more related to suicidal behavior rather than to depression per se.

It should also be mentioned that none of the studies described below had youth suicide as their focus.

A total of 11 studies have investigated the concentration of 5-HT, 5-HIAA, or both in several brain regions of suicide victims (12-22). In addition to measurements of the serotonergic system, 3 of the 11 studies also report findings for the noradrenergic and dopaminergic systems.

With regard to findings reported for the serotonergic system, 7 of 11 studies have reported significant decreases in the levels of 5-HT, 5-HIAA, or both. In general, decreases were noted in the area of the brain stem (Raphe Nuclei) and in other subcortical nuclei (e.g., hypothalamus). Lloyd et al. (15) measured 5-HT and 5-HIAA in Raphe Nuclei of five suicides and five controls. Three of the five suicides had died by drug overdose. They found no significant difference in 5-HIAA levels between the two groups. There was, however, a significant reduction in 5-HT levels for the suicide group. Pare et al. (14) determined norepinephrine, dopamine, 5-HT, and 5-HIAA levels in suicide victims who had died by carbon monoxide poisoning. They found no significant difference between the two groups for norepinephrine, dopamine, and 5-HIAA. They did report a significant reduction in brainstem levels of 5-HT, for the suicide group. Shaw et al. (12) found lower brainstem levels of 5-HT in suicide victims compared with controls, a statistically significant difference. However, it should be noted that about half of the suicide group died by barbiturate overdose and the other half died by carbon monoxide poisoning.

More recently, Korpi et al. (17) reported significant decreases in the hypothalamic concentration of 5-HT of suicide victims compared with nonsuicide controls. Similar findings were reported by Gillin et al. (16). They noted that 5-HT levels were significantly lower in the hypothalamus of suicide victims compared with controls.

Three studies have reported significant reductions in the levels of 5-HIAA in suicide victims. Bourne et al. (13) measured norepinephrine, 5-HT, and 5-HIAA in the hind-brain and found significantly lower levels only for 5-HIAA. Beskow et al. (18) measured dopamine, norepinephrine, 5-HT, and 5-HIAA in brainstem areas of suicide victims and controls. They noted significant reductions in 5-HIAA levels for the suicide group. The results of these studies are summarized in Table 1. (Tables and figures appear at the end of the chapter.)

In many of the foregoing studies, factors such as death by overdose or carbon monoxide poisoning, extensive post mortem delay, and lack of age-matched control groups figure significantly in the interpretation of these findings. These variables may also account in part for the lack of uniformity of findings among the post mortem studies. In addition to these potential sources of error, the levels of monoamines and their metabolites are known to be influenced by factors such as diet, acute drug use, alcohol, etc. While it is possible to control for the acute influence of these factors in CSF studies, for obvious reasons this is not the case in post mortem assessments. In an effort to minimize the impact of the aforementioned variable, we decided to examine a system--receptor binding--which has been shown to be generally nonresponsive to these acute influences.

Binding studies have shown that changes in the number of sites (or their density) can be induced by either chronic exposure to a chemical agent (e.g., antidepressants) or deprivation of the particular amine by its removal (e.g., lesioning). Recently, binding assays that appear to be associated with pre-(imipramine) and post-(spiroperidol) synaptic 5-HT neurons have been developed (23,24). Imipramine binding sites have been characterized in platelets and various regions of the brain. Some of the experimental evidence linking imipramine binding with 5-HT is that (1) radioautography studies of 3-H imipramine binding sites show distribution similar to serotonergic terminals (25); (2) chemical and electrolytic lesions of the Raphe nucleus cause a significant reduction in serotonin level and in the number of imipramine binding sites (26); (3) the use of an irreversible ligand results in reduced 3-H imipramine binding and serotonin uptake (27); (4) the potency of antidepressant drugs to inhibit serotonin uptake is significantly correlated with their potency to inhibit 3-H imipramine binding (28); (5) serotonin is the only neurotransmitter known to inhibit (^{3}H) imipramine binding (28,33); and (6) there is a similar pharmacologic profile between brain and platelet (^{3}H) imipramine binding sites (27).

The clinical significance of imipramine binding was provided by the studies of Langer and coworkers who reported decreases in the number of binding sites in the platelets of depressives (29). The combined association of imipramine binding with 5-HT function, as well as the significant reduction in binding density in depressives, suggested the possibility of alterations in imipramine binding in suicide victims. To test this hypothesis, Stanley et al. (30) determined imipramine binding in the brains of suicide victims and controls. Because of the problems previous research groups had encountered conducting post mortem studies, we took particular care in selecting cases for this study. Thus, there were no significant differences between the two groups with respect to age, sex and post mortem interval. The suicide victims chosen for this study had died in a determined manner (e.g., gunshot wound, hanging, jumped from height) and, as is the general practice of these researchers, the control group was chosen to match for sudden and violent deaths.

The findings indicated a significant reduction in the number of imipramine binding sites in frontal cortex (suicides B_{max} = 330 ± 39 fmole/mg/protein; controls B_{max} = 587 ± 75 fmole/mg/protein) with no difference in binding affinity (Kd) (Fig. 1). The results of this experiment seem to be consistent with the accumulating evidence suggesting the involvement of 5-HT in suicide. Specifically, reduced imipramine binding (associated with presynaptic terminals) may indicate reduced 5-HT release and agree with reports of reduced post mortem levels of 5-HT and 5-HIAA in suicides as well as lower levels of 5-HIAA in the CSF of suicide attempters.

Since the completion of this study, there have been four other studies that have measured imipramine binding either in suicide victims or in depressive persons who died from natural causes.

Paul and coworkers (31) measured imipramine binding in hypothalamic membranes from suicides and controls. Both groups were matched for age, gender, and post mortem interval. Imipramine binding was significantly lower in the brains of the suicide victims compared with controls. This group also measured desipramine binding in the same samples and noted no significant difference between the suicide and control group. They interpreted this finding as arguing against the possibility that the reductions they had observed in imipramine binding could be attributed to a drug-induced effect. Perry and colleagues (32) measured imipramine binding in the cortex and hippocampus of depressed individuals dying from nonsuicidal causes. They reported a significant reduction in imipramine binding in the depressive group relative to a nondepressed control group that had been matched for age, sex, and post mortem interval. Crow et al. (20) also reported a significant decrease in imipramine binding in

the cortex of suicide victims compared with controls. In contrast to the findings cited above, one study has reported an increase in imipramine binding in the brains of suicides compared with control (33). Possible explanations offered to address this discrepant finding include single point analysis instead of saturation isotherms and inadequate matching of factors such as age, gender and post mortem interval. In summary, five published post mortem studies have measured imipramine binding. Thus far, four of the five studies reported a decrease in imipramine binding and one study found an increase. And, as was the case in those post mortem studies that measured levels of 5-HT and 5-HIAA, none of the aforementioned studies had youth suicide as their focus (2).

In addition to assessing of post mortem presynaptic function of the 5-HT system in suicide, Stanley and Mann also measured post-synaptic 5-HT binding sites using ^{3}H-spiroperidol (5-HT2) (34). 5-HT2 binding in animals has been shown to change in response to chronic antidepressant treatment and lesioning of 5-HT nuclei (26,34).

In this study, suicide victims were compared with controls, and, as in previous studies, both groups were matched for age, sex, post mortem interval, and suddenness of death. Also, care was taken to select subjects who had died by nonpharmacologic means.

The study found significant increase in the number of 5-HT2 binding sites in the frontal cortex of suicide victims with no change in binding affinity (Fig. 2).

Because many of the brains had also been used in the previous report on imipramine binding by Stanley et al. (30), the researchers were interested in assessing the degree to which these measures of receptor function correlated. They found that the number of binding site (B_{max}) for 5-HT2 and imipramine was negatively correlated. This finding is of interest because it closely parallels the experimental observations noted in animal studies. Brunello et al. (26) lesioned the Raphe nucleus of rats using the 5-HT selective neurotoxin 5,7-dihydroxytryptamine. Two weeks following such lesions, 5-HT levels were significantly reduced. The same researchers found significant reductions in imipramine binding (associated with presynaptic serotonergic terminals) with significant increases in $5-HT_2$ binding (postsynaptic). They suggested that the increase in $5-HT_2$ binding might reflect a compensating increase in postsynaptic binding sites secondary to a loss of presynaptic input. Extrapolating to human data in suicide victims where Stanley et al. observed an increase in postsynaptic binding sites as well as a decrease in presynaptic binding sites, it may be that the functional consequences of this receptor arrangement could result in an overall hypofunction of this system. Thus, reduced levels of 5-HIAA in the CSF of suicide attempters as well as reduced levels of 5-HT and 5-HIAA in the brains of suicide victims would be a logical consequence of a hypofunctioning serotonergic systems.

Subsequent to the study done by Stanley et al. (34), there have been two additional reports of $5-HT_2$ binding in suicides. Owens et al. (19) reported an increase in $5-HT_2$ binding in nonmedicated suicide victims. Crow and colleagues (20) found no change in $5-HT_2$ binding between suicides and controls (2).

In addition to examining serotonergic binding sites in suicide victims, muscarinic binding in this group was also measured (35). The rationale for this assessment was based in part on the several lines of cholinergic sensitivity with affective disorders and the high incidence of individuals diagnosed as having an affective disorder who subsequently commit suicide.

In this study, muscarinic binding was estimated using the reversible antagonist 3-quinuclindyl benzilate (QNB). Samples of frontal cortex from 22 suicide and 22 controls matched for age, gender, post mortem interval and suddeness of death were used in this study. As previously, care was taken to chose a majority of cases where the cause of death

was nonpharmacological (3).

Scatchard analysis of the binding data indicated that there were no significant differences in the mean number of binding site (Bmax) between the two groups (suicide victims, 493 fmole/mg protein, and control subjects, 492 fmole/mg protein) (Kd) between the means of the two groups (suicide victims, 14 pM, and control subjects, 13.68 pM) (Figs. 3 and 4).

Correlations between B_{max} or K_d and either the suicide victims or control subjects were not significantly related to factors such as age and interval between death and autopsy. However, when both groups were combined, Bmax was significantly correlated with time between death and autopsy ($r = .35$, $p < .02$).

Comparisons between B_{max} values of suicide victims who died by violent means (gunshot wounds, hangings, or jumping from height) and of controls who had died either by violent or nonviolent methods revealed no significant differences. Variations in muscarinic cholinergic binding as a function of the time of day that individuals died have been reported (36). The Bmax values for the combined samples (suicide victims and control subjects) were examined at eight, separate 3-hour intervals by one-way analysis of variance; none of the intervals significantly differed from each other.

Two other studies have estimated QNB binding in suicides and controls. Kaufman et al. (37) determined QNB binding in three brain regions (including frontal cortex) in suicide victims and found no differences between the groups for any of the regions studied. In contrast to our findings and those of Kaufman's, Meyerson and colleagues (33) reported a significant increase in QNB binding in the frontal cortex of a small group of suicides not adequately matched for factors such as age, sex and post mortem interval (2).

More recently Mann et al. (38) have measured beta adrenergic receptors in suicide victims in the hope that such studies might indicate the functional status of central catecholamine neurons in suicidal behavior.

It has been suggested that down-regulation of beta adrenergic receptors may be linked with the therapeutic effect of antidepressants and that changes in these receptors may also relate to the neurochemical substrate of suicide and depression.

The researchers measured beta adrenergic receptor binding in the frontal cortex of suicide victims and controls using dihydroalphrenolol (DHA). There was a 73 percent increase in beta adrenergic receptor binding in suicide victims compared with controls.

In addition to this study, Zanko and Beigon (39) reported an increased number of binding sites (B_{max}) with no change in K_d in a small series of six suicide victims and matched controls. In contrast with the above studies, Meyerson et al. (33) reported no alteration in DHA binding in suicide victims. Thus, two of three studies measuring beta adrenergic receptors report an increase in binding in suicide victims. It should be noted that ante mortem use of antidepressants would not explain the receptor alterations we observed. Data from animal studies indicates that chronic antidepressant treatment causes a down-regulation of beta adrenergic receptors. Findings in suicide victims studied by Stanley et al. indicate alterations in receptor binding in the opposite direction from that which would be expected if drug effects had been present.

Having set forth the principal neurochemical findings in suicide research, it is important also to examine some factors that may exert an influence on some of the measures previously described in this review.

A preliminary analysis of 50 cases with an age range of 16 to 79 years revealed no significant relationship between age and 5-HT or 5-HIAA (2). However, imipramine was positively correlated with age. Severson et al. (40) recently published data on age effects and 5-HT and 5-HIAA levels as well as imipramine binding in human post mortem samples. They too noted that age did not appear to influence 5-HT or 5-HIAA levels.

They also found that the ratio of 5-HIAA/5-HT, an estimate of serotonin turnover, was uninfluenced by age. Severson did note a significant positive correlation between imipramine binding and age (range 17-100 years). Severson's and Stanley's findings of a positive correlation between these variables is of interest because the findings are in the opposite direction of those reported by Langer and coworkers (23) for imipramine binding in the platelet. Langer (23) reported that platelet imipramine binding decreases as a function of age. These discrepant findings are of interest because imipramine binding in the platelet and the brain were thought to be identical. Thus, findings such as these raise questions about the validity of peripheral measures as indices of central systems. A significant age-related decrease in 5-HT2 binding sites in frontal cortex ($r = -0.42$, $N = 34$, $p < .01$) was observed in the study of Mann and colleagues (38). A statistically significant increase in cortical DHA binding with age was seen in our study ($r = 0.60$, $N = 19$, $p < .01$) (38).

Another area that also represents a potential problem in post mortem research is that of post mortem interval (PMI) that time between death and the time the brain tissue is removed and frozen. The human post mortem studies conducted by Stanley et al. (41) assessed the influence of post mortem interval on 5-HT and 5-HIAA levels. Their post mortem interval was approximately 15 hours with a range of 6 hours to 45 hours. They found that there was a significant positive correlation between frontal cortex 5-HT levels and PMI. No significant findings were noted for 5-HIAA levels with PMI.

Severson and colleagues (40) also found that PMI was related to significant changes in 5-HT levels. However, their findings were in the opposite direction from that which Stanley and colleagues (41) observed-- namely, they reported a significant decline in 5-HT with increasing PMI. One possible explanation for this discrepancy may be the difference in the length of PMI between the two studies. In Stanley's study, the PMI was approximately 15 hours, while in Severson's study PMI averaged 36 hours (in some cases >72 hours). It may well be that while 5-HT levels appear to rise initially with a shorter PMI they subsequently fall with a more extensive delay (>1-1/2 days). In any case, previous research has shown that amines, such as DA and 5-HT, are more sensitive to PMI than are their acidic metabolites. Wilk and Stanley et al. (42) had previously published a study that assessed the influence of PMI and DA, DOPAC and HVA levels. They found that DA levels—not DOPAC or HVA— were more likely to be influenced by delay. Also, those same researchers published a similar study on the influence of PMI on 5-HT and 5-HIAA levels. Again, in general, they found a significant change in 5-HT, but not 5-HIAA, levels.

In contrast to variations in the concentrations of biogenic amines, it has been observed that most of the binding sites are uninfluenced by post mortem interval (30). Thus, with the exception of QNB, which displayed a modest decrease in binding density with increased post mortem delay, imipramine, 5-HT2, and beta adrenergic binding were not affected.

Another area of post mortem research that can result both in variations within and between studies, is nonspecific or "regional" dissections. In our animal studies (43), it had been our practice, and that of others, to analyze samples taken from general areas, e.g., frontal cortex. It occurred to us that our lack of precision in dissection might account for some of the variability we had observed from time to time.

In an attempt to investigate possible regional differences of 5-HT and 5-HIAA concentrations within the cortex, we dissected homogenous samples corresponding to frontal, temporal, and occipital cortex. In this experiment, the frontal cortex showed significantly higher concentrations of 5-HT and 5-HIAA compared with temporal or occipital samples. In a second experiment, three progressive 1 mm slices of the frontal cortex were examined in a rostral to caudal

fashion for regional concentration differences of 5-HT and 5-HIAA levels (43). Additional significant variation was noted within the frontal cortex with a rostral to caudal increase in 5-HIAA levels; 5-HT levels were consistent. Therefore, differences are found not only among the general areas of the cortex, i.e., frontal, temporal, and occipital, but significant differences can also be found within each area.

One of the potential criticisms of post mortem studies is that their findings lack a proven clinical utility, as no means of monitoring the alterations reported is provided. Thus, the clinical significance of post mortem findings must be inferred. (Both the ease and correctness with which these inferences are drawn remains largely untested.) Therefore, it would be useful to develop a method with clinical application that could be used in post mortem studies.

In ante mortem studies, biogenic amine metabolites in CSF are generally regarded as the best indicator of neuronal function in the brain. One way of testing the strength of this relationship is by simultaneously assessing the CSF and brain levels of the same metabolite in the same individual.

Stanley et al. (41) measured the acidic metabolites 5-HIAA and HVA, the principal metabolites of serotonin and dopamine, respectively, in the lumbar CSF and brains of the same individuals at autopsy. The post mortem lumbar punctures and samples of frontal cortex corresponding to Brodmann's Area 8-9 were obtained from 48 individuals (37 men and 11 women). The average age was 37 ($\pm$2.6, S.E.) years with a range of 16 to 78 years. The causes of death among the individuals in this study were generally sudden in nature, e.g., homicides, auto accidents, etc. The post mortem interval between death and tissue collection for the individuals in this study ranged from 285 to 1,815 minutes and averaged 891 $\pm$ 58 (S.E.) minutes.

Lumbar CSF samples were obtained. At autopsy, once the organs were removed from the chest and abdominal cavities, an 18 gauge spinal needle was inserted in the L-3, L-4 inter space. A 10 cc syringe with a leur-lock stop cock was attached to the needle and used to withdraw samples of CSF. (Figure 5)

The results of this study indicate the presence of a significant correlation between CSF and brain levels of 5-HIAA and HVA, r = 0.78, p <.001; r = 0.35, p <.02, respectively (Figs. 6 and 7).

In addition to the principal aim of the project presented above (i.e., the assessment of the relationship between metabolite levels in CSF and brain), Stanley et al. (41) were also interested in determining the degree to which post mortem CSF measures agreed with the CSF findings of ante mortem studies. In this regard, some of the findings that point out similarities between these results and those obtained from living individuals are: (1) a significant gradient in metabolite concentration in serial samples of CSF (Figs. 8 and 9); (2) the mean CSF concentrations of 5-HIAA (34.4 ng/ml) and HVA (71.6 ng/ml); (3) a significant correlation between the post mortem CSF concentrations of 5-HIAA and HVA (r = 0.69, p <.001) (Fig. 10); and (4) an inverse correlation between body height and CSF levels of 5-HIAA.

Thus, the relationship between metabolite levels in the brain and CSF provides direct evidence for the validity of using these CSF measures as an index of brain metabolism in the living. Further, this methodology could be used to examine the interrelationship between a biogenic amine or its metabolite and the status of the various receptors associated with the same neuronal system and to provide a means for applying post mortem finding to the clinical setting.

In summary, there are several lines of evidence suggesting that there may be a neurochemical component associated with the act of suicide. Thus far, the post mortem biochemical evidence tends to support the hypothesis that in individuals who commit suicide, there is some form of serotonergic dysfunction. With regard to youth suicide, it should be emphasized that no post mortem biochemical studies have been conducted on this age group. We are, therefore, left to speculate whether the alterations reported in adult suicide studies will also be found when appropriate youth suicide studies are conducted. As has been previously noted, some of the relevant neurochemical measures are known to be influenced by age, e.g., imipramine binding increases with age. Therefore, it will probably be necessary to conduct normative studies for many of these measures, either separately or in parallel with comparative studies of suicide victims.

One of the frequent criticisms of biochemical post mortem studies is that they fail to obtain diagnostic information. This information is critical if we hope to relate biochemical findings either directly to suicide behavior itself or to specific diagnostic groups.

It should be noted that this term "suicidal behavior" encompasses a complex array of symptoms. Previous studies describing a link between suicidal behavior and serotonin have also reported an association between this neurotransmitter and other behaviors. Specifically, Brown and colleagues (44) have reported a significant inverse correlation between individuals' history of aggressive behavior and their CSF levels of 5-HIAA. Linnoila et al. (45) found lower levels of CSF 5-HIAA in individuals who had engaged in violent and impulsive acts. To the extent that impulsivity and aggression can be regarded as risk factors that have an identifiable biochemical substrate, it will be important for future studies of suicide in youth to assess the degree to which these behaviors are present in this age group. Thus, it may be possible to systematically construct a behavioral and biochemical profile to aid the clinician in identifying individuals at high risk of committing suicide.

Recommendations for future studies of youth suicide should include projects that will integrate biochemical and behavioral factors. For post mortem research, this will necessitate interviewing next of kin to obtain the needed personality descriptors and diagnostic information that can then be assessed in the light of neurochemical findings. The priority for neurochemical studies should initially parallel studies that have already been conducted in adults. In an effort to maintain a link between post mortem findings and the clinical application of such findings, investigators should obtain samples of post mortem CSF where possible. Ante mortem studies should follow the same basic approach as described for post mortem investigations. Thus, normative behavioral/ diagnostic and biochemical data should be collected together so investigators can identify behaviors or clusters of behaviors that may correlate with biochemical findings.

Based on the results of the studies proposed above, it may be important to explore the use of various pharmacologic probes in the treatment of suicidal behavior. The biochemical findings in suicide to date seem to relate more to this specific behavior itself, rather than to any particular diagnostic group. Therefore, while it may be necessary to treat the symptoms associated with an individual's psychiatric syndrome, it may also be necessary to separately treat symptoms associated with their suicidal behavior.

REFERENCES

1. Suicide Surveillance, Centers for Disease Control, U.S. Dept. of Health and Human Services. Summary 1970-1980; Issued March 1985.

2. Stanley M, Mann JJ, Cohen L: Role of serotonergic system in the post mortem analysis of suicide. Psychopharm Bulletin 1986. (In press).

3. Asberg M, Thoren P, Traskman L, Bertilsson, Ringberger V: Serotonin depression: A biochemical subgroup within the affective disorders. Science 1976, 191:478-80.

4. Traskman-Bendz L: Depression and suicidal behavior: A biochemical and pharmacological study. Thesis, Stockholm, Sweden: Karolinska Institute, 1980.

5. van Pragg HM: CSF 5-HIAA and suicide in nondepressed schizophrenics. Lancet 1983; 2:977-8.

6. Mann JJ, Stanley M: Post mortem monoamine oxidase enzyme kinetics in the frontal cortex of suicide victims and controls. Acta Psychiat Scand 1984; 69:135-9.

7. Grote SS, Moses SG, Robins E, et al: A study of selected catecholamine metabolizing enzymes: A comparison of depressive suicides and alcoholic suicides with controls. J Neurochem 1974; 23:791-802.

8. Gottfries CG, Oreland L, Wilberg A, Winbland G: Lowered monoamine oxidase activity in brains from alcoholic suicides. J Neurochem 1975; 25:667-73.

9. Dorpat TL, Ripley HS: A study of suicide in the Seattle area. Compr Psychiatry 1960; 1(6):349-59.

10. Barraclough B, Bunch J, Nelson B, et al: A hundred cases of suicide: Clinical aspects. Br J Psychiatry 1974; 125:355-73.

11. Robins E, Murphy GE, Wilkinson RH, et al: Some clinical considerations in the prevention of suicide based on a study of 134 successful suicides. Am J Publ Health 1959; 49:888-99.

12. Shaw DM, Camps FE, and Eccleston EG: 5-hydroxytryptamine in the hind-brain of depressive suicides. Br J Psychiatry 1967; 113:1407-11.

13. Bourne HR, Bunney WE, Jr., Colburn RW, Davis JM, Shaw DM, Coppen AJ: Noradrenaline, 5-hydroxytryptamine, and 5-hydroxyindoleacetic acid in the hind-brains of suicidal patients. Lancet 1968; 805-8.

14. Pare CMB, Yeung DPH, Price K, and Stacey RS: 5-hydroxytryptamine, noradrenaline, and dopamine in brainstem, hypothalamus, and caudate nucleus of controls and of patients committing suicide by coal-gas poisoning. Lancet 1969; 133-5.

15. Lloyd KG, Fraley IJ, Deck JHN, Hornykiewicz O: Serotonin and 5-hydroxyindoleacetic acid in discrete areas of the brainstem of suicide victims and control patients. Advances in Biochemical Psychopharmacology, Vol. II. New York; Raven Press, 1974; 387-7.

16. Gillin JC, Nelson J, Kleinman J, et al: Studies of the cholinergic system in suicide and depression. Proceedings of the New York Acad of Sciences conference on psychobiology of Suicidal Behavior, 1985; 18-20.

17. Korpi ER, Kleinman JE, Goodman SJ, et al: Serotonin and 5-Hydroxyindoleacetic acid concentration in different brain regions of suicide victims: Comparison in chronic schizophrenic patients with suicide as cause of death. Presented at the meeting of the International Society for Neurochemistry, Vancouver, Canada, July 14, 1983.

18. Beskow J, Gottfries CG, Roos BE, and Winblad B: Determination of monoamine and monoamine metabolites in the human brain: Post mortem studies in a group of suicides and in a control group. Acta Psychiat Scand 1976; 53:7-20.

19. Owens F, Cross AJ, Crow TJ, et al: Brain 5-HT2 receptors and suicide. Lancet 1983; ii:1256.

20. Crow TJ, Cross AJ, Cooper SJ, et al: Neurotransmittor receptors and monoamine metabolites in the brains of patients with alzheimer-type dementia and depression and suicides. Neuropharmacology 1984; 23(12B):1561-9.

21. Cochrane E, Robins E, and Grote S: Regional serotonin levels in brain: A comparison of depressive suicides and alcoholic suicides with controls. Biological Psychiatry 1976; 11(3):283-294.

22. Stanley M, McIntyre I, and Gershon S: Post mortem serotonin metabolism in suicide victims, presented at 1983 ACNP, Puerto Rico.

23. Langer SF, Briley MS, Raisman R, et al: 3H-imipramine binding in human platelets: Influence of age and sex. Naunyn Schmiedebergs Arch Pharmacol 1980; 313:189-94.

24. Peroutka SJ, Snyder SH: Regulation of Serotonin (5HT2) receptors labeled with (3H) Sprioperidol by chronic treatment with antidepressant amitriptyline. Pharmacol Exp Ther 1980; 215:582-7.

25. Rainbow TC, Beigon, A: Distribution of imipramine binding sites in the rat brain studied by quantitative autoradiography. Neuro Sci Lett 1983; 37(3):209-14.

26. Brunello N, Chuang DM, Costa E: Different synaptic location of Mianserin and imipramine binding sites. Science 1982; 215:1112-5.

27. Rehavi M, Ittah Y, Price KL, et al: 2-Nitroimipramine: A selective irreversible inhibitor of (3H) serotonin uptake and (3H) imipramine binding in platelets. Biochem Biophys Res Comm 1981; 99:954.

28. Paul SM, Rehavi M, Rice KC: Does high affinity (3H) imipramine binding label serotonin reuptake sites in brain and platelet? Life Sci 1981; 28:2753-60.

29. Langer SF, Raisman R: Binding of (3H) imipramine and (3H) desipramine as biochemical tools for studies in depression. Neuropharmacology 1983; 22:407-13.

30. Stanley M, Virgilio J, Gershon S: Tritiated imipramine binding sites are decreased in the frontal cortex of suicides. Science 1982; 216:1337-9.

31. Paul SM, Rehavi M, Skolnick P, Goodwin FK: High affinity binding of antidepressants to a biogenic amine transport site in human brain and platelet; studies in depression. In: Post RM, Bellinger, JC, eds. Neurobiol of Mood Disorders. Baltimore: Williams and Wilkins, 1984; 845-53.

32. Perry EK, Marshall EF, Blessed G, Tomlinson BE, Perry RH: Decreased imipramine binding in the brains of patients with depressive illness. Br J Psychiatry 1983; 1412:188-92.

33. Meyerson LR, Wennogle LP, Abel MS: Human brain receptor alterations in suicide victims. Pharmacol Biochem Behav 1982; 17:159-63.

34. Stanley M, Mann JJ: Increased Serotonin - 2 Binding sites in frontal cortex of suicide victims Lancet 1983; 214-6.

35. Stanley M: Cholinergic binding in the frontal cortex of suicide victims. Am J Psychiatry 1984; 141:11.

36. Perry EK, Perry RH, Tomlinson BE: Circadian variations in cholinergic enzymes and muscarinic receptor binding in human cerebral cortex. Neurosci Lett 1977; 4:185-9.

37. Kaufman CA, Gillin JC, O'Laughlin T, et al: Muscarinic binding in suicides. In: New Research Abstracts, 136th Annual Meeting of the American Psychiatric Association. Washington DC, 1983.

38. Mann JJ, Stanley M: Unpublished data.

39. Zanko MT, Biegnon A: Increased adrenergic receptor binding in human frontal cortex of suicide victims. In: Abstract, Annual Meeting, Society for Neuroscience, Boston, MA, 1983.

40. Severson JA, Marwsson JO, Osterburg, HH: Elevated density of (3H) imipramine binding in aged human brain. J of Neurochem 1985; 45:1382-9.

41. Stanley M, Traskman-Bendz L, Dorovini-Zis K: Correlations between aminergic metabolites simultaneously obtained from samples of CSF and brain. Life Sciences 1985; 37:1279-86.

42. Wilk S, Stanley M: Dopamine metabolites in human brain. Psychopharmacology 1978; 57:77.

43. McIntyre IM, Stanley M: Post mortem and regional changes of Serotonin, 5 Hydroxyindoleacetic acid and tryptophan in brain. J of Neurochem 1984; 42:1588-92.

44. Brown GL, Goodwin FK, Ballenger JC, Joyer PF, Major LF: Aggression in humans correlates with cerebrospinal fluid amine metabolites. Psych Res 1979; 1:131-9.

45. Linnoila M, Virkkunen M, Scheinin M, Nuutila A, Rimon R, Goodwin FK: Low cerebrospinal fluid 5-hydroxyindoleacetic acid concentration differentiates impulsive from nonimpulsive violent behavior. Life Sciences 33:2609-14.

Post Mortem Neurotransmitter and Metabolite Studies in Completed Studies

Shaw et al. (12)	↓ Brainstem 5-HT
Bourne et al. (13)	↓ Brainstem 5-HIAA
Pare et al. (14)	↓ Brainstem 5-HT No change in brainstem 5-HIAA
Lloyd et al. (15)	↓ Brainstem 5-HT No change in brainstem 5-HIAA
Gillin et al. (16)	↓ Hypothalamus 5-HT Nucleus Acumbens 5-HIAA
Korpi et al. (17)	↓ Hypothalamus 5-HT
Beskow et al. (18)	↓ Brain 5-HIAA
Owens et al. (19)	No change in 5-HIAA levels in frontal cortex
Crow et al. (20)	No change in 5-HIAA levels in frontal cortex
Cochrane et al. (21)	No change in brain 5-HT
Stanley et al. (22)	No change in 5-HIAA or 5-HT levels in frontal cortex

Table 1.

Stanley et al. (30)	↓ ^{3}H-imipramine binding in cortex
Paul et al. (31)	↓ ^{3}H-imipramine binding in brain
Perry et al. (32)	↓ ^{3}H-imipramine binding* in cortex
Crow et al. (20)	↓ ^{3}H-imipramine binding in cortex
Meyerson et al. (33)	↑ ^{3}H-imipramine binding in cortex
Stanley and Mann (34)	↑ 5-HT$_2$ binding in cortex
Owen et al. (19)	↑ 5-HT$_2$ binding in cortex**
Crow et al. (20)	No change in 5HT$_2$ binding in cortex
Stanley (35)	No change in muscarinic cholinergic receptor binding in cortex
Kaufman et al. (37)	No change in muscarinic cholinergic receptor binding
Meyerson et al. (33)	↑ in muscarinic cholinergic receptor binding
Zanko and Biegon (39)	↑ in beta receptor binding
Mann and Stanley (6)	↑ in beta receptor binding
Meyerson et al. (33)	No change in beta receptor binding

* Depressed patients dying of natural causes

** Increased but not significantly

Table 2.

Characteristics of Suicide Victims (n=22) and Control Subjects (n=22) Whose Death was by Nonsuicidal Means

Subject	Age (years)	Sex	Cause of Death	Time Between Death and Autopsy (min.)	Number of Binding Sites (B_{max})	Binding A????? (K??)
Suicide Victims						
1	46	M	Hanging	1,440	191	17
2	13	M	Gunshot wound	1,140	197	15
3	15	M	Hanging	555	677	13
4	25	M	Gunshot wound	1,560	387	28
5	33	M	Gunshot wound	1,020	773	15
6	55	M	Jumping from height	1,140	388	16
7	25	M	Hanging	1,365	450	10
8	30	M	Hanging	1,320	640	11
9	34	M	Jumping from height	1,320	454	13
10	22	M	Gunshot wound	555	671	10
11	25	M	Drowning	1,005	498	8
12	80	M	Gunshot wound	1,335	555	24
13	18	M	Gunshot wound	1,055	505	16
14	30	M	Jumping from height	1,260	553	9
15	37	M	Drug overdose	795	605	11
16	64	M	Drug overdose	1,110	574	16
17	43	M	Gunshot wound	460	583	16
18	65	M	Jumping from height	1,110	406	10
19	30	F	Gunshot wound	1,290	621	12
20	72	F	Drug overdose	1,185	339	17
21	79	F	Drug overdose	1,080	543	12
22	18	F	Jumping from height	600	229	9
Control subjects						
1	45	M	Gunshot wound	1,650	232	8
2	21	M	Gunshot wound	1,205	242	17
3	22	M	Cardiovascular disease	750	735	14
4	20	M	Gunshot wound	1,570	411	23
5	31	M	Cardiovascular disease	880	423	11
6	47	M	Cardiovascular disease	1,200	526	13
7	28	M	Auto accident	735	439	8
8	18	M	Gunshot wound	805	649	19
9	39	M	Falling from height	1,245	510	11
10	30	M	Auto accident	460	527	10
11	26	M	Falling from height	1,350	652	12
12	53	M	Cardiovascular disease	860	393	36
13	24	M	Cardiovascular disease	1,305	485	12
14	23	M	Gunshot wound	1,035	563	10
15	39	M	Knife wound	600	597	11
16	40	M	Gunshot wound	735	606	16
17	33	M	Gunshot wound	435	593	13
18	82	M	Falling from height	770	382	8
19	23	F	Gunshot wound	865	640	10
20	45	F	Knife wound	1,020	592	19
21	73	F	Cardiovascular disease	1,440	279	10
22	50	F	Auto accident	630	343	10

Table 3.

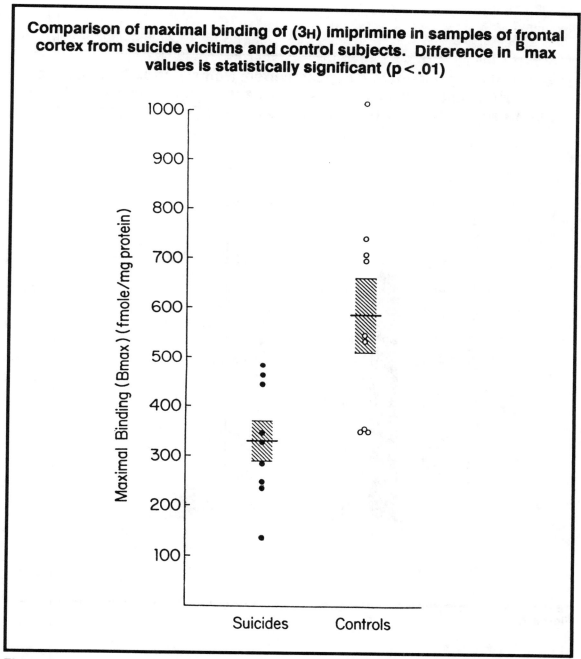

Comparison of maximal binding of (3H) imiprimine in samples of frontal cortex from suicide vicitims and control subjects. Difference in ^{B}max values is statistically significant (p < .01)

Figure 1.

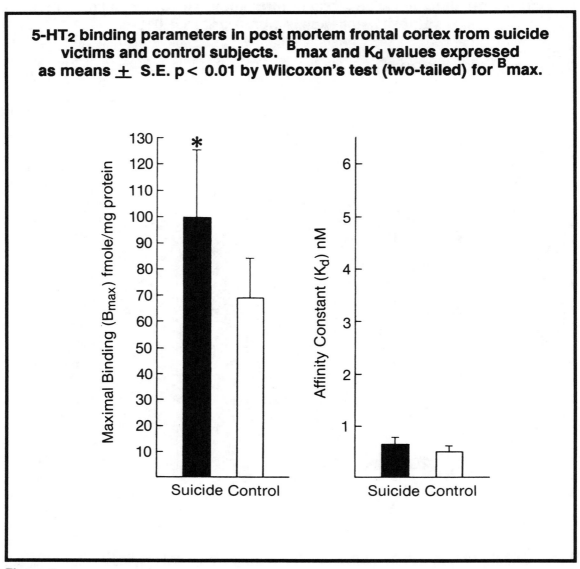

Figure 2.

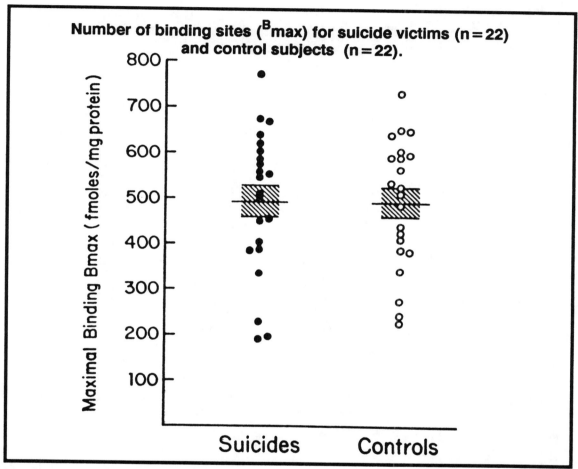

Figure 3.

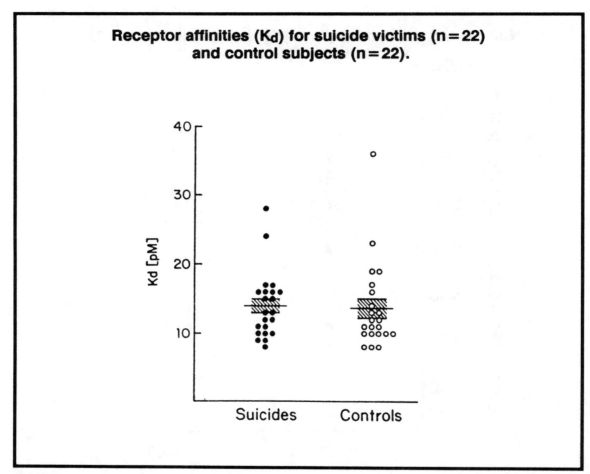

Figure 4.

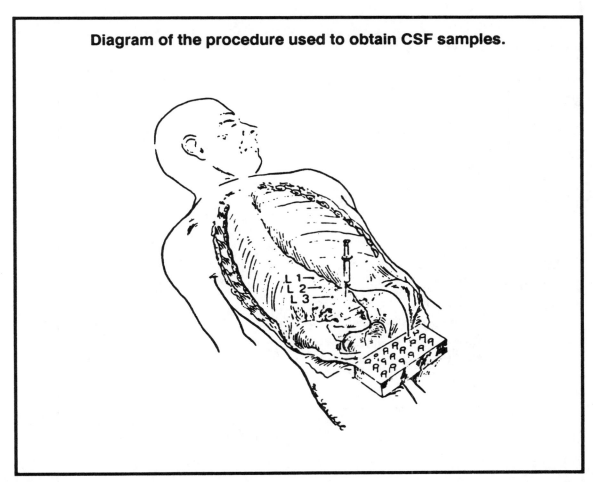

Diagram of the procedure used to obtain CSF samples.

L 1
L 2
L 3

Figure 5.

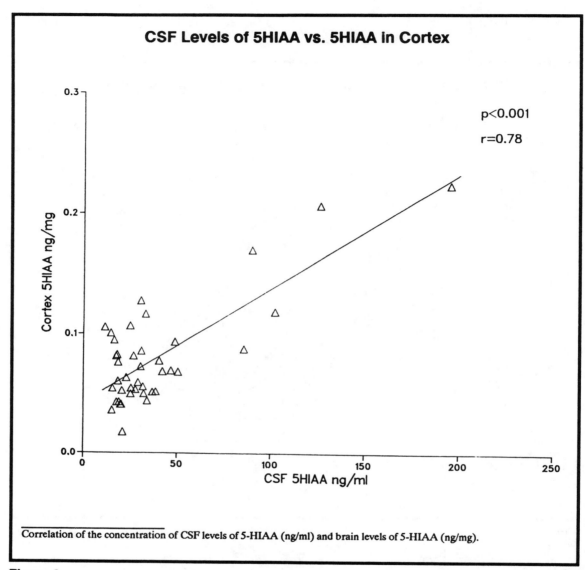

CSF Levels of 5HIAA vs. 5HIAA in Cortex

Correlation of the concentration of CSF levels of 5-HIAA (ng/ml) and brain levels of 5-HIAA (ng/mg).

Figure 6.

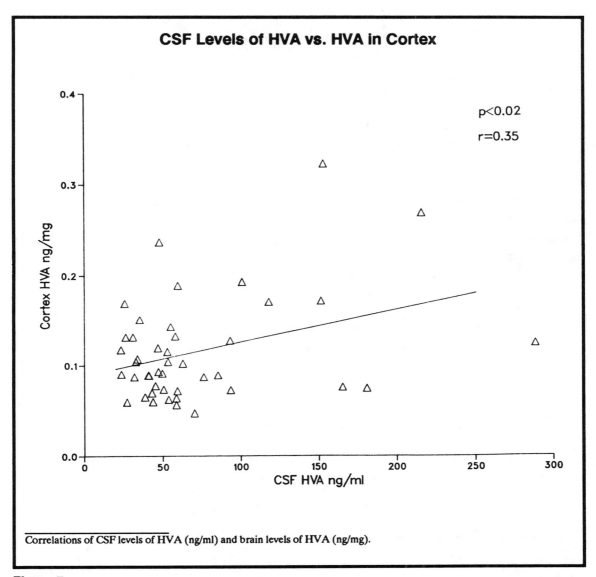

Correlations of CSF levels of HVA (ng/ml) and brain levels of HVA (ng/mg).

Figure 7.

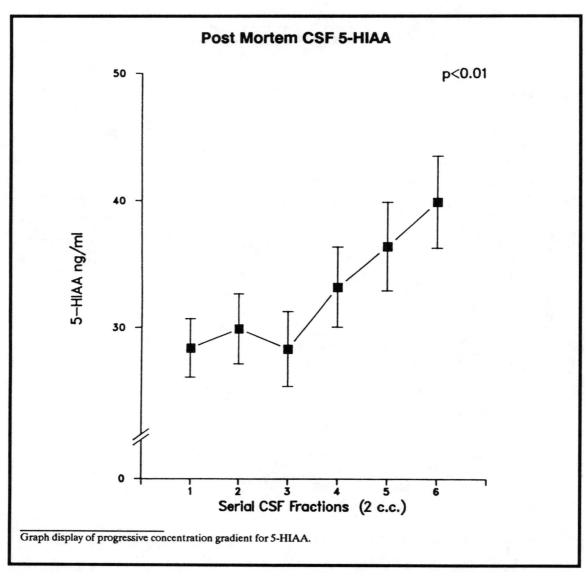

Post Mortem CSF 5-HIAA

$p < 0.01$

5-HIAA ng/ml

Serial CSF Fractions (2 c.c.)

Graph display of progressive concentration gradient for 5-HIAA.

Figure 8.

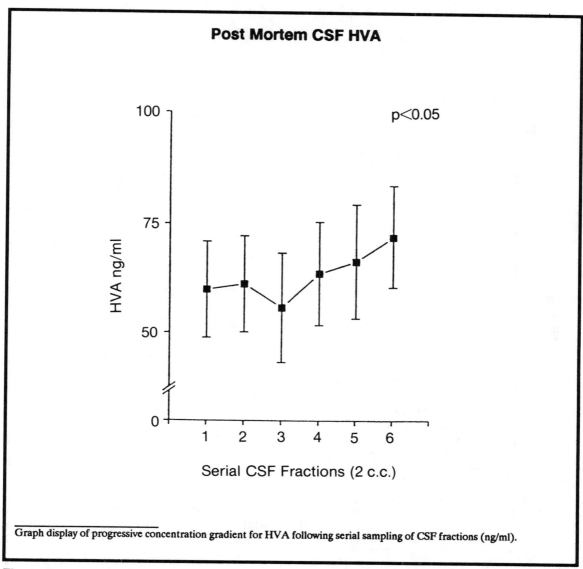

Graph display of progressive concentration gradient for HVA following serial sampling of CSF fractions (ng/ml).

Figure 9.

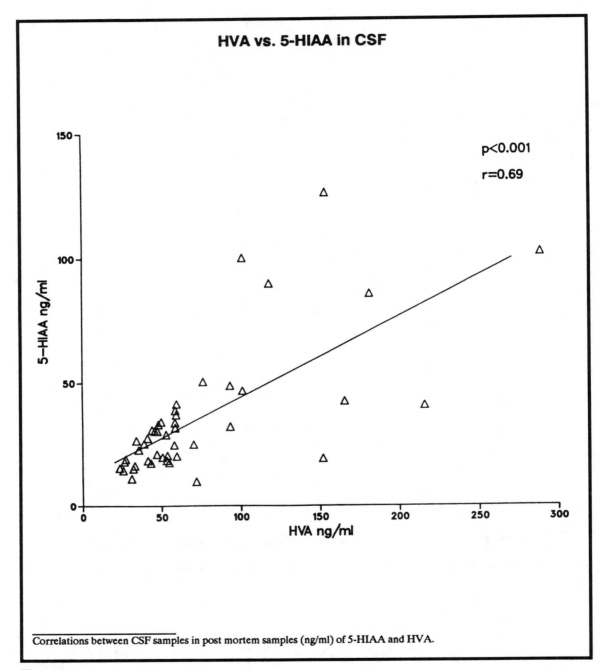

Correlations between CSF samples in post mortem samples (ng/ml) of 5-HIAA and HVA.

Figure 10.

THE NEUROENDOCRINE SYSTEM AND SUICIDE

Herbert Y. Meltzer, M.D., Bond Professor of Psychiatry, Department of Psychiatry, Case Western Reserve University, Cleveland, Ohio

Martin T. Lowy, Ph.D., Department of Psychiatry, Case Western Reserve University, Cleveland, Ohio

SUMMARY

Suicide is increased in frequency in Cushing's syndrome which is characterized by increased hypothalamic-pituitary-adrenal axis (HPA) activity. Several types of studies suggest increased HPA axis activity in depression or stress may be related to increased suicidal behavior: increased serum cortisol, increased 24 hour urinary free cortisol and an enhanced 5-hydroxytryptophan-induced increase in serum cortisol. However, these associations are weak and some cortisol measures do not relate to increased suicidal risk. The TRH-induced increase in TSH may be blunted in violent suicide but shows a positive relation to suicidal ideation. There is some evidence linking the HPA abnormalities and the blunted TSH response to serotonin, the neurotransmitter most closely linked to suicide. Suicide in adolescence may occur in the context of a rapidly changing and aroused neuroendocrine system. Hormonal markers of suicide risk and the role of hormones in altering neurotransmitter function appear to be worthy of further study.

INTRODUCTION

The endocrine system is of interest in relation to suicide for a variety of reasons. An increased likelihood of suicide is found in some endocrine disorders, e.g. Cushing's syndrome, and during corticosteroid therapy. As will be reviewed, the thyroid stimulating hormone (TSH) response to thyrotropin-releasing hormone (TRH) and the basal secretion of cortisol correlate with violent suicide or suicidal ideation. Perhaps more importantly, cortisol as well as other hormones can influence the activity of neurotransmitters such as serotonin (5-HT) which may have a more direct causal effect in suicide. Given that no one factor is likely to be the sole determinant of a complex behavior such as suicide, it is important to develop models of the etiology of suicide which integrate a variety of influences such as hormone secretion and neurotransmitter chemistry. We will attempt to do this by considering the hypothalamic-pituitary-adrenal (HPA) axis and the serotonergic system, considering the evidence relating both to suicide, and then the interaction between the two systems. We will also briefly consider other hormones that may contribute to suicide potential and hormone challenge tests that may predict suicide.

There is only minimal data concerning the endocrine status of adolescents who have made suicide attempts or putative biological markers of suicide in adolescents with psychiatric disorders. Therefore, this review will of necessity focus on studies in adult populations. How applicable these results are to adolescents remains to be determined.

In the one instance where data exists for adolescents and adults (the dexamethasone suppression test, DST), the findings are quite comparable. Suicide in both adolescents and adults often occurs as a consequence of major depression or schizophrenia, complicated by alcohol or drug abuse. Both adolescents and adults may suicide impulsively and as a consequence of severe stress. There is no a priori reason to consider any of these factors would act differently in adolescents, so it is most likely relevant to the task of this symposium on risk factors in adolescent suicide to consider the data concerning suicide in adults. This is not to say that unique biological, especially endocrine, factors are inoperative in adolescents or that they are less important than those common to suicide in both age groups. Rather, it is our belief that future studies on the biology of adolescent suicide may well use findings in older adults as appropriate guidelines for research to determine what are the most important influences on adolescent suicide.

ENDOCRINOPATHIES, CORTICOSTEROIDS AND SUICIDE

There are many aspects of the HPA axis which point toward its importance for understanding the biological contribution to suicide. Six of 35 consecutive patients with Cushing's syndrome, a group of disorders associated with large increases in glucocorticoid output, were reported to have suicidal thoughts and two of these made suicide attempts (Starkman and Schteingart, 1981). In another study, one of 29 cases of Cushing's syndrome made a suicide attempt (Cohen, 1980). Lewis and Smith (1983) reviewed the literature on exogenous corticosteroid-induced psychiatric syndromes and found that 3 percent of the cases for whom outcome was specified committed suicide. This data points towards a role of corticosteroids in increasing vulnerability to suicide. As will be discussed, this might occur because of effects of corticosteroids on neurotransmitter or neuromodulator physiology.

In addition to Cushing's syndrome, other endocrine disorders, various aspects of normal endocrine maturation, function and decline, and hormones other than glucocorticoids, may be associated with profound affective, cognitive and psychomotor disturbances. Hypo- and hyper- thyroidism, hypocortisolism (Addisonian syndrome), hypopituitarism (Simmond's disease), hyperpituitarism, pheochromocytoma, hypo- and hyperparathyroidism, hypo- and hyperglycemia, pancreatitis, pancreatic carcinoma, androgen excess and deficiency and estrogen-progesterone disorders associated with menarche, premenstrual syndrome, oral contraceptives, pregnancy and the postpartum period may produce highly disturbing changes in mental status that could figure in an individual's ability to function adequately, his sense of optimism concerning the future, the desirability of continuing to live, thoughts of suicide and capacity to carry out a suicide attempt. It is beyond the scope of this review to consider these conditions in detail. They are adequately described in textbooks of medicine and clinical endocrinology. Clearly, any adolescent presenting with suicidal ideation or a suicidal attempt should have a thorough medical workup to evaluate the possible presence of an endocrinopathy which might be causing symptoms that directly or indirectly compromise mental status. Conversely, adolescents with serious endocrinopathies such as juvenile diabetes, hypothyroidism or Cushing's syndrome may be at increased risk for suicide and a greater than usual index of suspicion concerning suicide might be advisable in such cases until adequate therapy was instituted.

TRH STIMULATION TEST AND SUICIDE

A blunted TSH response to TRH (<5 uU/ml) has been reported in about 25 percent of depressed patients (Loosen and Prange, 1980). Three studies have reported a relation between a blunted TSH response and violent suicide. Eight depressed patients with past, and three with recent, violent suicide attempts were found to have a low TSH response compared to patients who had made past (N=7) or current (N=7) nonviolent suicide attempts and 26 depressed patients without any suicide attempts (F=3.46, p< .005) (Linkowski et al., 1983). A two-way ANOVA showed a significant relationship of the TSH response to violence but not for recent vs. past attempts. Seven of 12 patients with an absent TSH response had a previous history of violent suicide attempts compared to four of 39 patients with a maximum TSH response above 1 mU/1 (p <.001). During a five year followup period, three committed suicide by violent means and one by overdose. All had an undetectable TSH response to TRH. Linkowski et al. (1984) subsequently reported similar findings in a slightly expanded sample. In agreement with this, Kjellman et al. (1985) reported that the TSH response to TRH was significantly lower in three depressed patients who made violent suicides than in 27 who had made no attempt or a nonviolent attempt. van Praag and Plutchick (1984) also report an association between violent suicide and a blunted TSH response to TRH.

The possibility that a blunted TSH response to TRH may have long term prognostic significance for suicide is intriguing. This could be mediated by a relationship between the blunted TSH response and specific neurotransmitter abnormalities such as diminished activity in 5-HT pathways. There is some evidence relating the TSH response to TRH to the serotonergic system. Cyproheptadine, a 5-HT antagonist, was found to inhibit the TSH response to TRH in two studies (Ferrari et al., 1976; Egge et al., 1977), but not in another (Goldstein et al., 1979). Cyproheptadine has multiple effects other than 5-HT antagonism and is not a particularly potent 5-HT antagonist. Gold et al. (1977) found a negative relationship between the TSH response and CSF 5-hydroxyindoleacetic acid (5-HIAA), the major metabolite of 5-HT in depressed patients, which suggests that diminished serotonergic activity might be associated with a larger TSH response. Thus, our TSH results indicating a

positive relation between the TSH response to TRH and suicidal ideation are consistent with a relation between diminished brain 5-HT and suicidal ideation. Krulich (1979) has reviewed the evidence from rodent studies which suggest that 5-HT may either inhibit or enhance TSH secretion. Krulich et al. (1979) found that quipazine, a 5-HT agonist, did not affect the TRH-induced increase in TSH in the rat but quipazine and 5-HT did inhibit endogenous TSH secretion. The relationship of brain 5-HT, the TSH response to TRH, and suicide requires further study. In light of these findings, we carried out a retrospective analysis of the relationship between suicide ratings and TSH response in a group of newly admitted psychiatric patients to our Mental Health Clinical Research Center who had had a TRH stimulation test (500 ug intravenously). TSH levels over the next 120 minute period was determined by radioimmunoassay. The subjects were drug-free for at least 7 days and consisted of 24 depressed patients (including six schizoaffective depressed, mainly affective), 13 schizophrenic patients (including three schizoaffective depressed, mainly schizophrenic patients), three manic patients and five with miscellaneous diagnoses. Patients were diagnosed according to Research Diagnostic Criteria. Suicidal behavior was assessed during the first week of hospitalization as part of the Schedule for Affective Disorders-Change (SADS-C) interview. Thirteen of the 45 patients admitted to slight or moderate suicidal ideation. Only two patients had made suicide attempts, not considered lethal in intent. There were no violent suicide attempts. We found a significant positive correlation between maximum TSH response to TRH (peak-minus-baseline) and suicide ratings (Spearman rho=0.30, N=45, p=0.044). The mean TSH response to TRH in this group was 9.8 ± S.D. 5.6 uU/ml. This is very similar to that found in 19 normal controls 8.9 ± S.D. 7.2 uU/ml. Ten of the 45 patients (22%) had a blunted TSH response (<5uU/ml). Of these, only three had any suicidal ideation, one mild, one slight, one moderate. Further study is needed to determine if current suicidal ideation is associated with a more robust TSH response but still within the normal limits.

There is conflicting data concerning the linkage between increased HPA axis activity and the blunted TSH response to TRH in depression. Kirkegaard and Carroll (1980), Asnis et al. (1981), Agren and Wide (1982) found no correlation between these two variables. We found no relationship between the TSH and 8 A.M. response to TRH plasma cortisol obtained within the same drug-free evaluation period that included the TRH stimulation test (Spearman rho=0.061, N=38, p=NS). Sixteen of the 45 patients had also undergone other neuroendocrine challenge test within the same three week drug-free period as the TRH test, e.g., the 5-hydroxytryptophan-induced increase in serum cortisol (Meltzer et al., 1984). We also examined the correlation between basal serum cortisol (obtained 60 minutes after catheter placement) and the TSH response in these 16 subjects. We found a highly significant negative correlation between these variables (Spearman rho=-0.65, N=16, p=0.007). This is consistent with the studies of Loosen et al. (1978) who reported a negative correlation between the TSH response to TRH and basal plasma cortisol just before a TRH infusion. The significant correlation between the TSH response to TRH basal and basal serum cortisol levels obtained during the 5-HTP study may be due to lesser influence of stress in the catheter study and the fact that both the TRH and 5-HTP studies were carried out at 10 A.M. Basal cortisol levels obtained at 8 A.M. may reflect the nocturnal surge of cortisol secretion. However, Asnis et al. (1981) did not observe any relationship between the TSH response to TRH and multiple measures of cortisol secretion, including plasma cortisol levels before and throughout the TRH infusion.

HYPOTHALAMIC-PITUITARY-AD RENAL AXIS AND SUICIDE

The presence or absence of a relationship between the TSH response to TRH and basal cortisol is directly relevant to consideration of the importance of TSH as a marker for suicide since there have been a variety of findings which indicate excessive activity of the HPA axis in suicide. Two early National Institute of Mental Health studies reported elevated urinary 24 hour 17-hydroxycorticosteriod (17-OHCS) levels in depressed patients who suicided. The enhanced cortisol secretion preceded the suicide attempts by several weeks (Bunney and Fawcett, 1965; Bunney et al., 1969). These findings were not replicated in subsequent studies of four patients who suicided but who did not evidence elevated 24 hr 17-OHCS prior to suicide with the period of study ranging from a day to eight months prior to suicide (Levy and Hansen, 1969; Fink and Carpenter, 1976). Agren and Wide (1982) found a negative correlation between Medical Lethality of Worst Ever Suicide Attempt and 24 hr urinary free cortisol in 76 patients with major depression. Ostroff et al. (1982), however, did find higher 24 hr urinary cortisol levels (as well as lower urinary norepinephrine-to-epinephrine levels) in three of 22 subjects, two of whom made lethal and one a near lethal suicide attempt.

In addition to urinary cortisol, which is a good measure of adreno-corticoid output, other studies have reported elevated plasma cortisol in suicide. Thus, Krieger (1974) reported that plasma cortisol in 13 patients who suicided during a two-year followup period (21.1 ± 5.6 ug/dl) was significantly higher than in 39 who did not (16.5 ± 2.4 ug/dl). However, single plasma samples, especially those obtained by venepuncture, may not be an accurate measure of cortisol output. Venepuncture may induce stress-related cortisol secretion. The results of Kreiger (1974) could indicate that individuals who are vulnerable to suicide may be particularly prone to stress-induced cortisol secretion.

We have recently examined plasma cortisol concentrations in relation to recent suicidal history (Meltzer et al., in preparation). Basal serum cortisol levels from unmedicated patients with major depression, mania or schizophrenia and normal controls who were part of a study of the cortisol response to 5-hydroxytryptophan (5-HTP) (Meltzer et al., 1984) were analyzed. In this study, subjects were fasted overnight and an indwelling venous catheter was inserted at 9 A.M. Thirty minutes later the first basal sample was withdrawn. Other samples were drawn 15 and 30 minutes later. The 10 A.M. sample (T_O) was related to the Hamilton Depression Rating scale (HDRS) suicide item (0-4) and the SADS-C suicide item (0-6). Serum cortisol (T_O) was significantly but weakly correlated with the HDRS suicide item for all subjects (Spearman rho=0.20, N=107, p=0.04). This included 61 depressives, 16 manics and 30 schizophrenics. The HDRS suicide rating was also correlated with T_O cortisol in the combined group of affective disorders (rho=0.23, N=77, p=0.05) but not in the depressed patients alone (rho=0.18, N=61, p=0.16). SADS-C suicide ratings and T_O cortisol were not significantly correlated in the affective disorder patients. The magnitude of the correlation between the HDRS suicide item and serum cortisol indicates only a small portion of the variance in suicide ratings can be attributed to elevated 10 A.M. cortisol levels. However, it is possible that this relationship is stronger at other times of the day. It would be of interest to examine the relationship between serum cortisol between 1 P.M. - 4 P.M. and suicide ratings,

since cortisol secretion during this period appears to best reflect 24 hour cortisol output (Halbreich et al., 1982). In the 61 depressed patients, T_O cortisol was significantly correlated with the Hamilton scale ratings of helplessness (rho=0.38, p=.003), depressed mood (rho=0.29, p=0.02), hopelessness (rho=0.27, p=0.03), paranoid symptoms (rho=-0.26, p=0.06) and work and activities (rho=0.25, p=0.06). These relationships are consistent with the conclusion that increased HPA axis activity is a state marker for severity of depression and as such could be an indicator of suicidality. This may be of some clinical value in patients who falsely deny suicidal ideation and intent.

We have also examined the relationship between basal cortisol levels and suicide attempts, both violent and nonviolent, together and separately, in these patients. As can be seen in Table 1, the 10 A.M. serum cortisol was not significantly different in any of these groups although the highest levels were found in the violent attempters, next in the nonviolent attempters and the lowest in the normal controls. No significant differences in basal serum cortisol were found when the two types of attempters were combined and compared to nonattempters and normal controls (data not presented). The trends evident in Table 1 for all psychiatric patients were more prominent in just the affective disorders (Table 2) but these differences were not significant either.

Basal Serum Cortisol in All Psychiatric Patients in Relation to Suicide Attempts		
Group	N	Basal Serum Cortisol (ug/dl)
Normals	21	11.5 ± 5.0*
No Attempts	73	12.0 ± 5.1
Nonviolent	11	12.7 ± 7.7
Violent	12	13.6 ± 6.1
* X ± S.D.		

Table 1.

Basal Serum Cortisol in Affective Disorders in Relation to Suicide Attempts		
Group	N	Basal Serum Cortisol (ug/dl)
Normals	21	11.5 ± 5.0*
No Attempts	55	11.7 ± 4.8
Nonviolent	9	13.5 ± 8.4
Violent	9	15.1 ± 6.4
* X ± S.D.		

Table 2.

223

We did find a trend for serum cortisol in the depressed and manic patients who had made an attempt (14.3 ± 7.3 ug/dl, N=18) to be higher than that of the nonattempters (11.6 ± 4.8 ug/dl, N=76, p=0.08). We examined whether serum cortisol levels above 20.0 ug/dl might have some value as a means of identifying suicide attempters but found no indication that was the case. Nevertheless, the trend in this data, considered in the context of the evidence for an association between excessive HPA axis activity and suicide, suggests that it would be of interest to carry out a prospective study in which serum cortisol was monitored in adolescents at high risk for suicide, e.g., those adolescents presenting at a clinical setting because of the suspicion of being suicidal or adolescent patients placed on suicide precautions in clinical or perhaps forensic settings.

In addition to plasma cortisol studies, there has been one study which related cerebrospinal fluid (CSF) cortisol to suicide. Traskman et al. (1980) reported no differences in CSF cortisol levels in five suicidal patients and 14 nonsuicidal depressives. There was also no relationship between a history of ever making a suicide attempt and high CSF cortisol. CSF cortisol was significantly correlated with urinary free cortisol (r=0.67, N=14, p<.01) which provides further evidence against a relationship between elevated urinary free cortisol and suicide. Nevertheless, further studies of CSF cortisol and suicide, especially violent suicide, would be of interest.

There have been eight published studies of the relationship between dexamethasone suppression test (DST) status at admission to hospital in psychiatric patients and prior suicidal activity. These are summarized in Table 3. Five of the eight found a significant relationship between suicidal activity and nonsuppression. Coryell and Schlesser (1981) found that all four patients who suicided out of a group of 205 unipolar depressions had been nonsuppressors. Carroll et al. (1981) reported that all five melancholic suicide completers were non-

suppressors whereas three completers with diagnoses other than major depression were suppressors.

They also noted eleven other suicide attempters who were nonsuppressors but failed to report how many other nonsuppressors were not suicidal. They proposed that the relationship between suicide and nonsuppression was restricted to melancholics. Banki and Arato (1983) and Targum et al. (1983) also found evidence that nonsuppression predicted suicidal activity. Robbins and Alessi (1985) studied 45 newly hospitalized adolescents, with various psychiatric disorders 23 of whom had attempted to commit suicide. Of the 39 suppressors, 17 (43.6%) made suicide attempts, none considered to have a lethal intent. However, all six nonsuppressors had made suicide attempts; of these, four were medically dangerous or lethal attempts. The two adolescents who had made nonmedically serious attempts and who were nonsuppressors subsequently made medically serious attempts, one of which was fatal. Thus, this study strongly supports a highly significant association of DST nonsuppression with lethal or potentially lethal suicidal behavior in adolescents.

Zimmerman et al. (1986) recently reported no relation between suicidal ideation, serious suicide attempts and nonsuppression in 187 major depressives. Brown et al. (1986) found no differences in the incidence of nonsuppression in 10 recent suicide attempters, 10 past attempters and 37 nonattempters. Moreover, nonserious suicide attempts were more common in suppressors than nonsuppressors. Meltzer et al. (in preparation) have recently reported no relation between violent, nonviolent and no suicide attempts and nonsuppression in 55 patients with major affective disorder. However, there was a trend for suicide attempters to be nonsuppressors (10/16, 62.5%) more commonly than nonattempters (16/39, 41%) (Fisher exact test, p=0.085). We also found that Hamilton Depression Scale suicide ratings were significantly higher in nonsuppressors (all diagnoses) than suppressors and that nonsuppressors had suicidal ideation significantly more frequently than suppressors. Differences in the number of days between the suicide attempt and the DST could account for some of the discrepencies between studies. However, Brown et al. (1986) found no such correlation in recent attempters. It is possible that the association between non-suppression and suicide may be confined to patients with endogenous depression as proposed by Carroll et al. (1981).

In addition to these studies of the relationship between suicidal ideation or acts and DST status, there are several other relevant reports. Two studies describe five patients who made suicide attempts within a few days of receiving dexamethasone as part of the DST (Beck- Freis et al., 1981; Asberg et al., 1981). Other investigators did not confirm this finding (Coryell, 1982; Kronfol et al., 1982). Yerevanian et al. (1983) reported an association between failure of the DST to normalize and subsequent suicide. Greden et al. (1980) also noted one such case.

Although there appears to be some evidence supporting a relationship between the DST and suicide, it is important that these results be interpreted cautiously because of the evidence that nonsuppression with the oral 1 mg test may be related to differences in dexamethasone pharmacokinetics. There are now several studies reporting lower dexamethasone levels in nonsuppressors than suppressors (Arana et al., 1984; Berger et al., 1984; Holsboer et al., 1986; Johnson et al., 1985; Lowy et al., in press). Differences in dexamethasone levels might produce both false positives and false negatives. Thus, there could be an association between low plasma dexamethasone levels and suicide rather than nonsuppression and suicide. In any event, it would appear prudent to assess DST status, including measurement of dexamethasone levels, in relation to suicidal activity. Such studies should include post-treatment repeat DST testing and long term followup to assess whether nonsuppression does have prognostic value for suicidal risk.

Suicide and the Dexamethasone Suppression Test

Authors	Patient Population	Suicide/ Attempt Suppression	Suicide/ Attempt NonSuppression	p	Comment
Coryell and Schlesser(1981)	UP Dep	0/109	4/96	0.06	1 suicidal neurotic NS.
Carroll et al (1981)	MDD21 Mixed 3	0/0	16/19		5/8 NS completers.
Banki and Arato(1983)	Mixed	2/20	12/37	<.10	
Targum et al (1983)	UP Dep	3/26	14/23	0.01	5 NS vs 0 S made subsequent attempt.
Robbins and Alessi(1985)	Adolescent. inpatients	17/22	6/6	0.01	4 NS made near lethal attempts. 5 made no serious attempts.
Zimmerman et al (1986)	MDD	12/127* 31/127+	2/60 5/60	NS 0.01	Nonserious more common in S.
Brown et al (1986)	MDD	18/37	9/20	NS	
Meltzer et al (in preparation)	Mixed	6/29	10/26	NS	

NS = nonsuppressor   S = suppressor
* serious suicide attempt   + nonserious suicide attempt
UP Dep = Unipolar depression   MDD = major depressive disorder.

Table 3.

It appears unlikely that nonsuppression at admission has noteworthy significance for suicide but it is possible that failure to normalize during treatment might. We have demonstrated that depression and nonsuppression may be related to glucocorticoid receptor subsensitivity (Gormley et al., 1985). These results have recently been replicated (Whalley et al., 1986). These studies involved measurement of glucocorticoid receptor concentration in lymphocytes. They could reflect similar changes in the HPA axis. Glucocorticoid influences on serotonergic neurons might mediate the relation between suicide and DST status. This will be discussed subsequently.

In addition to abnormalities in glucocorticoid output, we have raised the possibility that abnormalities in glucocorticoid response may be a factor in major depression and other psychiatric disorders (Lowy et al., 1984). Failure to suppress cortisol after dexamethasone may be a special instance of glucocorticoid receptor (GCCR) resistance. The lack of stigmata of Cushing's syndrome in psychiatric patients with excessive glucocorticoid output suggests some GCCR subsensitivity. Glucocorticoid receptor number or affinity may change in response to changes in the availability of glucocorticoids, e.g., administration of dexamethasone (1-24 mg) produces a decreased number of GCCR in lymphocytes from normal volunteers which can be detected as little as 12 hours after first administration (Bloomfield et al., 1981; Schlechte et al., 1982). GCCR down regulation following glucocorticoid administration can also occur in a selective manner within the brain (Meany and Aitken, 1985; Tornello et al., 1982). Alterations in the level of endogenous glucocorticoids can also modify GCCR number e.g., stress results in the decreased number of GCCR in both brain and liver (Loeb and Rosner, 1979; Sapolsky et al., 1984). Chrousos et al. (1983) has reported a familial glucocorticoid resistance in man characterized by a marked increase in serum cortisol levels, abnormal DST and no physical stigmata of glucocorticoid excess. A decreased number or affinity of the GCCR in lymphocytes was observed.

We have found decreased *in vivo* inhibition of the lymphocyte proliferative response to the mitogens conconavalin A (ConA) and phytohemaglutinin (PHA) following 1 mg dexamethasone in depressed patients who are nonsuppressors (Lowy et al., 1984). Depressed patients, especially nonsuppressors, also had lower binding of 3H-triamcinalone (Gormley et al., 1985). The failure to suppress serum cortisol following dexamethasone was associated with a smaller decrease in GCCR content. We measured serum dexamethasone levels and found significant negative correlations between the change in the PHA response, but not in the ConA response (Meltzer et al., 1984). We have also observed a subsensitivity of the lymphocytes of patients who were nonsuppressors to the inhibitory effect of 10-9 and 10-10M dexamethasone on the lymphoproliferative response to ConA (Lowy et al., in press). These concentrations of dexamethasone correspond to those present at 8 A.M. after a 1 mg dose. The difference between suppressors and nonsuppressors was observed only with ConA, not PHA.

Because of this, we thought it would be important to examine the relationship between suicide and subsensitivity to glucocorticoids as indicated by the *in vivo* responses to ConA and GCCR content. The presence of GCCR subsensitivity might counteract the effect of increased glucocorticoid output. The combination of the two factors might turn out to be a better predictor of suicide than measures of glucocorticoid output such as basal plasma cortisol or urinary free cortisol alone. We correlated Hamilton Depression Scale suicide ratings with these measures in unmedicated patients, the majority of whom met RDC for major depression. The results are preliminary because the number of subjects for whom data is available is small. We found no significant correlations between the change in the ConA and GCCR content following dexamethasone or basal GCCR concentration and the suicide rating. Since the group included only two subjects who had made a severe suicide attempt, further study is needed to rule out a relationship between GCCR resistance and suicide.

We have reported that the 5-HTP-induced increase in serum cortisol showed a significant positive correlation with HDRS suicide ratings at admission in 24 depressed and manic patients and that seven patients who made violent attempts had a larger cortisol response to 5-HTP than 33 who had not (Meltzer et al., 1984). We have continued this investigation using the same methodology with the exception that L-5-HTP 100 mg has been substituted for D,L-5-HTP, 200 mg. We have now examined our data in relation to suicidal attempts at any time in life, with information from the patient and informants. As can be seen in Table 4, patients with affective disorders who made violent attempts had the highest cortisol response, followed by those who made no attempt, a nonviolent attempt, and normal controls. The violent attempters had a significantly greater cortisol response than the nonviolent attempters (p=0.003) and the normal controls (p=0.0008) but just failed to differ from the nonattempters (p=0.08).

Glucocorticoids modulate the biosynthesis and functional activity of many neurotransmitters and neuromodulators. Thus, abnormalities in the GCCR could contribute to some of the known biochemical changes associated with depression. 5-HT, in particular, interacts with glucocorticoids in a variety of ways. 5-HT has a well known stimulatory effect on the adrenocortical system (Meltzer et al., 1984). Glucocorticoids, in turn, have been shown to have a facilitory effect on 5-HT biosynthesis and turnover (Rastogi and Signhal, 1978; deKloet et al., 1982). Glucocorticoids also modify 5-HT receptors (Bigeon et al., 1985) and various serotonergic drugs modify GCCR (Angelucci et al., 1982; Patacchioli et al., 1984). A decrease in glucocorticoid-mediated 5-HT synthesis due to a GCCR dysfunction could contribute to the postulated decreased level of 5-HT which occurs in some depressed patients. Recently, an association between the DST and platelet 5-HT uptake in depressed patients has been reported (Meltzer et al., 1983). In addition, dexamethasone has been shown to directly modify cerebrospinal fluid levels of the 5-HT metabolite, 5-hydroxyindoleacetic acid, in psychiatric patients (Banki et al, 1983).

Adrenalectomy increases $5-HT_1$ receptor binding in some regions of the hippocampus (Bigeon et al., 1985). Adrenalectomy also counteracted the stimulatory effect of vasoactive intestinal peptide (VIP) on $5-HT_1$ binding sites in the dorsal subiculum of the hippocampus, but not the inhibitory effect of VIP on the $5-HT_1$ binding sites in the suprachiasmatic nucleus. Other complex interactions between VIP and adrenal steroids on $5-HT_1$ binding were also reported (Rostene et al., 1985). Adrenalectomy also increases brain ^3H-imipramine binding (Arora and Meltzer, in press). Chronic corticosteroid administration appears to have mixed effects on 5-HT function (Dickson et al., 1985; Nausieda et al., 1982).

As discussed elsewhere in this symposium, 5-HT is thought to play an integral role in the biology of suicide, especially violent suicide, impulsivity or violence per se. In view of the above mentioned interactions between 5-HT and glucocorticoids, it will be important to obtain biological measures of both serotonin and glucocorticoid activity or function in individuals who have made suicide attempts or are considered high risks. Further basic re-

Cortisol Response to 5-Hydroxytryptophan in Patients with Major Affective Disorders		
Group	N	Cortisol Response (AUC)
Normal Controls	22	1624 ± 540
No Attempt	55	2112 ± 713
NonViolent Attempt	9	1776 ± 1046
Violent Attempt	9	2772 ± 846
$F = 6.10$, df = 3,89, p = 0.0008		

Table 4.

search on the interaction of these two systems is strongly indicated.

CONCLUSION

There is a possibility of neuroendocrine trait markers for violent or lethal suicide. A blunted TSH response, abnormal DST or increased UFC appears to be associated to past, current or future violent suicides. Similarly, the 5-HTP-induced increase in serum cortisol may be largest in patients who have made a violent suicide attempt anytime in life. Some, all or none of these neuroendocrine abnormalities may relate to decreased brain serotonergic activity. If they are related to decreased serotonergic activity, then the results would be consistent with a broad range of other biochemical studies summarized elsewhere in this report. Together the neuroendocrine studies suggest a concerted effort should be made to identify the abnormalities of 5-HT and the endocrine system in anyone who has made a violent suicide attempt and survived. The blunted TRH response may be related to increased HPA activity. More sophisticated ways of assessing increased HPA activity are now available to be applied to suicide research. A DST with measures of dexamethasone levels and a measure of glucocorticoid receptor sensitivity might prove a more sensitive index of suicidal activity. The 1-4 P.M. cortisol output, ACTH and CRF stimulation tests, measures of serum cortisol binding globulin and circadian rhythm disturbances are among the measures that might be evaluated. The aim of these studies would be to identify possible biological markers and to further develop an integrated neuroendocrine-neurotransmitter hypothesis of the etiology of suicide. For some biological factors that predispose to suicide, suicidal ideation, nonviolent, nonlethal intent attempts may represent a continuum. For other factors there may be a unique association with each level of suicidal intent or in relation to violence. A uniform way of collecting and presenting data in this regard might be useful. Methods for quantifying duration and intensity of ideation might help.

REFERENCES

1. Agren H, and Wide L: Patterns of depression reflected in pituitary- thyroid and pituitary-adrenal endocrine changes. Psychoneuroendo- crinology 7:(4)309-327, 1982.

2. Beck-Fries J, Aperia B, Kjellman B, Ljunggren J-G, Petterson J, Sara V, Sjolin A, Uden F, Wetterman L: Suicidal behavior and the dexamethasone suppression test. Am J Psych 138:(7)993-995, 1981.

3. Berger M, Pirke KM, Doerr P, Kreig JC, vonZerssen D: The limited utility of the dexamethasone suppression test for the diagnostic process in psychiatry. Brit J Psychiat 145:372-382, 1984.

4. Biegon A, Rainbow TC, McEwen BS: Corticosterone modulation of neurotransmitter receptors in rat hippocampus: A quantitative autoradiographic study. Brain Res 332:309-314, 1985.

5. Bloomfield DC, Smith KA, Peterson BA, Gajl-Peczalska K, Munck AU: In vitro glucocorticoid studies in human lymphoma: Clinical and biologic significance. J Steroid Biochem 15:275-284, 1981.

6. Bunney WE, and Fawcett JA: Possibility of a biochemical test for suicidal potential. Arch Gen Psychiat 13:232-239, 1965.

7. Bunney WE, Fawcett JA, David JM, Gifford S: Further evaluation of urinary 17-hydroxycorticosteroid in suicidal patients. Arch Gen Psychiat 21:138-150, 1969.

8. Carroll BJ, Greden JF, Feinberg M: Suicide, neuroendocrine dysfunction and CSF 5-HIAA concentrations in depression. Recent Adv. in Neuropsychopharmachology (eds) B Angrist, GD Burrows, M Lader, O. Lingjaerde, G Sedvall, P Wheatley. Pergamon Press, Oxford, pp 307-313, 1981.

9. Chrousos GP, Loriaux DL, Brandon D, Tomita M, Vingerholds ACM, Merriam G, Johnson EO, Lipsett, MB: Primary cortisol resistance: A familial syndrome and an animal model. J Steroid Biochem 19:567-575, 1983.

10. Coryell W: Suicidal behavior and the DST: Lack of association. Amer J Psychiatry 139:1214, 1982.

11. Coryell W, and Schlesser MA: Suicide and the dexamethasone suppression test in unipolar depression. Amer J Psychiat 138:1120-1121, 1981.

12. Cohen SI: Cushing's syndrome: A psychiatric study of 29 patients. Br J Psychiat 136:120-124, 1980.

13. deKloet ER, Kovacs GL, Sxabo G, Telegdy G, Bohus B, Versteeg DHG: Decreased serotonin turnover in the dorsal hippocampus of rat brain shortly after adrenalectomy: Selective normalization after corticosterone substitution. Brain Res 239:659-663, 1982.

14. Dickinson SL, Kennett GA, Curzon G: Reduced 5-hydroxytryptamine- dependent behaviour in rats following chronic corticosterone treatment. Brain Res 345:10-18, 1985.

15. Egge AC, Regol AD, Varma MM: Effect of cyproheptadine on TRH-stimulated prolactin and TSH release in man. J Clin Endocrinol Metab 44:210-213, 1977.

16. Ferrari C, Paracchi A, Rondena M, Beck-Peccoz P, Faglia G: Effect of two serotonin antagonists on prolactin and thyrotropin secretion in man. Clin Endocrinology 5:575-581, 1976.

17. Fink EB, and Carpenter WT: Further examination of a biochemical test for suicide potential. Dis Nerv Syst 37:341-343, 1976.

18. Gold PW, Goodwin FK, Wehr T, Rebar R: Pituitary thyrotropin response to thyrotropin releasing hormone in

affective illness: Relationship to spinal fluid amine metabolites. Am J Psychiat 134:1028-1031, 1977.

19. Goldstein J, Vanhaelst L, Bruno OD: Effect of cyproheptadine on thyrotropin and prolactin secretion in normal man. Acta Endocrinol 92:205-213, 1979.

20. Gormley GJ, Lowy MT, Reder AT, Hospelhorn VD, Antel JP, Meltzer HY: Glucocorticoid receptors in depression: Relationship to the dexamethasone suppression test. Am J Psychiat 142:1278-1284, 1985.

21. Greden JF, Albala AA, Haskett RF, James NM, Goodman L, Steiner M, Carroll BJ: Normalization of dexamethasone supression test: A laboratory index of recovery from endogenous depression. Biol Psychiat 15:449-458, 1980.

22. Halbreich J, Zumoff B, Kream J, Fukushima DK: The mean 1300-1600 hr plasma cortisol concentration as a diagnostic test for hypercortisolism. J Clin Endocrinol Metab 56:1262-1264, 1982.

23. Holsboer F, Wiedemann K, Gerken A, Boll E: The plasma dexamethasone variable in depression: Test-retest studies and early biophase kinetics. Psychiatry Res 17:97-103, 1986.

24. Johnson GF, Hunt G, Kerr K, Caterson I: Dexamethasone suppression test (DST) and plasma dexamethasone levels in depressed patients. Psychiatry Res 13:305-313, 1984.

25. Kirkegaard C, and Carroll BJ: Dissociation of TSH and adrenocortical disturbances in endogenous depression. Psychiatry Res 3:253-264, 1980.

26. Kjellman BF, Ljunggren J-G, Beck-Fries J, Wetterberg L: Effect of TRH on TSH and prolactin levels in affective disorders. Psychiatry Res 14:353-363, 1985.

27. Krieger G: The plasma level of cortisol as a predictor of suicide. Dis Nerv Syst 35:237-240, 1974.

28. Kronfol Z, Greden JF, Gardner R, Carroll BJ: Suicidal behavior and the DST: Lack of association. Amer J Psychiatry 139:1214, 1982.

29. Krulich L: Central neurotransmitters and the secretion of prolactin, GH, LH, and TSH. Ann Rev Physiol 41:603-615, 1979.

30. Krulich L, Grachetti A, Coppings RJ, McCann SM, Mayfield MA: On the role of central serotonergic system in the regulation of the secretion of thyrotropin and prolactin: Thyrotropin-inhibiting and prolactin-releasing effect of 5-hydroxytryptamine and quipazine. Endocrinology 105:276-283, 1979.

31. Levy B, and Hansen E: Failure of the urinary test for suicide potential: Analysis of urinary 17-hydroxycorticosteroids in suicidal patients. Arch Gen Psychiat 20:415-418, 1969.

32. Lewis DA, and Smith RE: Steroid-induced psychiatric syndromes: A report of 14 cases and a review of the literature. J Affect Dis 5:319-332, 1983.

33. Linkowski P, Van Wettere JP, Kerkhofs M, Brauman H, Mendlewicz J: Thyrotrophin response to thyreostimulin in affectively ill women: Relationship to suicidal behaviour. Br J Psychiat 143:401-405, 1983.

34. Linkowski P, Van Wettere JP, Kerkhofs M, Gregoire F, Brauman H, Mendlewicz J: Violent suicidal behavior and the thyrotropin- releasing hormone-thyroid-stimulating hormone test: A clinical outcome study. Neuropsychobiology 12:19-22, 1984.

35. Loeb JN, and Rosner W: Fall in hepatic cytosol glucocorticoid receptor induced by stress and partial hepatectomy: Evidence for separate mechanisms. Endocrinology 104:1003-1006, 1979.

36. Loosen PT, and Prange AJ, Jr: Thyrotropin releasing hormone (TRH): A useful tool for psychoneuroendocrine investigation. Psycho- neuroendocrinology 5:63-80, 1980.

37. Loosen PT, Prang AJ Jr, Wilson IC: Influence of cortisol on TRH-induced TSH response in depression. Am J Psychiat 135:244-246, 1978.

38. Lowy MT, Gormley GJ, Reder AT, Hospelhorn VD, Antel JP, Meltzer HY: Glucocorticoid receptor function in depression. In: Hormones and Depression (ed) U Halbreich and R Rose, Raven Press, New York, pp 91-112, 1987.

39. Lowy MT, Reder AT, Antel JP, Meltzer HY: Glucocorticoid resistance in depression: Relation between the DST and lymphocyte sensitivity to dexamethasone. Am J Psychiat 141:1365-1370, 1984.

40. Meaney MJ, and Aitken DH: (3H) dexamethasone binding in rat frontal cortex. Brain Res 328:176-180, 1985.

41. Meltzer HY, Arora RC, Tricou BJ, Fang VS: Serotonin uptake in blood platelets and the dexamethasone suppression test in depressed patients. Psychiatry Res 8:41-47, 1983.

42. Meltzer HY, Lowy MT, Koenig JI: The hypothalamic-pituitary-adrenal axis in depression. In: Hypothalamic, dysfunction in neuropsychiatric disorders (ed) FK Goodwin, Raven Press, New York, 165-182, 1987.

43. Meltzer HY, Perline R, Tricou BJ, Lowy M, Robertson AG: Effect of 5-hydroxytryptophan on serum cortisol levels in the major affective disorders. II. Relation to suicide, psychosis and depressive syndrome. Arch Gen Psychiat 41:379-387, 1984.

44. Meltzer HY, Umberkoman-Wiita B, Robertson AG, Tricou BJ, Lowy MT, Perline R: Effect of 5-hydroxytryptophan on serum cortisol levels in the major affective disorders I. Enhances response in depression and mania. Arch Gen Psychiat 41:366-374, 1984.

45. Nausieda PA, Carvey PM, Weiner WJ: Modification of central serotonergic and dopaminergic behaviors in the course of chronic corticosteroid administration. Eur J Pharmacol 78:335-343, 1982.

46. Ostroff R, Geller E, Bonese K, Ebersole E, Harkness L, Mason J: Neuroendocrine risk factors of suicidal behavior. Am J Psychiat 139:1323-1325, 1982.

47. Patacchioli FR, deKloet ER, Chiappini P, Chierichetti C, Scaccianoce S, Angelucci L: Brain serotonergic innervation in the regulation of stress response in the rat. In: Stress: The role of catecholamines and other neurotransmitters. Vol 2. (eds) E Usdin, R Kvetnensky, and J Axelrod, Gordon and Breach Science Publishers, New York, pp 787-793, 1984.

48. Rastogi RB, and Singhal RL: Adrenocorticoids control 5-hydroxy- tryptamine metabolism in rat brain. J Neural Transmission 42:63-71, 1978.

49. Robbins DR, and Alessi NE: Suicide and the dexamethasone suppression test in adolescence. Biol Psychiat 20:94-119, 1985.

50. Rostene WH, Fischette CT, Dussaillant M, McEwen BS: Adrenal steroid modulation of vasoactive intestinal peptide effect on serotonin binding sites in the rat brain shown by in vitro quantitative autoradiography. Neuroendocrinology 40:129-134, 1985.

51. Sapolsky RM, Krey LC, McEwen BS: Stress downregulates corticosterone receptors in a site-specific manner in the brain. Endocrinology 114:287-292, 1984.

52. Schlechte JA, Ginsberg BH, Sherman BM: Regulation of the glucocorticoid receptor in human lymphocytes. J Steroid Biochem 16:69-74, 1982.

53. Starkman MN, and Schteingart DE: Neuropsychiatric manifestations of patients with Cushing's syndrome. Arch Intern Med 141:215-219, 1981.

54. Targum SD, Rosen L, Capodanno AE: The dexamethasone suppression test in suicidal patients with unipolar depression. Am J Psychiatr 140:877-879, 1983.

55. Tornello S, Orti E, DeNicola AF, Rainbow TC, McEwen BS: Regulation of glucocorticoid receptors in brain by corticosterone treatment of adrenalectomized rats. Neuroendocrinology 35:411-417, 1982.

56. Traskman L, Tybring G, Asberg M, Bertilsson L, Lantto O, Schalling D: Cortisol in the CSF of depressed and suicidal patients. Arch Gen Psychiat 37:761-767, 1980.

57. vanPraag HM, and Plutchik R: Depression type and depression severity in relation to risk of violent suicide attempt. Psychiat Res 12:333-338, 1984.

58. Whalley LJ, Borthwick N, Copolov D, Dick H, Christie JE, Fink G: Glucocorticoid receptors and depression. Brit Med J 292:859-861, 1986.

59. Yerevanian BI, Olafsdottir H, Melanese E, Russotto J, Mallon P, Baciewicz G, Sagi E: Normalization of the dexamethasone suppression test at discharge: Its prognostic value. J Aff Dis 5:191-197, 1983.

60. Zimmerman M, Coryell W, Pfohl B: The validity of the dexamethasone suppression test as a marker for endogenous depression. Arch Gen Psychiat 43:347-355, 1986.

ACKNOWLEDGMENT

Supported in part by NIMH grants MH 41683 and MH 41684 and by the Cleveland Foundation. Dr. Meltzer is recipient of a Research Career Scientist Award, MH 47808 from NIMH.

GENETICS AND SUICIDAL BEHAVIOR

Alec Roy, M.B., Laboratory of Clinical Studies, Division of Intramural Clinical and Biological Research, National Institute on Alcohol Abuse and Alcoholism, Bethesda, Maryland

There are five lines of evidence about genetic factors in suicide. This paper will review the clinical, twin, Iowa-500, Amish, and Copenhagen adoption studies, all of which provide evidence about genetic factors in suicide. Most of these are studies of suicidal behavior among adults but it is likely that genetic factors for suicide are similar in both adolescents and adults.

CLINICAL STUDIES

A family history of suicide has been noted to be associated with suicidal behavior at all stages of the life cycle. There are five such studies among adolescents. In 1974 Shaffer (1) reported a comprehensive survey of all 31 suicides among children aged 14 years or younger in England and Wales during the seven years from 1962 to 1968. Suicidal behavior in a first degree relative had occurred in seven of these 31 youth suicides (22.6 percent). In four relatives this suicidal behavior had occurred before the child's suicide, but in three other cases a first degree relative attempted suicide after the child had committed suicide. There was also a high incidence of depression among the first degree relatives (20 percent).

In 1981 Tishler et al. (2) found that 22 percent of a series of 108 adolescents seen at a children's hospital emergency room after attempting suicide had a history that "at least one family member had exhibited suicidal behavior in the past."

In 1982 Garfinkel et al. (3) reported a review of the hospital charts of 505 children and adolescents who appeared at the emergency room of the Hospital for Sick Children in Toronto between January 1, 1970, and January 30, 1977, and had "deliberately inflicted self-injury with a documented conscious desire to die from the injury." A control group was derived by examining the charts of individuals of the same sex and of a similar age who did not have a history of attempting suicide but who had been admitted at about the same time to the same emergency room. The researchers found that significantly more of the youthful suicidal attempters, than their controls, had a family history of suicidal behavior (8.3 percent vs 1.1 percent) (Table 1).

Garfinkel et al. also used Weisman and Worden's Risk/Rescue Rating Scale (4) to obtain ratings of severity for the adolescent's suicide attempts. Interestingly, they found that significantly more of those who had made serious suicide attempts had a family history of suicide (Table 2).

As found in Shaffer's London study, the suicide attempters in Garfinkel et al.'s study also had a significant excess of relatives with mental illness and they concluded: "A strong genetic loading for affective disorder in families of individuals who attempt suicide is supported by our findings of an eight times higher rate of suicide attempts or suicide in the families of the index group and an absence of completed suicide in the families of the controls." They also noted: "Attempted suicide is on a continuum with completed suicide, as demonstrated by the finding that there was no family history of completed suicide in the control group and that the followup mortality rate from suicide in the index group surpassed the death rate for the controls."

In 1985 Shafii et al. (5) reported data derived from psychological autopsies carried out after lengthy home visits with the families of 20 children and adolescents who had committed suicide in Jefferson County, Louisville, between January 1980 and June 1983. Friends and significant others were also contacted and three extensive questionnaires were completed. Shafii et al. were able to match 17 of the suicide victims with controls drawn from among the suicide victim's closest friends. These controls, and their families, were interviewed using the same

methodology as was used with the families of the suicide victims. Shafii et al. also found that significantly more of the youth suicide victims, than controls, had a family history of suicide (Table 3). Again, there was a significant difference between the families of suicide victims and controls for emotional problems in the family. These workers concluded that "exposure to suicide or suicidal behavior of relatives and friends appears to be a significant factor in influencing a vulnerable young person to commit suicide."

In an ongoing study, Shaffer et al. (6) are performing extensive psychological autopsies on a consecutive series of youthful suicides under 19 years of age occurring in New York City. In a preliminary report of the first 52 suicide victims studied, they noted that a substantial number (20, 38 percent) had a rela-

Family History Differences Between Children and Adolescents Who Attempted Suicide and Controls

| | Suicide Attempters | | | Controls | | | Signif | | |
| | Available | With Charact. | | Available | With Charact. | | | | |
Characteristic	N	N	%	N	N	%	x^2	df	P
Family History of mental illness	442	228	51.6	452	74	16.4	122.3	1	.01
History of suicide	443	37	8.3	442	5	1.1	23.95	2	.01
Suicide attempts		26	5.9		5	1.1			
Completed suicide		11	2.5		0				

Reproduced with permission of the American Journal of Psychiatry.

Table 1.

Variables Discriminating the Severity of 604 Suicide Attempts by Children and Adolescents.

| | Percent of Attempts | | | Significance | | |
| | Low Danger | Moderate Danger | Severe Danger | | | |
Variable	(N = 385)	(N = 149)	(N = 70)	x^2	df	P
Family history of suicide	4.6	12.7	16.1			
No family history of suicide	95.4	87.3	83.9	13.09	4	.01

Reproduced with permission of the American Journal of Psychiatry

Table 2.

tive who had either committed or attempted suicide. Although cautioning that the family data are complex and are not yet fully explored, Shaffer et al. (7) consider that this aspect of these youthful suicides may represent an environmental rather than a genetic phenomenon; they may be imitative acts similar to the recently well publicized clustering of teenage suicides.

Among adults who exhibit suicidal behavior, there are also surprisingly few studies about the presence or absence of a family history of suicide. In an early study Farberow and Simon (15) reported that among 100 suicide victims in Vienna and Los Angeles, six had a parent who had killed himself, a rate more than 88 times the expected rate. Robins et al. (8) found that 11 percent of 109 suicide attempters had a family history of suicidal behavior. Murphy et al. (9) reported that one third of 55 callers to a suicide prevention center had a family history of suicidal behavior and that this was significantly more likely to be the case if the caller had himself at-

tempted suicide. Flinn and Leonard (10) noted that among 480 young nonpsychiatric subjects, those reporting their own suicidal behavior also reported more knowledge about suicidal behavior in others.

More recently, Murphy and Wetzel (11) systematically interviewed a random sample of all persons seen and admitted during a one-year period at the St. Louis County Hospital following a suicide attempt. Of the 127 patients in the study, 14 percent gave a family history of suicide, 24 percent a family history of attempted suicide, and 6 percent a family history of suicide threats. One or more of these family suicidal behaviors was reported by 36 percent of the suicide attempters. Among suicide attempters with a primary diagnosis of primary affective disorder, 17 percent had a family history of suicide and 17 percent a family history of suicide attempt (Table 4). As individuals with affective disorders comprise a larger proportion of suicides than individuals with personality disorders, Murphy and Wetzel predicted that

Significant Differences Between Children and Adolescents Aged 12-19 Who Committed Suicide and Matched-Pair Control Subjects.

Variable	Suicide Victims N = 20		Control Subjects N = 17		McNemar Test	
	N	%	N	%	(df = 1)	P
Family and environmental variables						
Exposure to suicide	13	65	3	18	6.12	< .008
Sibling's or friend's (attempted or completed suicide)	12	61	2	12	6.12	< .008
Parent's or adult relative's (suicidal ideation, threats, or attempts of completed suicide)	6	30	2	12	2.25	n.s[a]
Parent's emotional problems	12	60	4	24	5.14	< .02

x2 = 3.3, df = 1, P < .04
Reproduced with permission of the American Journal of Psychiatry

Table 3.

233

more of their patients with affective disorder could be expected to present a significant suicide risk in the future. Therefore, they concluded that a "systematic family history of such behavior coupled with modern clinical diagnosis should prove useful in identifying those attempters at increased risk for suicide."

The first study providing data about how commonly a family history of suicide is found among psychiatric patients was that of Pitts and Winokur (12). They found that among 748 consecutive patients admitted to a hospital, 37 reported a possible or definite suicide in a first degree relative (4.9 percent). In 25 (68 percent) of these 37 cases the diagnosis was an affective disorder, and these investigators noted that the statistical probability of this distribution occurring by chance was less than 0.02. When the probable diagnoses in the cases of the first degree relatives who suicided were considered, in 24 of the 37 patient-relative pairings, both members had affective disorders. Pitts and Winokur estimated that 79 percent of the suicides of the first degree relatives were associated with probable affective disorder.

In 1983, Roy (13) reported a study of all the 5,845 psychiatric patients admitted to the Clark Institute of Psychiatry in Toronto between January 1974 and June 1981. There were 243 inpatients with a family history of suicide (4.2 percent), a percentage very similar to the 4.9 percent reported by Pitts and Winokur nineteen years earlier. The patients with a family history of suicide were compared with the 5,602 inpatients without such a history. A family history of suicide was found to significantly increase the risk for an attempt at suicide in a wide variety of diagnostic groups (Table 5). Almost half (48.6 percent) of the patients with a family history of suicide had themselves attempted suicide. More than half (56.4 percent) of all the patients with a family history of suicide had a primary diagnosis of an affective disorder and more than a third (34.6 percent) had a recurrent unipolar or bipolar affective disorder.

Recently Linkowski et al. (14) investigated past suicidal behavior and family history of suicide among a consecutive series of 713 patients with affective disorder admitted over several years to the psychiatric department of the University of Brussels. They found that 123 of the depressed patients (17 percent) had a first or second degree relative who had committed suicide. They also found that a family history of suicide significantly increased the probability of a suicide attempt among the depressed women, especially the risk for a violent suicide attempt. Among the male depressives, a family history of suicide significantly increased the risk only for a violent suicide attempt (Tables 6 and 7). Linkowski et al. concluded that "a positive family history for violent suicide should be considered as a strong predictor of active suicidal attempting behavior in major depressive illness."

A family history of suicide has also been found significantly more among psychiatric patients who commit suicide (16). As manic-

Family History of Suicidal Behavior by Broad Diagnostic Groups				
		% with Family History of		
Diagnostic Group	F	Suicide	Attempt	Any[a]
Personality disorders	56	20	34	46
Primary affective disorder	29	17	17	38
Other diagnoses and none	42	5	17	21
All patients	127	14	24	36

[a]Any suicidal behavior includes suicide and attempted and threatened suicide.
Reproduced with permission of Journal of Nervous and Mental Diseases

Table 4.

depression is the psychiatric diagnosis most commonly found among suicide victims, it is not surprising to find that, across the various published series, approximately 10 percent of manic depressive patients have a family history of suicide (17-20).

A family history of suicide has also been noted to be associated with suicidal behavior among individuals in the last stages of the life cycle. Batchelor and Napier (21) found that among 40 consecutive cases of attempted suicide admitted to a general hospital, aged 60 years or over, a family history of suicide was present in 7 (17 percent) of the cases.

A consecutive series of 5845 inpatients admitted to the Clarke Institute of Psychiatry between January 1974 and June 1981. Patients, by diagnostic group, who attempted suicide comparing those with a family history of suicide with those without such a history.

Diagnostic Group	Second- or first-degree relative suicided			No family history of suicide		
	No. Attempted	(%)	No. of Attempts	No. Attempted	(%)	P
Schizophrenia	15/33	(45.4)	28	150/1114	(13.5)	<.0001
Unipolar	13/32	(41.6)	24	50/373	(13.4)	<.0001
Bipolar	22/58	(37.9)	48	56/405	(13.9)	<.0001
Depressive neurosis	26/47	(55.3)	45	221/715	(30.9)	<.0001
Personality disorder	33/48	(68.8)	89	328/1048	(31.3)	<.0001
Alcohol	3/7	(42.9)	3	42/147	(28.5)	NS
Others	6/18	(33.3)	16	378/1801	(21.0)	NS
Total	118/243	(48.6)	252	1225/5602	(21.8)	<.0001

Reproduced with permission of Archives of General Psychiatry

Table 5.

Clinical characteristics of the major depressive (MD) patients					
	MD with past violent suicidal attempt		MD with past non-violent suicidal attempt		MD with no suicidal attempt
	Males	Females	Males	Females	Males	Females
BP FH+*	3	6	0	7	14	14
FH−	10	11	9	19	72	79
UP FH+	4	12	1	19	16	27
FH−	16	15	23	84	92	160
Total	33	44	33	129	194	280

* FH+ patients with familial history of suicide
BP = bipolar; UP = unipolar
Reproduced with permission of Acta Psychiatrica Scandinavica

Table 6.

THE IOWA-500 STUDY

The Iowa-500 study is a followup study of just over 500 psychiatric patients consecutively admitted to the University of Iowa Psychiatric Hospital between 1934 and 1944. The 525 patients in the study were chosen because they met certain research criteria. They consisted of 200 schizophrenic, 100 manic, and 225 depressed patients. They were compared with a control group of 160 psychiatrically normal individuals admitted to the University of Iowa Hospital during the same period for appendectomy or herniography. Followup studies between 1972 and 1976 revealed that 30 of these 685 subjects subsequently committed suicide; 29 of the suicides were found among the 525 psychiatric patients and only 1 among the 160 normal controls (5.5 percent vs 0.6 percent) (30). This finding is impressive evidence for the close association of suicide with psychiatric disorder.

The Iowa-500 study has yielded other informative data (31) and Tsuang has recently reported the development of this study in another important direction. He and his associates not only followed up the psychiatric patients and controls but also their first degree relatives (32). The first degree relatives were interviewed, and Tsuang was interested in the answers to four questions which are relevant to the possible role of genetic factors in suicide. These questions were:

1. Are relatives of patients with schizophrenia and affective disorders subject to higher risk of suicide than relatives

Significances and relative odds ratios for the comparisons tested in subgroups of depressive attempters and non-attempters

	Comparison*					
	A		**B**		**C**	
	M	F	M	F	M	F
Significance of main effect**						
Polarity	n.s.	0.045	n.s.	n.s.	n.s.	0.021
Family history (FH +)	n.s.	0.004	n.s.	0.0003	0.010	0.010
Age	n.s.	n.s.	n.s.	n.s.	0.050	n.s.
Relative odds ratio***						
Polarity (BP vs UP)	0.65					2.43
Family history (FH + vs FH-)		2.02		3.53	14.96	2.68
Age, years						
31-45 vs 15-30					0.32	
46-60 vs 31-45					4.92	
>60 vs 46-60					2.19	
>60 vs 15-30					3.46	
No. of patients	260	453	260	453	66	173

*A) Presence versus absence of any suicidal attempts; B) violent versus non-violent attempt plus no suicidal attempt; C) violent versus non-violent attempts.
M = males; F = females
**All interactions between main effects (polarity x FH +, polarity x Age, and FH + x Age) non-significant.
***Given only for statistically significant main effects.
Reproduced with permission of Acta Psychiatrica Scandinavica

Table 7.

of nonpsychiatric control patients?

2. Are relatives of patients with schizophrenia and affective disorders who committed suicide subject to higher risks of suicide than relatives of patients who did not commit suicide?

3. Is the risk of suicide among relatives of schizophrenics different from that for relatives of manics and depressives?

4. Are the suicide risks different for male and female relatives of patients from different diagnostic categories?

The first degree relatives of the psychiatric patients were found to have a risk of suicide almost eight times greater than the risk in the relatives of the normal controls. When only deceased relatives were considered, the relatives of psychiatric patients were found to have a risk of suicide almost six times greater than the risk among the deceased relatives of the controls (Table 8).

Among the first degree relatives of the psychiatric patients, those who were the relative of one of the 29 patients in the Iowa-500 study who committed suicide themselves had a four times greater risk of committing suicide compared with the relatives of the patients who did not commit suicide. Among the deceased relatives, the suicide risk was three times greater (Table 9).

Next, the individual psychiatric diagnoses were examined. The risk of suicide was sig-

Risk of Suicide among Relatives of Patients and Controls					
				Relatives[a]	
		Suicides			
Subjects	N	N	%	BZ	MR(%) ± SE
Patients (N = 510)					
All relatives	3941	55	1.4	2348	2.3 ± 0.3[b]
Deceased relatives	2294	55	2.4	1338	4.1 ± 0.5[b]
Controls (N = 153)					
All relatives	1403	2	0.1	672	0.3 ± 0.2
Deceased relatives	589	2	0.3	305	0.7 ± 0.5

a. BZ = Bezugsziffer (age-adjusted size of the sample), MR = Morbidity risk.
b. P < .01 (comparison of patients with controls).
Reproduced with permission of Journal of Clinical Psychiatry

Table 8.

Risk of Suicide Among Relatives of Patients with and without Suicide					
				Relatives[a]	
		Suicides			
Subjects	N	N	%	BZ	MR(%) ± SE
Suicide (N = 29)					
All relatives	193	9	4.7	114	7.9 ± 2.5[a]
Deceased relatives	136	9	6.6	78	11.5 ± 3.6[a]
No suicide (N = 481)					
All relatives	3754	46	1.2	2234	2.1 ± 0.3
Deceased relatives	2158	46	2.1	1259	3./ ± 0.5

a. P < .05 (comparisons of suicide with no suicide).
Reproduced with permission of Journal of Clinical Psychiatry

Table 9.

nificantly greater among the first degree relatives of depressed patients than it was among the relatives of either schizophrenic or manic patients. When the relatives of patients who committed suicide were compared, the suicide risk was even higher, but it was equally high among the relatives of both depressed and manic patients (Table 10).

The suicide risk was also examined separately for the male and female relatives of the psychiatric patients. In general, the suicide risk was higher for male first degree relatives than it was for females (Table 11).

Thus, this followup of the first degree relatives of the subjects in the Iowa-500 study is

Risk of Suicide Among Living and Dead Relatives of Schizophrenics, Manics, and Depressives with Suicide and without Suicide.

Patients	Suicides			Relatives BZ	MR(%) ± SE
	N	N	%		
Schizophrenia (S)					
Suicide (N = 8)	41	0	0.0	23	0.0 ± 0.0
No Suicide (N = 187)	1159	9	0.8	723	1.2 ± 0.4
Total (N = 195)	1200	9	0.8	746	1.2 ± 0.4
Mania (M)					
Suicide (N = 6)	53	3	5.7	32	9.4 ± 5.2
No Suicide (N = 86)	748	4	0.5	426	0.9 ± 0.5
Total (N = 92)	801	7	0.9	458	1.5 ± 0.6
Depression (D)					
Suicide (N = 15)	99	6	6.1	59	10.2 ± 3.9
No Suicide (N = 208)	1847	33	1.8	1085	3.0 ± 0.5
Total (N = 223)	1946	39	2.0	1144	3.4 ± 0.5

Significant comparisons are as follows: Suicide, S vs M (P < .10), S vs D (P < .01); no suicide, S vs D (P < .01), M vs D (P < .01); and Total S vs D (P < .01), M vs D (P < .05).
Reproduced with permission of Journal of Clinical Psychiatry

Table 10.

Risk of Suicide Among Relatives of Schizophrenics, Manics, and Depressives by Sex

Diagnostic Group	Suicides			Relatives BZ	MR(%) ± SE
	N	N	%		
Schizophrenia					
Male relatives	601	9	1.5	359	2.5 ± 0.8[a]
Female relatives	590	0	0.0	394	0.0 ± 0.0
Mania					
Male relatives	395	5	1.3	221	2.3 ± 1.0
Female relatives	390	2	0.5	238	0.8 ± 0.6
Depression					
Male relatives	994	30	3.0	587	5.1 ± 0.9[a]
Female relatives	921	9	1.0	568	1.6 ± 0.5

a. P < .01 (comparison of males and females).
Reproduced with permission of Journal of Clinical Psychiatry

Table 11.

an important study and demonstrates that there are genetic factors in suicide. The main findings are summarized in Table 12.

TWIN STUDIES

Compelling evidence for the genetic transmission of manic-depression and schizophrenia is that the concordance rate for these psychiatric disorders is substantially higher among identical twins, who share the same genes, than it is among fraternal twins who share only 50 percent of their genes (22). Thus, if the propensity to commit suicide was genetically transmitted, concordance for suicide should be found more frequently among identical than fraternal twins. This was well stated by Kallman (23): "If hereditary factors play a decisive role we should find a concordant tendency to suicide more frequently in one-egg than in two-egg pairs regardless of ordinary differences in environment. If the main emphasis is placed on certain constellations of nongenetic factors, concordance should be expected in some twin pairs of either type, who shared the same environment and responded to a similar degree of distress with the same type of psychosis."

Kallman had collected 2,500 twin index cases from mental institutions, TB hospitals, old age homes, and other parts of the population of New York State. In 1947, he reported that among this clinical material, there were 11 twin pairs where one twin was known to have committed suicide. Three of these 11 twin pairs were monozygotic and 8 dizygotic. In none of these 11 twin pairs had the other twin committed suicide (24). This negative finding led him to conclude that "there is no statistical evidence for the popular notion that the tendency to commit suicide recurs in certain families as the result of a special hereditary trait or of a particular type of genetically determined personality deviation."

However, 20 years later in 1967, Haberlant (25,26) pooled the accumulated data from twin studies from different countries. By then, 149 sets of twins had been reported in which one twin was known to have committed suicide. Among these twin pairs there were nine sets of twins where both twins had committed suicide. All of these nine twin pairs were identical twins; there was no set of fraternal twins concordant for suicide (Table 13).

Four of these nine monozygotic twin sets concordant for suicide came from the Danish Psychiatric Twin Register and their case histories revealed that in three of them the twins were also concordant for manic-depressive disorder (27). In another of these nine monozygotic twin sets, the twins were also concordant for schizophrenia. Since Haberlandt's review, Zair (28) has reported a tenth pair of identical twins who both com-

	Summary of Morbidity Risks of Suicide in Patients and Relatives								
	Patients			**Relatives**			**Relatives of Suicides**		
Diagnostic Group	**N**	**BZ**	**MR%**	**N**	**BZ**	**MR%**	**N**	**BZ**	**MR%**
Schizophrenia	8	125	6.4	9	746	1.2	0	23	0.0
Mania	6	62	9.7	7	458	1.5	3	32	9.4
Depression	15	173	8.7	39	1144	3.4	6	59	10.2
Control	1	97	1.0	2	672	0.3	0	7	0.0

BZ = Benzugsziffer (age-adjusted size of the sample)
MR = Morbidity risk
Reproduced with permission of Journal of Clinical Psychiatry

Table 12.

mitted suicide. Again there was an association with affective disorder as both twins had killed themselves during a depressive episode and both their parents and a grandmother had also been treated for depression.

Approximately 1 in 250 live births is an identical twin and between 0.5 and 1 percent of all deaths among the general population are due to suicide. Thus, it is somewhat surprising that only 10 pairs of monozygotic twins concordant for suicide have been reported in the 173 years since the first report of suicide in twins (29). Also, in 5 of these 10 twin pairs, the twins were also concordant for either depression or schizophrenia. Thus, although twin data provide evidence for the genetic transmission of suicide, this evidence may be partly confounded by the issue of the genetic transmission of psychiatric disorders themselves.

Suicide in Twins		
Type of twins	Number of twin pairs	Number of twin pairs where both twins committed suicide (%)
Identical	51	9* (17.7%)
Fraternal	98	0 (0%)

P <0.0001
* Four of these 9 sets of twins have been reported twice. They are included in Haberlant's 1967 review (26) and have also been reported in detail in 1970 by Juel-Nielsen and Videbech. (27)
Reproduced with permission of Diseases of the Nervous System (22)

Table 13.

THE AMISH STUDY

In 1985 Egeland and Sussex (33) made their first report on the suicide data obtained from the study of affective disorders among the Old Order Amish community of Lancaster County in southeastern Pennsylvania. This is a continuing study into the genetics and course of illness of the affective disorders among this population (34). Suicide research among the Amish is of great interest

for several reasons. They are an Anabaptist, nonviolent, pacifist society where there are no violent crimes and where there has been no known murder. Alcohol is prohibited and there is no alcoholism. Also, the Amish are a wealthy farming community among whom there is no unemployment. Their strong religious beliefs foster a tightly knit community, and three generations commonly live together under the same roof. Family life is valued and divorce precluded. Social isolation is rare and the cohesive nature of their community offers social support for individuals who encounter stress or adverse life events. Thus, several of the important social risk factors for suicide among individuals in the general population such as unemployment, divorced or separated marital status, social isolation, and alcoholism are risk factors not commonly found among these Amish (35-38). This means that genetic factors for suicide may play a larger part in suicides occurring among the Amish.

Not surprisingly, suicide is a relatively rare event among this group of Amish. In fact Egeland and Sussex were only able to find 26 suicides over the 100 years from 1880 to 1980. Over these 100 years the suicide rates among these Amish have consistently been substantially lower than the rates for the rest of the United States.

Egeland and Sussex's team used the Schedule for Affective Disorders and Schizophrenia-Lifetime Version (SADS-L). They conducted an average of six interviews, with various family members, for each of the 26 suicide victims. A five-member psychiatric board used the Research Diagnostic Criteria (RDC) to make psychiatric diagnoses based on these interviews and supplemented by information from other sources. The first important finding of the study was that 24 of the 26 suicide victims met RDC criteria for a major affective disorder. Eight had bipolar I, four bipolar II, and 12 unipolar affective disorder. A further case met the diagnostic criteria for a minor depression. Furthermore, most of the suicide victims had a heavy family loading for affective disorders.

For example, among the eight bipolar I suicide victims the morbidity risk for affective disorders among their 110 first degree relatives was 29 percent compared with the 1 to 4 percent found among the general population.

The second finding of the study was that almost three quarters of the 26 suicide victims were found to cluster in four family pedigrees, each of which contained a heavy loading for affective disorders and suicide. Figure 1 shows a very heavy loading for affective disorders in one family where there have been seven suicides. All seven suicide victims were found among individuals with definite affective disorder. Figure 2 shows a second pedigree, also with a heavy loading for affective disorders, where there have been six suicides, five of which were found among individuals with definite affective dis-

order.

Interestingly, the converse was not true as there were other family pedigrees with heavy loadings for affective disorder but without suicides. It is also of note that the morbidity risk for affective disorders among 170 first degree relatives in other bipolar I pedigrees without suicide was, similar to that found in bipolar pedigrees with suicide, also in the 20 percent range. Thus, in this study, a familial loading for affective disorders was not in itself a predictor for suicide.

The third finding of the study was that only six of the 26 suicide victims (23 percent) had received any psychiatric treatment despite the fact that 24 of them had severe affective disorders whose natural history is usually that of recurrent episodes. The other 20 suicide victims had either never received any medi-

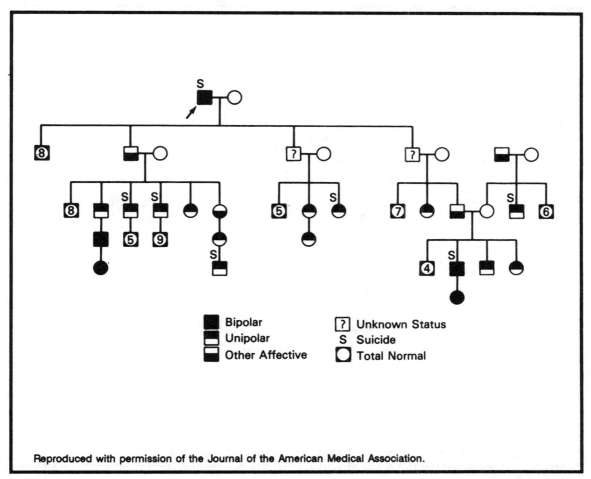

Figure 1.

cal treatment for their psychiatric disorder, or they were seeing a family doctor at the time they committed suicide, or they were planning to seek help for themselves.

Egeland and Sussex concluded: "Our study replicates findings that indicate an increased suicidal risk for patients with a diagnosis of major affective disorder and a strong family history of suicide." They also noted: "Bipolar and unipolar illness conveying a high risk as a diagnostic pattern in pedigrees. The number not receiving adequate treatment for manic-depressive illness (among the suicides) supports the common belief that intervention for these patients at risk is recommended. It appears most warranted in those families in which there is a family history of suicide. The clustering of suicides in Amish pedigrees follows the distribution of affective illness in the kinship and suggests the role of inheritance."

DANISH-AMERICAN ADOPTION STUDIES

The strongest evidence that we have for the presence of genetic factors in suicide comes from the adoption studies carried out in Denmark by Schulsinger, Kety, Wender, and Rosenthal (39-41). The strength of the adoption strategy is that it is one of the best ways to tease apart "nature" from "nurture" issues. This is because individuals separated at birth, or shortly afterwards, share their genes, but no subsequent environmental experiences, with their biological relatives. In contrast, adoptees share their environmental experiences through childhood and adolescence with their adopting relatives but they

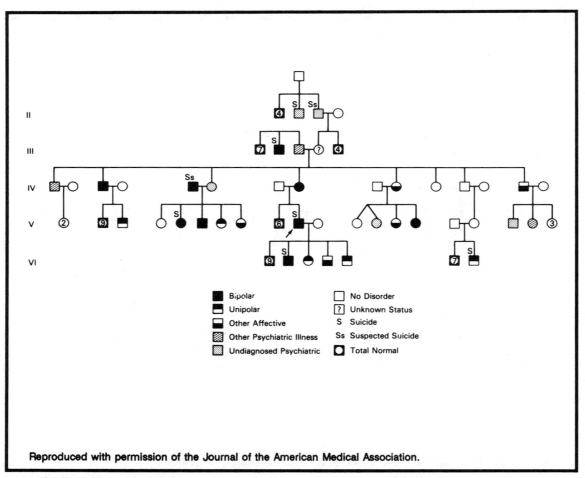

Reproduced with permission of the Journal of the American Medical Association.

Figure 2.

242

share no genes with them.

The Psykologisk Institut has a register of the 5,483 adoptions that occurred in greater Copenhagen between 1924 and 1947. A screening of the registers of causes of death revealed that 57 of these adoptees eventually committed suicide. They were matched with adopted controls for sex, age, social class of the adopting parents, and time spent both with their biological relatives and in institutions before being adopted. Searches of the causes of death revealed that 12 of the 269 biological relatives of these 57 adopted suicides had themselves committed suicide compared with only 2 of the 269 biological relatives of the 57 adopted controls. This is a highly significant difference for suicide between the two groups of relatives (Table 14). None of the adopting relatives of either the suicide or control group had committed suicide.

Also, these striking results are of additional interest because the suicides were largely independent of the presence of psychiatric disorder. Schulsinger and coworkers also investigated whether or not the names of the 12 biological relatives who committed suicide appeared on the psychiatric case registers. They found that 6 of these biological suicide relatives had had no contact with the psychiatric services and thus presumably did not suffer from one of the major psychiatric disorders commonly found among suicide victims--manic-depression, schizophrenia, or

alcoholism--as these are chronic disorders with frequent relapses usually requiring psychiatric hospitalization. Schulsinger et al. (39) therefore proposed that there may be a genetic predisposition for suicide independent of, or additive to, the major psychiatric disorders associated with suicide.

Wender et al. (41,42) went on to study another group of the Danish adoptees. These were the 71 adoptees identified by the psychiatric case register as having suffered from an affective disorder. They were matched with 71 control adoptees without affective disorder. The results of this study showed that significantly more of these adoptees with affective disorder, than their controls, had committed suicide. Thus this study, too, demonstrates that there is a genetic component to suicide (Table 15).

Of further interest in this study was the examination of the adoptee suicide victims and their biological relatives by the type of affective disorder suffered by the suicide victim. It was particularly adoptee suicide victims with the diagnosis of "affect reaction" who had significantly more biological relatives who had committed suicide than controls. The diagnosis of "affect reaction" is used in Denmark to describe an individual who has affective symptoms accompanying a situational crisis--often an impulsive suicide attempt (Table 16). These findings led Kety (42) to suggest that a genetic factor in suicide may be an inability to control impulsive behavior which

Incidence of Suicide in the Relatives of Adoptees Who Committed Suicide and Their Controls				
Adoptees	Biological Relatives		Adoptive Relatives	
57 adoptees died by suicide	12/269	(4.5%)	0/148	(0%)
57 matched control adoptees	2/269	(0.7%)	0/150	(0%)

P < 0.01
Reproduced with permission of Williams and Wilkins

Table 14.

Incidence of Suicide in the Relatives of Adoptees Who Have Suffered a Depressive Illness and Their Controls				
Adoptees	Biological Relatives		Adoptive Relatives	
71 adoptees with depression	15/407	(3./%)	1/187	(0.5%)
71 matched control adoptees	1/360	(0.3%)	2/171	(0%)

P < 0.01
Published with permission of Williams and Wilkins

Table 15.

has its effect independently of, or additively to, psychiatric disorder. Psychiatric disorder, or environmental stress, may serve "as potentiating mechanisms which foster or trigger the impulsive behavior, directing it toward a suicidal outcome (42)."

Kety (42) also noted that there has been much recent work on the biology of impulsivity and that disturbances in central serotonin systems have been described in relation to suicidal behavior in personality disordered individuals and in patients with various other psychiatric disorders (reviewed in this volume by Asberg). In this regard it is noteworthy that Buchsbaum et al. (44) found that significantly more college students with low levels of the enzyme monoamine oxidase (MAO) in their blood platelets had a family history of suicidal behavior compared with students with high platelet MAO levels. This enzyme is involved with the metabolism of serotonin. Furthermore, as there is some evidence that lithium may be useful in impulsive and aggressive individuals (43), Kety (42) also suggested that controlled trials of drugs acting on central serotonin system might be informative among patients who exhibit suicidal behaviors.

SUMMARY

Suicide, like so much else in psychiatry, tends to run in families. The question is what is being transmitted. No doubt in some youthful suicide victims what is transmitted is not a genetic factor but a psychological factor. The family member who has committed suicide may serve as a role model to identify with, and the option of committing suicide becomes one possible "solution" to intolerable psychological pain. However, the family, twin, and adoption studies reviewed here show that there are genetic factors in suicide. In many suicide victims, these will be genetic factors involved in the genetic transmission of manic depression, schizophrenia, and alcoholism--the psychiatric disorders most commonly associated with suicide. However, the Copenhagen adoption studies strongly suggest there may be a genetic factor for suicide independent of, or additive to, the genetic transmission of psychiatric disorder. Interestingly, support for this possibility comes from the recent Amish studies, which showed that suicide was much more likely to occur when an individual had genetic vulnerabilities to both suicide and to affective

Incidence of suicide in the biological relatives of depressive and control adoptees		
Diagnosis in Adoptee	Incidence of suicide in biological relatives	Significance
Affective reaction	$\frac{5}{66}$ (7.6%)	P <0.0004*
Neurotic depression	$\frac{3}{127}$ (2.4%)	P <0.056
Bipolar depression	$\frac{4}{75}$ (5.3%)	P <0.0036
Unipolar depression	$\frac{3}{139}$ (2.2%)	P <0.06/
No mental illness	$\frac{1}{360}$ (0.3%)	

* compared with biological relatives of control adoptees with no known history of mental illness
Reproduced with permission of Williams and Wilkins

Table 16.

illness.

There is a possible practical implication for the prevention of youth suicide arising from this review. It is that an adolescent who develops a depressive episode, or who exhibits suicidal behavior, and who has a family history of suicide might be considered to be at risk of committing suicide. Such an individual might, therefore, be more closely assessed and followed, particularly with a view to determining whether he is developing a recurrent affective disorder for which psychopharmacological intervention might be appropriate.

REFERENCES

1. Shaffer D: Suicide in childhood and early adolescence. J Child Psychol Psychiatry, 1974;5:275-291.

2. Tishler C, McKenry P, Morgan K: Adolescent suicide attempts: Some significant factors. Suicide Life Threat Behav, 1981;11:86-92.

3. Garfinkel B, Froese A, Hood J: Suicide attempts in children and adolescents. Am J Psychiatry, 1982;139:1257-1261.

4. Weissman A, Worden J: Risk-rescue rating in suicide assessment. Arch Gen Psychiatry, 1972;26:553-560.

5. Shafii M, Carrigan S, Whittinghill R, Derrick A: Psychological autopsy of completed suicides in children and adolescents. Am J Psychiatry, 1985;142:1061-1064.

6. Shaffer D, Gould M, Traubman P: Suicidal behavior in children and young adults. Paper presented at the Conference on Psychobiology of Suicidal Behavior, New York Academy of Sciences, New York, September 1985.

7. Shaffer D: Quoted in Clinical Psychiatry News, 1985.

8. Robins E, Schmidt E, O'Neal P: Some interrelations of social factors and clinical diagnosis in attempted suicide. Am J Psychiatry, 1957;114:221-231.

9. Murphy G, Wetzel R, Swallow C, McClure J: Who calls the suicide prevention center: A study of 55 persons calling on their own behalf. Am J Psychiatry, 1969;126:314-324.

10. Flinn D, Leonard C: Prevalence of suicidal ideation and behavior among basic trainees and college students. Milit Med, 1972;137:317-320.

11. Murphy G, Wetzel R: Family history of suicidal behavior among suicide attempters. J Nerv Ment Dis, 1982;170:86-90.

12. Pitts F, Winokur F: Affective disorder. Part 3 (Diagnostic correlates and incidence of suicide). J Nerv Ment Dis, 1964;139:176-181.

13. Roy A: Family history of suicide. Arch Gen Psychiatry, 1983;40:971-974.

14. Linkowski P, Maertelaer de V, Mendlewicz J: Suicidal behavior in major depressive illness. Acta Psychiatr Scand, 1985;72:233-238.

15. Farberow N, Simon M: Suicide in Los Angeles and Vienna: An intercultural study of two cities. Public Health Rep, 1969;84:389-403.

16. Roy A: Risk factors for suicide in psychiatric patients. Arch Gen Psychiatry, 1982;39:1089-1095.

17. Roy A: Genetics of suicide. Psychobiology of suicidal behavior. Annals New York Academy of Science, 1986; in press.

18. Roy A: Family history of suicide in affective disorder patients. J Clin Psychiatry, 1985;46:317-319.

19. Roy A: Family history of suicide in manic-depressive patients. J Affect Disorders, 1985;8:187-189.

20. Roy A: Genetic factors in suicide. Psychopharm Bull, 1986; in press.

21. Batchelor I, Napier M: Attempted suicide in old age. Br Med J, 1953;2:1186-1190.

22. Tsuang M: Genetic factors in suicide, Dis Nerv Syst, 1977;38:498-501.

23. Kallman F, Anastasio M: Twin studies on the psychopathology of suicide. J Nerv Ment Dis, 1947;105:40-55.

24. Kallman F, DePorte J, DePorte E, Feingold L: Suicide in twins and only children. Am J Human Genetics, 1949;2:113-126.

25. Haberlandt W: Der suizid als genetisches problem (zwillings und familien analyse). Anthrop Anz, 1965;29:65-89.

26. Haberlandt W: Aportacion a la genetica del suicido. Folia Clin Int, 1967;17:319-322.

27. Juel-Nielsen N, Videbech T: A twin study of suicide. Acta Genet Med Gemellol, 1970;19:307-310.

28. Zaw K: A suicidal family. Br J Psychiatry, 1981;189:68-69.

29. Williams S: Cit Lowenberg, 1941;1918.

30. Tsuang MT: Suicide in schizophrenia, manics, depressives, and surgical controls: A comparison with general population suicide mortality. Arch Gen Psychiatry, 1978;35:153-155.

31. Tsuang MT, Woolson RF: Excess mortality in schizophrenia and affective disorders: Do suicides and accidental deaths solely account for this excess? Arch Gen Psychiatry, 1978;35:1181-1185.

32. Tsuang MT: Risk of suicide in the relatives of schizophrenics, manics, depressives, and controls. J Clin Psychiatry, 1983;44:396-400.

33. Egeland J, Sussex J: Suicide and family loading for affective disorders. JAMA; 1985;254:915-918.

34. Egeland JA, Hostetter AM: Amish study: I. Affective disorders among the Amish, 1976-1980. Am J Psychiatry 1983;140:56-61.

35. Robins E, Murphy G, Wilkinson R, Gassner S, Kays J: Some clinical observations in the prevention of suicide based on a study of 134 successful suicides. Am J Public Health, 1959;49:888-889.

36. Dorpat T, Ripley H: A study of suicide in the Seattle area. Compr Psychiatry, 1960;1:349-359.

37. Barraclough B, Bunch J, Nelson B, Sainsbury P: A hundred cases of suicide. Clinical Aspects Br J Psychiatry, 1974;125:355-373.

38. Murphy G, Robins E: Social factors in suicide. JAMA, 1967;199:303-308.

39. Schulsinger R, Kety S, Rosenthal D, Wender P: A family study of suicide. In Origins, Prevention and Treatment of Affective Disorders. M. Schou & E. Stromgren (eds). 277-287 Academic Press Inc. New York.

40. Schulsinger F, Kety S, Rosenthal D, Wender P: 1981. A family study of suicide. Paper presented at the Third World Congress of Biological Psychiatry, Stockholm, Sweden.

41. Wender P, Kety S, Schulsinger F: Arch Gen Psychiat (in press).

42. Kety S: Genetic Factors in Suicide. Chapter in Suicide. A. Roy (ed). 1986, Williams and Wilkins, Baltimore.

43. Shard M, Marini J, Bridges C, Wagner E: The effect of lithium on impulsive aggressive behavior in man. Am J Psychiatry, 1976;133:1409-1413.

44. Buchsbaum M, Coursey R, Murphy D: The biochemical high-risk paradigm: Behavioral and familial correlates of low platelet monoamine oxidase activity. Science, 1976;339-341.

SUMMARY AND OVERVIEW OF RISK FACTORS IN SUICIDE

*Frederick K. Goodwin, M.D., Scientific Director, National Institute of Mental Health,
NIH Clinical Center, Bethesda, Maryland*

*Gerald L. Brown, M.D., Senior Investigator, Biological Psychiatry Branch, Intramural
Research Program, National Institute of Mental Health, Bethesda, Maryland*

INTRODUCTION

This conference brings together two independent traditions in the study of suicide--the psychosocial and the psychiatric-biomedical. Although we focus here primarily on potential biological risk factors, we also highlight opportunities for interdisciplinary cooperation that could enhance scientific understanding and lead to improvements in treatment and prevention. The educational efforts that we hope will grow from this conference should, wherever possible, be based on firmly established knowledge, rather than simply belief systems--however compelling they may seem. Much of the apparent disparity among the different schools of thought represented at this conference might be due to the fact that different approaches focus on different populations. By and large, psychosocial studies have focused on individuals with suicidal ideation who contact suicide prevention programs, whereas the psychiatric-biomedical studies have focused on actual suicides or major suicide attempts, largely among individuals with a major psychiatric diagnosis.

Biological investigations of suicidal behavior have been most active in the following areas of study: brain chemistry as measured through cerebrospinal fluid (CSF); postmortem analyses of tissues from individuals who

have committed suicide; neuroendocrine correlates; and genetics. Each of these subjects has been well reviewed by the previous authors, Asberg (1), Stanley (2), Meltzer (3), and Roy and Kety (4). Rather than covering the same ground again, we will briefly summarize these excellent reviews and then add some comments of our own.

CSF BIOCHEMICAL STUDIES

Asberg reports that several studies have found an increased rate of suicide attempts in psychiatric patients with low CSF concentrations of the serotonin metabolite, 5-hydroxyindoleacetic acid (5-HIAA). Many of the study populations were depressed patients, but similar studies involving populations with other psychiatric diagnoses, such as personality disorders (5,6) and schizophrenia (7,8), suggest that the association between low levels of CSF 5-HIAA and suicide is not confined to depression. The association may not, however, be present in manic-depressive patients.

Asberg notes that evidence to date also suggests that low concentrations of CSF homovanillic acid (HVA), a metabolite of dopamine, are associated with suicide attempts in depressed patients. This association has not been found in other psychiatric populations.

Asberg points out that CSF metabolites are only indirect measures of amine turnover in the brain. She notes some confounding influences on such measures--age, sex, body height, concentration gradient, circadian and seasonal rhythms, drug effects, medical diseases, diet, and physical activity. Methodological problems include lumbar-puncture location and subject position, amount of CSF drawn, handling and storage, assay methods, and within-subject stability of CSF 5-HIAA. Despite these problems, the biochemical methodology is elegant compared to measures of suicidal behavior. Among problematic methodological factors Asberg notes, is the lack of clear definitions of **suicide attempt** in most studies and the assumption made in "life history" measure-

ments of behavior that biological systems remain stable over time.

Asberg characterizes low CSF 5-HIAA as an indicator of vulnerability rather than as a marker of the **state** of depression. She cites longitudinal CSF studies as well as genetic evidence in support of this conclusion.

The mechanisms by which serotonin function influences suicidal behavior are unknown, but Asberg points out that some evidence links impulsivity and difficulties in handling aggression to suicide attempts. Formulations of such a link come from animal studies, classical psychoanalytic observations, and behavioral and biochemical studies in clinical populations.

Asberg suggests that including lumbar punctures to obtain CSF is a reasonable part of the clinical assessment in some psychiatric patients. In conclusion, she proposes a

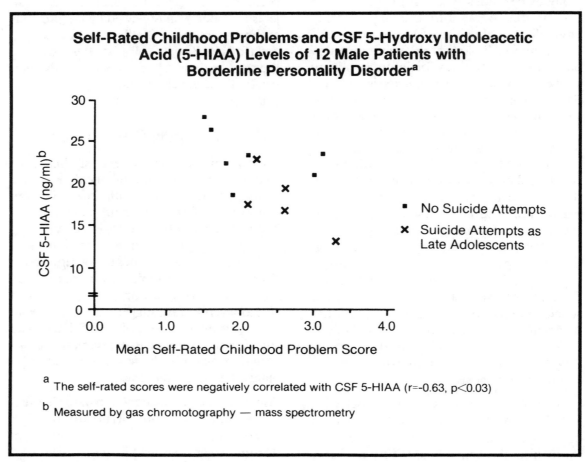

Self-Rated Childhood Problems and CSF 5-Hydroxy Indoleacetic Acid (5-HIAA) Levels of 12 Male Patients with Borderline Personality Disorder[a]

■ No Suicide Attempts

✕ Suicide Attempts as Late Adolescents

Mean Self-Rated Childhood Problem Score

CSF 5-HIAA (ng/ml)[b]

[a] The self-rated scores were negatively correlated with CSF 5-HIAA ($r=-0.63$, $p<0.03$)

[b] Measured by gas chromotography — mass spectrometry

Figure 1.

model of interaction between biological vulnerability and psychiatric symptoms (e.g., depression), psychological factors, adverse environmental occurrences, and childhood history.

Of most interest to us is the factor that implies a **trait**, a relatively stable characteristic that changes little, if at all, with clinical condition, in contrast to the factor that changes with clinical **state**. Our data (5,6,9) show that young adults with a history of aggressive and impulsive behavior (including a childhood history) have low levels of CSF 5-HIAA. Such evidence suggests that these behaviors reflect, in part, certain trait characteristics, which may be relatively independent of changing environments and personal relationships. More ambiguous are data linking CSF 5-HIAA levels to Asberg's categories of nonviolent and violent suicide, the latter usually associated with the lowest levels of CSF 5-HIAA. Is the violent behavior a reflection of an isolated **state** or is it one episode in a long-time history of similar behavior, not all of which may have been self-destructive or suicidal?

Some studies indicate that young children have higher levels of CSF 5-HIAA than do adults. It is unclear whether this difference relates to the observations that serious suicidal behaviors are more common in adults and adolescents than in young children. In our replication study, young adults and late adolescents with the lowest levels of CSF 5-HIAA had childhood histories that included many affective-impulsive symptoms, but no reported incidence of childhood suicidal attempts. (Figure 1)

POSTMORTEM STUDIES

Stanley reviews postmortem studies of biogenic amines, their metabolites and enzymes, and receptor binding. He points out that available information indicates that suicide victims are diagnostically heterogenous, so that differences in neurochemistry found at autopsy may be more related to suicidal behavior than to depression per se. He also cautions that none of the postmortem studies he reviews focus on youth.

Postmortem enzyme studies of suicide reveal no consistent patterns. Stanley's own group found no differences between suicidal subjects and controls in either the A or B forms of monoamine oxidase (MAO). Previous findings of lowered brain MAO activity among suicide victims may have been related to alcoholism.

Earlier studies of serotonin and its metabolite 5-HIAA generally found decreased levels in subcortical nuclei, including the hypothalamus and parts of the brain stem. Some of the variability in these studies is undoubtedly due to confounding variables, such as manner of death (e.g., drug overdose), and the extent of delay between death and autopsy ("postmortem interval").

Receptor-binding studies may be less influenced by these variables. Stanley's group controlled for age, sex, and postmortem interval, as well as the manner of death, which in each case was sudden and violent. They found significantly fewer imipramine-binding sites in the frontal cortex of suicide victims, a finding consistent with the association between suicide and low central serotonin function since imipramine binding is a marker for presynaptic serotonin nerve terminals. Of the four other imipramine-binding studies published, three have replicated the findings of Stanley and his colleagues. However, generalizing from these results in adults to suicide in the young is risky because some relevant neurochemical measures, such as imipramine binding, are known to be influenced by age. Thus, Stanley's call for studies of young people, both normal controls and suicide victims, is well taken. He points to the need for better diagnostic information and greater specificity in reporting related aggressive, violent, and impulsive behavior. He closes by suggesting a behavioral-biochemical profile to help clinicians identify patients at high risk for suicide.

Issues that seem important to us include the fact that subjects in most postmortem studies of serotonin (5-HT) and its metabolite (5-HIAA) are predominantly depressed patients. None of the reports indicate any attempt to determine a history of aggressive behaviors. This absence of data on aggressive-impulsive behavior in completed suicides seems especially to highlight the importance of collecting careful psychological autopsy data in conjunction with the biological assessments in postmortem studies.

A curious discrepancy is apparent in this literature. The lowered 5-HT functioning in the frontal cortex suggested by receptor studies has not been subjected to postmortem analysis, which is so aptly suited to anatomical localization. Older studies have, however, shown lower levels of 5-HT and/or 5-HIAA in the midbrain-brainstem area, the nucleus acumbens, and hypothalamic area, the latter of which has also been shown to have increased 5-HT presynaptic receptor changes (10,11,12). These apparent inconsistencies may be clarified as postmortem and receptor studies move beyond the preliminary stage. Catecholamine neurotransmitter-metabolite studies are not consistent and relevant receptor data are lacking; the same can be said for the cholinergic systems.

NEUROENDOCRINE STUDIES

A link between suicide and hormonal functioning is strongly suggested by the suicidal behavior of individuals with endocrinopathies, particularly Cushing's syndrome. In his review of endocrine abnormalities in suicide, Meltzer suggests that they may serve as weak markers for suicide, but further research is more likely to show their role in influencing neurotransmission, which in turn may be more directly associated with causal factors.

Although urinary corticosteroids were the original biological variable associated specifically with suicidal behavior (13), plasma and CSF studies are still too few to warrant any conclusion. An association between dexamethasone suppression test (DST) non-suppression and suicidal behavior seemed to be positive in earlier studies, but more recent studies bring this association into question. Some earlier indications that the administration of the test dose of dexamethasone might increase the risk of suicidal behavior seem not to be borne out in the more recent analyses.

Meltzer discusses new work on glucocorticoid-receptor-resistance (GCCR) studies. In an earlier report, he indicated that the plasma 5-hydroxytryptophan (5-HTP)-induced cortisol response was negatively correlated with CSF 5-HIAA; such a correlation might link the urinary and plasma cortisol findings with CSF 5-HIAA in suicidal patients. In ongoing studies of patients with major affective disorders, the elevated cortisol response to 5-HTP seems particularly linked to a history of violent suicide attempts.

Early studies in patients with histories of violent suicidal attempts showed a blunted thyroid-stimulated-hormone (TSH) response to thyrotropin-releasing hormone (TRH); more recent work, including some of Meltzer's, does not always confirm the early reports, however. Evidence that the TSH response is negatively related to CSF 5-HIAA is consistent with a relationship between low levels of brain serotonin and suicidal ideation, which had been shown to be positively related to the TSH response.

It seems particularly important to us that continued efforts be made to integrate the neuroendocrine and the 5-HT data. Animal studies indicate that increased plasma cortisol decreases 5-HT synthesis in the CNS via activation of liver tryptophan hydroxylase, which shifts peripheral tryptophan to the kynurenine pathway from its availability to the CNS for 5-HT synthesis (14). Humans with carcinoid syndrome (5-HT-secreting tumors in the small intestine) are often depressed, insomniac, and irritable, if not overtly aggressive; they may have a decreased 5-HT synthesis in the CNS secondary to decreased availability of the precursor, tryptophan. If so, the treatment of these patients with para-chlorophenylalanine (PCPA), a 5-HT synthesis inhibitor that crosses the blood-brain barrier (12), might be expected to worsen their CNS symptoms, as has been reported (15,16).

GENETIC STUDIES

Roy and Kety point out that suicidal behavior and depression are common in first-degree relatives of children and adolescents who commit suicide--both before and after the suicide. A significantly higher rate of psychiatric illness has also been found. In his ongoing study, Shaffer has found that 38 percent of suicidal adolescents have a family history of suicide. Increased incidence of suicidal behavior has also been shown in relatives of suicidal adults; a recent, controlled study found that among 127 patients admitted to a hospital following suicide attempts, 24 percent gave a family history of suicide attempts. Psychiatric diagnoses commonly associated with a family history of suicide are personality disorders and affective illness, especially manic-depressive illness.

The familial association with suicidal behavior is clear enough, but it begs the question of its source--in psychosocial or biomedical-genetic factors or some combination of them. First one must know what is transmitted: is it suicide per se, a vulnerable personality (i.e., aggressive/impulsive), or an illness (i.e., affective disorder)? Secondly, one must know whether proneness to suicide is transmitted genetically or environmentally through learning.

Twin and adoption studies address both of these questions. Evidence from all the twin studies together appears to show a genetic vulnerability both toward suicidal behavior and severe mental illness.

The Danish adoption study provides especially strong evidence for a genetic factor in suicide, and further, the data indicate that this genetic vulnerability to suicide can be inherited independently of overt psychiatric illness. Among the adoptees who committed suicide, half had a major psychiatric illness among their biological first-degree relatives; the remainder had family histories of suicide without a major psychiatric diagnosis but often with a history of aggressive/impulsive symptoms. Psychiatric and/or suicidal histories were virtually absent among the adoptive families or their relatives. The Amish study has shown that a heavy loading for affective disorder and for suicide can be somewhat independent of each other.

It seems to us particularly important to pursue the identification or clarification or possible biological differences within special families or populations with known, epidemiologically characterized behavioral vulnerabilities. An example of such work is the ongoing attempt to clarify how chromosome 11 may be related to the occurrence of affective disorders (and possibly to suicidal behavior) in the Amish population, and whether this finding can be characterized in other populations. Clearly, genetic factors are involved in suicidal behavior, but that is not to say that environmental (learning) factors are not operating.

RESEARCH STRATEGIES

Before proposing research strategies, we will briefly summarize the five categories of risk factors that ought to be considered.

Behavior

Longitudinal history from childhood to the present. As noted above, not only does a history of aggressive and impulsive behavior seem to be associated with vulnerability to suicide, but affective or impulsive symptoms in childhood are related to low levels of CSF 5-HIAA in adolescence, which in turn is associated with increased suicidal behavior. In addition, differences in drug states may be relevant to behavioral predispositions. The natural history of an illness should also be taken into account; for example, manic-depressive illness--a condition with a high risk for suicide--has been hypothesized to begin when a genetic vulnerability interacts with an environmental stressor, and once such an interaction begins, it takes on a life of its own, eventually requiring little environmental stress to produce recurrences.

Aggression history. The single best predictor for aggressive behavior is a history of such behavior, just as the best single predictor for suicidal behavior is a history of it (17,18).

Family History

The data reviewed here make a strong case for the importance of assessing family history of both suicidal and aggressive-impulsive-violent behaviors as well as of psychiatric illnesses.

Psychiatric History and Diagnoses

The evidence further argues for determining whether a psychiatric illness is present in individuals who are prone to self-destructive behavior. Indeed, the number of individuals who actually kill themselves in the absence of a psychiatric illness would appear quite low. As noted earlier, the psychosocial focus of the suicide prevention movement has primarily derived its experience from working with people who threaten or attempt suicide, while the clinical-medical focus on suicide as an integral part of major psychiatric illness has primarily derived its experience from working with patients with completed or nearly completed suicide. Although the domains of attempters and completers do overlap somewhat, by and large they represent different populations (19). The major affective illnesses, particularly manic-depressive illness, alcoholism, schizophrenia, and other psychoses all have substantially higher associations with suicidal behavior than one would expect for a normal population. Individuals suffering from these major psychiatric disturbances make up the majority of completed suicides. To this we can now add that the risk is increased when one of these disorders occurs in an individual with aggressive/impulsive "personality" traits. On a practical level, a proper diagnosis can lead to appropriate treatment for the specific

disorder, and indeed we believe that this will turn out to be the single best approach to preventing actual suicides.

Medical History

The presence of a major medical illness is a risk factor for suicide. In addition, some specific medical disorders have been associated with a higher incidence of suicidal or aggressive behavior. Most are associated with disturbances in corticosteroid or serotonin metabolism. They include:

- Endocrinopathies, particularly Cushing's syndrome (corticosteroids).
- Metabolic disorders, i.e., carcinoid syndrome (serotonin), Lesch-Nyhan syndrome (serotonin alteration and aggressive behavior (20), incidence of suicide is unknown).
- Neurological disorders, i.e., Parkinson's disease (21,22) and epilepsy (low CSF 5-HIAA) (23,24) and Gilles de la Tourette syndrome (sometimes associated with low CSF 5-HIAA and, often, aggressive behavior (25), but incidence of suicide in unknown).

Biological Parameters

In the future, we should do studies to clarify the seasonality of suicide (26), receptor studies *in vivo*, controlled pharmacological studies of suicidal and aggressive behaviors, and seriously consider doing lumbar punctures as part of the psychiatric assessment in some patients. Very few of such studies are being done now. The development of a clinical-risk profile for suicidal behavior might be very useful to clinicians. An important and unanswered clinical-scientific question related to the biological factors that may contribute to the high incidence of suicide in manic-depressive illness, given the fact that the association between low levels of the serotonin metabolite and a history of suicide, consistent across a wide variety of disorders, does not hold for manic-depressive patients. Nevertheless, the tripartite relationship between suicide, aggression, and affective illness remains an important cornerstone on which to build further understanding. (Figure 2)

One of our stated goals in the introduction was to promote and foster interdisciplinary collaboration and mutual cooperation in the pursuit of scientific knowledge in the service of public health. Some of the areas of research most likely to support such a goal include:

- Genetic research, especially of special populations (e.g., Amish, Indians, Greenlanders, Hungarians), offers opportunities for further dissection of genetic and environmental factors.

- Much could be gained from pursuing psychological-autopsy data with the same methodological vigor that has been applied to the biological postmortem studies. In such studies we need to assign as much importance to measures of "personality" dimensions as we do to formal psychiatric diagnoses. In this regard, we should evaluate the relationship between formal psychiatric profiles--e.g., sensation-seeking (27)--and relevant biological measures.

- Longitudinal studies are particularly important if we are to tease apart whether some behaviors are strongly dependent upon an environmental stimulus or whether some individuals tend to repeat the same kinds of behaviors independent of a particular environment. The state vs. trait issues cannot be confidently elaborated without such studies.

- Powerful statistical methods should follow well thoughtout hypotheses rather than blindly applied in the hope of uncovering significant associations among large samples. When such findings do occur, they must be replicated with a fresh sample.

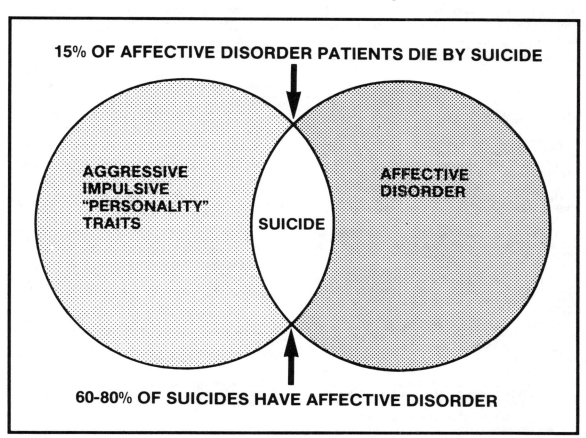

Figure 2.

- Few studies have examined the importance of drug states as predispositions to suicidal behavior.

SUMMARY

Certain principles should underlie our attempts to make a significant and meaningful difference in dealing with the major public health problem of suicidal behavior, particularly in youth. Recommendations receiving the highest priority should be based on sound, scientific data. Second priority should be assigned to activities that will promote the development of needed data (e.g., well-controlled epidemiological studies). For services, the highest priority should go to programs that provide direct treatment to high-risk individuals--those with a psychiatric or medical disorder known to be associated with a high rate of completed suicide (as distinct from suicidal ideation), those who have made previous suicidal attempts, and those with a strong family history of suicidal behavior. Obviously, preference must be given to treatments for which efficacy is based on actual data, rather than impressions or hopes.

REFERENCES

1. Asberg M: Neurotransmitter metabolites in CSF. In: The Report of the Secretary's Task Force on Youth Suicide (DHHS). Government Printing Office, Washington, D.C. 1987.

2. Stanley M: Post-mortem studies of suicide. In: The Report of the Secretary's Task Force on Youth Suicide (DHHS). Government Printing Office, Washington, D.C. 1987.

3. Meltzer HY, Lowry MT: The neuroendocrine system and suicide. In: The Report of the Secretary's Task Force on Youth Suicide (DHHS). Government Printing Office, Washington, D.C. 1987.

4. Roy A, Kety S: Genetics and suicidal behavior. In: The Report of the Secretary's Task Force on Youth Suicide (DHHS). Government Printing Office, Washington, D.C. 1987.

5. Brown GL, Goodwin FK, Ballenger JC, Goyer PF, Major LF: Aggression in humans correlates with cerebrospinal fluid amine metabolites. Psychiatry Res 1:131-139, 1979.

6. Brown GL, Ebert ME, Goyer PF, Jimerson DC, Klein WJ, Bunney WE Jr, Goodwin FK: Aggression, suicide, and serotonin: Relationship to CSF amine metabolites. Am J Psychiatry 139:741-746, 1982.

7. Van Praag H: CSF 5-HIAA and suicide in non-depressed schizophrenics. Lancet 2:977-978, 1983.

8. Roy A, Ninan P, Mazonson A, Pickar D, van Kammen D, Linnoila M, Paul S: CSF monoamine metabolites in chronic schizophrenic patients who attempt suicide. Psychol Med 15:335-340, 1985.

9. Brown GL, Kline WJ, Goyer PF, Minichiello MD, Kreusi MJP, Goodwin FK: Relationship of childhood characteristics to cerebrospinal fluid 5-hydroxyindoleacetic acid in aggressive adults. In: Shagass et al (eds) IV World Congress of Biology and Psychiatry, Elsevier Press, pp. 177-179, 1986.

10. Paul SM, Rehavi M, Skolnick P, Goodwin FK: High affinity binding of antidepressants to biogenic amine transport sites in human brain and platelet: Studies in depression. Post PM, Ballenger JC (eds) Neurobiology of Mood Disorders, pp. 846-853, Williams & Wilkins, Baltimore, 1984.

11. Korpi ER, Kleinman JE, Goodman SJ et al: Serotonin and 5-hydroxyindoleacetic acid concentration in different brain regions of suicide victims: Comparison in chronic schizophrenic patients with suicide as cause of death. Presented at the meeting of the Int. Soc. for Neurochemistry, Vancouver, Canada, July 14, 1983.

12. Gillin JC, Nelson J, Kleinman J et al: Studies of the cholinergic system in suicide and depression. New York Acad of Sciences Conference on Psychobiology of Suicidal Behavior, Sept 18-20, 1985.

13. Bunney WE Jr, Fawcett JA: Possibility of a biochemical test for suicidal potential. Arch Gen Psychiatry 13:232-239, 1965.

14. Curzon G: Effects of adrenal hormones and stress on brain serotonin. Am J Clin Nutri 24:830-834, 1971.

15. Major LE, Brown GL, Wilson WP: Carcinoid and psychiatric symptoms. South Med J 66:787--790, 1973.

16. Sjordsma A, Lovenberg M, Engelman K, Carpenter WT, Wyatt RJ, Gessa GL: Serotonin Now. Clinical implications of inhibiting its synthesis wih para-chlorophenylalanine (PCPA). Combined Clinical Staff Conference at the National Institutes of Health. Ann Intern Med 73:607-629, 1970.

17. Pokorny AD: Prediction of suicide in psychiatric patients: Report of a prospective study. Arch Gen Psychiatry 40:249-257, 1983.

18. Robins LN: Deviant Children Grown Up: A Sociological and Psychiatric Study of Sociopathic Personality. Williams & Wilkins, Baltimore, 1966.

19. Clayton PJ: Suicide. In: Roy A, (ed) Symposium on Self-Destructive Behavior, The Psychiatric Clinics of North American, WB Saunders Co, 8(2):203-214, 1985.

20. Ciaranello RB, Anders TF, Barchas JD, Berger PA, Cann HM: The use of 5-hydroxytryptophan in a child with Lesch-Nyhan syndrome. Child Psychiatry Hum Dev 7:127-133, 1976.

21. Bunney WE Jr, Janowsky DS, Goodwin FK, Davis JM, Brodie HKH, Murphy DL, Chase TN: Effects of L-DOPA on depression. Lancet 1:885, 1969.

22. Brown GL, Wilson WP, Green RL: Mental aspects of Parkinsonism and their management. In: Parkinson's Disease: Rigidity, Akinesia, Behavior, Selected Communications on Topic. Vol 2, Siegfried, J (ed). Verlag Hans Huber, Bern, pp. 265-278, 1973.

23. Matthews WS, Barabas G: Suicide and epilepsy: A review of the literature. Psychosomatics 22:515-524, 1981.

24. Chadwick D, Jenner P, Reynolds EH: Amines, anticonvulsants, and epilepsy. Lancet 1:473-476, 1975.

25. Cohen DJ, Shaywitz BA, Capapulo BK, Young JG, Bowens MB Jr: Chronic, multiple tics of Gilles de la Tourettes' disease. Arch Gen Psychiatry 35:245-250, 1978.

26. Bolander A-M: Nordic suicide statistics. In: Waldenstrom J, Larsson T, Ljungstedt N (eds). Suicide and Attempted Suicide. Stockholmi Nordiska Bokhandelns Forlag, 1972.

27. Rapoport J, Elkins R, Langer DH, Sceery W, Buchsbaum MS, Gillin JC, Murphy DL, Zahn TP, Lake R, Ludlow C, Mendelson W: Childhood Obsessive-Compulsive Disorder. Am J Psychiatry 138:1545-1554, 1981.